Black's Picturesque Tourist of Scotland

BLACK'S

PICTURESQUE TOURIST

OF

SCOTLAND.

EDINBURGH: PRINTED BY T. CONSTABLE,
PRINTER TO HER MAJESTY.

BLACK'S

PICTURESQUE TOURIST

OF

SCOTLAND.

WITH AN ACCURATE TRAVELLING MAP;

ENGRAVED CHARTS AND VIEWS OF THE SCENERY;

PLANS OF EDINBURGH AND GLASGOW;

AND A COPIOUS ITINERARY.

SECOND EDITION.

EDINBURGH:

ADAM AND CHARLES BLACK, 27, NORTH BRIDGE,

BOOKSELLERS AND PUBLISHERS TO THE QUEEN.

M.DCCC.XLII.

B.9138,42,3
9463.43

1860, July 13.
Pickman Bequest.

PREFACE.

THE plan and execution of the present volume will be found, in an important respect, to differ from any other work upon the same subject. In the compilation of Guide-Books, it appears to the Publishers that much eloquence has often been needlessly expended in elaborate eulogiums on the beauty or grandeur of natural scenery, of which no adequate idea can be conveyed to the mind by any written description, however graphic and minute. In the present work, therefore, no attempt has been made to write up to the attraction of the subject. A plain and intelligible account has been given of the scenery most worthy of the attention of strangers, without dictating the amount of admiration with which any given prospect is to be contemplated. Instead of the fine writing thus suppressed, there has been incorporated a large amount of Traditionary, Historical, and Literary illustration, by which it is conceived a recollection of the scenery will be more permanently fixed in the memory of the tourist, than by any original description of its features which the author could himself have given.

Neither labour nor expense has been spared to give

the work the greatest possible degree of accuracy. With this view, the several sheets, in their progress through the press, have been transmitted to individuals conversant with the topography of the respective districts, while the descriptions of Edinburgh, Glasgow, and Aberdeen, have been wholly contributed by natives of these cities.

To enumerate all the improvements made upon the present edition, or duly to acknowledge the important assistance rendered by numerous contributors, would exceed the limits of a preface. The publishers may, however, advert to a few of the more prominent additions now introduced. Among these may be mentioned,

I. A TOUR TO THE LAND OF BURNS—comprehending those parts of the country more particularly associated with his history, or celebrated in his works.

II. A TOUR TO THE HIGHLANDS OF DEESIDE AND THE CAIRNGORM MOUNTAINS—conducting to the grandest combination of mountain scenery in the kingdom.

III. A DESCRIPTION OF THE LINE OF RAILWAY BETWEEN EDINBURGH AND GLASGOW, (included in the Itinerary.)

IV. A DESCRIPTION OF THE TOWN OF ABERDEEN—written on the same plan as the Descriptions of Edinburgh and Glasgow, in which all the objects of interest are visited in successive ' Walks.'

V. Many valuable additions to the THIRD, NINTH, and TENTH TOURS, and to the Descriptions of PERTH, DUNDEE, LANARK, and the vicinity of the FALLS OF CLYDE.

VI. ROAD CHARTS of the FIRST, SEVENTH, EIGHTH, and THIRTEENTH TOURS, and of the TOUR TO DEESIDE ; with numerous amendments upon the Charts given in the First Edition, and upon the Travelling Map.

VII. Several new Views of Picturesque Scenery, and of Public Buildings, engraved on wood and steel. Among these are included Abbotsford, Loch Katrine, Bracklinn Bridge, and the more interesting portions of Edinburgh.

With these additions, it is believed the work will fully supply all the information required by the Tourist.

The Itinerary at the end of the volume, which includes all the more important roads in Scotland, will be found peculiarly valuable, as it not only gives the distances, but also contains brief marginal notices of the interesting objects along the several roads. By inspecting this portion of the work as he passes along, the Tourist may therefore ascertain, without the trouble of enquiry, the names of all the objects of interest on each side of the road.

To those desiring a more minute knowledge of the northern part of Scotland, the Guide to the Highlands, by George and Peter Anderson, Esquires, occasionally quoted in the following pages, may be recommended as a manual equally interesting and accurate.

EDINBURGH, 27, NORTH BRIDGE, }
1st July 1842.

NOTE

REGARDING THE ADMISSION OF VISITORS

TO

EDINBURGH GAOL AND BRIDEWELL.

————

Since the following pages were printed, Edinburgh Gaol and
Bridewell have been consolidated into one Prison, under a special
Board of Management. Admission is granted only to those strangers
who are accompanied by one of the Commissioners.

CONTENTS.

TABLE OF THE DISTANCES

OF THE PRINCIPAL TOWNS IN SCOTLAND FROM EACH OTHER AND FROM LONDON, GENERALLY CALCULATED BY THE MAIL ROADS.

Town	EDINBURGH and chain of towns	DISTANCE FROM LONDON
	EDINBURGH	398
Aberdeen	109 Aberdeen	503
Arbroath	60 49 Arbroath	452
Ayr	77 177 128 Ayr	394
Banff	154 45 94 222 Banff	546
Berwick-on-Tweed	56 164 115 132 209 Berwick-on-Tweed	337
Campbelton	177 276 228 90 262 232 Campbelton	489
Cupar Fife	30 79 30 107 124 85 261 Cupar Fife	422
Dunbarton	58 150 106 47 195 113 108 81 Dunbarton	410
Dumfries	71 180 131 59 240 108 205 101 96 Dumfries	386
Dundee	43 66 17 116 111 98 221 13 99 114 Dundee	435
Elgin	169 63 99 206 34 224 231 125 190 240 119 Elgin	561
Falkirk	24 127 84 56 159 79 156 54 37 83 67 157 Falkirk	416
Fochabers	100 54 90 212 25 215 240 116 108 231 108 9 163 Fochabers	552
Forres	156 75 101 200 46 211 290 134 174 227 118 12 151 21 Forres	546
Fort Augustus	130 133 120 180 104 185 161 116 133 205 110 70 117 79 59 Fort Augustus	522
Glasgow	44 143 100 83 175 99 133 74 14 72 83 173 22 179 187 127 Glasgow	395
Greenock	66 165 122 45 197 121 111 96 12 94 105 195 45 201 189 149 22 Greenock	418
Haddington	17 126 77 94 171 38 194 47 75 88 60 186 41 177 173 147 61 83 Haddington	375
Hamilton	37 146 97 38 186 92 134 56 21 61 90 184 22 190 178 138 11 33 54 Hamilton	361
Inverary	104 169 125 53 207 153 73 108 46 132 106 173 83 182 162 103 60 58 121 71 Inverary	455
Inverness	127 194 174 173 135 Inverness	549
Jedburgh	47 156 107 98 201 33 222 77 103 73 90 216 71 207 203 177 89 111 46 78 149 204 Jedburgh	354
John o' Groat's House	814 235 294 329 206 369 329 294 279 365 294 172 877 181 160 162 239 315 331 304 296 131 361 John o' Groat's House	706
Kelso	43 152 103 120 212 23 220 73 101 33 86 212 67 203 199 173 87 109 36 80 147 200 10 357 Kelso	364
Kirkcudbright	99 208 160 64 253 135 115 129 119 28 254 233 225 225 96 120 116 90 157 256 109 391 112 Kirkcudbright	364
Lanark	31 140 91 51 185 86 158 61 29 58 74 199 32 191 187 152 25 47 48 14 85 187 64 213 62 82 Lanark	375
Montrose	72 37 12 149 82 127 210 42 119 148 29 93 96 85 105 141 112 134 89 123 137 135 129 296 115 171 103 Montrose	464
Paisley	52 151 108 34 183 107 127 82 9 80 91 181 31 127 175 152 8 16 69 19 54 170 97 201 95 106 23 120 Paisley	407
Peebles	22 131 82 62 176 61 179 52 60 56 65 191 46 182 178 152 46 63 20 35 106 179 41 236 32 78 27 94 54 Peebles	373
Perth	40 83 39 94 129 95 159 22 68 111 32 129 45 120 116 90 61 83 57 72 86 114 87 272 83 139 71 51 69 62 Perth	432
Port Patrick	135 242 193 56 264 182 60 163 103 78 172 282 112 268 256 216 89 111 150 92 149 231 155 382 126 55 95 201 95 135 150 Port Patrick	421
St. Andrews	42 84 29 117 126 95 191 16 91 111 12 124 64 126 147 126 84 106 57 77 118 146 87 304 83 139 71 41 92 62 32 173 St. Andrews	432
Stirling	35 118 73 60 146 90 155 47 34 90 56 146 11 152 140 109 27 42 52 38 90 135 52 296 78 125 37 85 35 57 34 116 57 Stirling	427
Thurso	316 263 312 354 234 371 367 295 307 387 293 200 305 209 188 191 321 342 333 332 294 159 363 20 359 415 331 294 329 338 273 410 305 294 Thurso	708
Wick	296 242 291 333 213 350 346 274 286 366 274 179 284 188 167 170 300 322 312 311 273 138 342 19 338 394 310 273 308 317 252 389 284 273 21 Wick	687
Wigton	105 214 165 50 258 106 93 135 97 55 148 256 121 262 250 210 83 95 122 34 142 245 128 404 138 31 70 176 83 85 144 37 145 116 403 382 Wigton	395
Carlisle	92 201 151 92 246 88 180 122 109 27 135 261 116 252 248 222 95 117 109 84 155 249 53 366 63 63 74 164 106 77 132 120 132 116 406 387 94 Carlisle	391

☞ The names of the various towns are arranged at each end of the line of figures, and the angle where the perpendicular and horizontal lines meet, gives the distance of the respective towns from each other.

THE

PICTURESQUE TOURIST

OF

SCOTLAND.

ORIGIN OF THE NAME—EXTENT—GENERAL ASPECT—NATURAL DIVI-
SIONS—MOUNTAINS—VALES—RIVERS—LAKES—MINERAL PRODUCE
—CLIMATE AND SOIL—AGRICULTURE—ANIMAL KINGDOM—FISHER-
IES—MANUFACTURES—COMMERCE—INTERNAL COMMUNICATION—
REVENUE—CONSTITUTION—RELIGIOUS INSTITUTIONS—ADMINISTRA-
TION OF JUSTICE—POPULATION.

SCOTLAND is the northern and smaller division of the
Island of Great Britain. The origin of the term is
involved in much obscurity. That part of the country
which lies beyond the Firths of Forth and Clyde received
from the Romans the appellation of Caledonia, and its
inhabitants were denominated Caledonians. They were
afterwards known by the name of Picts, and from them
the country was for some centuries called Pictland. The
term Scotland began to come into use, for the first time,
in the eleventh century, and this name is supposed to have
been derived from a colony of Scots, who had previously
left Ireland, and planted themselves in Argyleshire and
the West-Highlands.

EXTENT.—The longest line that can be drawn in Scotland, is from its most southerly point, the Mull of Galloway, in lat. 54° 38′ N., long. 4° 50′ W., to Dunnet Head, its most northerly point, in lat. 58° 40′ 30″ N., long. 3° 29′ W., or about 285 miles; but the longest line that can be drawn in about the same parallel of longitude, is from the former point to Cape Wrath, in lat. 58° 36′ N., long. 4° 56′ W., a distance of 275 miles. The breadth is extremely various. From Buchanness point to the point of Ardnamurchan in Argyleshire, the distance is 160 miles; but from the bottom of Loch Broom to the Firth of Dornoch, it is only twenty-four miles. The whole coast is so much penetrated by arms of the sea, that there is only one spot throughout its whole circuit upwards of forty miles from the shore. The area of the mainland is computed at 25,520 square miles of land, and 494 of fresh water lakes; the islands are supposed to contain about 4080 square miles of land, and about 144 of water.

GENERAL ASPECT.—The surface of the country is distinguished for variety, and, compared with England, it is, generally speaking, rugged and mountainous. It is supposed, that estimating the whole extent of the country, exclusive of lakes, at 19,000,000 acres, scarcely so many as 6,000,000 are arable,—that is less than one-third; whereas in England, the proportion of arable land to the entire extent of the country exceeds three-fourths. With the exception of a few tracts of rich alluvial land along the courses of the great rivers, Scotland has no extensive tracts of level ground, the surface of the country being generally varied with hill and dale.

NATURAL DIVISIONS.—Scotland is naturally divided into Highlands and Lowlands. The former division comprehends, besides the Hebrides, the Orkney and Shetland islands, the counties of Argyle, Inverness, Nairn, Ross, Cromarty, Sutherland, and Caithness, with parts of Dumbarton, Stirling, Perth, Forfar, Kincardine, Aberdeen, Banff, and Moray or Elgin, with the exception, however, of the level ground on the eastern coast to the south of the Moray Firth. The Highlands, again, are divided into two unequal portions, by the chain of lakes occupying the Glenmore-nan-albin, or " Great glen of Caledonia," stretching north-east and south-east across the island, from Inverness to Fort William, now connected together, and forming the Caledonian Canal. The northern division of the Highlands is decidedly the more barren and unproductive of the two, though the other division contains the highest mountains. In the eastern parts of Ross and Cromarty there are level tracts of considerable fertility. The Lowland division of the kingdom, though comparatively flat, comprises also a great deal of mountainous country.

MOUNTAINS.—Of the Highland mountains, the most celebrated is the chain of the Grampians. It commences on the south side of Loch Etive in Argyleshire, and terminates between Stonehaven and the mouth of the Dee on the eastern coast. The most elevated part of this range lies at the head of the Dee. Ben Macdui, the highest mountain in Scotland, rises to the height of 4418 feet, and the adjoining mountains of Cairngorm, Cairntoul, and Ben Avon, are respectively 4050, 4245, and 3967 feet high. The other principal summits of the Grampian chain are, Schehallion, near the east end of Loch Rannoch, 3613 feet above the level of the sea ; Ben Lawers, on the north side of Loch Tay, 3945 ; Ben More, at the head of Glendochart, 3818 ; Ben Lomond, on the side

of Loch Lomond, 3191 ; and Ben Cruachan, at the head
of Loch Awe, 3390.   Ben Nevis, till recently reputed
the highest of the British mountains, lies immediately to
the east of Fort William, being separated from the Grampians by the moor of Rannoch ; it rises 4358 feet above
the level of the sea, and its circumference at the base is
supposed to exceed twenty-four miles.   To the south of
the Grampians, and running parallel to them across the
island, there is a chain of hills divided by the valleys of
the Tay and Forth into three distinct portions, and bearing the names of the Sidlaw, Ochil, and Campsie hills.
The low country between them and the Grampians is
called the valley of Strathmore.   In the Lowland division
of the country, the Cheviots form the principal range.
These hills are situate partly in England and partly in
Scotland.   They separate Northumberland from Roxburghshire, stretch through the latter county in a westerly direction, keeping to the north of Liddisdale, then
bending north-west towards the junction of the counties
of Roxburgh, Selkirk, and Dumfries, they unite with the
Lowther Hills, an extensive group, which, having Ettrick
water, near the above-mentioned junction, for its eastern
boundary, spreads over the southern portion of the counties
of Selkirk, Peebles, and Lanark, and the north of Dumfries-shire, and in the west of the latter county joins the
ridges, which passing through Kirkcudbrightshire, Wig-
tonshire, and the south of Ayrshire, terminate at Loch
Ryan in the Irish Channel.   Of these hills the highest
lie on the confines of the counties of Dumfries, Peebles,
Lanark, and Selkirk ; Broadlaw, in the parish of Tweedsmuir, the most elevated mountain in the south of Scotland, is 2741 feet above the level of the sea ; Hartfell,
contiguous to Broadlaw, is 2635 feet above the level of

the sea, and several of the neighbouring hills rise to the height of about 2000 feet.

VALES.—The most important level tracts in Scotland are, the Carse of Stirling and Falkirk, which occupies the country on both sides the Forth, from Borrowstounness on the south, and Kincardine on the north, westward to Gartmore ; the tract between Dundee and Perth, bounded by the Sidlaw hills on the north, and the Tay on the south, denominated the Carse of Gowrie ; the Merse of Berwickshire, extending from the Leader water along the Tweed to Berwick ; and the valley of Strathmore, which comprises a considerable portion of the counties of Perth and Angus, stretching from Methvin in the former to the vicinity of Laurencekirk in Kincardineshire, and from thence, under the name of *The How of the Mearns*, to within a short distance of Stonehaven. Besides these, there are several smaller straths, such as Teviotdale in Roxburghshire, Tynedale in East Lothian, and the *How of Fife*.

RIVERS.—The principal rivers of Scotland are, the Tweed, the Forth, the Tay, the Spey, and the Clyde. The Tweed rises in Tweedsmuir about six miles from Moffat. It runs first north-east to Peebles, then east, with a little inclination to the south, to Melrose ; it next passes Kelso and Coldstream, and pursuing a north-easterly direction, falls into the sea at Berwick. During the latter part of its course, the Tweed forms the boundary between England and Scotland. The descent from its source to Peebles is 1000 feet, and thence to Berwick about 500 feet more. Including windings, its length is reckoned at rather more than 100 miles. Its principal tributaries are, the Ettrick, which it receives near Selkirk ; the Gala a little above, and the Leader a little below

Melrose; the Teviot at Kelso; the Till at Tillmouth; and the Adder near Berwick.

The Forth rises on the east side of Ben Lomond, and runs in an easterly direction, with many windings, till it unites with the Firth of Forth at Kincardine. Its most important tributary is the Teith, which it receives a short way above Stirling. The Tay conveys to the sea a greater quantity of water than any other river in Britain. It has its source in the western extremity of Perthshire, in the district of Breadalbane, on the frontiers of Lorn in Arygle-shire. At first it receives the name of the Fillan. After a winding course of eight or nine miles it spreads itself out into Loch Dochart, and, under the appellation of the Dochart, flows in an easterly direction through the vale of Glendochart, at the eastern extremity of which, having previously received the waters of the Lochy, it expands into the beautiful long narrow lake, called Loch Tay. Issuing thence, it speedily receives a great augmentation by the river Lyon, and running north and east at Logierait, about eight miles above Dunkeld, it is joined by the Tummel. It now takes a direction more towards the south, to Dunkeld, where, on its right bank, it receives the beautiful river Bran. On leaving Dunkeld, it runs east to Kinclaven, and after receiving a considerable augmentation to the volume of its waters by the accession of the Isla, the Shochie, and the Almond, it flows in a south-westerly course to Perth. A short way below Perth, it assumes the appearance of a Firth or estuary. At the foot of the vale of Strathearn, it receives on its right bank its last great tributary, the Earn; and, gradually expanding its waters, it flows in a north-easterly direction past Dundee, till it falls into the sea, between Tentsmoor Point and Buttonness.

The Spey is admitted to be the most rapid of the Scottish rivers, and, next to the Tay, to discharge the greatest quantity of water. It has its source in Loch Spey, within about six miles of the head of Loch Lochy. It runs in a north-easterly direction through Badenoch and Strathspey, to Fochabers, below which it falls into the Moray Firth, at Garmouth. During its course, it receives numerous mountain streams, but no important tributary. From its source to its mouth, the distance is about seventy-five miles; but following its windings, its course is about ninety-six miles. Owing to the origin and course of its tributary waters, the Spey is very liable to sudden and destructive inundations. It flows through the best wooded part of the Highlands, and affords a water carriage for the produce of the extensive woods of Glenmore and Strathspey, large quantities of which are floated down to the seaport of Garmouth.

The Clyde is, in a commercial point of view, the most important river of Scotland. It has its origin in the highest part of the southern mountain land, at no great distance from the sources of the Tweed and the Annan. It flows at first in a northerly direction, with a slight inclination to the east, as far as Biggar. Being joined by the Douglas, near Harperfield, it takes a north-west course by Lanark, Hamilton, and Glasgow, falling into the Firth of Clyde, below Dumbarton. Following its windings, the course of the Clyde, from its source to Dumbarton, is about seventy-three miles, but the length of the river, in a direct line, is only about fifty-two miles. Its principal tributaries are, the Douglas, Nethan, Avon, Mouse, Kelvin, Cart, and Leven. Of the celebrated falls of the Clyde, two are above, and two below Lanark; the uppermost is Bonnington Linn, the height of which is about thirty feet; the second fall is Cora Linn, where the water dashes over the rock in three distinct leaps; Dundaff Fall is ten feet high, and at Stonebyres there are three distinct falls, altogether measuring about seventy-six feet in height. The Clyde is navigable at high water, as far as Glasgow, and large sums of money have been expended, especially of late, in improving and deepening the channel. The Forth and Clyde Canal falls into the latter river, at Dunglass, a little above Dumbarton.

LAKES.—The chief lakes of Scotland are—Loch Lomond, lying between Dumbartonshire and Stirlingshire; Loch Ness, in Inverness-shire; Loch Maree, in Ross-shire; Loch Awe, in Argyleshire; Lochs Tay, Rannoch, and Ericht, in Perthshire, &c.

MINERAL PRODUCE.—The minerals of Scotland are numerous and valuable. The great coal-field of Scotland extends, with little interruption, from the eastern to the western coast. The most valuable part of this field, is situated on the north and south sides of the Forth, about the average breadth of ten or twelve miles on each side, and on the north and south sides of the Clyde, ranging through Renfrewshire, part of Lanarkshire, and the north of Ayrshire. Detached coal-fields have also been found in various other parts of Scotland. Lime is very generally diffused throughout the country. Iron abounds in many parts, particularly in the coal-field. Lead-mines are wrought to a great extent at Leadhills, and. Wanlockhead, in Dumfries-shire. In the soil which covers these fields, particles of gold have occasionally been found; copper-ore is found at Blair Logie, Airthrie, and at Fetlar, in Orkney; antimony at Langholm; manganese in the neighbourhood of Aberdeen; silver has been wrought at Alva, in Clackmannanshire, and at

Leadhills in Lanarkshire; there are extensive slate-quarries in Aberdeenshire, Argyleshire, Perthshire, and Peebles-shire; marble is found in Argyleshire, Sutherland, and the Hebrides; sandstone abounds generally throughout the country; and granite, and other primitive rocks, within the limits of the Grampians.

MINERAL SPRINGS.—There are numerous medicinal mineral springs in various parts of Scotland. " The most remarkable of these are—the sulphurous waters of *Strathpeffer*, near Dingwall, Ross-shire; *Muirtown*, in the same neighbourhood; *Moffat*, in Dumfries-shire; and *St. Bernard's*, at Stockbridge, a suburb of Edinburgh: the chalybeats of *Hartfell*, near Moffat; *Vicar's Bridge*, near Dollar, Stirlingshire; and *Bonnington*, near Edinburgh: the saline waters of *Dunblane*, near Stirling; *Airthrie*, also near Stirling; *Pitcaithly*, near Perth; and *Innerleithen*, near Peebles. At *St. Catharine's*, in the parish of Liberton, near Edinburgh, there is a spring which yields asphaltum in considerable quantities."[*]

CLIMATE.—The climate of Scotland is extremely variable. Owing to its insular situation, however, neither the cold in winter, nor the heat in summer, are so intense as in similar latitudes on the continent. The annual average temperature may be estimated at from 44° to 47° of Fahrenheit. The quantity of rain which falls on the east coast of Scotland, varies from 22 to 26 inches, while on the west coast, and in the Hebrides, it ranges from 35 to 46 inches. The average number of days, in which either rain or snow falls in parts situated on the west coast, is about 200, on the east coast about 145. The winds are more variable than in England, and more violent, especially about the equinoxes. Westerly winds

---

[*] Malte Brun and Balbi Abridged. Edin., 1841.

generally prevail, particularly during autumn, and the early part of winter, but north-east winds are prevalent and severe, during spring and the early part of summer.

AGRICULTURE.—The soils of the various districts of Scotland are exceedingly diversified. The general average is inferior to that of England, although many of the valleys are highly productive.   In Berwickshire, the Lothians, Clydesdale, Fifeshire, the Carses of Stirling, Falkirk, and now particularly in the Carse of Gowrie, Strathearn, Strathmore, and Moray, there are tracts of land not inferior to any in the empire.   The inferiority of the climate and soil, as compared with England, is exhibited by contrasting the phenomena of vegetation in the two countries. Notwithstanding the very advanced state of agriculture in many districts of Scotland, the crops are not reaped with the same certainty as in England, nor do the ordinary kinds of grain arrive at the same perfection. Thus, although Scotch and English barley may be of the same weight, the former does not bring so high a price ; it contains less saccharine matter, and does not yield so large a quantity of malt. Various fruits, also, which ripen in the one country, seldom arrive at maturity in the other, and never reach the same perfection ; while different berries acquire in Scotland somewhat of that delicious flavour which distinguishes them in still higher parallels.

The following tables, exhibiting the proportion which the cultivated parts of the soil bear to the uncultivated, were digested by Sir John Sinclair from his Statistical Account :—

PROPORTION OF CULTIVATED AND UNCULTIVATED SOIL.

	Eng. Acres.
Number of acres fully or partially cultivated, .	5,043,450
Acres uncultivated, including woods and plantations,	13,900,550
Total extent of Scotland in English acres, . .	18,944,000

EXTENT OF WOODS AND PLANTATIONS.

	Eng. Acres.
Extent of plantations, ...	412,226
Extent of natural woods, ...	501,469
Total,	913,695

NATURE OF THE PRODUCTIVE SOILS.

	Eng. Acres.
Sandy soils, ...	263,771
Gravel, ...	681,862
Improved mossy soils, ...	411,096
Cold, or inferior clays, ...	510,265
Rich Clays, ...	987,070
Loams, ...	1,869,193
Alluvial haugh, or carse land, ...	320,193
	5,043,450

Since these tables were compiled, however, extensive tracts of waste lands, particularly in the interior, have been planted with wood, and immense improvements have taken place in every department of agriculture.

ANIMAL KINGDOM.—The domestic animals common to Scotland, are the same as those of England, with some varieties in the breeds. Among the wild animals, the roe, and the red-deer are most worthy of notice. The golden-eagle, and other birds of prey, are found in the mountainous districts, and the country abounds with all kinds of moor-game, partridges, and water-fowl.

FISHERIES.—There are many valuable fisheries in Scotland; the salmon fisheries, especially, produce a large revenue to their owners, but, during late years, they have experienced an extraordinary decline.

The herring fishery is carried on to a considerable extent, on the east coast of Scotland, and there are most productive and valuable fisheries of ling and cod,. in the neighbourhood of the Shetland and Orkney Islands.

MANUFACTURES.—The manufactures of Scotland, especially those of linen and cotton, are extensive and flourishing. The making of steam-engines, and every other sort of machinery, is carried on to a great extent, and vast quantities of cast-iron goods are produced, especially at Carron, in Stirlingshire.

COMMERCE.—The commerce of Scotland has increased with astonishing rapidity, especially within a comparatively recent period, and a vast trade is now carried on, particularly with America and the West Indies. It is supposed, that since 1814, the increase in the principal manufactures and trades carried on in the country, and in the number of individuals employed in them, amounts to at least 30, or 35 per cent.

INTERNAL COMMUNICATION.—Carriage roads extend over every part of the country ; and " in consequence of the excellent materials which abound in all parts of Scotland, and of the greater skill and science of Scottish trustees and surveyors, the turnpike-roads in Scotland are superior to those in England."* The irregularity of surface is not favourable to artificial inland navigation. Among the most important Canals are *The Caledonian Canal*, connecting the Lakes Ness, Oich, and Lochy, with the Beauly Firth on the north, and with Loch Eil on the south ; the *Forth and Clyde* or *Great Canal*, extending from the Firth of Forth at Grangemouth, to Bowling Bay on the Firth of Clyde ; and *the Union Canal* commencing at Edinburgh, and terminating in the Great Canal at Port Downie near Falkirk. Besides these, there are several

---

* Sir H. Parnell on Roads, p. 313.

others which may be noticed in describing the localities through which they pass. Among the Railways of Scotland, the most important is that between Edinburgh and Glasgow. There are many other undertakings of this kind completed or in progress, but limited space prevents our noticing them more particularly.

REVENUE.—The increase in the revenue has fully kept pace with the increasing prosperity of the country. At the period of the Union, the revenue amounted only to £110,696; in 1788, it was £1,099,148; in 1813, it amounted to £4,204,097, and in 1831, to £3,525,114.

CONSTITUTION.—Under the Reform Act of 1832, Scotland returns fifty-three members to the Imperial Parliament, of whom, thirty are for the shires, and twenty-three for the cities, boroughs, and towns; twenty-seven counties return one member each, and the counties of Elgin and Nairn, Ross and Cromarty, and Clackmannan and Kinross, are combined in pairs, each of which returns one member. Of the cities, boroughs, and towns—seventy-six in number—Edinburgh and Glasgow return two members each; Aberdeen, Paisley, Dundee, Greenock, and Perth, one each; the remaining burghs and towns are combined into sets or districts, each set, jointly, sending one member. The county population is 1,500,107, and the number of electors 33,115, giving one elector in every forty-five persons, whilst in the boroughs, the population being 865,007, and the electors 31,332, the proportion is one in every twenty-seven persons. The Scottish Peers choose sixteen of their number to represent them in the House of Lords. The Peers, like the Commoners, hold their seats for only one Parliament.

RELIGIOUS INSTITUTIONS.—Scotland is divided into 1023 parishes, (including parishes *quoad sacra,*) each of which is provided with one minister, or, in a few instances in towns, with two.   The number of parishes, *quoad sacra*, has been increased of late, but down to January 1836, the number before mentioned was the total amount. The stipends of the endowed clergy, with the glebe and manse, probably average from £260, to £300 a year. The government of the Church is vested in kirk-sessions, presbyteries, synods, and the General Assembly.   The number of churches belonging to Dissenters, of all denominations, amounts to 800, besides a considerable number of missionary stations.   The incomes of the Dissenting clergy are wholly derived from their congregations ; they average, probably, from £120, to £130, a year, including a house and garden.   In many cases, however, the income is considerably larger. Scotland has four Universities, that of St. Andrews, founded by Papal authority in 1413; that of Glasgow, by the same authority, in 1450; that of Aberdeen, also with the sanction of the Pope, in 1494, though education did not commence there till 1500 ; and that of Edinburgh, the only one instituted since the Reformation, in 1582.   None of these colleges or universities can be said to be liberally endowed.   St. Andrews has eleven professorships ; Glasgow nineteen ; King's College, Aberdeen, nine ; Marischal College, twelve ; and Edinburgh thirty.   The aggregate number of students in these universities is at present 2515, of which Edinburgh has 1051, Glasgow 792, Aberdeen 550, and St. Andrews 122.   In every parish there is at least one school, for teaching the ordinary branches of education.   The emoluments of the schoolmaster are derived from a small annual salary, with a free house and garden, provided by the landed proprietors, and moderate school fees.   Private schools, also, are very numerous, and it is supposed, on good authority, that the total number of schools of every kind in Scotland, amounts to about 5162.*

ADMINISTRATION OF JUSTICE.—The supreme *civil* court of Scotland, is called the Court of Session. It holds, in Edinburgh, two sessions annually. The number of judges was formerly fifteen, but is now thirteen; they are styled Lords of Session, and sit in two courts or chambers, called the first and second divisions, which form, in effect, two courts of equal and independent authority. The Court of Justiciary, the supreme *criminal* court of Scotland, consists at present of six judges, who are also judges of the Court of Session. The president of the Court is the Lord Justice Clerk. The Court holds sittings in Edinburgh during the recess of the Court of Session; and twice a year, in the spring and autumn vacations, the judges hold circuits in the chief provincial towns, two going each circuit. There was formerly a Court of Exchequer, for the trial of cases connected with the revenue, but it is now abolished as a separate establishment, and the duties are devolved on one of the judges of the Court of Session. There are also inferior courts of law, viz. the courts of the boroughs, of the justices of peace, and of the sheriffs.

POPULATION.— The population of Scotland at the period of the Union, in 1707, is supposed not to have exceeded 1,050,000. In 1755, it amounted to 1,265,380, and in 1831, it had increased to 2,365,114; of which, 1,114,816 were males, and 1,250,298 females. The

---

* From returns made to the House of Commons, it appears that the voluntary schools are to the established schools nearly as four to one, or about 4000 to 1162. The aggregate attendance is calculated to amount to about 230,600; and, adding to this number the pupils instructed in female seminaries, private boarding schools for boys, &c., we shall find that about a ninth part of the total population is receiving the benefit of education.

average population of Scotland, per square mile, is 70·7. During the ten years ending with 1820, the entire population of Scotland increased 16 per cent., and during the ten years ending with 1830, 13 per cent.; while the population of the great towns increased during the same periods, 26¼ and 26½ per cent. The population of Scotland has increased less rapidly than that of England, and much less so than that of Ireland; and, in consequence, the Scotch have advanced more rapidly than the English or Irish, in wealth, and the command of the necessaries and conveniences of life. Their progress in this respect has indeed been quite astonishing. The habits, diet, dress, and other accommodations of the people, have been signally improved. It is not too much to affirm, that the peasantry of the present day are better lodged, better clothed, and better fed than the middle classes of landowners a century ago!

The approach to Scotland by Tourists from other countries, must, of course, be determined by the particular views and circumstances of individuals. Those who enter the kingdom by the western road may either proceed to Glasgow, and assume it as their starting point, or to Edinburgh, visiting, on the way, the classic banks of the Tweed, Teviotdale, the valleys of Ettrick and Yarrow, with Melrose, Dryburgh, and Abbotsford. The great majority of Tourists come at once to the metropolis; and to all who, for the first time, approach Scotland on the east coast, this plan possesses many advantages. Edinburgh is not only easily reached from London, Hull, and Newcastle, but is in itself, with its environs, an object of very great interest and curiosity, and by the increased fa-

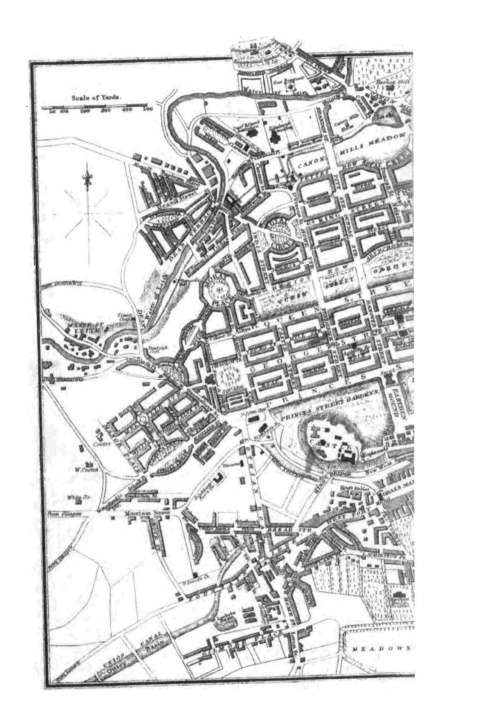

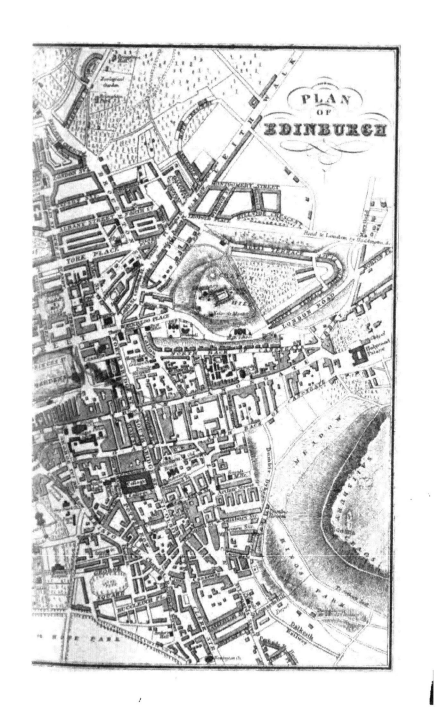

cilities of travelling, is placed cheaply within from one to two days' journey of the finest scenery of Perth, Stirling, Dumbarton, and Argyleshires; while the approach to all of these scenes lies through those lowland districts which abound the most in landscape beauty, and in historical and traditionary interest. We shall therefore assume Edinburgh as our first great starting point, and commence our description with a notice of that city and its interesting environs.

EDINBURGH.

SITUATION—ARCHITECTURE—POPULATION—LEGAL PROFESSION—MA-
NUFACTURES—SOCIAL ADVANTAGES.

THE metropolis of Scotland is situated in the northern part of the County of Mid-Lothian, and is about two miles distant from the Firth of Forth.* Its length and breadth are nearly equal, measuring about two miles in either direction. Its site is generally admitted to be un-equalled in panoramic splendour by any capital in Europe, and the prospect from the elevated points of the city and neighbourhood is of singular beauty and grandeur. The noble estuary of the Forth, expanding from River into Ocean; the solitary grandeur of Arthur's Seat; the varied park and woodland scenery which enrich the southward prospect; the pastoral acclivities of the neigh-bouring Pentland Hills, and the more shadowy splendours

* The precise geographical position of the centre of the city, is 55° 57′ 58″ north latitude, and 3° 11′ 55″ west longitude.

of the Lammermoors, the Ochils, and the Grampians, form some of the features of a landscape combining, in one vast expanse, the richest elements of the beautiful and the sublime.

> " Traced like a map the landscape lies
>   In cultured beauty stretching wide ;
> There Pentland's green acclivities ;
>   There Ocean, with its azure tide ;
> There Arthur's Seat ; and, gleaming through
> Thy southern wing, Dunedin blue !
> While in the orient, Lammer's daughters,
>   A distant giant range, are seen,
>   North Berwick-Law, with cone of green,
> And Bass amid the waters." *

To most of the great cities in the kingdom the approaches lie through mean and squalid suburbs, by which the stranger is gradually introduced to the more striking streets and public buildings. The avenues to Edinburgh are, on the contrary, lined with streets of a highly respectable class, the abodes of poverty being, for the most part, confined to those gigantic piles of buildings in the older parts of the city, where they so essentially contribute to the picturesque grandeur of the place.

The general architecture of the city is very imposing, whether we regard the picturesque confusion of the buildings in the Old Town, or the symmetrical proportions of the streets and squares in the New.† Of the public buildings it may be observed, that, while the greater

---

* Delta.

† " A more striking contrast than exists between these two parts of the same city could hardly be imagined. On one side, a succession of splendid squares, broad and well-paved streets, columns, statues, and clean side-walks, thinly promenaded, and by the well-dressed exclusively—a kind of wholly grand and half-deserted city, which has been built too ambitiously for its population ;—and on the other, an antique wilderness of streets and ' wynds,' so narrow and lofty

number are distinguished by chaste design and excellent masonry, there are none of those sumptuous structures, which, like St. Paul's or Westminster Abbey, York Minster, and some other of the English provincial Cathedrals, astonish the beholder alike by their magnitude and their architectural splendour. But in no city of the kingdom is the general standard of excellence so well maintained. If there be no edifice to overwhelm the imagination by its magnificence, there are comparatively few to offend taste by their deformity or meanness of design. Above all, Edinburgh is wholly exempt from such examples of ostentatious deformity as, in London, may be seen to mingle with some of the most graceful specimens of domestic architecture in the Regent Park.

The resemblance between Athens and Edinburgh, which has been remarked by most travellers who have been so fortunate as to have visited both capitals, has conferred upon the Scottish Metropolis the honorary title of " The Modern Athens." Stuart, author of " The Antiquities of Athens." was the first to draw attention to this resemblance, and his opinion has been confirmed by the testimony of many later writers. Dr. Clarke

---

as to shut out much of the light of heaven; a thronging, busy, and particularly dirty population; side-walks almost impassable from children and other respected nuisances; and, altogether, between the irregular and massive architecture, and the unintelligible jargon agonising the air about you, a most outlandish and strange city. Paris is not more unlike Constantinople, than one side of Edinburgh is unlike the other. Nature has properly placed ' a great gulf' between them."—WILLIS's *Pencillings by the Way.*

We may be allowed to observe, in reference to this extract, that the " dirty population" in the Old Town, must be understood merely as an antithesis to the " well-dressed" in the New. We deny that the inhabitants, even of the meanest streets of the Old Town, are deserving of special remark in this particular. Without question, there is much squalor, as well as poverty, but we cannot admit that there is more disregard of cleanliness among the humbler ranks of Edinburgh, than is always found associated with poverty in populous and crowded cities.

remarks, that the neighbourhood of Athens is just the Highlands of Scotland enriched with the splendid remains of art; and Mr. W. H. Williams observes, that the distant view of Athens from the Ægean Sea, is extremely like that of Edinburgh from the Firth of Forth, *" though certainly the latter is considerably superior."*

Nor are the natural or artificial beauties of the place its only attractions, for many of its localities teem with the recollections of " the majestic past," and are associated with events of deep historical importance. Other of its localities have been invested with an interest no less engrossing by the transcendant genius of Sir Walter Scott, whose novels have not only refreshed and embellished the incidents of history, but have conferred on many a spot formerly unknown to fame, a reputation as enduring as the annals of history itself.

In literary eminence, also, Edinburgh claims a distinguished place. At the comencement of the present century, its University displayed an array of contemporaneous talent unequalled by any similar institution either before or since,* and many of the present professors honourably uphold its scientific and literary reputation.

By the last population returns, made in 1831, the inhabitants of Edinburgh, with Leith, its sea-port, amounted to 161,909.† Of this number, a large proportion is engaged in literary and professional pursuits, a circumstance which gives an elevated tone to the general society of the place. Some idea may be formed of the large proportion which the professional and other liberally

---

* We have only to remind our readers of the names of Robertson, Playfair, Black, Cullen, Robison, Blair, Dugald Stewart, Gregory, and Monro, to vindicate what might otherwise appear a sweeping assertion.

† It is generally believed that the population has not increased since these returns were made.

educated classes bear to the other orders of society, by comparing the population returns of Edinburgh with those of five other of the large towns of the kingdom.

NAMES of TOWNS AND THEIR SUBURBS.	TOTAL POPU-LATION.	MALES TWENTY YEARS OF AGE.					MALE SERVANTS.	FEMALE SERVANTS.
		Employed in Manu-factures, or in making Manufac. Machiny.	Employed in Retail or Handi-craft Trades.	Capitalists, Bankers, Profession-al, and other liberally educated Men.	Labourers employed in Labour not Agri-cultural.	Other Males (except Ser-vants.)		
EDINBURGH and Leith.	161,909	792	19,764	7463	4448	2396	1422	12,429
GLASGOW.	202,426	19,913	18,832	2723	574	4012	946	8006
LIVERPOOL and Toxteth Park.	189,242	359	21,206	8201	16,095	1214	363	9033
MANCHEST. and Salford.	182,812	15,342	17,231	2821	7629	1696	398	3965
BRISTOL and Barton-Regis.	103,886	415	11,270	2654	7312	1867	814	5702
BIRMING-HAM.	146,986	5028	19,469	2366	5899	1371	966	5233

This table, compiled from Parliamentary documents, not only demonstrates the large proportion borne by the educated ranks to the general mass of the population, but, from the number of male and female domestic servants, it is also obvious that the average number of families in comfortable circumstances must exceed that of any of the other large towns of the empire. It must not, however, be concluded that there are many of the inhabitants of Edinburgh in circumstances of great opulence; in this respect it cannot be compared with the other towns in the table, but competence is as generally possessed and comfort as widely diffused as in any other community of like magnitude.

The prosperity of the city essentially depends upon its

College and Schools, and still more essentially upon the Courts of Judicature. The former attract many strangers who desire to secure for their families a liberal education at a moderate expense; the latter afford employment for the gentlemen of the Legal Profession, whose number is so great that they may be said to form one-third of the population in the higher and middle ranks of society.*

As there are no very extensive manufactures, the city is exempt from those sudden mercantile convulsions pro-

---

* The great family of Lawyers may be divided into the following classes. The first class consists of the Judges of the Court of Session. Their nomination is with the Crown : they are now invariably chosen from among the Advocates, and, before their appointment, they must have been practising at the bar for at least five years. Their number was formerly 15, but is now reduced to 13. The Advocates (*Anglice* Barristers) form the second class. They are united into a Society or Incorporation called the Faculty of Advocates, and possess the privilege of pleading before every Court in Scotland, and also before the House of Lords. The present number of the body is about 450, but there are not one-third of them in practice, and probably not one-fifth of them subsist solely by their professional gains. A considerable number of them are gentlemen wholly independent of their profession, but who have joined the body on account of the status which they acquire from the learning and accomplishment of its members. The next class consists of the Writers to the Signet, who also form an Incorporation. They were originally called Clerks to the Signet, from their having been employed in the Secretary of State's office in preparing summonses, and other writs which received the Royal Signet, and they have still the sole privilege of preparing such writs. They are in other respects similar to the English Attorneys or Solicitors, and they are the oldest, most numerous, and most wealthy body of Law Practitioners in Scotland. Before admission to the body an apprenticeship of five years is required, and an attendance of two Sessions at one of the Universities, independent of four courses of the Law Classes. The number of the Society is at present nearly 700, of whom about 450 are in practice. The Solicitors before the Supreme Court, and Advocates' First Clerks, form another section of this class, their duties being the same as the Writers to the Signet, with the exception of their not being entitled to sign writs passing the Signet. These three classes, along with certain functionaries connected with the Court, form the College of Justice, which possesses certain privileges, the members being exempted from most of the local taxes ; among others, from poors'-rates, and the annuity levied for payment of the stipend of the Clergy of Edinburgh. They are not amenable to the jurisdiction of any inferior Court, excepting the Small Debt Court held by the Sheriff. The Solicitors at Law, (who practise before the inferior Courts,) the Accountants, and others, who pass under the more general name of Writers, are also included in the great family of Lawyers, but their distinctive peculiarities we think it unnecessary to mention here.

ductive of so much misery in many other of the great towns of the kingdom. Printing and publishing are carried on to a large extent. In this department of industry Edinburgh far surpasses all the towns of the kingdom, London only excepted; many of the most valuable and popular works of the age emanating from the Edinburgh press.* Shawls and ale are also among the celebrated productions of the place; and there has recently been established, on the banks of the Union Canal, a very extensive manufactory for the spinning of silk. Printing papers are manufactured to a large extent in the neighbourhood, but none of the mills are in the immediate vicinity of the city. Although there are several other branches of manufacture, they are, for the most part, on an insignificant scale.

As a place of family residence, Edinburgh possesses many advantages. The climate, although it cannot be called mild or genial, is yet eminently salubrious. The annual quantity of rain is moderate, compared with the fall upon the western coast. The violent winds, to which the city is exposed by its elevated situation, are by no means unfavourable to general health, as they carry the benefit of a thorough ventilation into the close-built lanes and alleys of the Old Town. The facilities of education, and the advantages of cultivated society, have been already alluded to. In the former of these particulars, we believe it to be unequalled in the kingdom, and in the latter it can be surpassed by London alone.

* The Edinburgh Review, the Encyclopædia Britannica, Blackwood's Magazine, Tait's Magazine, the Medical Journal, the Journal of Agriculture, and the Philosophical Journal, are some of the more important periodical publications. In circulation it is worthy of remark, that both Blackwood's and Tait's Magazines far exceed any of their London contemporaries.

There are twelve newspapers, of which two are published thrice a-week, five twice a-week, and the rest weekly.

The markets are liberally supplied with all the necessaries and luxuries of the table. White fish are more especially abundant, cod, haddocks, and, at certain seasons, herrings, being sold at a very low price. Coal of good quality is found in the immediate neighbourhood of the city, and there is a copious supply of excellent water. Upon the whole, it would be difficult to name a city which unites so many social advantages, and where a person of cultivated mind and moderate fortune could pass his time more agreeably.

The most convenient mode of imparting information to strangers, is to select a particular district of the city to be perambulated, describing the objects of interest on the way. With this view, we shall visit all the more important public buildings and institutions in successive walks, adding in notes such collateral or subordinate information as may appear necessary to convey a more accurate idea of the city and its institutions, as well as other matter which may tend to enliven the dulness of dry topographical details.

WALK FIRST.

REGISTER-HOUSE—THEATRE-ROYAL—STAMP OFFICE—POST OFFICE—PRISON—BRIDEWELL—CALTON HILL—STEWART'S MONUMENT—OBSERVATORY—PLAYFAIR'S MONUMENT—CAMERA OBSCURA—NELSON'S MONUMENT—NATIONAL MONUMENT—HIGH SCHOOL—BURNS'S MONUMENT—HOLYROOD PALACE—HOLYROOD ABBEY—ARTHUR'S SEAT—HOUSE OF JOHN KNOX—NORTH BRIDGE.

THE central situation of the building, and the large number of hotels in its neighbourhood, points out

THE REGISTER HOUSE

as an appropriate starting point.   This handsome edifice,
designed by the celebrated Robert Adam, is the Depo-
sitory of the Public Records.*   It forms a square of 200

* This important establishment includes various offices, such as the offices
of the Clerks and Extractors of the Court of Session, of the Jury Court, and
of the Court of Justiciary, the office of the Great and Privy Seal, of the Chan-
cery, the Lord Lyon's office, the Bill-Chamber, &c. But it is most celebrated
for the different Registers which are there kept, and from which it derives its
name. The most important and useful of these are the Registers of Sasines,
of Inhibitions, and of Adjudications.

When a party wishes either to dispose absolutely of a landed estate in Scotland, or to grant a security over it, (such as an heritable bond,) it is necessary
for him not only to grant a conveyance of the property to the purchaser or
creditor, as the case may be, but also to give him Infeftment or Sasine, which is
a symbolical delivery of the lands. An instrument of Sasine is then written out
by a notary, which must be recorded within sixty days in the Register of Sasines.
And, in the case of a competition, it is not the party whose conveyance or instrument of Sasine is *first in date*, but the party whose Sasine is *first recorded*, who
is preferred to the property. The Sasine may be recorded either in the General
Register for all Scotland, which is kept in the Register-House at Edinburgh, or
in the particular Register for the County where the lands lie. These County
Registers are transmitted at stated periods to the Keeper of the Records in
Edinburgh.

This is the manner in which a party *voluntarily* divests himself of his lands ;
but there are also two kinds of diligence,—Inhibition and Adjudication,—by
which an individual's heritable property may be affected without his consent. By
the former, a debtor is prohibited from conveying or burdening his property to
the prejudice of the creditor using the inhibition ; by the latter, he is divested of
the property, which, by a decree of the court, is declared to belong to his creditor, in satisfaction of his debt. An inhibition must be recorded within forty
days of its date, either in the General Register of Inhibitions at Edinburgh, or
in the Particular Register for the County, which, like the County Registers of
Sasines, are transmitted at stated periods to the Keeper of the Records at
Edinburgh. An abbreviate of a decree of adjudication must be recorded within
sixty days of its date, in a register kept in the Register-House for that purpose,
called the Register of Abbreviates of Adjudication.

A party, therefore, who wishes either to purchase a property or make a loan
over it, may, by a search of the Registers of Sasines, Inhibitions, and Adjudications, ascertain whether there has been any previous sale or conveyance of it
by the proprietor or his predecessors—to what extent it may be burdened with
heritable debts—whether the proprietor has been prohibited by inhibition from
granting any voluntary conveyance—or whether there has been any judicial
assignation of it by adjudication. It is a principle of the Scotch law, that no
party who has possessed a property upon an heritable title for forty years, shall
be disquieted in his possession thereafter ; and, also, that any party who may
have possessed a title to a property without insisting in or prosecuting it for
a period of forty years, shall be held to have abandoned his right. A forty

feet, surmounted by a dome of fifty feet diameter. It contains upwards of 100 apartments for the transaction of public business. Among these the great room, in which the older records are deposited, is distinguished for its handsome proportions. Admission can only be obtained by an introduction to some of the public officers.

Directly opposite the east end of the Register House, stands

THE THEATRE ROYAL.

Its exterior is plain almost to meanness, but its internal accommodation is excellent. Its management is unexceptionable, the manager, Mr. W. H. Murray, being equally esteemed for his distinguished ability in his profession, and for the virtues and accomplishments of his private life.*

Proceeding due east we enter Waterloo Place, and on the right pass successively the STAMP OFFICE, and the POST OFFICE. The lightness of the open colonnades on either side of the street are generally much admired by English strangers. It was upon entering this street, and contemplating the Calton Hill before him, that George IV. exclaimed, in royal rapture, " How superb !" Still advancing in the same direction, we reach the stair leading to the Calton Hill, from the top of which may be seen, in the churchyard across the street, the circular tower erected as a monument to David Hume, the Historian. THE PRISON is immediately to the east of the churchyard,

years' search of the records, showing no incumbrances, is therefore generally considered sufficient evidence that the property is not liable to any burden or ground of eviction, and that any one may with safety either purchase it or lend money on its security. No such assurance of the safety of a transaction, relative to landed property, can be obtained in England, nor probably in any other country in Europe.

* A smaller theatre, under the same management, is open during the summer months. It stands at the head of Leith Walk, but possesses no architectural attraction.

and a little further along, in the same direction, is
BRIDEWELL. To both of these institutions strangers are
admitted, by orders from any of the magistrates of the
city, which there is no difficulty in procuring.

Upon the left hand, in ascending the second flight of
steps to the hill, is the graceful MONUMENT to DUGALD
STEWART, a reproduction, with some variations, of the
Choragic monument of Lysicrates. For the design of
this monument, Edinburgh is indebted to the classical
taste of Mr. Playfair. Close by are THE OBSERVATORY,
and MONUMENT to PROFESSOR PLAYFAIR. In the OLD
OBSERVATORY, an unshapely building, occupying a prominent position a little to the west, is a CAMERA OBSCURA,
accessible to strangers by an order from any of the subscribers. Upon the summit of the hill stands NELSON'S
MONUMENT, a structure more ponderous than elegant,
" modelled exactly after a Dutch skipper's spy-glass, or
a butter churn,"* but which, from the grandeur of its site,
and greatness of dimensions, must be admitted to possess
those attributes of sublimity which are independent of
grandeur of design. The prospect from the top of the
monument is very fine ; the admission fee is threepence
for each person. Near Nelson's Monument are the
twelve columns of the NATIONAL MONUMENT. The object proposed by the erection of this structure, was the
commemoration of the heroes who fell at Waterloo.
The splendour of the intended building, (which was to
be a literal restoration of the Parthenon,) was worthy of
so patriotic a cause, but, unfortunately, the architectural
taste of the projectors was far in advance of the pecu-
niary means at their disposal, and the monument consequently remains unfinished. It cannot fail to be lamented,

* The Modern Athens. By a Modern Greek. London, 1825.

not only by all Scotsmen, but by every man of taste, that this attempt to restore one of the "glories of the antique world," upon a site worthy of its fame, should thus be defeated by the want of funds. How long the structure is destined to languish in its present condition it is impossible to calculate—probably till some auspicious occasion, when Her Majesty may be pleased to visit her Scottish Metropolis, and to acknowledge a royal interest in the progress of the work. So far as the building has proceeded the workmanship is masterly, affording a very fine example of Edinburgh masonry. The view with which our text is illustrated, represents the existing condition of this modern ruin.

On the southern slope of the hill, overlooking the buildings of the Old Town,

THE HIGH SCHOOL

occupies a site worthy of its architectural beauty. The business of the school is conducted by a Rector, four Classical Masters, a French Teacher, a Teacher of Writing, and a Teacher of Arithmetic and Mathematics.

Of these, the first five have a small endowment from the city in addition to the Class-fees. Although essentially a classical seminary, due consideration is given to those collateral branches of learning which form a necessary part of a liberal education. The extent of the building affords ample accommodation for conducting the business of instruction upon the most approved principles; and the play-ground, extending to nearly two acres, commands a fine prospect of the Old Town, Arthur's Seat, and the adjacent country.* Opposite the High School, close upon the road side, stands BURNS's MONUMENT, with a statue of the Poet by Flaxman. The monument is open during the summer months, the admission-fee being sixpence for each visitor.

From this point a descent may be made by a footpath to the North Back of the Canongate, at the lower end of which the stranger will reach

HOLYROOD PALACE.

This ancient residence of Scottish Royalty is a handsome building of a quadrangular form, with a central court

* In 1823, the increasing population of the city appeared to demand the institution of another seminary for the same branches of learning as the High School. THE NEW ACADEMY was accordingly then founded in the northern suburbs of the city, by an influential body of the inhabitants, and its situation renders it more convenient for those residing in that neighbourhood. In both institutions the instruction of the pupils is conducted with the utmost zeal and success, many of them, after completing their curriculum of study, carrying off the highest honours in the Universities of Oxford and Cambridge. Still more recently has been instituted THE SOUTHERN ACADEMY, for the convenience of the inhabitants of that quarter of the city. Here also the instruction of the pupils is most judiciously superintended. To the admirable mental culture these institutions afford, may principally be imputed the advanced intelligence which distinguishes the great body of the inhabitants of the Scottish Metropolis, great proportion of the children of the higher and middle classes receiving their education in one or other of these seminaries. Besides the public Institutions, there are many admirably conducted private schools. Those interested in the instruction of the humbler ranks, would do well to visit DR. BELL's SCHOOL in Niddry Street, where a very large number of children of both sexes receive the benefit of a useful education.

ninety-four feet square. Its front is flanked with double castellated towers, imparting to the building that military character which the events of Scottish History have so often proved to have been requisite in her Royal residences.

The changes which from time to time the edifice has undergone, renders it a matter of difficulty to affix a precise date to any part of it. The towers of the north-west corner, built by James V., are understood to be the most ancient portion of the present building. In 1822, previous to the visit of George IV., some improvements were made in its internal accommodation, and since that time its walls have undergone a thorough repair at the expense of the Crown. The most interesting relic is the BED OF QUEEN MARY, which remains in the same state as when last occupied by that unhappy Princess. The CLOSET where the murderers of Rizzio surprised their victim, is also an object of interest to visitors. This bloody tragedy was acted on the 9th of March, 1566. " The Queen was seated at supper in a small cabinet adjoining to her bedroom, with the Countess of Argyle, Rizzio, and one or two other persons. Darnley suddenly entered the apartment, and, without addressing or saluting the company, gazed on Rizzio with a sullen and vindictive look ; after him followed Lord Ruthven, pale and ghastly, having risen from a bed of long sickness to be chief actor in this savage deed ; other armed men appeared behind. Ruthven called upon Rizzio to come forth from a place which he was unworthy to hold. The miserable Italian, perceiving he was the destined victim of this violent intrusion, started up, and, seizing the Queen by the skirts of her gown, implored her protection. Mary was speedily forced by the King from his hold. George Douglas, a

bastard of the Angus family, snatched the King's own
dagger from his side, and struck Rizzio a blow; he was
then dragged into the outer apartment, and slain with
fifty-six wounds. The Queen exhausted herself in prayers
and entreaties for the wretched man's life; but when
she was at length told that her servant was slain, she
said, ' I will then dry my tears, and study revenge.'
During the perpetration of this murder, Morton, the
chancellor of the kingdom, whose duty it was to enforce
the laws of the realm, kept the doors of the Palace with
160 armed men, to insure the perpetration of the
murder."*

Stains are still shown at the door of the apartment,
said to be produced by the blood of the murdered man.†

---

* SCOTT's Scotland, vol. ii., p. 105.

† A pleasant story, suggested by these reputed blood-marks, occurs in the
introductory chapter to the Second Series of Chronicles of the Canongate.
Our readers, we are assured, will thank us for enlivening our narrative by here
introducing it.

"My long habitation in the neighbourhood," says Mr. Chrystal Croftangry,
"and the quiet respectability of my habits, have given me a sort of intimacy
with good Mrs. Policy, the housekeeper in that most interesting part of the
old building, called Queen Mary's Apartments. But a circumstance which
lately happened has conferred upon me greater privileges; so that, indeed,
I might, I believe, venture on the exploit of Chatelet, who was executed for
being found secreted at midnight in the very bedchamber of Scotland's mistress.

"It chanced, that the good lady I have mentioned, was, in the discharge of her
function, showing the apartments to a Cockney from London;—not one of your
quiet, dull, commonplace visitors, who gape, yawn, and listen with an acquies-
cent nymph, to the information doled out by the provincial cicerone. No such
thing—this was the brisk, alert agent of a great house in the city, who missed
no opportunity of doing business, as he termed it, that is, of putting off the goods
of his employers, and improving his own account of commission. He had
fidgeted through the suite of apartments, without finding the least opportunity
to touch upon that which he considered as the principal end of his existence.
Even the story of Rizzio's assassination presented no ideas to this emissary of
commerce, until the housekeeper appealed, in support of her narrative, to the
dusky stains of blood upon the floor.

"' These are the stains,' she said; ' nothing will remove them from the place
—there they have been for two hundred and fifty years—and there they will remain while the floor is left standing—neither water nor any thing else will ever
remove them from that spot.'

The largest apartment in the Palace is the Picture Gallery, which measures 150 feet long, by 27 broad. Upon the walls of this room are suspended the portraits of 106 Scottish Kings, in a style of art truly barbarous. They

" Now, our Cockney, amongst other articles, sold Scouring Drops, as they are called, and a stain of two hundred and fifty years' standing was interesting to him, not because it had been caused by the blood of a Queen's favourite, slain in her apartment, but because it offered so admirable an opportunity to prove the efficacy of his unequalled Detergent Elixir. Down on his knees went our friend, but neither in horror nor devotion.

" ' Two hundred and fifty years, ma'am, and nothing take it away ? Why, if it had been five hundred, I have something in my pocket will fetch it out in five minutes. D'ye see this elixir, ma'am ? I will show you the stain vanish in a moment.'

" Accordingly, wetting one end of his handkerchief with the all-derging specific, he began to rub away on the planks, without heeding the remonstrances of Mrs. Policy. She, good soul, stood at first in astonishment, like the Abbess of St. Bridget's, when a profane visitant drank up the vial of brandy which had long passed muster among the relics of the cloister for the tears of the blessed saint. The venerable guardian of St. Bridget probably expected the interference of her patroness—She of Holy Rood might, perhaps, hope that David Rizzio's spectre would arise to prevent the profanation. But Mrs. Policy stood not long in the silence of horror. She uplifted her voice, and screamed as loudly as Queen Mary herself, when the dreadful deed was in the act of perpetation—

' Harrow now out! and walawa !' she cried.

" I happened to be taking my morning walk in the adjoining gallery, pondering in my mind why the kings of Scotland, who hung around me, should be each and every one painted with a nose like the knocker of a door, when lo ! the walls once more re-echoed with such shrieks, as formerly were as often heard in the Scottish Palaces as were sounds of revelry and music. Somewhat surprised at such an alarm in a place so solitary, I hastened to the spot, and found the well-meaning traveller scrubbing the floor like a housemaid, while Mrs. Policy, dragging him by the skirts of the coat, in vain endeavoured to divert him from his sacrilegious purpose. It cost me some trouble to explain to the zealous purifier of silk-stockings, embroidered waistcoats, broad-cloth, and deal planks, that there were such things in the world as stains which ought to remain indelible, on account of the associations with which they are connected. Our good friend viewed every thing of the kind only as the means of displaying the virtue of his vaunted commodity. He comprehended, however, that he would not be permitted to proceed to exemplify its powers on the present occasion, as two or three inhabitants appeared, who, like me, threatened to maintain the housekeeper's side of the question. He therefore took his leave, muttering that he had always heard the Scots were a nasty people, but had no idea they carried it so far as to choose to have the floors of their palaces blood-boltered, like Banquo's ghost, when to remove them would have cost but a hundred drops of the Infallible Detergent Elixir, prepared and sold by Messrs. Scrub and Rub, in five shilling and ten shilling bottles, each bottle being marked with the initials of the inventor, to counterfeit which would be to incur the pains of forgery."

appear to be " mostly by the same hand, painted either from the imagination, or porters hired to sit for the purpose." * In the olden time many a scene of courtly gaiety has enlivened this gloomy hall; among the last were the balls given by Prince Charles Edward in 1745. The election of the representative Peers of Scotland is now the only ceremony performed within its walls. In the south side of the quadrangle is the Hall of State fitted up for the levees of George IV. in 1822; and in the eastern side is the suite of apartments occupied by Charles X. (of France) and his family in 1830–33. The Palace is shown to strangers by the domestics of the Duke of Hamilton, hereditary keeper. Three different persons used to be employed to exhibit the Palace and Abbey, the gratuities being left to the discretion of visitors. It is presumed that no claim ought now to be made by the exhibitors of the Palace, as Mr. Hume, when referring in the House of Commons to the estimate for the repairs of the Royal Palaces in Scotland, observed, that " he held in his hand a letter from the Duke of Hamilton, stating that orders had been given for the opening of Holyrood Palace free of charge to the public."

On the north side of the Palace, are the ruins of the
ABBEY OF HOLYROODHOUSE.
This Abbey was founded in 1128, by David I., a prince whose prodigal liberality to the clergy drew from James VI. the pithy observation that he was " a sair sanct for the Crown."† Of this building nothing now remains but

* Humphrey Clinker.
† Tradition gives the following account of the foundation of the Abbey:— The pious David having been out hunting, was placed in the utmost peril by the attack of a stag. When defending himself from his assailant, a cross miraculously slipped from heaven into his hand, upon seeing which the stag instantly fled. The sequel is more credible. In a dream which visited the slumbers of the monarch, he was commanded to erect an abbey on the spot of his remarkable preservation, and in obedience to the heavenly mandate, he founded the Abbey of Holyroodhouse.

the mouldering ruins of the chapel, situated immediately
behind the palace. "It was fitted up by Charles I. as
a chapel royal, that it might serve as a model of the
English form of worship, which he was anxious to introduce into Scotland. He was himself crowned in it in
1633. James II. (VII. of Scotland) afterwards rendered
it into a model of Catholic worship to equally little purpose. Since the fall of the roof in 1768, it has been a
ruin."* In the south-east corner are deposited the remains of David II., James II., James V., and Magdalen
his Queen, Henry Lord Darnley, and other illustrious
persons. The precincts of the Abbey, including Arthur's
Seat and Salisbury Crags, are a sanctuary for insolvent
debtors. The limit of the privileged territory, on the side
next the town, extends to about a hundred yards from
the Palace.†

The immediate proximity of Arthur's Seat may induce
many tourists to ascend the hill from this point, the most
favourable which can be selected for the purpose. Its
height is 822 feet above the level of the sea, and the
ascent being neither difficult nor dangerous, the tourist
is amply rewarded for his slight exertion, by the magnificent prospect from the summit. "A nobler contrast
there can hardly exist than that of the huge city, dark
with the smoke of ages, and groaning with the various
sounds of active industry or idle revel, and the lofty and
craggy hill, silent and solitary as the grave; one exhibiting the full tide of existence, pressing and precipitating
itself forward with the force of an inundation; the other
resembling some time-worn anchorite, whose life passes
as silent and unobserved as the slender rill, which escapes

* CHAMBERS' Picture of Scotland.
† In Croftangrie, a narrow lane close by the Abbey, is a house said to have
been occupied by the Regent Murray.

unheard, and scarce seen, from the fountain of his patron saint. The city resembles the busy temple, where the modern Comus and Mammon held their court, and thousands sacrifice ease, independence, and virtue itself, at their shrine ; the misty and lonely mountain seems as a throne to the majestic but terrible genius of feudal times, where the same divinities dispensed coronets and domains to those who had heads to devise, and arms to execute bold enterprises."* On the left of the footpath leading up the hill stand the ruins of St. Anthony's Chapel,† and upon the right is the semicircular ridge of bold and precipitous rocks known by the name of Salisbury Crags. Those who are disinclined to ascend the hill, may either walk along the top of the Crags or along the promenade immediately below.‡ From this walk may be seen the

* Sir Walter Scott—Introduction to the Chronicles of the Canongate.

† The spot where Jeanie Deans is represented to have met with the ruffian Robertson may be seen in ascending the hill, although no remains of the cairn are now visible. " It was situated," says the novelist, " in the depth of the valley behind Salisbury Crags, which has for a background the north-western shoulder of the mountain, called Arthur's Seat, on whose descent still remain the ruins of what was once a chapel, or hermitage, dedicated to Saint Anthony the Eremite. A better site for such a building could hardly have been selected ; for the chapel, situated among the rude and pathless cliffs, lies in a desert, even in the immediate vicinity of a rich, populous, and tumultuous capital ; and the hum of the city might mingle with the orisons of the recluses, conveying as little of worldly interest as if it had been the roar of the distant ocean. Beneath the steep ascent on which these ruins are still visible, was, and perhaps is still pointed out, the place where the wretch Nicol Muschat had closed a long scene of cruelty towards his unfortunate wife, by murdering her with circumstances of uncommon barbarity. The execration in which the man's crime was held, extended itself to the place where it was perpetrated, which was marked by a small *cairn* or heap of stones, composed of those which each passenger had thrown there in testimony of abhorrence, and on the principle, it would seem, of the ancient British malediction, ' May you have a cairn for your burial-place.' "—*Heart of Mid-Lothian.*

‡ " If I were to choose a spot from which the rising or setting sun could be seen to the greatest possible advantage, it would be that wild path winding around the foot of the high belt of semi-circular rocks, called Salisbury Crags, and marking the verge of the steep descent which slopes down into the glen on the south-eastern side of the City of Edinburgh. The prospect, in its general outline, commands a close-built, high-piled city, stretching itself out in a form

site of the cottage of Davie Deans, and other objects rendered imperishably interesting by the novels of Sir Walter Scott.

Retracing our steps to Holyrood and proceeding up the Canongate, we reach, upon the left, QUEENSBERRY HOUSE, a large dull looking structure, erected by William, first Duke of Queensberry. The building is now converted into an hospital. A little farther up the street, on the opposite side, approached by a narrow archway, is the WHITE HORSE CLOSE, a singular looking group of houses, which, in ancient times, was a well frequented *hostelrie*. The White Horse Inn is understood to be the oldest place of the kind in the city, of which the premises remain in their original integrity, although now partitioned into dwelling-houses of the lowest class.* Continuing to ascend the street, we pass, upon the same side, the ungainly fabric called the CANONGATE KIRK, and next reach the Court-Room and Jail of the Canongate. In a niche of the latter building are painted the arms of the

which, to a romantic imagination, may be supposed to represent that of a dragon; now a noble arm of the sea, with its rocks, isles, distant shores, and boundary of mountains; and now, a fair and fertile champaign country, varied with hill, dale, and rock, and skirted by the picturesque ridge of the Pentland Mountains. But as the path gently circles around the base of the cliffs, the prospect, composed as it is of these enchanting and sublime objects, changes at every step, and presents them blended with, or divided from each other, in every possible variety which can gratify the eye and the imagination. When a piece of scenery so beautiful, yet so varied—so exciting by its intricacy, and yet so sublime—is lighted up by the tints of morning or of evening, and displays all that variety of shadowy depth, exchanged with partial brilliancy, which gives character even to the tamest of landscapes, the effect approaches near to enchantment. This path used to be my favourite evening and morning resort, when engaged with a favourite author, or new subject of study."—*Heart of Mid-Lothian.*

The solid and commodious pathway which has now superseded the winding footpath above described, was suggested by this glowing eulogy of the surrounding landscape.

* A modern proprietor has had the singularly bad taste to change the name of this antique court to *Davison's Close.* Surely the Antiquarian Society, or some other competent tribunal, should be armed with power to avenge such affronts upon antiquity.

JOHN KNOX'S HOUSE.

Canongate, with the motto, "*Sic itur ad astra*," as if the worthy inhabitants of this ancient burgh regarded the prison as the best avenue to heaven. A little further up the street, on the left, is MORAY HOUSE, the ancient mansion of the Earls of Moray, erected in 1618. From the balcony in front of the building, the Marquis of Argyle and his family saw the Marquis of Montrose conducted to prison, from whence he was shortly afterwards led to execution. Still ascending the street, we pass, upon the right and left, Leith Wynd and St. Mary's Wynd, two narrow streets, dedicated to the sale of old clothes. At the head of the Netherbow, where it expands into the High Street, stands the HOUSE OF JOHN KNOX. Over the door is an inscription, at present totally eclipsed by the numerous signboards of the inhabitants, but which, if visible, would run thus :

LUFE . GOD . ABOVE . AL . AND . YOUR . NICHBOUR . AS . YOUR . SELF.

Close beneath the window from which Knox is said to have preached to the populace, there has long existed a rude effigy of the Reformer stuck upon the corner in the attitude of addressing the passers by.* After having

---

* "Of this, no features were, for a long time, discernible, till Mr. Dryden,† about three years ago, took shame to himself for the neglect it was experiencing, and got it daubed over in glaring oil-colours, at his own expense. Thus a red nose, and two intensely black eyes, were brought strongly out upon the mass of the face; and a pair of white-iron Geneva bands, with a new black gown, completed the resuscitation. A large canopy of Chinese fashion, hung at the edges with tassels, was spread over the preacher's head, making him look much finer than he had ever done in his life-time, and a demure precentor was placed underneath his yellow pulpit, in order to prevent strangers from taking up an idea that our great Reformer, like the poor itinerant Methodists of modern times, had to direct the singing as well as the doctrine of his hearers. The precentor, however, was not very well used in his station, for, provoking only the laughter of the spectators, while the preacher excited their veneration, he was

† An intelligent tonsor, occupying the house at the time Mr Chambers visited the premises. The house is now possessed by a member of the same family, who cherishes the effigy of the Reformer with similar affection, and displays a more classical taste in its colouring and decorations.

sufficiently admired this grotesque specimen of sculpture, the stranger will pursue his way up the High Street. The stupendous height of many of the houses, and the air of antique majesty which, in spite of some modern innovations, still distinguishes the street, cannot fail to strike the attention of visitors. From either side descend numerous lanes or *closes*, of a width frequently limited to six feet, and so steep as to be of very laborious ascent. In these closes are the squalid abodes of some of the lowest of the population.

Upon reaching the North Bridge, our first walk will terminate by returning to the Register Office. If the stranger desires to prolong it, he will continue to ascend the High Street, commencing with the Tron Church. For the sake of arrangement, however, we must designate the next division of his progress the Second Walk.

WALK SECOND.

TRON CHURCH—ROYAL EXCHANGE—ST. GILES'S CATHEDRAL—PARLIA- MENT HOUSE—ADVOCATES' LIBRARY—SIGNET LIBRARY—COUNTY HALL—BANK OF SCOTLAND—CASTLE—GEORGE IV. BRIDGE— HERIOT'S HOSPITAL.

PROCEEDING as before from the Register Office, the stranger will now walk along the North Bridge. This bridge was founded in 1763, and completed in 1769. On the 3d of August in the latter year, the arches of

soon after taken down. There is a stone in the building, at a little distance from the diminutive pulpit, and pointed at by the preacher, bearing the name of the Deity in Greek, Latin, and English, carved upon it, from which rays seem to diverge upon the side next the effigy, and clouds upon the side most remote

three vaults in the south abutment, in consequence of an error in construction, gave way with a tremendous crash, and filled the whole city with alarm. Five persons were killed by the accident. There is a floating tradition that a similar catastrophe is once more destined to occur. From the parapet, on each side, is an extensive view of the city towards the east and the west. The spacious area seen immediately below, when looking over the western parapet, contains the fish, fruit, and vegetable markets. From these, an ascent by stairs conducts to the butcher market and poultry market, which are situate upon successive terraces communicating with each other. Proceeding to the upper end of the North Bridge, the stranger again reaches the High Street, part of which he traversed in the preceding walk. Its length from the Castle to Holyrood Palace is about a mile.* At the point where the High Street and the North and South Bridges cross each other, stands the Tron Church, an edifice of no architectural pretension. It derived its name from a *tron* or weighing beam in its immediate neighbourhood, to which, in former times, it was customary to nail false notaries and other malefactors by the ears. Its clock is provided with a dial plate of dimmed glass, which is lighted with gas from the inside after nightfall.

Ascending the High Street,

from his irradiating finger. Some ingenuity seems to have been exercised here in painting the radiance of a bright saffron, while the reprobate clouds are treated with a villanous dark green—a distinction of wonderful delicacy, considering what the rays and the clouds are intended to emblematise. The modern possessor, to whom the general thanks of Scotland are due, takes care to paint the whole piously over every second of May."—*Traditions of Edinburgh*, vol. i., p. 243.

* Although we have here given the general designation of High Street to this imposing line of buildings, its various divisions, commencing at the Castle, are severally known by the names, *Castle Hill—Lawnmarket—High Street—Netherbow* and *Canongate.*

THE ROYAL EXCHANGE BUILDINGS

lie upon the right hand side of the way opposite St. Giles's Cathedral. The Council Chamber, for the meetings of the Magistracy, and various other apartments for the transaction of municipal business, occupy that side of the quadrangle opposite the entrance. Parties proposing to visit the Crown Room in the Castle, will here obtain orders of admission on the terms mentioned on page 53 of the present work. The spot where the city Cross formerly stood is now indicated by a radiated pavement about twenty-five yards from the entrance to the Exchange.

ST. GILES'S CATHEDRAL

is nearly opposite the Royal Exchange. It derives its name from its patron, St. Giles, abbot and confessor, and tutelar saint of Edinburgh.* The date of its foundation

* Mr. Stark, in his very accurate work, relates that the legend regarding St. Giles, describes him as "a native of Greece born in the sixth century. On the

is unknown. It is first mentioned in the year 1359, in a charter of David II. In 1466, it was made a collegiate church, and no fewer than forty altars were at this period supported within its walls. The Scottish poet, Gavin Douglas, (the translator of Virgil,) was for some time Provost of St. Giles. After the Reformation it was partitioned into four places of worship, and the sacred vessels and relics which it contained, including the arm-bone referred to in the preceding note, were seized by the magistrates of the city, and the proceeds of their sale applied to the repairing of the building. In 1603, before the departure of James VI. to take possession of the throne of England, he attended divine service in this church, after which he delivered a farewell address to his Scottish subjects, assuring them of his unalterable affection. "His words were often interrupted by the tears of the whole audience, who, though they exulted at the King's prosperity, were melted into sorrow by these tender declarations." * On the 13th October 1643, the Solemn League and Covenant was sworn to and subscribed within its walls by the Committee of Estates

---

death of his parents, he gave all his estate to the poor, and travelled into France, where he retired into the deep recess of a wilderness, near the conflux of the Rhone with the sea, and continued there for three years, living upon the spontaneous produce of the earth and the milk of a doe. Having obtained the reputation of extraordinary sanctity, various miracles were attributed to him ; and he founded a monastery in Languedoc, long after known by the name of St. Giles. In the reign of James II. Mr. Preston of Gourton, a gentleman whose descendants still possess an estate in the county of Edinburgh, procured a supposed arm bone of this holy man, which relic he most piously bequeathed to the Church of St. Giles in Edinburgh. In gratitude for this invaluable donation, the magistrates of the city, in 1454, considering that the said bone was 'freely left to oure moyer kirk of Saint Gele of Edinburgh, withoutyn ony condition makyn,' granted a charter in favour of Mr. Preston's heirs, by which the nearest heir of the name of Preston was entitled to the honour of carrying it in all public processions. This honour the family of Preston continued to enjoy till the Reformation."—*Picture of Edinburgh*, p. 217.

* ROBERTSON's History of Scotland.

of Parliament, the Commission of the Church, and the English Commission. The Regent Murray and the Marquis of Montrose are interred near the centre of the south side of the church, and on the outside of its northern wall is the monument of Napier of Merchiston, the inventor of lagarithms.

The cathedral is now divided into three places of worship, viz. the High Church, the Tolbooth Church, and a Hall, originally intended for the meetings of the General Assembly, but which, after its completion, was found to be unfit for the purpose. In the High Church the Magistrates of the City, the Judges of the Court of Session, and the Barons of Exchequer, attend divine service in their official robes. The patronage of these, as well as of all the other city churches, is vested in the Magistrates and Town Council. The remains of John Knox, the austere Ecclesiastical Reformer, were deposited in the cemetery of St. Giles, which formerly occupied the ground where the buildings of the Parliament Square now stand.

With the exception of the spire, the whole of the external walls of the Cathedral have in recent years been renovated—a circumstance which has materially impaired the venerable aspect of the building.

In the centre of the Parliament Square, of which the Cathedral just described may be said to form the northern side, stands THE EQUESTRIAN STATUE OF CHARLES II., which, in vigour of design and general effect, still maintains its rank as the best specimen of bronze statuary which Edinburgh possesses.

The Chambers of the Court of Exchequer, the Parliament House, and the Libraries of the Faculty of Advocates and of the Writers to the Signet, form the eastern, western, and southern sides of the Square.

THE PARLIAMENT HOUSE

is situated in the south-west angle. The large hall, now known by the name of the *Outer-House*, is the place in which the Scottish Parliament met before the Union. This hall is 122 feet long by 49 broad. Its roof is of oak, arched and handsomely finished. It contains two statues—one of Henry Dundas, the first Lord Melville, and the other of that eminent lawyer, Lord President Blair, who died in 1811. At the south end of the Outer-House are four small chambers or Courts, in which the Lords Ordinary sit. Entering from the east side, are two larger Courts of modern and elegant structure, appropriated to the First and Second Divisions of the Court, before whom are tried those cases which are of unusual importance or difficulty, or where the judgment of a Lord Ordinary has been brought under review of the Court by a reclaimer or appeal. Adjoining to the Court-Rooms of the Divisions is another Court-Room of nearly similar appearance, in which sits the High Court of Justiciary, the supreme criminal tribunal of Scotland.

In session time, and during the hours of business, the Outer-House presents a very animated scene. As all the Courts open into it, it affords a very convenient promenade or lounging place for those counsel or agents whose cases are not then actually going on in Court. The well-employed advocates may be seen flitting from bar to bar, or Court to Court, while agents, whose causes have just been called, may be observed pressing through the crowd, with anxious face and hurried step, looking out for the counsel, whose absence from the debate might be fatal to their clients. Occasionally may be seen some unfortunate litigant, listening, with all reverence and humility, to an opinion on the merits of his case from one

of the fathers of the bar, his countenance unequivocally
expressing the hopes or fears engendered by the communication. The less employed and unemployed counsel
and agents, and a number of loungers who make this
hall a place of resort, may be seen in groups conversing
together, in every variety of tone and manner, from the
gravity of consultation to the gaiety of uncontrolled
merriment.

THE ADVOCATES' LIBRARY

adjoins the Parliament House, with which it has a communication. It contains the most valuable collection
of books in Scotland, the printed works amounting to
150,000 volumes, and the manuscripts to 1700. The
collection of Scottish poetry is exceedingly rare and
curious. The volumes in this department amount to
nearly 400, and the number is likely to be still further
increased by the zeal and research of Dr. Irving, the
present librarian, who devotes unremitting attention to
augment its treasures. Of the manuscripts, the most
valuable are those relating to the civil and ecclesiastical
history of Scotland. The funds of the Library are chiefly
derived from the fees paid by each advocate, upon his
entering as a member of the Faculty. It is also one of
the five libraries which receive from Stationers' Hall a
copy of every new work published in Great Britain or
Ireland. No public institution in Great Britain is conducted with greater liberality. Strangers are freely admitted without introduction; and no one who is at all
known, is ever denied the privilege of resorting to, and
of reading or writing in the Library. The members are
entitled to borrow twenty-five volumes at one time, and
to lend any of the books so borrowed to their friends.
The literary wealth of the library is at present deposited

in a suite of apartments neither spacious, elegant, nor commodious. It is proposed to build a new library in the neighbourhood for their reception. The office of principal librarian has been held by men eminently distinguished in the world of letters, Thomas Ruddiman, David Hume, and Adam Ferguson, having honoured the institution by filling this situation; and David Irving, LL.D., who at present holds the appointment, is an accomplished scholar, a learned civilian, and eminently skilled in ancient Scottish history, biography, and poetry.

THE SIGNET LIBRARY

is also immediately adjoining to the Parliament House. It possesses two handsome rooms, one of which was acquired a few years ago from the Advocates' Library. These rooms, more especially the upper one, are well worthy the attention of strangers. This Library is peculiarly rich in the department of history, more especially in British and Irish history. The total number of volumes it contains may be estimated at 50,000. It is supported exclusively by the contributions of the Writers to Her Majesty's Signet, and the same liberality which distinguishes the Advocates' Library, also prevails in the management of its affairs. The present librarian, Mr. David Laing, is distinguished by the extent and accuracy of his bibliographical knowledge. He also possesses that general acquaintance with literature which forms one of the most valuable qualifications for the office which he holds.

THE COUNTY HALL stands at the western termination of the Libraries above described. The general plan is taken from the Temple of Erectheus at Athens, and the principal entrance, from the Choragic Monument of

Thrasyllus. The Hall is decorated with a Statue of Lord Chief Baron Dundas, by Chantrey.

THE OLD TOLBOOTH, which the inhabitants sometimes quaintly called " The Heart of Mid-Lothian," and which, under this name, has become so renowned in the novel of Sir Walter Scott, formerly stood in the middle of the High Street, at the north-west corner of St. Giles's Church.* This gloomy looking building was built in 1561. From that period till the year 1640, it served for the accommodation of Parliament and the Courts of Justice, as well as for the confinement of prisoners; but after the erection of the present Parliament House, it was employed only as a prison. Its situation, jammed as it was into the middle of one of the chief thoroughfares of the city, was signally inconvenient, and in 1817, when the New Prison was prepared for the reception of inmates, the ancient pile of the Tolbooth was demolished. The great entrance-door, with its ponderous padlock and key, were removed to Abbotsford, the seat of Sir Walter Scott, where they are now to be seen with the other curiosities of the place.†

Proceeding up the High Street, we pass, upon the left, George the Fourth's Bridge, and on the right, Bank Street, at the foot of which stands THE BANK OF SCOT-

---

* A chartist orator, in recently addressing an audience upon the Calton Hill, commenced with the inauspicious phrase, " Men of the Heart of Mid-Lothian !" The compliment, which unquestionably belongs to the class called " left-handed," was, of course, acknowledged by a unanimous burst of laughter from the crowd.

† Alluding to the removal of these relics, Sir Walter observes, " it is not without interest, that we see the gateway through which so much of the stormy politics of a rude age, and the vice and misery of later times, had found their passage, now occupied in the service of rural economy. Last year, to complete the change, a tom-tit was pleased to build her nest within the lock of the Tolbooth—a strong temptation to have committed a sonnet, had the author, like Tony Lumpkin, been in a concatenation accordingly."

LAND, an edifice of high architectural merit, erected at an expense of £75,000.* At the head of the High Street, upon a precipitous rocky eminence, stands

THE CASTLE,

the most prominent building in the city, and one of the four fortresses which, by the Articles of Union, are to be kept constantly fortified.† The period of its foundation is unknown. There is no doubt, however, that it can boast a more remote antiquity than any other part of the city, and that it has formed the nucleus around which Edinburgh has arisen. The earliest name by which it is recognised in history, is *Castrum Puellarum,* or " The Camp of the Maidens," from the daughters of the Pictish kings being educated and brought up within its walls. It consists of a series of irregular fortifications, and although, before the invention of gunpowder, it might be considered impregnable, it is now a place of more apparent than real strength. It can be approached only upon the eastern side. The other three sides are very preci-

---

* The Bank of Scotland has the merit of having originated and established the distinctive principles of the Scotch Banking System. It is the earliest establishment of the kind in Scotland, having been incorporated by Act of the Scotch Parliament in 1695. The capital of the Bank—originally £100,000—is now £1,500,000; of which sum £1,000,000 has been paid up. In the year 1704, it commenced the issue of £1 notes—a practice now universally adopted by Scottish Banks, and found to be attended with great public convenience.

With the exception of the *Bank of Scotland,* the *Royal Bank of Scotland,* and the *British Linen Company,* all of which possess large capitals, there are no chartered banking associations in Scotland *with limited responsibility.* In all the other institutions of the kind, *the partners are jointly and severally liable for the debts of the company, to the whole extent of their fortunes.* And when, in addition to this security, it is considered that there is no limitation to the number of partners of which a banking company in Scotland may consist, and that the public records afford the means of ascertaining, with absolute certainty, the real and heritable estate of which the partners may be possessed, it is obvious that the banking establishments of the country possess a solidity of basis highly advantageous to the community at large.

† The other fortresses included in this provision, are the Castles of Dumbarton, Blackness, and Stirling.

pitous; some parts, as an English friend of our own observed, being *more than perpendicular*. Its elevation is 383 feet above the level of the sea, and, from various parts of the fortifications, a magnificent view of the surrounding country may be obtained. It contains accommodation for 2000 soldiers, and its armoury affords space for 30,000 stand of arms. Facing the north-east is the principal or Half-Moon Battery, mounted with twelve, eighteen, and twenty-four pounders, the only use of which, in these piping times of peace, is to fire on holidays and occasions of public rejoicing. The architectural effect of the Castle has been much marred by a modern addition on its western side, designed in a style most uncongenial to the character of a fortress.

In the earlier periods of Scottish history, this fortress experienced the vicissitudes common to the times, and was frequently taken and re-taken by various conflicting parties. In the present work, we can only advert to one or two of the more striking events in its annals.

In 1296, during the contest for the crown between Bruce and Baliol, it was besieged and taken by the English. It still remained in their possession in 1313, at which time it was strongly garrisoned and commanded by Piers Leland, a Lombard. This governor having fallen under the suspicion of the garrison, was thrown into a dungeon, and another appointed to the command, in whose fidelity they had complete confidence. It has frequently been remarked, that in capturing fortresses, those attacks are generally most successful which are made upon points where the attempt appears the most desperate. Such was the case in the example now to be narrated. Randolph, Earl of Moray, was one day surveying the gigantic rock, and probably contemplating the possibility of a successful assault upon the fortress, when he was accosted by one of his men-at-arms with the question, " Do you think it impracticable, my lord ? " Randolph turned his eyes upon the querist, a man a little past the prime of life, but of a firm, well-knit figure, and bearing in his bright eye, and bold and open brow, indications of an intrepidity which had already made him remarkable in the Scottish army.

" Do you mean the rock, Francis ? "* said the earl ; " perhaps not, if we could borrow the wings of our gallant hawks."

" There are wings," replied Francis, with a thoughtful smile, " as strong, as buoyant, and as daring. My father was keeper of yonder fortress."

" What of that ? you speak in riddles."

" I was then young, reckless, high-hearted; I was mewed up in that convent-like castle ; my mistress was in the plain below—"

" Well, what then ? "

" 'Sdeath, my lord, can you not imagine that I speak of the wings of love ? Every night I descended that steep at the witching hour, and every morning before the dawn I crept back to my barracks. I constructed a light twelve-foot ladder, by means of which I was able to pass the places that are perpendicular ; and so well, at length, did I become acquainted with the route, that in the darkest and stormiest night, I found my way as easily as when the moonlight enabled me to see my love in the distance, waiting for me at her cottage door."

" You are a daring, desperate, noble fellow, Francis ! However, your motive is now gone ; your mistress—"

* The soldier's name was William Frank. Mr. Leitch Ritchie here uses the novelist's license in dealing with the name, and in throwing the story into the form of a dialogue, but the events are faithfully narrated.

" She is dead : say no more ; but another has taken her place."

" Ay, ay, it is the soldier's way. Woman will die, or even grow old ; and what are we to do ?   Come, who is your mistress now ? "

" MY COUNTRY. What I have done for love, I can do again for honour ; and what *I* can accomplish, you, noble Randolph, and many of our comrades, can do far better. Give me thirty picked men, and a twelve-foot ladder, and the fortress is our own ! "

The Earl of Moray, whatever his real thoughts of the enterprise might have been, was not the man to refuse such a challenge. A ladder was provided, and thirty men chosen from the troops ; and in the middle of a dark night, the party, commanded by Randolph himself, and guided by William Francis, set forth on their desperate enterprise.

By catching at crag after crag, and digging their fingers into the interstices of the rocks, they succeeded in mounting a considerable way ; but the weather was now so thick, they could receive but little assistance from their eyes ; and thus they continued to climb, almost in utter darkness, like men struggling up a precipice in the night- mare. They at length reached a shelving table of the cliff, above which the ascent, for ten or twelve feet, was perpendicular ; and having fixed their ladder, the whole party lay down to recover breath.

From this place they could hear the tread and voices of the " check-watches" or patrol above ; and surrounded by the perils of such a moment, it is not wonderful that some illusions may have mingled with their thoughts. They even imagined that they were seen from the battle- ments ; although, being themselves unable to see the warders, this was highly improbable. It became evident, notwithstanding, from the words they caught here and there, in the pauses of the night-wind, that the conversation of the English soldiers above, related to a surprise of the castle; and, at length, these appalling words broke like thunder on their ears: "Stand! I see you well!" A fragment of the rock was hurled down at the same instant; and, as rushing from crag to crag, it bounded over their heads, Randolph and his brave followers, in this wild, helpless, and extraordinary situation, felt the damp of mortal terror gathering upon their brow, as they clung, with a death-grip, to the precipice.

The startled echoes of the rock were at length silent, and so were the voices above. The adventurers paused, listening breathless; no sound was heard but the sighing of the wind, and the measured tread of the sentinel, who had resumed his walk. The men thought they were in a dream, and no wonder; for the incident just mentioned, which is related by Barbour, was one of the most singular coincidences that ever occurred. The shout of the sentinel, and the missile he had thrown, were merely a boyish freak; and while listening to the echoes of the rock, he had not the smallest idea that the sounds which gave pleasure to him, carried terror, and almost despair, into the hearts of the enemy.

The adventurers, half uncertain whether they were not the victims of some illusion, determined that it was as safe to go on as to turn back; and, pursuing their laborious and dangerous path, they at length reached the bottom of the wall. This last barrier they scaled by means of their ladder; and leaping down among the astonished check-watches, they cried their war-cry, and, in the midst of answering shouts of "treason! treason!" notwith-

standing the desperate resistance of the garrison, captured
the Castle of Edinburgh." *

Robert Bruce then entirely demolished its fortifications,
that it might not again be occupied by a hostile power.
The wisdom of this policy was subsequently proved by
the conduct of Edward III. who, on his return from Perth,
caused it to be rebuilt and strongly garrisoned. But his
possession of it was destined to be of short duration. One
of those stratagems characteristic of the adventurous spirit
of the times, was successfully resorted to for its deliverance. In 1341, Sir William Douglas, with three other
gentlemen, waited upon the governor. One of them,
professing to be an English merchant, informed him that
he had a vessel in the Forth richly laden with wine,
beer, and biscuits exquisitely spiced, and produced at the
same time samples of the cargo. The governor, pleased
with their quality, agreed for the purchase of the whole,
which the pretended captain requested permission to deliver early next day to avoid interruption from the Scots.
He accordingly arrived at the time appointed, attended
by a dozen of armed followers, disguised as seamen, and
the gates being opened for the reception of the provisions,
they contrived, just in the entrance, to overturn one of
the carriages, thus effectually preventing the closing of
the gates. The porter and guards were then put to the
sword, and the assailants being re-inforced by Douglas
and his party, who lay in ambush near the entrance, the
English garrison was overpowered, and expelled from the
castle.

During the reign of Queen Mary, when the country
was distracted by intestine wars, this fortress was gal-

* HEATH's Picturesque annual. *Scott and Scotland*, pp. 174-7

lantly defended for the Queen by Kircaldy of Grange.
The rest of Scotland had submitted to the authority of
Morton the Regent, Kircaldy alone, with a few brave
associates, remaining faithful to the cause of his Royal
Mistress.   Morton was unable, with the troops at his
command, to reduce the garrison, but Elizabeth having
sent Sir William Drury to his aid with 1500 foot, and a
train of artillery, trenches were opened, and approaches
regularly carried on against the castle.   For three and
thirty days Kircaldy gallantly resisted the combined forces
of the Scots and English, nor did he demand a parley till
the fortifications were battered down, and the wells were
dried up or choked with rubbish.   Even then, with a
heroism truly chivalrous, he determined rather to fall
gloriously behind the ramparts, than surrender to his
enemies.   But his garrison were not animated with the
same inflexible courage.   Rising in a mutiny, they compelled him to capitulate.   Drury, in the name of his
mistress, engaged that he should be honourably treated ;
but Elizabeth, insensible alike to the claims of valour, and
to the pledged honour of her own officer, surrendered
Kircaldy to the Regent, who, *with her consent*, hanged
the gallant soldier and his brother at the Cross, on the
3d of August 1573.

   In 1650, the castle was besieged by the Parliamentary
army, under Cromwell ; and capitulated on honourable
terms.   In 1745, although Prince Charles Stuart held
possession of the city, he did not attempt the reduction
of the castle.   In modern times, some of the prisoners
during the French war, were confined within its walls.
The Scottish Regalia are exhibited in the Crown-Room
every day from twelve till three o'clock.   Visitors are
gratuitously admitted by an order from the Lord Provost,

which may be obtained by applying at the City Chambers between twelve and three o'clock. Persons procuring orders are required to sign their names and places of residence in a book kept in the City Chambers for this purpose, and the order is available only upon that day on which it is dated. These insignia of Scottish Royalty consist of a Crown, a Sceptre, and Sword of State.* Along with them is also shown the Lord Treasurer's Rod of Office, found deposited in the same strong oak chest in which the Regalia were discovered. The room where Queen Mary gave birth to James VI., in whom the crowns of England and Scotland were united, will be an object of interest to many strangers. The gigantic piece of artillery called MONS MEG, from being cast at Mons in Flanders, is mounted on an elegant carriage on

* " Taking these articles in connection with the great historical events and personages that enter into the composition of their present value, it is impossible to look upon them without emotions of singular interest, while, at the same time, their essential littleness excites wonder at the mighty circumstances and destinies which have been determined by the possession or the want of possession of what they emblematise and represent. *For* this diadem did Bruce liberate his country; *with* it, his son nearly occasioned its ruin. It purchased for Scotland the benefit of the mature sagacity of Robert II.—did not save Robert III. from a death of grief—procured, perhaps, the assassination of James I.—instigated James IV. to successful rebellion against his father, whose violent death was expiated by his own. Its dignity was proudly increased by James V. who was yet more unfortunate, perhaps, in his end, than a long list of unfortunate predecessors. It was worn by the devoted head of Mary, who found it the occasion of woes and calamities unnumbered and unexampled. It was placed upon the infant brow of her son, to the exclusion of herself from all its glories and advantages, but not to the conclusion of the distresses in which it had involved her. Her unfortunate grandson, for its sake, visited Scotland, and had it placed upon his head with magnificent ceremonies; but the nation whose sovereignty it gave him was the first to rebel against his authority, and work his destruction. The Presbyterian solemnity with which it was given to Charles II. was only a preface to the disasters of Worcester; and afterwards, it was remembered by this monarch, little to the advantage of Scotland, that it had been placed upon his head with conditions and restrictions which wounded at once his pride and his conscience. It was worn by no other monarch, and the period of its disuse seems to have been the epoch from which we may reckon the happiness of our monarchs, and the revival of our national prosperity."—CHAMBERS' *Walks in Edinburgh*, p. 49.

the Bomb Battery. It was employed at the siege of Norham, and afterwards burst, when firing a salute to the Duke of York in 1682, since which time it has never been repaired. On the north side of the esplanade stands the Statue of the late Duke of York, erected to commemorate his services as Commander-in-Chief of the Forces.

In returning from the Castle, an opening upon the left, immediately upon leaving the esplanade, conducts to the house of Allan Ramsay, the author of " The Gentle Shepherd," a pastoral drama of charming simplicity, and still highly popular among the rural population of Scotland.

The stranger will now retrace his steps to

GEORGE IV. BRIDGE,

which spans the Cowgate, and forms an important feature in the modern improvements of the city. At its northern end is the WEST Bow, which, before the erection of this bridge, presented an aspect highly interesting to the lover of antique buildings. Although now a place of small consideration, it is not 100 years since the Assembly Rooms of Edinburgh were situate within its precincts. Before the erection of the North and South Bridges, it was also the principal avenue by which wheel-carriages reached the more elevated streets of the city. It " has been ascended by Anne of Denmark, James I., and Charles I., by Oliver Cromwell, Charles II., and James II. How different the avenue by which George IV. entered the city ! " * But the West Bow has also been the scene of many more mournful processions. Previous to the year 1785, criminals were conducted through the

* CHAMBERS' Traditions of Edinburgh, vol. L, p. 140.

Bow to the place of execution in the Grassmarket, and the murderers of Porteous, after securing their victim, hurried him down this street to meet the fate they had destined for him.*   The spot where the city gibbet stood is now indicated by a cross upon the causeway of the market-place, in the middle of the street, between No. 104 on the one side, and No. 123 on the other; the centre of the cross covering the precise spot in which the socket-stone of the gallows-tree was sunk. About the middle of the Bow, where the roadway now

* The murder of Captain Porteous forms an event so memorable, not only in the annals of the city, but in what might be termed the philosophy of mobs, that it would be an unpardonable omission to pass it over unnoticed. We need hardly remind our readers that it forms one of the most striking incidents in the Heart of Mid-Lothian.

John Porteous was the son of a tailor in Edinburgh; his father intended to breed him up to his own trade, but the youthful profligacy of the son defeated the parent's prudent intention, and he enlisted into the Scotch corps at that time in the service of the States of Holland. Here he learned military discipline, and, upon returning to his own country in 1715, his services were engaged by the magistrates of Edinburgh to discipline the City Guard. For such a task he was eminently qualified, not only by his military education, but by his natural activity and resolution; and, in spite of the profligacy of his character, he received a captain's commission in the corps.

The duty of the Edinburgh City Guard was to preserve the public peace when any tumult was apprehended. They consisted principally of discharged veterans, who, when off duty, worked at their respective trades. To the rabble they were objects of mingled derision and dislike, and the numerous indignities they suffered, rendered them somewhat morose and austere in temper. At public executions they generally surrounded the scaffold, and it was on an occasion of this kind that Porteous their captain committed the outrage for which he paid the penalty of his life.

The criminal, on the occasion in question, had excited the commiseration of the populace by the disinterested courage he displayed in achieving the escape of his accomplice. At this time it was customary to conduct prisoners under sentence of death to attend divine service in the Tolbooth Church. Wilson, the criminal above alluded to, and Robertson, his companion in crime, had reached the church, guarded by four soldiers, when Wilson suddenly seized one of the guards in each hand, and a third with his teeth, and shouted to his accomplice to fly for his life. Robertson immediately fled, and effected his escape. This circumstance naturally excited a strong feeling of sympathy for Wilson, and the magistrates, fearing an attempt at rescue, had requested the presence of a detachment of infantry in a street adjoining to that where the execution was to take place, for the purpose of intimidating the populace. The introduction of another military force than his own into a quarter of the city where no drums

passes, stood the HOUSE OF MAJOR WEIR, the celebrated
necromancer, who, along with his sister, suffered death

but his own were ever beat, highly incensed Captain Porteous, and aggravated
the ferocity of a temper naturally surly and brutal. Contrary to the appre
hension of the authorities, the execution was allowed to pass undisturbed, but
the dead body had hung only a short time upon the gibbet when a tumult
arose among the multitude ; stones and other missiles were thrown at Porteous
and his men, and one of the populace, more adventurous than the rest, sprang
upon the scaffold, and cut the rope by which the criminal was suspended.

Porteous was exasperated to frenzy by this outrage on his authority, and leaping from the scaffold, he seized the musket of one of the guards, gave the word
to fire, and, discharging his piece, shot the man dead upon the spot. Several
of his soldiers also, having obeyed his order to fire, six or seven persons were
killed, and many others wounded. The mob still continuing their attack, another volley was fired upon them, by which several others fell, and the scene of
violence only closed when Porteous and his soldiers reached the guard-house in
the High Street. For his reckless and sanguinary conduct in this affair, Captain Porteous was arraigned before the High Court of Justiciary, and sentence
of death was passed upon him. His execution was appointed to take place on
the 8th of September 1736.

The day of doom at length arrived, and the ample area of the Grassmarket
was crowded in every part with a countless multitude, drawn together to gratify
their revenge or satisfy their sense of justice by the spectacle of the execution.
But their vengeance met with a temporary disappointment. The hour of execution was already past, without the appearance of the criminal, and the expectant
multitude began to interchange suspicions that a reprieve might have arrived.
Deep and universal was the groan of indignation which arose from the crowd,
when they learned that such was indeed the fact. The case having been represented to her Majesty Queen Caroline, she intimated her royal pleasure that the
prisoner should be reprieved for six weeks. The shout of disappointed revenge
was followed by suppressed mutterings and communings among the crowd, but
no act of violence was committed ; they saw the gallows taken down, and then
gradually dispersed to their homes and occupations.

Night ushered in another scene ; a drum was heard beating to arms, and the
populace promptly answered its summons by turning out into the streets. Their
numbers rapidly increased, and, separating into different parties, they took
possession of the city gates, posting sentinels for their security. They then disarmed the City Guard, and, having thus possessed themselves of weapons, they
were the uncontrolled masters of the city. During the progress of the riot,
various efforts were made to communicate with the Castle, but the vigilance of
the insurgents defeated all such attempts. The Tolbooth was now invested,
and a strong party of the rioters having surrounded it, another party proceeded
to break up the doors. For a considerable time the great strength of the place
rendered their efforts fruitless, but, having brought fire to their aid, they burned
the door, and rushed into the prison.

Porteous, elated with his escape from the sentence he so richly merited, was
regaling a party of his boon companions within the building, when the assault
was made upon its gates. The wretched man well knew the hatred with which
he was regarded by the populace, and was at no loss to comprehend the motive
for their violence. Escape seemed impossible. The chimney was the only place

for witchcraft in 1670. The fate of Weir is chiefly remarkable from his being a man of some condition, (the son of a gentleman, and his mother a lady of family in Clydesdale,) which was rarely the case with those who were the victims of such accusations. Whether the crimes which he confessed were the diseased fancies of an imagination labouring under temporary insanity, or whether he was in reality a man of atrociously depraved life, does not very clearly appear. After his condemnation, he doggedly refused to have recourse to prayer, " arguing, that as he had no hope whatever of escaping Satan, there was no need of incensing him by vain efforts at repentance." * The modern improvements in this part of the city have now swept away all vestiges of the house, which, ever after the death of Weir, enjoyed the reputation of being haunted. So general was the horror entertained for the crimes of the man and the terrors of

of concealment that occurred to him, and, scrambling into it, he supported himself by laying hold of the bars of iron with which the chimnies of a prison-house are crossed to prevent the escape of criminals. But his enemies soon dragged him from his hiding-place, and, hurrying him along the streets, they brought him to the very spot, where, that morning, he ought to have paid the forfeit of his life. The want of a rope was now the sole obstacle to the accomplishment of their purpose, and this want was soon supplied by breaking open a shop where the article was sold ; a dyer's pole served in room of a gallows, and from t they suspended the unhappy man. Having thus propitiated the spirit of offended justice, they threw down the weapons of which they had possessed themselves, and quietly dispersed to their respective homes.

It has been justly observed, that the murder of Porteous has more the character of a conspiracy than of a riot. The whole proceedings of the insurgents were marked by a cool and deliberate intrepidity, quite at variance with the accustomed conduct of rioters. No violence was perpetrated either upon person or property, save the single act of vengeance executed upon Porteous. So studious were the insurgents to avoid every appearance of prædial outrage, that a guinea was left upon the counter of the shop from which they took the rope to hang their victim. None of the offenders were ever discovered, although government made the most strenuous exertions, and offered large rewards for their apprehension. There can be little doubt, however, that many of the participators in that night's transactions were of a class unaccustomed to mingle in scenes of vulgar tumult.

* SIR WALTER SCOTT's Letters on Demonology and Witchcraft, p.330.

his abode, that no family was ever found hardy enough
to occupy the house as a residence.

In the Grassmarket—situated, as we have already
mentioned, at the foot of the Bow—a weekly market is
held on Wednesday for grain, horses, cattle, and sheep.
At its south-west corner it is entered by the WEST PORT;
the scene of the appalling atrocities of the monster Burke.
As the name of this wretched man is now generally employed to distinguish the crime for which he suffered, we
need scarcely remind our readers that his victims were
destroyed by strangulation, and that his object was not
to possess himself of their property, for they were all of
a humble rank in life, but to convert their bodies into a
source of gain by selling them to the anatomist.

Proceeding along the Bridge, Heriot's Hospital will be
seen occupying a fine situation on the right. Upon
reaching the southern end of the Bridge, and proceeding
a short way up the Candlemaker-Row, we reach upon
the right the entrance to THE GREYFRIAR'S CHURCHYARD,
in ancient times the garden belonging to the monastery of
Greyfriars, which was situated in the Grassmarket. In
this church yard are interred George Buchanan, the accomplished Latin poet, and preceptor of James VI.,
Allan Ramsay, the Scottish poet, Principal Robertson the
historian, Dr. Black, the distinguished chemist, Dr. Hugh
Blair, and Colin Maclaurin. There are two churches in
the burying-ground under one roof, known by the name
of Old Greyfriars, and New Greyfrairs. Of the former,
Principal Robertson was pastor for many years. Leaving
the churchyard, and still ascending the Candlemaker-Row,
the entrance to the CHARITY WORK-HOUSE is the next
opening upon the right. The grounds around the house
are laid out as a kitchen garden for the establishment,

and the inmates are frequently employed in its cultivation. The house itself is a large building of the plainest description. The funds by which the institution is supported are derived from an assessment on house property, collections at the church doors, and occasional donations and voluntary contributions from the citizens. The average number of inmates is about 750.*

Leaving the Work-house grounds by the entrance from Laurieston, a short walk conducts us to

HERIOT'S HOSPITAL.

This handsome edifice owes its foundation to George Heriot, jeweller to James VI., whose name will probably be more familiar to the ear of strangers as the " jingling Geordie" of " The Fortunes of Nigel." † The design, which is attributed to Inigo Jones, is in that mixed style which dates its origin from the reign of Elizabeth, examples of which are afforded by Drumlanrig Castle in Dumfries-shire, Northumberland House in the Strand, and many other edifices throughout the kingdom. Its form is quadrangular, the sides each measuring forty feet, and enclosing a court of ninety-four feet square. The building was commenced in 1628, and completed in 1660, and the erection is said to have cost £27,000. The chapel, occupying the south side of the quadrangle, a few years ago presented nothing but a clay floor and bare walls, round which there was a stone seat, to accommodate the boys when assembled for morning and evening service.

---

* Besides this institution, the parish of St. Cuthberts and the Canongate have each a house for the reception of paupers, with peculiar funds, and separate boards of management.

† " For the wealth God has sent me, it shall not want inheritors while there are orphan lads in Auld Reekie."—*Fortunes of Nigel, Chapter IV.*

A brief outline of the benevolent founder's history is given in the Note to Chapter II. of the same work.

ST. JOHN'S HOSPITAL, FROM THE GREENBANK.

It is now fitted up in a very different style, and with its splendid pulpit, fine oaken carvings, and richly adorned ceiling, forms one of the principal attractions of the place. The object of this splendid institution is the maintenance and education of " poor and fatherless boys," or boys whose parents are in indigent circumstances, " freemen's sons of the town of Edinburgh," of whom 180 are accommodated within its walls. The course of instruction consists of English, Latin, Greek, Writing, Arithmetic, Book-keeping, Mathematics, and Geography. To these branches have recently been added French, Drawing, the Elements of Music, and Practical Mechanics. Boys are admitted between the age of seven and ten, and generally leave at fourteen, unless superior scholarship appears to fit them for prosecuting some of the learned professions, in which case the period of their stay is extended, with the view of preparing them for the studies of the University. All the boys, upon leaving the hospital, receive a bible, and other useful books, with two suits of clothes of their own choice. Those going out as apprentices are allowed £10 annually for five years, and £5 at the termination of their apprenticeship. Those destined for any of the learned professions are sent to college for four years, during which period they receive £30 a-year. In 1836, an act was obtained from Parliament, empowering the Governors to extend the benefits of the Institution, and employ their surplus funds in establishing Free Schools in the different parishes of the city. Seven of these schools are already in full operation, in which upwards of 2000 children, of both sexes, are instructed in the usual branches of a parochial education, the females being, in addition, taught sewing and knitting.

This great scheme of instruction, when complete, must prove of incalculable benefit to the community, as the advantages of a substantial education will be brought within the reach of every citizen, however humble. In addition to these liberal provisions for the instruction of youth, there are also ten bursaries, or exhibitions, open to the competition of young men not connected with the institution. The successful competitors for these bursaries receive £20 *per annum*, for four years. The princely provision thus made for the welfare of his countrymen, amply justifies the sentiment put into the mouth of the founder by Sir Walter Scott, " I think mine own estate and memory, as I shall order it, has a fair chance of outliving those of greater men." The management. is vested in the Town Council and Clergy of the city, and visitors are admitted by an order from any of the Governors.

Retracing our steps to the entrance to the Charity Work-House, the Meadow Walk will be seen exactly opposite. In a field, upon the right hand, a short way down the walk, stands

GEORGE WATSON'S HOSPITAL.

This hospital is for the benefit of the children and grand-children of decayed merchants of the city of Edinburgh. The building is plain, but commodious. Boys are received into this hospital between seven and ten, and remain till fifteen years of age. The number of boys amounts to about eighty, and the education they receive very much resembles that of Heriot's Hospital. Each boy, after leaving the hospital, receives £10 a-year, for five years ; and, upon attaining the age of twenty-five, if unmarried and well-conducted, he receives a further sum of £50. Those who prefer an academical education, receive £20 a-year, for five years. The management is vested in the Master, Assistants, and Treasurer of the Merchant Company of Edinburgh, the ministers of the Old Church, and five members of the Town Council. A little to the west of George Watson's Hospital stands the Merchant Maiden Hospital, but as it does not come within the scope of any of our walks, we think it better to include the description of it, and of the other more important hospitals which we do not pass in our progress, in a foot-note.*

* *The Merchant Maiden Hospital* was founded in 1695, for the maintenance and education of the daughters of merchant burgesses in the city. Nearly 100 girls are maintained in this hospital. They are admitted between seven and eleven years of age, and leave at seventeen. The course of instruction includes English, Writing, Arithmetic, Geography, French, Music, Drawing, Dancing, and Needle-work. Upon leaving the hospital, each girl receives £9, 6s. 8d. The original edifice stood in Bristo Street; the present building is agreeably situated in Lauriestoon, a little to the west of George Watson's Hospital.

The Trades' Maiden Hospital stands on the south side of Argyle Square. The girls eligible for admission into this institution, are the daughters of decayed tradesmen. It supports about fifty girls, who are admitted at the same age, and instructed in the same branches as in the Merchant Maiden Hospital. They go out at the age of seventeen, each girl receiving £5, 11s. and a bible.

The Orphan Hospital maintains and educates about 150 children of both sexes. The old building, situated near Trinity College Church, was abandoned as unhealthy, and a handsome new edifice was erected in 1833, on the property of Dean. The benefits of the institution are extended to the whole of Scotland.

John Watson's Institution is a spacious and showy edifice, also situated on the property of Dean. The purpose of the endowment, is the maintenance and education of destitute children. About 190 children are maintained in it. They are admitted between the ages of five and eight, and leave at fourteen.

Cauvin's Hospital is pleasantly situated at Duddingston, a village about a mile and a half to the east of Edinburgh. The children enjoying the benefit of this institution are, "the sons of respectable but poor teachers," and, "of poor but honest farmers; whom failing, the sons of respectable master-printers or booksellers," and, "of respectable servants in the agricultural line." Twenty boys are maintained in it. They are admissible from six to eight years of age, and are retained in the hospital for six years.

Trinity College Hospital, the oldest charitable institution in the city, stands at the foot of the lane called Leith Wynd. It was founded in 1461 by Mary of

Immediately adjoining to the Meadows, on the south-west, are Bruntsfield Links, (*anglice*, Downs,) where many of the inhabitants are accustomed to amuse themselves with the national game of golf. The game is played with a club and ball. The club is formed of ash, flexible and finely tapered, measuring from three to four feet long, according to the player's height or length of arm. The head is faced with horn and loaded with lead. The ball is about the size of a common tennis ball, made of feathers compressed into a very hard but slightly elastic leathern shell or cover. The game consists in striking the ball successively into a certain number of small holes, about a quarter of a mile apart, the player who does so in the smallest number of strokes being the victor. Each player carries an assortment of clubs varying in elasticity, and thus adapted to the distance the ball is to be driven, the best club for a long stroke being laid aside for one less elastic when the distance becomes

Gueldres. Its benefits are conferred on "burgesses, their wives or children not married, nor under the age of fifty years." Forty persons are maintained within the walls of the hospital, and about ninety out-pensioners receive £6 a-year.

Gillespie's Hospital enjoys a fine situation on the south-west confines of the city. The founder was a tobacconist in Edinburgh, who devoted the greater part of his property to endow an hospital for the maintenance of indigent old men and women, and for the elementary education of 100 poor boys. The number of the aged inmates is between thirty and forty. None are admitted under the age of fifty-five, a preference being given to servants of the founder or persons of his name.

Besides the endowments for the relief of the destitute, there are many other charitable associations maintained by private subscription. Among them may be mentioned, The House of Refuge—The House of Industry—The Strangers' Friend Society—The Society for Relief of the Destitute Sick—The Society for the Relief of Indigent Old Men, and two similar institutions for the Relief of Indigent Old Women—The Seamen's Friend Society—and the Society for Clothing the Industrious Poor.

There are also many public Dispensaries and a Lying-in Hospital, where medicines and medical attendance are gratuitously afforded to the poor; but a further enumeration of such institutions does not appear to be required for the purposes of the present publication.

shortened. An expert player will strike a ball from 130 *to* 150 yards.

Returning from the Links to that point of the Meadows where the walks cross each other, the stranger will be in the immediate neighbourhood of

GEORGE'S SQUARE.

This is the only large square in the Old Town. Towards the close of the last century, it was the principal place of residence of the higher ranks: The Duchess of Gordon, the Countess of Sutherland, the Countess of Glasgow, Viscount Duncan, the Hon. Henry Erskine, and many other persons of rank residing there. The house of Walter Scott, Esq., W.S., father of the novelist, was on the west side of the Square.

E

Passing along Charles Street and Bristo Street, and turning to the right into Lothian Street, two places of worship will be observed upon the left hand, the one a Roman Catholic, and the other a Baptist Chapel, the two being built upon a mutual gable. Proceeding along Lothian Street and South College Street, and then turning to the right a short distance along Nicolson Street, the stranger will arrive in front of the fine portico of

THE ROYAL COLLEGE OF SURGEONS.

In classic elegance, few buildings will be found to surpass this handsome structure, although its effect is much impaired by the uncongenial architecture of the surrounding houses. The principal portion of the building is occupied with an extensive museum of anatomical and surgical preparations. The arrangement is, in every respect, admirable, and a praiseworthy liberality is exhibited in the admission of strangers. Although, by the strict letter of the regulations, a member's order is requisite, yet even this form is, in most cases, dispensed with. A little further south, on the same side of the street, is the Asylum for the Industrious Blind.

Returning northward, the next object of importance is

' THE UNIVERSITY.

No regular University existed in Edinburgh till the year 1582, although long previous to this period, teachers of philosophy and divinity had been established in the city. On the 24th of April of that year, King James VI. issued the charter for its foundation, and in the following year the course of instruction was commenced. By the liberality of James, and private benefactions, the University rapidly advanced in importance, and, as its revenues increased, its sphere of usefulness was extended by the additión of new professorships, till, in the 18th century, it attained a celebrity unsurpassed by any academical institution in Europe.

The present structure is of modern erection. The old buildings were both unsightly and incommodious, and a subscription having been set on foot, the foundation of the present handsome and spacious edifice was laid in 1789. The local subscriptions, however, were insufficient to accomplish the object; and, upon the case being brought before Parliament, an annual grant of £10,000 was obtained to complete the undertaking. The plan is by Mr. Robert Adam, with some subsequent modifications, principally in the internal arrangement, by Mr. W. H. Playfair. The buildings are of a quadrangular form, the sides measuring 358 by 255 feet, with a spacious court in the centre. The eastern front is adorned with a portico, supported by Doric columns, twenty-six feet in height, each formed of a single block of stone.

No test of any description is required from the students; they are not resident within the College, nor are they distinguished by any peculiarity of dress. In pursuing their studies they are at perfect liberty to select the classes they attend—a certain curriculum of study is, however, requisite in taking degrees in Medicine and Arts,—those who intend to qualify for a degree in the latter being required to attend the Classes of Humanity, Greek, Logic, Rhetoric, Moral Philosophy, Natural Philosophy, and Mathematics. The number of students attending the University during the present session (1840-41,) is about 1050.

There are 34 foundations for bursaries, the benefit of

which is extended to 80 students. The greater number of these bursaries do not exceed in value £10 per annum.

The Museum contains a large collection of specimens in the various departments of Natural History. The Ornithological department is peculiarly valuable, both from its extent and admirable classification. Visitors are admitted upon payment of one shilling each. There is also an Anatomical Museum, where the professional visitor will be highly interested by the variety and beauty of the preparations.

The Library occupies the south side of the building. The principal apartment is equally distinguished by the symmetry of its proportions, the chasteness of its decorations, and its admirable adaptation to the purpose for which it is intended. It is incomparably the finest library-room in Scotland; measuring 187 feet in length, by 50 in breadth, with an arched roof from 50 to 58 feet high. A small collection of paintings, bequeathed to the University by Sir James Erskine of Torry, adorns the west end of the room.

Proceeding northward, upon leaving the University,

THE ROYAL INFIRMARY

is situated in the first street upon the right. A detailed account of this institution does not appear to be necessary in the present work. The last annual report shows that 3832 patients received the benefit of the institution within the year, of whom 782 were fever patients. Besides the relief afforded to patients, clinical lectures, or discourses on the cases in the several wards, are delivered within the walls by certain Professors of 'the University. The professor of clinical surgery also lectures upon the more important surgical cases in the wards under his inspection.

Besides the professorial lectures, the ordinary physicians and surgeons of the institution deliver clinical discourses on the cases under their immediate care. Journals are regularly kept, recording the symptoms, progress, and result of the cases, with the various remedies employed. To these journals the students have access.

The fees paid by students for the right to attend the medical and surgical practice in the Hospital, are five guineas for an annual, or twelve guineas for a perpetual ticket.

Proceeding along the South Bridge, an open railing, for a short distance on either side, affords a view of the Cowgate, with which the tourist will, in all probability, have no wish to cultivate a closer acquaintance. The Register House will again come into view on reaching the Tron Church, thus terminating our Second Walk.

WALK THIRD.

ROYAL INSTITUTION—NEW CLUB—ST. JOHN'S CHAPEL—ST. CUTHBERT'S CHURCH—CHARLOTTE SQUARE—ST. GEORGE'S CHURCH—DEAN BRIDGE—AINSLIE PLACE—MORAY PLACE—HERIOT ROW—PITT MONUMENT—GEORGE FOURTH'S MONUMENT—ASSEMBLY ROOMS—PHYSICIAN'S HALL—ST. ANDREW'S SQUARE—MELVILLE MONUMENT—ROYAL BANK.

In this walk we shall conduct the stranger through the principal streets of the New Town, adverting to all the more striking objects in our progress.

Proceeding to the westward the buildings of the High Street will be seen upon the left, towering to the heavens like the habitations of a race of Titans. These buildings, standing upon a steep and lofty ridge, with tributary lanes or closes descending abruptly to the valley beneath, produce an effect highly picturesque and majestic.   The interjacent valley extending westward to the end of Prince's Street, and now tastefully laid out in pleasure-grounds, was formerly a stagnant pond or marsh, known by the name of the Nor-Loch.   The monument to Sir Walter Scott, of which an engraving illustrates our text, is to be erected within the railing of the pleasure-grounds opposite the foot of St. David's Street.   The Earthen Mound, formed by the deposition of the rubbish accumulated in digging the foundations of the houses in the New Town, is a convenient avenue of communication between the New Town and the Old.   Its southern end has for many years been disfigured by wooden structures of all shapes and sizes, erected for successive exhibitions of wild beasts, horsemanship, wax-works, and panoramas. At its northern extremity stands

THE ROYAL INSTITUTION,

One of the handsomest modern buildings of which Edinburgh can boast.   The expense of driving the piles upon which this fine structure is built, exceeded £1600.   The Royal Society, the Royal Institution for the Encouragement of the Fine Arts in Scotland, the Board of Trustees for the Improvement of Manufactures, and the Society of Antiquaries, have apartments within its walls.   To the Museum of the Antiquarian Society strangers are admitted by an order from any of the members.   Among the relics of antiquity preserved in this collection may be mentioned the colours carried by the Covenanters during the civil war; the stool which Jenny Geddes, in her zeal against Prelacy, launched at the head of the

Bishop of Edinburgh, in St. Giles's Church ; and the *Maiden,* or Scottish guillotine, with which the Earl of Morton, the Marquis of Argyle, Sir Robert Spottiswood, and many other distinguished persons, were beheaded.* The paintings of the Scottish Artists are exhibited in the Institution during the spring months,† and the native manufactures are also exhibited here for a short period during the same season. The Royal Society holds its meetings once a fortnight during the winter months, when papers connected with the varied departments of science

* It is very generally believed, that it was the Earl of Morton who introduced the Maiden into Scotland. This opinion, however, has been proved to be erroneous, entries in the Council Records showing that it was in use long before his time. Michael Wing-the-wind, in "The Abbot," refers to this instrument during his conversation with Adam Woodcock in Holyrood Palace. " Herod's daughter," says Michael, " who did such execution with her foot and ancle, danced not men's heads off more cleanly than this Maiden of Morton. 'Tis an axe, man—an axe, which falls of itself like a sash window, and never gives the headsman the trouble to wield it."

† The Scottish School of Painting is at present in a most prosperous condition. Two associations have been formed in Edinburgh, by means of which many members of the community, who could in no other way be expected to contribute to the support of Art, are rendered willing and efficient patrons. These associations each possess a numerous body of subscribers. The amount of the annual subscriptions is expended in the purchase of pictures, which are distributed among the members by lottery. The only essential distinction between these two associations, consists in the purchase of pictures, in the one case, being made by a Committee ; while, in the other, the purchase is made by the prizeholders themselves.

The advantage of the former plan, appears to consist in the encouragement which it holds out to Artists to devote their talents to the production of works in the higher walks of Art, for which private purchasers are necessarily few in number. The advantage of the second scheme consists, in the first place, in the choice of pictures being devolved upon the prizeholders themselves, whereby each individual is enabled to gratify his personal taste ; and, secondly, in the protection it affords to the subscribers, from the danger of unreasonable prices being affixed to their pictures by those Artists who have personal friends on the Committee of Management.

A very general impression prevails, that the prices which, in some instances, have been paid by the Committee of the former association, are altogether disproportioned to the merit of the pictures bought ; and it may reasonably be questioned, whether such liberality is not in effect injurious to the very parties deriving the temporary advantage, by encouraging an exaggerated view of their merit, and a false notion of the value of their works, which must ultimately be highly prejudicial to their professional success.

and learning, falling within the scope of the Society's plan, are read by the several members.

Continuing our walk towards the west, we pass on the right THE NEW CLUB, an association of Noblemen and Gentlemen, partaking of the character of a joint-stock Hotel and Reading Room, for the exclusive accommodation of members. These are elected by ballot, the number being limited to 660. The entrance-money is thirty-five guineas, and the annual subscription five guineas.

The frowning grandeur of the Castle Rock now becomes very imposing, and presents a vivid contrast to the tranquil beauty of the green sward and shrubberies of the valley beneath. These pleasure-grounds, endowed with natural features of the most varied character, and improved by all the resources of modern Horticulture, form one of the chief ornaments of the City.

Upon reaching the west end of Princes Street, ST. JOHN'S CHAPEL and ST. CUTHBERT'S CHURCH will be seen upon the left, the former an elegant structure of the florid Gothic order, the latter in a style of architecture, which can be referred to no school, nor age, nor country. It has, however, the merit of being the largest church in Edinburgh, and is furnished with an upper and lower gallery. St. John's is one of the places of worship belonging to the Scottish Episcopal Communion, and is embellished with all those graces of internal and external architecure, by which the English Church usually distinguishes the edifices dedicated to her religious service.*

* The other Episcopal Chapels in Edinburgh are St. Paul's, York Place, a Gothic structure of singular elegance; St. George's, also in York Place, a small but commodious place of worship; St. James's, Broughton Place; St. Paul's, Carrubber's Close; St. Peter's, Roxburgh Place; and Trinity Chapel, near the Dean Bridge.

Turning to the north, the stranger will now enter Charlotte Square, a spacious quadrangle of excellent houses. In the centre of its western side stands St. George's Church, the handsomest modern place of worship in the Scotch Establishment. Its erection cost £33,000.

After passing along the narrow lane by the side of St. George's, and through Charlotte Place, turn to the right, and proceed by Melville Place, Randolph Crescent, and Lynedoch Place, through the Toll-Bar, to

THE DEAN BRIDGE.

For this fine bridge Edinburgh is principally indebted to the enterprize of one individual, who contributed largely to the expense of its erection, for the improvement of his property on the northern side of the river. The road-way passes at the great height of 106 feet above the bed of the stream.* The arches are four in number, each 96 feet span, the breadth between the parapets being 39 feet, and the total length of the bridge 447 feet.

As no object of any interest occurs on the river side, the stranger may retrace his steps to Randolph Crescent, through which he will pass to Great Stuart Street, Ainslie Place, and

MORAY PLACE.

This is the quarter of the city most celebrated for the

* This is the stream which Richie Moniplies, in the Fortunes of Nigel, represents as a navigable river superior to the Thames. Strangers, who have seen both, will be enabled to estimate how far Richie's patriotism had obscured his power of memory.

"I suppose you will tell me next" (said Master Heriot) "that you have at Edinburgh as fine a navigable river as the Thames, with all its shipping?"

"The Thames!" exclaimed Richie, in a tone of ineffable contempt—"God bless your honour's judgment, we have at Edinburgh the Water of Leith and the Nor-Loch!"

architectural magnificence of its buildings. The ground
is the property of the Earl of Moray, and the various
streets, squares, and crescents erected upon it, are in ac-
cordance with a uniform plan designed by Mr. Gillespie
Graham, architect.* By some persons it has been objected
that the severe simplicity of style and massive solidity
of structure which particularly distinguish these buildings,
impart an aspect of solemnity and gloom repugnant to
the character of domestic architecture. Even the harmony of design and uniformity of plan have offended
some critics. " The New Town of Edinburgh," says
Dr. James Johnson, in his work entitled ' The Recess,' †
" is beautifully monotonous, and magnificently dull."
Until philosophers shall succeed in establishing a uniform standard of taste, it will be vain to contend with
such cavillers. We therefore leave them in peaceful
possession of their opinions, and shall only observe, that
the massive dignity of the architecture in this quarter of
the City, has called forth the admiration of the large
majority of intelligent visitors. Nor is the substantial
comfort of the dwellings to be overlooked. The walls
are of the most solid and durable masonry ; both the
building materials and workmanship being of the best
description.

The rent of the houses in Moray Place, varies from
£140 to £160, and in Ainslie Place, from £100 to
£130.

Leaving Moray Place by Darnaway Street, Heriot

---

* The annual *feu-duty* or ground-rent of the houses, in this quarter of the
city, varies from 20s. to 40s. per foot of frontage.

† " The learned SMELFUNGUS travelled from Boulogne to Paris—from Paris
to Rome—and so on—but he set out with the spleen and jaundice, and every
object he passed by was discoloured or distorted.—He wrote an account of
them, but 'twas nothing but the account of his miserable feelings."—STERNE's
Sentimental Journey.

Row introduces us to another *suite* of those pleasure-grounds, which tend so much to beautify the city. Ascending the first opening on the right we reach Queen Street, which runs parallel with Heriot Row, and overlooks the interjacent pleasure-grounds. Through the openings formed by the streets running to the north, a noble prospect is obtained of the Firth of Forth, the shores of Fife, and the Ochil Hills, and, in some states of the atmosphere, the peaks of the Grampians may be seen in the distance.

THE PITT STATUE

occupies the spot where George's Street is intersected by Frederick Street. It is executed by Chantrey, and possesses considerable dignity of expression. Proceeding eastward along George's Street, THE ASSEMBLY ROOMS will be seen upon the right. Their external appearance is plain and unpretending, the only approach to ornament being the four Doric columns, doing duty as a portico in the front of the building. In these Rooms are held the public Balls and Concerts,* and other meetings of various kinds. The principal ball-room is 92 feet long, 42 feet wide, and 40 feet high. There are also various other

---

* Although there is no want either of taste or capacity for music in Scotland, the inhabitants of Edinburgh cannot be said to be distinguished for their practical devotion to the art. Vocal music in parts, or concerted instrumental music, is rarely met with in private society; the Glee Club, and the associations formed, from time to time, for orchestral music, being almost wholly dependent upon the professional musicians. The higher styles of ecclesiastical music may be said to be unknown, except from the performances at the two musical festivals of 1815 and 1824. The organ is excluded both from the churches of the establishment and from the chapels of the most numerous of the Dissenting bodies, and in few congregations is there even a band of professional singers. The psalmody is, for the most part, led by the precentor alone, who is followed by the whole congregation, vociferating the melody " without remorse or mitigation of voice." The want of chorus-singers, arising from the abject state of sacred music, renders it almost impossible to hold a musical

apartments of smaller dimensions. A little to the east stands

GEORGE IV. STATUE.

. It is also executed by Chantrey. The attitudinal majesty of the monarch must be admitted to be somewhat exaggerated. The figure is so far thrown back, as to give it the appearance of leaning for support upon the drapery behind, an expedient suggesting some particulars in the natural history of the kangaroo, which by no means contribute to aggrandize the effect. It must, however, be granted, that by caricaturing the Monarch the artist has exalted the Minister, for the exaggerated pomp of the one statue, powerfully contrasts with the intellectual elevation of the other.

Continuing our progress eastward, ST. ANDREW'S CHURCH stands upon the left. It possesses a portico, supported by four Corinthian columns, and a handsome spire, rising to the height of 168 feet. Among the numerous spires in Edinburgh, this is the only one at all remarkable for lightness of design, or elegance of proportion. Upon the opposite side of the street stands the PHYSICIANS' HALL, with a portico in front, supported by four Corinthian columns.

THE MELVILLE MONUMENT,

which graces the centre of St. Andrew's Square, was erected to the memory of the late Lord Melville. What-

festival in the city; and, although efforts have been making, by some of the professional vocalists, to discipline a body of singers to supply this want, Edinburgh is still immeasurably behind the cathedral towns, and even some of the manufacturing towns of England, in that indispensable requisite of the oratorio —an efficient chorus.

The Professional Society of Edinburgh includes, among its members, many highly respectable musicians; but the more liberal encouragement held out in London, to the first order of talent, deprives the city of most of its best professors in this as well as other walks of art.

ever difference of opinion may prevail as to the political views of this nobleman, it will be admitted by all parties, that, in the exercise of his patronage, the claims of his own countrymen were never overlooked. This handsome column records their gratitude for his services. It rises 136 feet high, to which the statue adds other 14 feet. The design is that of the Trajan column, the shaft being fluted, instead of ornamented with sculpture, as in the ancient model.

In the centre of the east side of the square, standing apart from the other buildings, is THE ROYAL BANK. In front of the bank is an equestrian STATUE OF THE EARL OF HOPETOUN.

Passing through St. Andrew Street, we again reach Princes Street, and terminate our Third Walk, by returning to the Register House.

WALK FOURTH.

ROYAL TERRACE—LEITH WALK—(LEITH—NEWHAVEN)—INVER-LEITH ROW—EXPERIMENTAL GARDENS—BOTANIC GARDENS.

IN the three preceding walks, we have exhausted most of the objects of interest in the city, and if the stranger should with them close his perambulations, he sacrifices very little worthy of notice. But, in order to render our Hand-book more complete, we find it necessary to give a short description of Leith, and a passing notice of New-haven. By omitting both of these places, the circuit of the present walk is very materially abridged, without any corresponding diminution of its interest ; we shall, therefore,

print the description of Leith and Newhaven in a smaller
type, that the reader may more readily distinguish the
portion of the text which relates to them, and which may
be read or passed over at pleasure.

Proceeding from the Register House down Greenside
Street, nothing worthy of remark occurs till we reach the
head of LEITH WALK, one of the most splendid roads in
the kingdom. Turning to the right at this point, a noble
range of buildings called the ROYAL TERRACE, partly
obscured by an unsightly church of recent erection, will
be seen occupying the northern side of the Calton Hill.
These buildings command a magnificent prospect of the
Firth of Forth, and the opposite shores, with all the interjacent country.

Tourists proposing to visit Leith, will continue their progress
down Leith Walk. Omnibuses ply between Edinburgh and Leith
every half hour, and, as there is nothing of peculiar interest to be
seen upon the way, time will be saved by taking advantage of one
of these vehicles.

LEITH,

The sea-port of Edinburgh, is distant about a mile and a half
from the centre of the metropolis. It was not only the first, but,
for several centuries, the only port in Scotland, traces of its existence being found in documents of the 12th century. During its
early history, few places have so often been the scene of military
operations. " In 1313, all the vessels in the harbour were burned
by the English, and again in 1410. In 1544, it was plundered and
burned, its pier destroyed, and its shipping carried off, by the Earl
of Hertford, to avenge the insult which Henry VIII. conceived
the Scotch had offered him, by refusing to betroth their young
queen, Mary, to his son Prince Edward. Three years subsequent
to this, it was again plundered and burned by the English, under
Hertford, then Duke of Somerset, and its whole shipping, together

with all that in the Forth, entirely annihilated by the English admiral, Lord Clinton. Four years after this, the town was fortified by Desse, a French general, who came over with 6000 men to assist the Queen-Regent in suppressing the Reformation. On the completion of these fortifications, which consisted in throwing a strong and high wall, with towers at intervals, around the town, the Queen-Regent took up her residence there, and, surrounded with her countrymen, hoped to be able to maintain her authority in the kingdom. These measures, however, had only the effect of widening the breach between her and her subjects, till they finally took up arms, and besieged her in her stronghold. In October 1559, the Lords of the Congregation invested Leith with an army, but, after various ineffectual attempts to gain access to the town by scaling the walls, they were driven back with great slaughter by a desperate sally of the besieged.

" In the month of April in the succeeding year, the forces of the Congregation again invested the town, being now aided by an army of 6000 men, under Lord Grey of Wilton, dispatched to their assistance by Elizabeth. On this occasion, the contest was protracted and sanguinary. For two months, during which the town suffered dreadfully from famine, as well as from the more violent casualties of war, the struggle continued, without any decisive advantage being gained by either side; at the end of that period, both parties being heartily tired of the contest, a treaty was entered into, by which it was stipulated that the French should evacuate the kingdom, that they should be allowed to embark unmolested, and that the English army should, upon the same day, begin its march to England. Immediately after the conclusion of this treaty, the walls of Leith were demolished by order of the Town Council of Edinburgh, and no vestige of them now remains."* In 1561, when Queen Mary came from France to take possession of the throne of her ancestors, she landed upon the pier of Leith; but of this pier no vestiges now remain. In 1650, the town was occupied by Cromwell, who exacted an assessment from the inhabitants. In 1715, the citadel was taken by a party of the adherents of the Stuart family, but, upon being threatened by the Duke of Argyle, it was speedily evacuated. George IV., upon visiting Scotland in 1822, landed at a spot a little to the north of the New Drawbridge,

---

* Encyclopædia Britannica, Seventh Edition. Article LEITH.

where an inscribed plate has been inserted in the pavement to commemorate the event.

Leith presents few antiquities of any interest. Among those
which remain, may be mentioned the Parish Church of South Leith,
a Gothic edifice, built previous to the year 1496, and the old
church of North Leith, founded in 1493. In the Links, upon the
south-east side of the Town, may be seen several mounds, raised,
for the purpose of planting cannon, by the besieging army, in 1560.

The town " is for the most part irregularly and confusedly built,
and a great portion of it is extremely filthy, crowded, and inele-
gant. Some parts of it, again, are the reverse of this, being spacious,
cleanly, and handsome. Such are two or three of the modern
streets, and various ranges of private dwellings, erected of late years
on the eastern and western skirts of the town.

" The modern public buildings worthy of remark are the Exchange Buildings, a large and elegant structure in the Grecian style
of architecture, containing a spacious and handsome assembly-
room, a commodious hotel, and public reading-room. ` The expense
of the erection was £16,000. The Custom-House, situated in
North Leith, is also a very splendid building; it was erected in
1812, at an expense of £12,000. The Leith Bank, a neat little
edifice, erected in 1805-6. The New Court House, by far the
most elegant building in the town, and forming altogether, whether
the chasteness of the design or the neatness of the workmanship
be considered, a very favourable specimen of modern architecture
on a small scale."* The Parish Church of North Leith is a handsome though unpretending structure, surmounted by a tasteful spire;
—the living is one of the best in the Church of Scotland.

The chief manufactures are ropes and cordage, sail-cloth, bottles,
soap, and candles. There are several breweries and a distillery,
and ship-building is carried on to a considerable extent.

Leith is the most important naval station on the east coast of
Scotland, and a considerable traffic is carried on at the port, the
gross revenues of which average above £20,000 a-year: but " it
is universally admitted that the harbour, in its present state, is very
inadequate to the accommodation of the trade of Edinburgh and
of the Firth of Forth, especially to the important branches of steam
navigation and the ferry communication between the opposite shore

* Encyclopædia Britannica.

of the Firth."* Large sums have been expended, from time to time, with the view of improving the harbour and docks, but they are still considered inadequate to the trade. Government, in the arrangement of the affairs of the City of Edinburgh, by an Act passed in July 1838, made provision for making an extensive improvement in the harbour, which, it is hoped, will ere long be carried into effect.

Leith, with Musselburgh, Portobello, and Newhaven, returns a Member to Parliament. The population, which we have included under that of Edinburgh, amounted, in 1831, to 25,855.

NEWHAVEN

Is a small fishing village, with a stone and chain pier, situate about a mile farther up the Forth than Leith. Its chief importance is derived from the steamers which ply from its piers. Of these piers, however, neither the one nor the other has sufficient depth of water to admit of the approach of steamers of large size. The London boats, accordingly, now land and take on board their passengers at Granton, a little farther up the Firth, where a low-water pier has recently been constructed by the Duke of Buccleuch.

The inhabitants of Newhaven are a laborious and hardy race. They form a distinct community, rarely intermarrying with any other class. The male inhabitants are almost all fishermen, and the females are constantly occupied in vending the produce of their husbands' industry in the markets or streets of Edinburgh.

* Parliamentary Report, July 1835.

F

When provoked, the *fishwives* display resources of abuse quite equal
to their Billingsgate contemporaries. They are also celebrated for
the exorbitant prices they demand for their goods, very frequently
asking three or four times the sum they finally consent to take.
Other traders, when purchasers are cheapening their wares, or
offering a price which they consider much below their value, are
therefore in the habit of saying, " What ! would you mak' a fishwife o' me ?" Although a very hard-working people, they do not
indulge in an excessive use of ardent spirits. The quantity they
consume is, indeed, very considerable, but the prodigious loads with
which they are burdened, may be allowed to form some apology for
the occasional use of such a stimulus, and their constant exercise
in the open air appears to prevent any injurious effects from following the indulgence. They are, for the most part, tidy in their
habits, and, in these days, when one dull uniformity pervades the
dress of all classes, it is refreshing to the lover of the picturesque
to contemplate the gaudy garb of the rosy, hearty, mirth-making
fishwife.*

Returning to the head of Broughton Street, the neat
Gothic front of the ROMAN CATHOLIC CHAPEL will be
observed on the west side of the street, close by the
Adelphi Theatre. At the end of York Place stands ST.
PAUL'S CHAPEL, an elegant Gothic structure, one of the
places of worship of the Episcopal communion. Continuing to proceed down Broughton Street, the stranger
will next pass the chapel of the sect called Rowites,
whose vagaries made so much noise in the religious world
some years ago. Immediately contiguous to this place
of worship, is ALBANY STREET CHAPEL, belonging to

* Those tourists who visit Leith and Newhaven, will require to invert the
order of the subsequent pages of this walk. The arrangement of the objects
to which attention is directed will therefore be as follows :—BOTANIC GARDENS,
CANONMILLS, ST. MARY'S CHURCH, ST. JAMES'S CHAPEL, ALBANY STREET
CHAPEL, ST. PAUL'S CHAPEL, ROMAN CATHOLIC CHAPEL.

the Independents, a body more commonly known in England by the name of Congregationalists. At the corner of Broughton Place is St. James's Chapel, an Episcopal place of worship, and at the east end of the same street is the principal chapel of the Burghers, the most numerous dissenting body in Scotland. Continuing to proceed northwards, by Mansfield Place and Bellevue Crescent, St. Mary's Church will be seen terminating the northern extremity of the latter street. It is one of the neatest of the Edinburgh Churches, possessing a portico and spire, respectable in design and of excellent masonry. At the northern end of Claremont Street— the range of lofty houses opposite St. Mary's Church— are the Zoological Gardens. They are pleasantly situ- ated, and laid out with good taste. The collection being only of recent formation, is not so considerable as in a few years it is likely to be.

From St. Mary's Church the road now declines towards the village of Canonmills. After passing this squalid suburb,* the stranger crosses the Water of Leith, by Canonmills Bridge. Upon his left he will observe some massive and singular looking buildings, erected, some years ago, by an oil gas company. The speculation was soon abandoned as an unprofitable one, and the buildings are now occupied as warehouses. At the further end of Howard Place are the Experimental Gardens, and upon the same side of the road, considerably farther along, is the Botanic Garden. To the latter, strangers are freely

---

* The general character of the place has one redeeming feature. Dr. Neill's pleasant suburban residence, " like a jewel of gold in a swine's snout," is situ- ated on the confines of the village, his garden bordering on the loch, though separated from it by a wall. The proprietor is a distinguished botanist and naturalist, his gardens displaying a variety of botanical rarities, as well as many choice living specimens of interesting objects in the animal kingdom.

admitted, but the hot-houses are open to the public only on Saturday, between the hours of twelve and four.

The garden embraces an extent of 14½ English acres; and presents every facility for prosecuting the study of Botany. Immediately upon his entrance the stranger is struck with the luxuriance and vigour of the evergreens, to the cultivation of which, Mr. M'Nab, the able superintendent, has devoted much attention. On the southern side of the garden there is a large collection of hardy plants, arranged according to the Natural System of Jussieu, such as ferns, grasses, labiate, cruciform, and leguminous plants, &c. Close to this collection is a small pond containing rushes, water lilies, &c., and a ditch containing those plants which thrive best in such a situation. To the north of this arrangement is a collection of British plants, arranged according to the Linnæan or artificial system, with the name attached to each species. On the eastern side are the plants peculiar to Scotland, and on the west a few which are peculiar to England and Ireland. A little to the east of this British arrangement is a collection of roses. Proceeding northwards, we come to a general collection of hardy evergreens, chiefly exotic, to the east of which is a small collection of Medical plants, with the names attached. We then reach the Greenhouses, which have of late been much increased by a liberal grant from Government. These houses contain a large collection of exotics, which thrive admirably. The western division contains heaths, epacrideæ, dryandras, proteas, grevillias, diosmas, &c., while in the eastern division, we have a stove with a northern exposure, in which epiphytes and parasites are cultivated with great success. The peculiar forms of these plants, and their remarkable mode of growth, attract the attention of all.

In the other greenhouses of the front range, there are many interesting plants; among these may be noticed Plantains, which bear fruit well, Papaw tree, Pitcher-plant, Papyrus, Indian rubber fig, cacti, cinnamon, tea plants, camphor tree, Astrapæa, some of the Fig tribe growing suspended in the air, amaryllides, arums, euphorbias, &c. In front of this range of houses is a piece of ground, on which many of the plants of warmer regions, such as palms, acacias, &c., are cultivated in the open air, being carefully protected during winter. Behind these houses is a smaller range in which numerous seedlings are cultivated, and a large Palm-house about 45 feet high, in which are found Plantains and Bananas, Sago Palms, Fan Palms, European Palms, Cabbage Palms, Date Palms, Cocoa Nut Trees, Sugar Cane, Bamboos, Screw Pine, Elephant's foot, &c. The houses are heated partly by hot water and partly by steam. From the top of the boiler-house there is a very fine view of Edinburgh. On the high northern wall of the garden, many valuable exotics are trained, as Magnolias, Myrtles, Eucalypti, &c.

The garden is surrounded by trees on the west, south, and eastern sides, and, among these, there are some of considerable interest. Many of them were removed, in their full grown state, from the former garden in Leith Walk, and, under the judicious management of Mr. M'Nab, they have all succeeded. To the west of the general European collection is an old Yew, which has been twice transplanted; having been transferred, first, from the old Physic Gardens, below the North Bridge, to the garden in Leith Walk, and afterwards removed to its present situation. Beside the British collection is a magnetic observatory, superintended by the Professor of Natural Philosophy. The class-room of the Professor of Botany, and the house of the superintendent, are situated on the right-hand side of the entrance.

In returning, the stranger may vary his route by turning to the right, immediately after recrossing Canonmills Bridge, and proceeding by Brandon Street, Pitt Street, and Dundas Street, to George's Street, from which he may pursue the same line of progress to the Register House, as in the preceding walk.

The objects of interest in the City being now exhausted, we proceed to introduce the tourist so some spots in the vicinity more particularly worthy of notice. Among these we may observe, that Roslin is generally regarded as the most attractive, although we have commenced with Habbie's Howe, as the best geographical arrangement.

ENVIRONS OF EDINBURGH.

HABBIE'S HOWE.

A very delightful excursion may be made from Edinburgh to Newhall, distant about twelve miles, supposed, with great probability, to be the scene of Allan Ramsay's celebrated pastoral, " The Gentle Shepherd."

Leaving Edinburgh by Burntsfield Links, the tourist passes on the right MERCHISTON CASTLE, the birth-place of the celebrated Napier, the inventor of Logarithms. A little further on is the village of Morningside, and a number of villas and country boxes. Two miles from Edinburgh is the Hermitage of Braid, (J. Gordon, Esq. of Clunie,) situated at the bottom of a narrow and thickly wooded dell, through which a small rivulet, called the Braid Burn, strays. Braid once belonged to a family called Fairly, and the Laird of Braid, during the Reformation, was a personal friend and zealous defender of John Knox. The road now skirts the rocky eminences called the Hills of Braid, which command a most beautiful view of the Scottish metropolis, with the Firth of Forth, its islands, and the shores of Fife in the background. The more northern side, called Blackford Hill, the property of Richard Trotter, Esq. of Mortonhall, is the spot mentioned in " Marmion."

> " Still on the spot Lord Marmion stay'd,
> For fairer scene he ne'er survey'd," &c.

The space of ground which extends from the bottom
of Blackford Hill to the suburbs of Edinburgh, was formerly denominated the Borough Moor.   We are informed
by historians that it was studded with magnificent oaks
at the time when James IV. arrayed his army upon it,
previous to his departure on the fatal expedition which
terminated in the Battle of Flodden.   The HARE STONE,
in which the Royal Standard was fixed, is still to be seen
built into the wall, which runs along the side of the footpath at the place called Boroughmoor-head.   At about
half a mile's distance to the southward, there is another
stone called the Buck Stone, upon which the proprietor
of the barony of Pennycuik is bound, by his charter, to
place himself, and to wind three blasts of a horn, when
the king shall visit the Borough Moor.   On the right, at
some distance, is Dreghorn (A. Trotter, Esq.,) the village
of Colinton, delightfully situated at the bottom of the
Pentland Hills, and Colinton House, (Lord Dunfermline.)
About five miles from Edinburgh, on the southern slope
of the Pentland Hills, is WOODHOUSELEE, the seat of
James Tytler, Esq., surrounded by fine woods.   The
ancient house of the same name, once the property of
Bothwellhaugh, the assassin of the Regent Murray, was
four miles distant from the present site.   Woodhouselee
had been bestowed upon Sir James Ballenden, one of
the Regent's favourites, who seized the house, and turned
out Lady Bothwellhaugh naked, in a cold night, into the
open fields, where, before next morning, she became
furiously mad.*   The ruins of the mansion are still to be
seen in a hollow glen beside the river.   Popular report
tenants them with the restless ghost of the lady.   The

* This event forms the subject of Sir Walter Scott's fine ballad of " Cadyow
Castle," which will be found quoted entire in the SEVENTH TOUR.

road now passes the hamlet of Upper Howgate, and a little farther on Glencorse Church, embosomed in a wood. On the right is the vale of Glencorse, watered by a little rill, called Logan Water, or, more commonly, Glencorse Burn. The head of this valley is supposed by some to be the scene of Allan Ramsay's Pastoral Drama, " The Gentle Shepherd," but the appearance of the scenery, as well as the absence of all the localities noticed by Ramsay, render this opinion extremely improbable. The sequestered pastoral character of this valley, however, renders it well worthy of a visit. After crossing Glencorse Burn, the road passes House-of-Muir, in the neighbourhood of which is the place where the Covenanters were defeated, 28th November 1666. The insurrection, which ended in this skirmish, began in Dumfries-shire, where Sir James Turner was employed to levy the arbitrary fines imposed for not attending the Episcopal churches. The people rose, seized his person, disarmed his soldiers, and, having continued together, resolved to march towards Edinburgh, expecting to be joined by their friends in that quarter. In this they were disappointed, and being now diminished to half their numbers, they drew up on the Pentland Hills, at a place called Rullion Green. They were commanded by one Wallace, and here they awaited the approach of General Dalziel of Binns, who, having marched by Calder to meet them on the Lanark road, and finding that, by passing through Colinton, they had got to the other side of the hills, crossed the mountains, and approached them. The Covenanters were drawn up in a very strong position, and withstood two charges of Dalziel's cavalry, but upon the third shock they were broken, and utterly dispersed. There were about fifty killed, and as many made prison-

ers.   Passing through the village of Silver Burn, the road
reaches

NEWHALL,

on the banks of the North Esk, about three miles from
Pennycuik House, and twelve south-west from Edinburgh.   Newhall is now the property of Robert Brown,
Esq.   At the era of Ramsay's drama, it belonged to Dr.
Alexander Pennycuik, a poet and antiquary.   In 1703, it
passed into the hands of Sir David Forbes, a distinguished
lawyer ; and, in Ramsay's time, was the property of Mr.
John Forbes, son to Sir David, and cousin-german to
the celebrated President Forbes of Culloden.   The scenery
around Newhall answers most minutely to the description
in the drama.   Near the house, on the north side of the
·vale, there is a crag (called the Harbour Crag, from having afforded refuge to the Covenanters,) which corresponds
exactly with the first scene of the first act :

> " Beneath the south side of a craggy bield,
>   Where chrystal springs the halesome waters yield."

Farther up the vale, and behind the house, there is a
spot beside the burn, which corresponds to the description of the second scene :

> " A flow'ry howm between twa verdant braes,
>   Where lasses used to wash and spread their claes ;
>   A trottin' burnie wimplin' through the ground,
>   Its channel pebbles shining smooth and round."

A little farther up the vale there is a place called the
Howe Burn, where the stream forms a small cascade,
and where the scenery in every respect corresponds with
the exquisite description of the spot called " Habbie's
Howe,"

> " Gae farer up the burn to Habbie's Howe,
>   Where a' the sweets o' spring and summer grow,

There, 'tween twa birks, out ower a little linn,
The water fa's and mak's a singand din ;
A pule breast deep, beneath as clear as glass,
Kisses wi' easy whirls the bordering grass."

Still farther up the vale, at a place called the Carlops,* a tall rock shoots up on each side. At this spot, near an old withered solitary oak tree, is the site of Mause's cottage, described in the second scene of the second act :

" The open field, a cottage in the glen,
An auld wife spinnin' at the sunny end.
At a sma' distance, by a blasted tree,
Wi' faulded arms and half raised look, ye see
               Bauldy his lane."

PENNYCUIK HOUSE, the seat of Sir George Clerk, Bart., is well worthy of a visit. The neighbouring scenery is extremely beautiful, and the pleasure-grounds are highly ornamented. The house contains an excellent collection of paintings, with a number of Roman antiquities found in Britain, and, amongst other curiosities, the buff-coat worn by Dundee at the battle of Killiecrankie. The principal apartment, called Ossian's Hall, has a ceiling beautifully decorated with paintings by Runciman.

———

ROSLIN.

Another interesting scene, visited more frequently than any other by the inhabitants of Edinburgh, is ROSLIN CHAPEL, situated about seven miles from the city, on

* A contraction of Carline's Loups, in consequence, it is said, of a witch or carline having been frequently observed to leap, by night, from the rock at one side over to that at the other.

the banks of the North Esk. The vale of Roslin is one of
those beautiful and sequestered dells which so often occur
in Scotland, abounding with all the romantic varieties of
cliff, and copsewood, and waterfall. Its beautiful Gothic
chapel is one of the most entire and exquisitely decorated
specimens of ecclesiastical architecture in Scotland. It
was founded, in 1446, by William St. Clair, Earl of
Orkney, and Lord of Roslin. At the revolution of 1688,
part of it was defaced by a mob from Edinburgh, but it
was repaired in the following century by General St. Clair.
The late Earl of Rosslyn, some years ago, undertook the
restoration of its more dilapidated parts, and the present
Earl still continues the repairs, with scrupulous attention
to preserve the original character of the structure. "This
building," says Mr Britton, "may be pronounced unique,
and I am confident it will be found curious, elaborate,
and singularly interesting. The Chapel of King's College, St. George, and Henry VII., are all conformable to
the styles of the respective ages when they were erected;
and these styles display a gradual advancement in lightness and profusion of ornament: but the Chapel of Ros-
lyn combines the solidity of the Norman with the minute
decorations of the latest species of the Tudor age. It is
impossible to designate the architecture of this building
by any given or familiar term: for the variety and eccen-
tricity of its parts are not to be defined by any words of
common acceptation." The central aisle is bold and
lofty, enclosed as usual by side aisles, the pillars and
arches of which display a profusion of ornament, executed
in the most beautiful manner. The "Prentice's Pillar"
in particular, with its finely sculptured foliage, is a piece
of exquisite workmanship. It is said that the master-
builder of the Chapel, being unable to execute the design

of this pillar from the plans in his possession, proceeded to Rome, that he might see a column of a similar description which had been executed in that city. During his absence, his apprentice proceeded with the execution of the design, and, upon the master's return, he found this finely ornamented column completed. Stung with envy at this proof of the superior ability of his apprentice, he struck him a blow with his mallet, and killed him on the spot. Upon the architrave uniting the Prentice's Pillar to a smaller one, is the following sententious inscription from the book of Apocryphal Scripture, called Esdras:—
"*Forte est vinum, fortior est rex, fortiores sunt mulieres; super omnia vincit veritas.*" Beneath the Chapel lie the Barons of Roslin, all of whom were, till the time of James VII., buried in complete armour.*

---

* This circumstance, as well as the superstitious belief that, on the night before the death of any of these barons, the chapel appeared in flames, is beautifully described by Sir Walter Scott, in his exquisite ballad of Rosabelle:—

> O listen, listen, ladies gay!
>   No haughty feats of arms I tell;
> Soft is the note, and sad the lay,
>   That mourns the lovely Rosabelle.
>
> "Moor, moor the barge, ye gallant crew!
>   And gentle ladye deign to stay!
> Rest thee in Castle Ravensheuch,
>   Nor tempt the stormy firth to-day.
>
> "The blackening wave is edged with white;
>   To inch and rock the sea-mews fly;
> The fishers have heard the Water-Sprite,
>   Whose screams forbode that wreck is nigh.
>
> "Last night the gifted Seer did view
>   A wet shroud swathed round ladye gay;
> Then stay thee, Fair, in Ravensheuch:
>   Why cross the gloomy firth to-day?"—
>
> "'Tis not because Lord Lindesay's heir
>   To-night at Roslin leads the ball,
> But that my ladye-mother there
>   Sits lonely in her castle-hall.

Admission to the Chapel is now limited to Wednesday and Saturday of each week.*

The mouldering ruin of ROSLIN CASTLE, with its

" 'Tis not because the ring they ride—
And Lindesay at the ring rides well—
But that my sire the wine will chide,
If 'tis not fill'd by Rosabelle."—

O'er Roslin, all that dreary night,
A wonderous blaze was seen to gleam ;
'Twas broader than the watch-fire's light,
And redder than the bright moon-beam.

It glared on Roslin's castled rock,
It ruddied all the copsewood glen ;
'Twas seen from Dryden's groves of oak,
And seen from cavern'd Hawthornden.

Seem'd all on fire that chapel proud,
Where Roslin's chiefs uncoffin'd lie,
Each baron, for a sable shroud,
Sheathed in his iron panoply.

Seem'd all on fire within, around,
Deep sacristy and altar's pale ;
Shone every pillar foliage-bound,
And glimmer'd all the dead men's mail.

Blazed battlement and pinnet high,
Blazed every rose-carved buttress fair—
So still they blaze, when fate is nigh
The lordly line of high St. Clair.

There are twenty of Roslin's barons bold
Lie buried within that proud chapelle ;
Each one the holy vault doth hold—
But the sea holds lovely Rosabelle.

And each St. Clair was buried there,
With candle, with book, and with knell ;
But the sea caves rung, and the wild winds sung,
The dirge of lovely Rosabelle.

* On the same days *Dalkeith Palace* is open to strangers, and upon Wednesday *Hawthornden* may also be visited, by obtaining an order as directed on page 97. Wednesday is thus the only day upon which *all the three places* can be seen, and tourists will, of course, endeavour to devote this day to the purpose. For the consolation of those who cannot accomplish this, it may be stated, that a very good idea of the picturesque attractions of Hawthornden may be formed, from the scenery of the Esk nearest Roslin, which can be seen without an order.

tremendous triple tier of vaults, stands upon a peninsular rock, overhanging the picturesque glen of the Esk, and is accessible only by a bridge of great height, thrown over a deep cut in the solid rock, which separates it from the adjacent ground. This castle, the origin of which is involved in obscurity, was long the abode of the proud family of the St. Clairs, Earls of Caithness and Orkney. In 1544, it was burned down by the Earl of Hertford; and, in 1650, it surrendered to General Monck. About sixty or seventy years ago, the comparatively modern mansion, which has been erected amidst the ruins of the old castle, was inhabited by a genuine Scottish laird of the old stamp, the lineal descendant of the high race who first founded the pile, and the last male of their long line. He was Captain of the Royal Company of Archers, and Hereditary Grand Master of the Scottish Masons. At his death, the estate descended to Sir James Erskine St. Clair, father of the present Earl of Rosslyn, who now represents the family.

The neighbouring moor of Roslin was the scene of a celebrated battle, fought 24th February 1302, in which the Scots, under Comyn, then guardian of the kingdom, and Simon Fraser, attacked and defeated three divisions of the English on the same day.*

After leaving Roslin, we pass the caves of Gorton,

* " Three triumphs in a day!
     Three hosts subdued by one !
   Three armies scatter'd like the spray
     Beneath one summer sun.—
   Who, passing 'mid this solitude
     Of rocky streams, and leafy trees,—
   Who, gazing o'er this quiet wood,
     Would ever dream of these ?
   Or have a thought that ought intrude,
     Save birds and humming bees ?"

Δ

situated in the front of a high cliff on the southern side of the stream.   These caverns, during the reign of David II., while Scotland was overrun by the English, afforded shelter to the gallant Sir Alexander Ramsay of Dalwolsey, with a band of chosen patriots.

Passing through scenery of great natural beauty, the footpath down the river conducts the tourist to

HAWTHORNDEN,

the classical habitation of the poet Drummond, the friend of Shakspeare and Jonson ; it is now the property of Sir Francis Walker Drummond. " This romantic spot seems to have been formed by nature in one of her happiest moments.   All the materials that compose the pictu-resque seem here combined in endless variety : stupen-dous rocks, rich and varied in colour, hanging in threa-tening aspect, crowned with trees that expose their bare branching roots ; here the gentle birch hanging midway, and there the oak, bending its stubborn branches, meeting each other ; huge fragments of rocks impede the rapid flow of the stream, that hurries brawling along unseen, but heard far beneath, mingling in the breeze that gently agitates the wood."   Being built with some view to de-fence, the house rises from the very edge of the grey cliff, which descends sheer down to the stream.   An in-scription, on the front of the building, testifies that it was repaired by the poet in 1638.   It is well known, that Ben Jonson walked from London, on foot, to visit Drummond, and lived several weeks with him at Haw-thornden.   Under the mansion are several subterraneous caves, hewn out of the solid rock with great labour, and connected with each other by long passages ; in the court-yard there is a well of prodigious depth, which

communicates with them. These caverns are supposed
to have been constructed as places of refuge, when the
public calamities rendered the ordinary habitations un-
safe. The walks around the house are peculiarly fine,
but admission to them is limited to Wednesday of each
week, and can only be obtained by an order from the
proprietor, application for which must be made at the
office of Walker and Melville, Esquires, Writers to the
Signet, 110, George Street.

Farther down the river is the pretty village of LASS-
WADE, the name of which is said to be derived from a
young woman, or *lass*, who, in former times, waded across
the stream, carrying upon her back those whose circumstances enabled them to purchase the luxury of such a
conveyance. In a cottage in the vicinity, Sir Walter
Scott spent some of the happiest years of his life. At a
short distance is

MELVILLE CASTLE,

the seat of Viscount Melville. The building was erected
by the celebrated Harry Dundas, first Viscount Melville.
The park contains some fine wood. Two miles farther
is the town of DALKEITH, and in its immediate neighbourhood, situated on an overhanging bank of the North Esk,
a little to the east of the town, stands

DALKEITH PALACE,

a seat of the Duke of Buccleuch. It is a large, but by
no means elegant structure, surrounded by an extensive
park, through which the rivers of North and South Esk
flow, and unite their streams a short way below the
house. The first proprietors of Dalkeith upon record
are the Grahams ; from them it passed, in the reign of
David II., by a daughter, into the possession of Sir Wil-

liam Douglas, ancestor of the Earls of Morton. In the reign of Queen Mary, Dalkeith was the head quarters of the celebrated Regent Morton, and, after resigning his regency, he retired to this stronghold, which, from the general idea entertained of his character, acquired, at that time, the expressive name of the Lion's Den. In the year 1642, the estate was purchased from the Earl of Morton by Francis, Earl of Buccleuch. Anne, Duchess of Buccleuch and Monmouth, after the execution of her unhappy husband, substituted the modern for the ancient mansion, and lived here in royal state, and, for more than a century, it has formed the residence of the Buccleuch family. Since the union of the crowns, Dalkeith House has twice been the temporary residence of royalty,— namely, of King Charles, in 1633, and of George IV., in 1822. It is worthy of notice, that Froissart, the historian of chivalry, visited the Earl of Douglas, and lived with him several weeks at the Castle of Dalkeith. There is a popular belief current, that the treasure unrighteously amassed by the Regent Morton lies hidden somewhere among the vaults of the ancient building; but Godscroft assures us, that it was expended by the Earl of Angus in supporting the companions of his exile in England, and that, when it was exhausted, the Earl generously exclaimed, " Is it, then, all gone ? let it go ; I never looked it should have done so much good !" Dalkeith Palace is shown to strangers, when the family is not residing there, on Wednesday and Saturday. The environs of Dalkeith are interesting, and the tourist may be conveyed thither from Edinburgh, by the railroad, in a short space of time, and at a very low rate.*

* The beautiful scenes through which the North and South Esk flow, and the various seats that adorn the banks of these streams, are very happily described by Sir Walter Scott, in his ballad of the Grey Brother :—

About a mile south-west from Dalkeith, on the northern bank of the South Esk, is

NEWBATTLE ABBEY,

a seat of the Marquis of Lothian.   This mansion stands on the spot formerly occupied by the abbey of Newbattle, founded by David I. for a community of Cistercian monks. An ancestor of the present noble proprietor was the last abbot, and his son, Mark Ker, got the possessions of the abbey erected into a temporal lordship, in the year 1591. The house contains a number of fine paintings and curious manuscripts, and the lawn is interspersed with some straggling trees of great size.

About two miles higher up the South Esk, is

DALHOUSIE CASTLE,

a modernized building in the castellated form.   The original structure was of vast antiquity, and great strength. The present possessor, the Earl of Dalhousie, is the lineal

" Sweet are the paths,—O, passing sweet !
   By Esk's fair streams that run,
O'er airy steep, through copsewoods deep,
   Impervious to the sun.

There the rapt poet's step may rove,
   And yield the Muse the day,
There Beauty, led by timid Love,
   May shun the tell-tale ray.

From that fair dome where suit is paid,
   By blast of bugle free, *
To Auchendinny's hazel glade,
   And haunted Woodhouselee.

Who knows not Melville's beechy grove,
   And Roslin's rocky glen,
Dalkeith, which all the virtues love,
   And classic Hawthornden."

* Pennycuik. See ante, p. 83.

descendant of the celebrated Sir Alexander Ramsay. The scenery around Dalhousie is romantic and beautiful.

Passing ARNISTON, the residence of the celebrated family of Dundas, the tourist, at the distance of about eleven miles from Edinburgh, comes in sight of BORTHWICK CASTLE, an ancient and stately tower, rising out of the centre of a small but well cultivated valley, watered by a stream called the Gore. This interesting fortress is in the form of a double tower, seventy-four feet in length, sixty-eight in breadth, and in height ninety feet from the area to the battlements. It occupies a knoll, surrounded by the small river, and is enclosed within an outer court, fortified by a strong outward wall, having flanking towers at the angles. The interior of the castle is exceedingly interesting. The hall is a stately and magnificent apartment, the ceiling of which consists of a smooth vault of ashler work. Three stairs, ascending at the angles of the building, gave access to the separate stories; one is quite ruinous, but the others are still tolerably entire. The licence for building Borthwick Castle was granted by James I. to Sir William Borthwick, 2d June 1430. It was to Borthwick that Queen Mary retired with Borthwell, three weeks after her unfortunate marriage with that nobleman, and from which she was obliged, a few days afterwards, to flee to Dunbar in the disguise of a page. During the civil war, Borthwick held out gallantly against the victorious Cromwell, and surrendered, at last, upon honourable terms. The effect of Cromwell's battery still remains, his fire having destroyed a part of the freestone facing of the eastern side of the castle. Borthwick is now the property of John Borthwick, Esq., of Crookstone, a claimant of the ancient peerage of Borthwick, which has remained in abeyance since the death of the ninth Lord Borthwick, in the reign of Charles II. The valley of Borthwick is a sober, peaceful, sequestered, and exquisitely rural spot, and its manse and church, farm-houses and cottages, are in complete harmony with its prevailing character. In the manse of Borthwick, Dr. Robertson, the historian, was born.

A mile and a quarter to the eastward of Borthwick Castle, and within sight of its battlements, stands CRICHTON CASTLE, on the banks of the Tyne, twelve and a half miles south from Edinburgh, and about two miles above the village of Pathhead, on the Lauder road. The foot-path which leads from Borthwick to Crichton meanders delightfully through natural pastures and rushy meadows, among dwarf hazel, and alder and blackthorn bushes, broom and brackens, till walled in by a nearly impene-trable wilderness of furze roughly clothing the bank. The waters divide hereabouts,—the infant Tyne running eastward, while the Borthwick burn, descending from the southward heights, flows west till it falls into the Esk. Crichton Castle was built at different periods, and forms, on the whole, one large square pile enclosing an interior court-yard. A strong old tower, which forms the east side of the quadrangle, seems to have been the original part of the building. The northern quarter, which ap-pears to be the most modern, is built in a style of remark-able elegance. The description of the castle given by Sir Walter Scott, in his poem of Marmion, is so minutely accurate, that we transcribe it in preference to any re-marks of our own.

> That Castle rises on the steep
>   Of the green vale of Tyne ;
> And, far beneath, where slow they creep
> From pool to eddy, dark and deep,
> Where alders moist, and willows weep,
>   You hear her streams repine.

The towers in different ages rose:
Their various architecture shows
   The builders' various hands;
A mighty mass, that could oppose,
When deadliest hatred fired its foes,
   The vengeful Douglas' bands.

Crichtoun! though now thy miry court
   But pens the lazy steer and sheep,
   Thy turrets rude, and tottered Keep,
Have been the minstrel's loved resort.
Oft have I traced, within thy fort,
   Of mouldering shields the mystic sense,
   Scutcheons of honour, or pretence,
Quarter'd in old armorial sort,
   Remains of rude magnificence.
Nor wholly yet hath time defaced
   Thy lordly gallery fair;
Nor yet the stony cord unbraced,
Whose twisted knots with roses laced,
   Adorn thy ruin'd stair.
Still rises, unimpaired, below,
The court-yard's graceful portico;
Above its cornice, row and row
   Of fair hewn facets richly show
     Their pointed diamond form,
   Though there but houseless cattle go,
     To shield them from the storm.
And, shuddering, still may we explore,
   Where oft whilom were captives pent,
The darkness of thy Massy More;*
     Or, from thy grass-grown battlement,
May trace, in undulating line,
The sluggish mazes of the Tyne.

Crichton was the patrimonial estate and residence of the
celebrated Sir William Crichton, Chancellor of Scotland,
during the minority of James II., and whose influence

* The pit or prison-vault.

contributed so much to destroy the formidable power of the Douglas family. On the forfeiture of William, third Lord Crichton, the castle and barony of Crichton was granted to Sir John Ramsay, a favourite of James III. The defeat and death of James involved the ruin of Ramsay. He in his turn was proscribed, exiled, and his estate forfeited, and the castle and lordship of Crichton were granted anew to Patrick Hepburn, third Lord Hales, who was created Earl of Bothwell. He was ancestor of the infamous James Earl of Bothwell, who exercised such an unhappy influence over the fortunes of Queen Mary. On his outlawry, Crichton was conferred by James VI. on his kinsman Francis Stewart, Earl of Bothwell, so noted for the constant train of conspiracies and insurrections in which he was engaged. Since that period, Crichton has passed through the hands of about a dozen proprietors, and is now the property of William Burn Callander, Esq. The ancient church of Crichton still exists, at the distance of half a mile to the north of the castle. It is a small but venerable building in the shape of a cross, with a low and truncated belfrey. The west end has been left unfinished.

Returning to the road, about half a mile from Path-head, stands OXENFORD CASTLE, a residence of the Earl of Stair. It is situate on the north bank of the Tyne, in the midst of an extensive park.

About three miles south from Edinburgh are the ruins of CRAIGMILLAR CASTLE, situate on the top of a gentle eminence, and surrounded with some fine old trees. " There is nothing to shew at what age or by what hand it is built;"* but the rampart wall which surrounds the castle appears, from a date preserved on it, to have been

* CHALMERS's Caledonia, Vol. ii. page 570.

built in 1427. Craigmillar, with other fortresses in Mid-Lothian, was burned by the English after Pinkey fight in 1555, and Captain Grose surmises, with great plausibility, that much of the building, as it now appears, was erected when the castle was repaired after that event.

In point of architecture and accommodation, Craigmillar surpasses the generality of Scottish castles. It consists of a strong tower, flanked with turrets, and connected with inferior buildings. There is an outer court in front, defended by the battlemented wall already mentioned, and beyond these there was an exterior wall, and in some places a deep ditch or moat. In 1813, a human skeleton was found enclosed, in an upright position, in a crevice of the vaulting of the Castle. Upon being exposed to the air, it shortly crumbled to dust.

Being so near Edinburgh, Craigmillar was often occupied as a royal residence. Here John, Earl of Mar, younger brother of James III., was imprisoned in 1477. James V. occupied it occasionally during his minority, and it was so often the residence of Queen Mary, that the adjacent village acquired the name of Little France, from her French guards being quartered there.

The castle and estate of Craigmillar were acquired by Sir Simon Preston in 1374, from one John de Capella, and they continued in the possession of the Preston family till about the period of the Revolution, when they were purchased by Sir Thomas Gilmour, the great lawyer, to whose descendant, Walter Little Gilmour, Esq., they still belong.

EDINBURGH to PEEBLES, SELKIRK, MELROSE, KELSO & BERWICK.

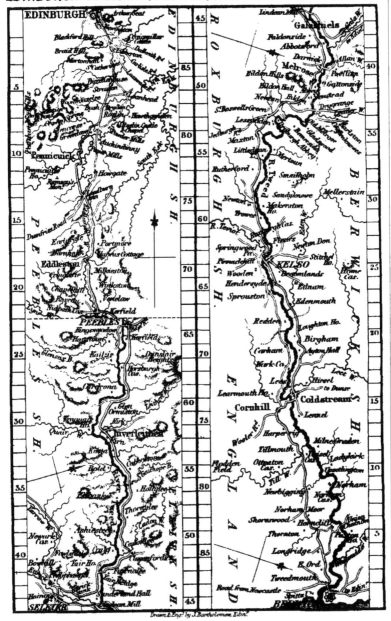

Drawn & Engd by J. Bartholomew, Edin.r

Edinburgh, Published July 1, 1841 by Adam & Charles Black 27 North Bridge.

FIRST TOUR.

LEAVING Edinburgh by Nicolson Street, the tourist sees on an eminence, a short distance to the left, the ruins of CRAIGMILLAR CASTLE, an interesting edifice, of which a description is given on the preceding page. A little farther on, and nearer the road, stand the village and church of Libberton, pleasantly situated on a rising ground, and commanding a splendid view of Edinburgh and the surrounding scenery. Passing on the right, Morton Hall, (Richard Trotter, Esq.,) and upon the left, Gracemount, (Mrs. Hay,) and St. Catherine's (Sir William Rae,) we reach the small village of Burdiehouse, a corruption of Bourdeaux House, the name conferred on it by a native of that port in France. A little farther on is the village of Straiton, near which was fought the second of three conflicts which took place in one day, in 1303, styled the battle of Roslin. Six miles from Edinburgh we pass Bilston toll-bar, where a road strikes off on the left to Roslin. About a mile farther the tourist passes Greenlaw, built as a depôt for French prisoners during the late war, and on the right, Glencorse House and church. A little beyond are Auchindinny House,

once the residence of Henry Mackenzie, author of the
Man of Feeling; and Auchindinny paper-mill. At the
distance of other two miles the road enters PENNYCUIK
VILLAGE, ten miles distant from Edinburgh. In the immediate vicinity are the extensive paper-mills of Messrs.
Cowan and Sons. On the right stands Pennycuik House,
the seat of Sir George Clerk, Bart., a fine specimen of
modern architecture, surrounded by beautiful woods.
At the top of the hill, south of Pennycuik, a new road
has been opened, leading to Linton and Biggar. Three
miles from Pennycuik the tourist enters Peebles-shire,
where the direct road to Dumfries parts off on the
right. The tract of country around is bleak and moorish.
Three miles from Kingside Edge is The Cottage, (W. F.
Mackenzie, Esq. of Portmore, M.P.,) and a mile beyond
this, Eddlestone village. Passing in succession, Darnhall,
(Lord Elibank,) Cringletie, (Murray, Esq.,) Winkstone,
(M'Gowan, Esq.,) Rosetta, (Dr. Young,) and Venelaw,
(Erskine, Esq.,) the tourist enters the royal burgh of

PEEBLES,

the county town, beautifully situated on the Tweed,
twenty-two miles distant from Edinburgh. Peebles is
a town of great antiquity, and must, from a very early
period, have been a seat of population, as is indicated by
its name, which, in British, signifies shielings or dwelling
places; it is certain that at the end of the 11th century
there were at this place, a village, a church, a mill, and
a brewhouse. Owing to its situation in the midst of a
fine hunting country, and on the direct road to the royal
forest of Ettrick, it became at an early period the
occasional residence of the Kings of Scotland, and is the
scene of the celebrated poem of James I., entitled
" Peblis to the Play." On account of its sequestered

situation this town figures little in Scottish history, and
seems to have taken no part in any great historical event.
It was, however, burnt and laid waste oftener than once
during the invasions of the English. Peebles is divided
into two districts,—the old and new town. A bridge of
great antiquity, consisting of five arches, connects the
town with an extensive ·suburb on the opposite bank.
The appeárance of the whole is very pleasing, and the
surrounding scenery is extremely beautiful. Peebles is
a town possessed of very little commerce or manufacture.
It has a weekly market, and seven annual fairs. At the
end of the fifteenth century Peebles possessed no fewer
than eleven places of worship, out of which the remains
of only two are now visible. There is a large edifice of
a castellated appearance still existing, known to have
belonged to the Queensberry family, which is believed to
be the scene of a highly romantic incident thus related
by Sir Walter Scott. There is a tradition in Tweeddale,
that when Nidpath Castle, near Peebles, was inhabited by
the Earls of March, a mutual passion subsisted between
a daughter of that noble family, and a son of the laird of
Tushielaw, in Ettrick forest. As the alliance was thought
unsuitable by her parents, the young man went abroad.
During his absence the young lady fell into a consumption,
and at length, as the only means of saving her life, her
father consented that her lover should be recalled. On
the day when he was expected to pass through Peebles,
on the road to Tushielaw, the young lady, though much
exhausted, caused herself to be carried to the balcony
of a house in Peebles, belonging to the family, that she
might see him as he rode past. Her anxiety and eagerness gave such force to her organs, that she is said to have
distinguished his horse's footsteps at an incredible dis-

tance.   But Tushielaw, unprepared for the change in
her appearance, and not expecting to see her in that place,
rode on without recognizing her, or even slackening his
pace.   The lady was unable to support the shock, and,
after a short struggle, died in the arms of her attendants.

The vale of the Tweed, both above and below Peebles,
contained a chain of strong castles to serve as a defence
against the incursions of English marauders.   These
castles were built in the shape of square towers, and
usually consisted of three stories—the lower one on the
ground floor being vaulted and appropriated to the reception of horses and cattle in times of danger.   They
were built alternately on both sides of the river, and in
a continued view of each other.   A fire kindled on the
top of these towers was the signal of an incursion, and,
in this manner, a tract of country seventy miles long
from Berwick to the Bield, and fifty broad, was alarmed
in a few hours.

> ——— " A score of fires, I ween,
> From height, and hill, and cliff were seen,
> Each with warlike tidings fraught,
> Each from each the signal caught ;
> Each after each they glanced in sight,
> As stars arise upon the night :
> They gleam'd on many a dusky tarn,
> Haunted by the lonely earn,*
> On many a cairn's grey pyramid,
> Where urns of mighty chiefs lie hid."
> *Lay of the Last Minstrel.*

The strongest and the most entire of these fortresses
is NIDPATH CASTLE, situated about a mile west from the
town of Peebles, on a rock projecting over the north
bank of the Tweed, which here runs through a deep

* The Scottish Eagle.

narrow glen, once well wooded on both sides. Nidpath was at one time the chief residence of the powerful family of the Frasers, from whom the families of Lovat and Salton in the north are descended. The last of the family in the male line was Sir Simon Fraser, who, in 1302, along with Comyn, then guardian of the kingdom, defeated three divisions of the English, on the same day, on Roslin Moor. Sir Simon left two daughters co-heiresses, one of whom married Hay of Yester, an ancestor of the Marquis of Tweeddale. The second Earl of Tweeddale garrisoned Nidpath, in 1636, for the service of Charles II., and it held out longer against Cromwell than any place south of the Forth. The Tweeddale family were so much impoverished by their exertions in the royal cause, that they were obliged, before the end of the reign of Charles II., to dispose of their barony of Nidpath to William, first Duke of Queensberry, who purchased it for his son the first Earl of March. On the death of the last Duke of Queensberry, in 1810, the Earl of Wemyss, as heir of entail, succeeded to the Nidpath estate. The castle is now falling fast to decay. It was formerly approached by an avenue of fine trees, all of which were cut down by the late Duke of Queensberry to impoverish the estate before it descended to the heir of entail. The poet, Wordsworth, has spoken of this conduct with just indignation in the following sonnet:—

> " Degenerate Douglas! oh, the unworthy Lord!
> Whom mere despite of heart could so far please,
> And love of havoc, (for with such disease
> Fame taxes him,) that he could send forth word
> To level with the dust a noble horde,
> A brotherhood of venerable Trees,
> Leaving an ancient dome, and towers like these,
> Beggar'd and outraged!—Many hearts deplored

The fate of those old Trees ; and oft, with pain,
The traveller, at this day, will stop and gaze
On wrongs, which Nature scarcely seems to heed :
For shelter'd places, bosoms, nooks, and bays,
And the pure mountains, and the gentle Tweed,
And the green silent pastures, yet remain."

Leaving Peebles, the tourist proceeds along the northern bank of the Tweed, and passing in succession
Kerfield (Gillespie, Esq.)—on the opposite bank of the
river, King's Meadows and Hayston, (Sir Adam Hay,
Bart.)—the ruins of Horsburgh Castle, the property of
the ancient family of the Horsburghs now resident at
Pirn—Kailzie, (R. N. Campbell, Esq.) Nether Horsburgh (Campbell, Esq.,) Cardrona, the seat of the old
family of Williamson, and Glenormiston House (Stewart,
Esq. ;) six miles below Peebles reaches the village of

INNERLEITHEN,

situated about a quarter of a mile from the mouth of
Leithen water. It occupies a pleasant situation at the
bottom of a sequestered dell, environed on the east and
west by high and partially wooded hills, and having the
Tweed rolling in front. Till little more than thirty years
ago, Innerleithen was one of the smallest and most
primitive hamlets in this pastoral district. But, about
the beginning of the present century, its mineral spring
began to attract notice, and it has now become a favourite watering-place, much frequented in the summer
and autumn by visitors from Edinburgh. The healthi-
ness of the climate—the beauty of the situation—its
proximity to St. Mary's Loch in Yarrow, and various
trouting streams, as well as other advantages connected
with its locality, render Innerleithen a very delightful
residence. A handsome wooden bridge leads across the
Tweed to the hamlet of Traquair and Traquair House,

the seat of the Earl of Traquair. At a short distance, at the base of a hill overlooking the lawn, a few birch trees may be seen, the scanty remains of the famed " Bush aboon Traquair." A few years ago an association was instituted at Innerleithen, called the St. Ronan's Border Club, consisting of a number of gentlemen connected with all parts of the country, who hold an annual festival for the performance of games and gymnastic exercises.

Leaving Innerleithen, at a short distance upon the right, is Pirn ; and three miles farther on, the road enters Selkirkshire, passing, on the left, Holylee (Ballantyne, Esq.) A mile beyond, on the opposite side of the river, are the ruins of Elibank Tower, from which Lord Elibank takes his title. Two miles farther on is Ashestiel (Col. Russell,) once the residence of Sir Walter Scott. A mile beyond this the road crosses Caddon Burn, and, at the village of Clovenfords, joins the road from Edinburgh to Selkirk. Two miles beyond, it passes Fairnielie (Pringle of Clifton) and Yair, the seat of Alexander Pringle, Esq. of Whytbank, M.P., one of the loveliest spots in Scotland, closely surrounded by hills most luxuriantly wooded. The road then crosses the Tweed at Yair Bridge, and, two miles farther on, crosses the Ettrick, and enters the royal burgh of

SELKIRK,

situated on a piece of high ground overhanging the Ettrick. Selkirk is a town of neat appearance, and the beautiful woods surrounding The Haining, the seat of Robert Pringle, Esq. of Clifton, form an excellent back ground to it. The population of the town and parish is 2883. It gives the title of Earl to a branch of the Douglas family.

A party of the citizens of Selkirk, under the command

of their town-clerk, William Brydone, behaved with
great gallantry at the battle of Flodden, when, in revenge for their brave conduct, the English entirely destroyed the town by fire. A pennon, taken from an
English leader by a person of the name of Fletcher, is
still kept in Selkirk by the successive deacons of the
weavers, and Brydone's sword is still in the possession
of his lineal descendants. The well-known pathetic
ballad of " The Flowers of the Forest," was composed on the loss sustained by the inhabitants of Ettrick
Forest at the fatal battle of Flodden. The principal
trade carried on in Selkirk at the time of the battle, and
for centuries afterwards, was the manufacture of thin or
single-soled shoes.* Hence, to be made a sutor of Selkirk
is the ordinary phrase for being created a burgess, and a
birse or hog's bristle is always attached to the seal of the
ticket.

[Those tourists, whose time does not admit of their visiting the
vales of Ettrick and Yarrow, may pass over the following chapter,
which, forming a sort of episode in the tour, we have printed in a
smaller type.]

ETTRICK AND YARROW.

" By Yarrow stream still let me stray,
  Though none should guide my weary way ;
  Still feel the breeze down Ettrick breaks,
  Though it should chill my wither'd cheeks."
                            SIR WALTER SCOTT.

Leaving Selkirk, the tourist will retrace his steps to the bridge
over the Ettrick, and turn up the north bank. The large level
plain on the northern side of the river, is Philiphaugh, the scene of
the defeat of Montrose, by General Leslie, 13th September 1645.
Montrose himself had taken up his quarters, with his cavalry, in

* Up wi' the Souters o' Selkirk,
    And down wi' the Earl o' Home ;
  And up wi' a' the braw lads
    That sow the single-soled shoon.

the town of Selkirk, while his infantry, amounting to about twelve or fifteen hundred men, were posted on Philiphaugh. Leslie arrived at Melrose the evening before the engagement, and next morning, favoured by a thick mist, he reached Montrose's encampment without being descried by a single scout. The surprisal was complete, and when the Marquis, who had been alarmed by the noise of the firing, reached the scene of the battle, he beheld his army dispersed in irretrievable rout. After a desperate but unavailing attempt to retrieve the fortune of the day, he cut his way through a body of Leslie's troopers, and fled up Yarrow and over Minchmoor towards Peebles. This defeat destroyed the fruit of Montrose's six splendid victories, and effectually ruined the royal cause in Scotland. The estate of Philiphaugh is the property of Colonel Murray, the descendant of the " Outlaw Murray," commemorated in the beautiful ballad of that name. At the head of Philiphaugh the Yarrow comes out from Newark's " birken bower" to join the Ettrick. At the confluence of these streams, about a mile above Selkirk, is Carterhaugh, the supposed scene of the fairy ballad of " Tamlane." The vale of Yarrow parts off from the head of Philiphaugh towards the right, that of Ettrick towards the left. The whole of this tract of country was, not many centuries ago, covered with wood, and its popular designation still is " the Forest." A native of Selkirk, who died about eighty years ago at an advanced age, used to tell that he had seen a person older than himself who said he had in his time walked from that town to Ettrick, a distance of eighteen miles, and never once all the way escaped from the shadow of trees. Of this primeval forest no vestige is now to be seen.

> " The scenes are desert now, and bare,
> Where flourish'd once a forest fair,
> Up pathless Ettrick and on Yarrow,
> Where erst the outlaw drew his arrow."
>   SCOTT.

Turning up the vale of Ettrick, the first object of interest that occurs is Oakwood, the residence of the hero of the ballad called " The Dowie Dens of Yarrow," and, from time immemorial, the property of the Scotts of Harden ; it is supposed, also, to have been the mansion of the famous wizard Michael Scott. Two or three miles farther up the glen is the village of Ettrick-brig-end, and, about six miles above, the remains of the tower of Tushielaw may be discerned upon the hill which rises from the north bank of the

H

river. Tushielaw was the residence of the celebrated freebooter
Adam Scott, called the King of the Border, who was hanged by
James V. in the course of that memorable expedition in 1529 which
proved fatal to Johnnie Armstrong, Cockburn of Henderland, and
many other marauders; the elm tree on which he was hanged still
exists among the ruins. Opposite to Tushielaw the Rankleburn
joins the Ettrick. The vale of Rankleburn contains the lonely farm
of Buccleuch, supposed to have been the original property of the
noble family of that name. There are remains of a church and burial
ground and of a kiln and mill in this district, but no traces of a
baronial mansion. Farther up are the ruins of Thirlestane Castle,
and, close by, the modern mansion of Thirlestane, the seat of Lord
Napier, the lineal descendant of the old family of the Scotts of
Thirlestane, as well as of the still more famous one of the Napiers
of Merchiston. Sir John Scott of Thirlestane, his paternal ancestor, was the only chief willing to follow James V. in his invasion
of England, when the rest of the Scottish nobles, encamped at
Fala, obstinately refused to take part in the expedition. In memory of his fidelity, James granted to his family a charter of arms
entitling them to bear a border of fleurs-de-luce similar to the treasure in the royal arms, with a bundle of spears for the crest, motto,
" ready, aye ready."—(See Lay of the Last Minstrel, canto iv.)
Thirlestane is surrounded with extensive plantations, and its late
noble and benevolent owner employed for many years his whole
time and talents in carrying on, at great expense, important improvements in this district. About a mile farther up stand the
kirk and hamlet of Ettrick. A cottage near the sacred edifice is
pointed out as the birth-place of the Ettrick Shepherd. The
celebrated Thomas Boston was at one time minister of Ettrick,
and, in the church-yard, a handsome monument has been erected
to his memory since the commencement of the present century.

   Crossing the hills which bound the vale of Ettrick on the right,
the tourist descends into the celebrated vale of Yarrow. At the
head of the vale is the beautiful sheet of water called St. Mary's
Loch, four miles long, and nearly one broad.

> —— " lone St. Mary's silent lake,
> ———————— nor fen nor sedge,
> Pollute the pure lake's crystal edge.
> Abrupt and sheer the mountains sink,
> At once upon the level brink;

And just a trace of silver sand
Marks where the water meets the land.
Far in the mirror bright and blue,
Each hill's huge outline you may view;
Shaggy with heath, but lonely bare,
Nor tree, nor bush, nor brake, is there,
Save where of land yon slender line
Bears 'thwart the lake the scatter'd pine.
Yet even this nakedness has power,
And aids the feeling of the hour:
Nor thicket, dell, nor copse you spy,
Where living thing conceal'd might lie:
There's nothing left to fancy's guess,
You see that all is loneliness;
And silence aids—though the steep hills
Send to the lake a thousand rills;
In summer tide, so soft they weep,
The sound but lulls the ear asleep;
Your horse's hoof-tread sounds too rude,
So stilly is the solitude." *

The river Yarrow flows from the east end, and a small stream connects the Loch of the Lowes with its western extremity. In the winter it is still frequented by flights of wild swans; hence Wordsworth's lines:

"The swans on sweet St. Mary's lake,
Float double—swan and shadow!"

In the neighbourhood is the farm of Blackhouse, adjacent to which are the remains of a very ancient tower in a wild and solitary glen, upon a torrent named Douglas Burn, which issues from the hills on the north, and joins the Yarrow, after passing a craggy rock, called the Douglas-craig. This wild scene, now a part of the Traquair estate, formed one of the most ancient possessions of the renowned family of Douglas, and is said by popular tradition to be the scene of the fine old ballad of "The Douglas Tragedy." Near the eastern extremity of St. Mary's Loch are the ruins of Dryhope Tower, the birth-place of Mary Scott, famous by the traditional name of the "Flower of Yarrow," and a mile westward, is the ancient burying-ground of St. Mary's Kirk, but the Church has long ago disappeared.

—— "Though in feudal strife, a foe
Hath laid Our Lady's chapel low,
Yet still beneath the hallow'd soil,
The peasant rests him from his toil,·

* Marmion. Introduction to Canto II.

> And, dying, bids his bones be laid,
> Where erst his simple fathers pray'd." *

A funeral in a spot so very retired, has an uncommonly striking
effect. At one corner of the burial-ground, but without its precincts, is a small mound, said by tradition to be the grave of Mass
John Birnam, the former tenant of the chaplainry.

> " That wizard priest, whose bones are thrust,
> From company of holy dust."

In the adjacent vale of Megget, is Henderland Castle, the residence of Cockburn, a border freebooter, who was hanged over the
gate of his own tower by James V. Tradition says that Cockburn
was surprised by the king while sitting at dinner. A mountain torrent called Henderland Burn, rushes impetuously from the hills
through a rocky chasm, named the Dow-glen, and passes near the
site of the tower. To the recesses of this glen, the wife of Cockburn is said to have retreated, during the execution of her husband,
and a place called the *Lady's Seat*, is still shown, where she is said
to have striven to drown, amid the roar of a foaming cataract, the
tumultuous noise which announced the close of his existence. The
beautiful pathetic ballad, entitled " The Lament of the Border
Widow," was composed on this event. On the north side of St.
Mary's Loch is a hill called the Merecleuchhead, over which there
is a scarcely visible track, termed the King's Road, leading over
the hills into Ettrick.† At the head of the Loch of the Lowes,
on the east, is Kirkenhope, and on the west, Chapelhope, the
scene of the tale of " The Brownie of Bodsbeck." A few miles
farther on through the hills, is a small house called Birkhill, opposite the door of which, Claverhouse shot four Covenanters, whose
grave-stones were discernible in Ettrick churchyard a few years
ago. Opposite the house at Birkhill, is a hill called the Watch
Hill, from the circumstance of the Covenanters stationing one of
their number there, to give notice of the approach of the soldiers ;
and a little below is a hideous gully, containing a waterfall, called
Dobbs Linn, and a cave which served as a place of retreat for the

---

* Marmion. Introduction to Canto II.
† An old song opens with this stanza :—

> " The king rade round the Merecleuchhead,
> Booted and spurr'd, as we a' did see ;
> Syne dined wi' a lass at Mossfennan yett,
> A little below the Logan Lee."

persecuted remnant. Near the head of Moffat Water, is the " dark Loch Skene," a mountain lake of considerable size. The stream into which it discharges itself, after a short and hurried course, falls from a cataract of immense height, and gloomy grandeur, called from its appearance The Grey Mare's Tail. The water is precipitated over a dark rugged precipice, about 300 feet high. A little way from the foot of the cataract, is a sort of trench, called " The Giant's Grave," which has evidently been a battery designed to command the pass. The character of the surrounding scenery is uncommonly savage and gloomy, and the earn or Scottish eagle, has for many ages built its nest yearly upon an islet in Loch Skene. This rude and savage scene is well described in the introduction to the second canto of Marmion.'

> " There eagles scream from isle to shore ;
> Down all the rocks the torrents roar ;
> O'er the black waves incessant driven,
> Dark mists infect the summer heaven ;
> Through the rude barriers of the lake
> Away its hurrying waters break
> Faster and whiter, dash and curl,
> Till down yon dark abyss they hurl.
> Rises the fog-smoke, white as snow
> Thunders the viewless stream below.
> *   *   *
> ——————— the bottom of the den,
> Where, deep deep down and far within,
> Toils with the rocks the roaring linn ;
> Then issuing forth one foamy wave,
> And wheeling round the Giant's Grave,
> White as the snowy charger's tail,
> Drives down the pass of Moffatdale."

The vale of Moffat, although less celebrated by its literary associations, is by no means inferior in picturesque attraction to its more favoured rivals, the Ettrick and Yarrow. To within a short distance from the village of Moffat the valley is strictly pastoral ; and although its upper extremity, from its great elevation, is not unfrequently shrouded in mist, a day of sunshine discloses scenery of a highly pleasing and romantic character.

The Grey Mare's Tail is nearly ten miles north-east from the village of Moffat, noted for its mineral well.

Returning to the Vale of Yarrow, a short way below St. Mary's Loch, is Mount Benger, at one time occupied by the Ettrick Shepherd ; and " The Gordon Arms " Inn, about thirteen miles from Selkirk, where a bridge over the Yarrow leads to Altrive, near the east

end of the lake, where the poet died. The next object of interest
that occurs is the Church of Yarrow, a neat little edifice, erected
about the time of Cromwell. On the moor, a little way west from
the kirk, two tall unhewn masses of stone, about eighty yards apart
from each other, mark the scene of the duel fought between John
Scott of Tushielaw and his brother-in-law, Walter Scott, third son
of Robert Scott of Thirlestane, in which the latter was slain. The
proposal of the lady's father, to endow her with half his property,
upon her marriage with a warrior of such renown, is alleged to
have been the cause of this unnatural quarrel. The incident has
given rise, directly or indirectly, to ballads, songs, and poems innumerable. The most famous, are the old ballad called "The
Dowie Dens of Yarrow," and those composed by Hamilton of
Bangour and Logan; and, more recently, the three charming poems
of Wordsworth,—Yarrow Unvisited, Yarrow Visited, and Yarrow
Revisited. A few verses of Yarrow Visited may here be quoted,
as, in addition to the beauty of the poetry, they give an excellent
description of the scenery.

"And is this—Yarrow?—*This* the
   stream
Of which my fancy cherish'd,
So faithfully, a waking dream?
   An image that hath perish'd!
O that some minstrel's harp were near
   To utter tones of gladness,
And chase this silence from the air
   That fills my heart with sadness.

Yet why?—a silvery current flows
   With uncontroll'd meanderings;
Nor have these eyes, by greener hills
   Been soothed in all my wanderings.
And, through her depths, St. Mary's
   Lake
Is visibly delighted;
For not a feature of those hills
   Is in the mirror slighted.

Where was it that the famous Flower
   Of Yarrow Vale lay bleeding?
His bed, perchance, was yon smooth
   mound
On which the herd is feeding:
And, haply, from this crystal pool,
   Now peaceful as the morning,
The water-wraith ascended thrice,
   And gave his doleful warning.

Delicious is the lay that sings
   The haunts of happy lovers;
The path that leads them to the grove,
   The leafy grove that covers:
And Pity sanctifies the verse
   That paints, by strength of sorrow,
The unconquerable strength of love;
   Bear witness, rueful Yarrow!

But thou, that didst appear so fair
   To fond imagination,
Dost rival in the light of day
   Her delicate creation:
Meek loveliness is round thee spread,
   A softness still and holy;
The grace of forest charms decay'd,
   And pastoral melancholy.

That region left, the vale unfolds
   Rich groves of lofty stature,
With Yarrow winding through the
   pomp
   Of cultivated nature;
And, rising from these lofty groves,
   Behold a Ruin hoary!
The shatter'd front of Newark's
   Tower,
   Renown'd in Border story."

Farther down the vale is the village of Yarrowford, near which are the remains of the strong and venerable Castle of Hangingshaw, one of the possessions of the Outlaw Murray, and, till within these few years, of his descendants. It stood in a romantic and solitary situation, and was the scene of the beautiful old ballad called "The Sang of the Outlaw Murray."* When the mountains around Hangingshaw were covered with the wild copse which constituted a Scottish forest, a more secure stronghold for an outlawed baron can hardly be imagined. A little beyond is the handsome modern mansion of Broadmeadows, (—— Boyd, Esq.,) commanding a delightful view; and a mile below are the romantic ruins of NEWARK CASTLE, standing on an eminence overhanging the Yarrow, with dark wooded hills rising closely around on both sides. It is scarcely necessary to remind the tourist, that this is the mansion in which Anne Duchess of Buccleuch and Monmouth is made to listen to the "Lay of the Last Minstrel." At Newark, Leslie, after the battle of Philiphaugh, caused a number of his prisoners to be executed in cold blood. The spot where this atrocious deed was perpetrated is still called the "Slain-men's-lee." Opposite Newark is the farm of Foulshiels, where Mungo Park, the celebrated African traveller, was born. Farther down, at the mouth of the vale on the right, is Bowhill, a summer residence of the Duke of Buccleuch, standing on the face of an eminence, embowered amidst its beautiful new woods; and on the left Philiphaugh House, (Colonel Murray,) situated on a hill overlooking Carterhaugh and the confluence of the Ettrick and Yarrow. The road now passes Philiphaugh and enters the town of Selkirk.

* The scene is, by the common people, supposed to have been the Castle of Newark, but this is highly improbable, as Newark was always a royal fortress; and Mr. Plummer, who, at one time, held the office of sheriff-depute of Selkirkshire, assured Sir Walter Scott that he remembered the *insignia* of the unicorns, &c., so often mentioned in the ballad, in existence upon the old tower at Hangingshaw. The house was burnt down by accident, about seventy or eighty years ago, to the great grief of the people, who loved the proprietor on account of his numerous virtues. As a trait of the hospitality practised at Hangingshaw, it is recorded by tradition, that whosoever called at the house, was treated with a draught of stout ale from a capacious vessel, called "the Hangingshaw Ladle."

CHART OF THE VALES OF TEVIOT AND TWEED.

Leaving Selkirk for Melrose, the road leads along the
south bank of the Ettrick, and, at the distance of about a
mile, enters Roxburghshire.   Near this spot is the secluded burying-ground of Lindean, to which a church
was formerly attached.   Three miles from Selkirk, the
Ettrick flows into the Tweed.   At this spot bridges have
lately been thrown over both rivers.   Proceeding along
the banks of the Tweed, the tourist, at the distance of
a mile and a half, reaches

ABBOTSFORD,

the seat of Sir Walter Scott, Bart., situated on a bank

overhanging the south side of the Tweed, which at this place makes a beautiful sweep around the declivity on which the house stands. It is surrounded by flourishing plantations, and commands an interesting though not extensive view.

ABBOTSFORD.

The house is of very extraordinary proportions, and though irregular as a whole, produces a very striking effect. The entrance to the house is by a porchway, adorned with petrified stags' horns, into a hall, which is perhaps the most interesting of all the apartments. The walls are pannelled with richly carved oak from the palace of Dunfermline, and the roof consists of painted arches of the same material. Round the cornice there is a line of coats armorial richly blazoned, belonging to the families who kept the borders,—as the Douglasses, Kers, Scotts, Turnbulls, Maxwells, Chisholms, Elliots, and Armstrongs. The floor is of black and white marble from the Hebrides, and the walls are hung with an-

cient armour, and various specimens of military imple-
ments. From the hall you proceed to the armoury, a
narrow low-arched room, which runs quite across the
house, having a blazoned window at either extremity,
and filled with smaller pieces of armour and weapons.
This apartment communicates with the drawing-room on
the one side, and the dining-room on the other. The
former is a large and lofty saloon with wood of cedar.
Its antique ebony furniture, carved cabinets, &c. are all
of beautiful workmanship. The dining-room is a very
handsome apartment, with a roof of black oak richly carved. It contains a fine collection of pictures; the most
interesting of which are the head of Queen Mary in a
charger the day after she was beheaded, and a full length
portrait of Lord Essex on horseback, of Oliver Cromwell,
Claverhouse, Charles II., Charles XII. of Sweden, and,
among several family pictures, one of Sir Walter's great
grandfather, who allowed his beard to grow after the
execution of Charles I. The breakfast parlour is a small
and neat apartment, overlooking the Tweed on the one
side, and the wild hills of Ettrick and Yarrow on the
other. It contains a beautiful and valuable collection of
water-colour drawings, chiefly by Turner and Thomson
of Duddingston, the designs for the magnificent work
entitled " Provincial Antiquities of Scotland." The
library, which is the largest of all the apartments, is a
magnificent room, fifty feet by sixty. The roof is of carved oak, chiefly after models from Roslin. The collection of books in this room amounts to about 20,000 volumes, many of them extremely rare and valuable. From
the library there is a communication with the study, a
room of about twenty-five feet square by twenty feet
high, containing of what is properly called furniture no-

thing but a small writing-table in the centre, a plain arm-chair covered with black leather, and a single chair besides. There are a few books, chiefly for reference, and a light gallery of tracery work runs round three sides of the room, which contains only one window, so that the place is rather sombre. From this room you enter a small closet, containing what must be viewed by all with the deepest interest—the body-clothes worn by Sir Walter previous to his decease.* The external walls of the house, as well as those of the adjoining garden, are enriched with many old carved stones, which have originally figured in other and very different situations. The door of the old tolbooth of Edinburgh, the pulpit from which Ralph Erskine preached, and various other curious and interesting relics, may also be seen. Through the whole extent of the surrounding forests there are a number of beautiful winding walks, and near the waterfalls in the deep ravines are benches or bowers commanding the most picturesque views. The mansion of Abbotsford and its woods have been entirely created by its late proprietor, who, when he purchased the ground about thirty years ago, found it occupied by a small onstead called " Cartley Hole." The first purchase was made from the late Dr. Douglas of Galashiels. It is said that the money was paid by instalments, and that the letter enclosing the last remittance contained these lines :

" Noo the gowd's thine,
And the land's mine."

* " After showing us the principal rooms, the woman opened a small closet adjoining the study, in which hung the last clothes that Sir Walter had worn. There was the broad-skirted blue coat with large buttons, the plaid trowsers, the heavy shoes, the broad-rimmed hat, and stout walking-stick,—the dress in which he rambled about in the morning, and which he laid off when he took to his bed in his last illness. She took down the coat, and gave it a shake and a wipe of the collar, as if he were waiting to put it on again!"—WILLIS's Pencillings by the Way.

Various other "pendicles" were purchased at different times from the neighbouring bonnet-lairds, at prices greatly above their real value. In December 1830, the library, museum, plate, and furniture of every description were presented to Sir Walter as a free gift by his creditors, and he afterwards bequeathed the same to his eldest son, burdened with a sum of L.5000 to be divided among his younger children. The proceeds of a subscription set on foot in London a considerable time ago, are to be applied to the payment of this debt, so as to enable the trustees to entail the library and museum as an heir-loom in the family, and it is expected that the mortgage on the lands will be liquidated by the profits of the new edition of Sir Walter's works, and thereby enable the executors to complete an entail of the entire property.

A little to the east of Abbotsford, and on the opposite bank of the river, the Allan or Elwand water runs into the Tweed. There can be little doubt that the vale of the Allan is the true "Glendearg" of the Monastery.* The banks on each side are steep, and rise boldly over the eccentric stream which jets from rock to rock, rendering it absolutely necessary for the traveller to cross and recross it, as he pur-

* "When we had ridden a little time on the moors, he said to me rather pointedly, ' I am going to show you something that I think will interest you ;' and presently, in a wild corner of the hills, he halted us at a place where stood three small ancient towers, or castellated houses, in ruins, at short distances from each other. It was plain, upon the slightest consideration of the topography, that one (perhaps any one) of these was the tower of Glendearg, where so many romantic and marvellous adventures happen in The Monastery. While we looked at this forlorn group, I said to Sir Walter that they were what Burns called 'ghaist-alluring edifices.' ' Yes,' he answered, carelessly, ' I dare say there are many stories about them.' As we returned, by a different route, he made me dismount and take a footpath through a part of Lord Somerville's grounds, where the Elland runs through a beautiful little valley, the stream winding between level borders of the brightest green sward, which narrow or widen as the steep sides of the glen advance or recede. The place is called the Fairy Dean, and it required no cicerone to tell, that the glen was that in which Father Eustace, in The Monastery, is intercepted by the White Lady of Avenel."—Letter of Mr. Adolphus—LOCKHART's Life of Scott, vol. v.

sues his way up the bottom of the narrow valley. " The hills also rise at some places abruptly over the little glen, displaying at intervals the grey rock overhung with wood, and farther up rises the mountain in purple majesty—the dark rich hue contrasting beautifully with the thickets of oak and birch, the mountain ashes and thorns, the alders and quivering aspens which chequered and varied the descent, and not less with the dark green velvet turf which composed the level part of the narrow glen." At a short distance from Abbotsford is the small village of Bridgend, which received its name from a bridge erected over the Tweed by David I., to afford a passage to the Abbey of Melrose. It consisted of four piers, upon which lay planks of wood ; and in the middle pillar was a gateway large enough for a carriage to pass through, and over that a room in which the toll-keeper resided. It was at a ford below this bridge that the adventure with the White Lady of Avenel befell Father Philip, the sacristan of the Monastery. (See Monastery, Vol. I.) From this bridge the Girthgate, a path to the sanctuary of Soutra, runs up the valley of Allan Water, and over the moors to Soutra Hill. Between Bridgend and Darnick is a place called Skinnersfield (a corruption for Skirmishfield,) where a battle was fought in 1526 between the Earl of Angus and the Laird of Buccleuch, for possession of the person of James V., which terminated in favour of Angus.* The road now

* " The Earl of Angus, with his reluctant ward, had slept at Melrose, and the clans of Home and Kerr, under the Lord Home, and the barons of Cessford and Fairnihirst, had taken their leave of the king, when, in the grey of the morning, Buccleuch and his band of cavalry, comprehending a large body of Elliots, Armstrongs, and other broken clans, were discovered, hanging like a thunder cloud upon the neighbouring hill of Haliden. The encounter was fierce and obstinate, but the Homes and Kerrs returning at the noise of the battle, bore down and dispersed the left wing of Buccleuch's little army. The hired banditti fled on all sides, but the chief himself, surrounded by his clan, fought desperately in the retreat. The laird of Cessford, chief of the Roxburgh

passes the village of Darnick, in which there is an ancient tower, built during the fifteenth century, and a little farther on reaches

MELROSE,

situated on the south side of the Tweed, near the base of the Eildon Hills.   It is thirty-six miles from Edinburgh, thirteen from Jedburgh, and fourteen from Kelso. " The vale of the Tweed is everywhere fertile and beautiful, and here grandeur is combined with beauty and fertility. The eye is presented with a wide range of pleasing and impressive scenery—of villages and hamlets—the river winding rapidly among smiling fields and orchards, the town with its groves, and gardens, and neat rural church, wooded acclivities, and steep pastoral slopes crowned with the shapely summits of majestic hills, forming a richly diversified and striking panorama, not to speak of the elegant and graceful remains of the ancient Abbey, the sight of which conveys a deep interest to the mind, carries it back through ages and events long past, and leads to sober reflections on the vicissitude of human affairs, and the instability of human institutions."*   Near the village are the remains of the famous Abbey, which afford the finest specimen of Gothic architecture and Gothic sculpture ever reared in this country.   The stone of which it is built, though it has resisted the weather for so many ages, retains perfect sharpness, so that even the most minute ornaments seem as entire as when newly wrought.   The

Kerrs, pursued the chase fiercely, till, at the bottom of a steep path, Elliot of Stobs turned and slew him, with a stroke of his lance. When Cessford fell the pursuit ceased, but his death, with those of Buccleuch's friends who fell in the action, to the number of eighty, occasioned a deadly feud betwixt the clans of Scott and Kerr, which cost much blood upon the marches."—See *Introduction to Minstrelsy of the Scottish Border*, and *Lay of the Last Minstrel.*

* Monastic Annals of Teviotdale, p. 196.

other buildings being completely destroyed, the ruins of the church alone remain to indicate the ancient magnificence of this celebrated monastery. It is in the usual form of a Latin cross, with a square tower in the centre, eighty-four feet in height, of which only the west side is standing. The parts now remaining of this structure are the choir and transept—the west side, and part of the north and south walls of the great tower, part of the nave, nearly the whole of the southmost aisle, and part of the north aisle. The west gable being in ruins, the principal entrance is by a richly moulded Gothic portal in the south transept. Over this doorway is a magnificent window, twenty-four feet in height and sixteen in breadth, divided by four bars or mullions, which branch out or interlace each other at the top in a variety of graceful curves. The stone work of the whole window yet remains perfect. Over this window are nine niches, and two on each buttress, which formerly contained images of our Saviour and his Apostles. Beneath the window is a statue of John Baptist, with his eye directed upward, as if looking upon the image of Christ above. The carving upon the pedestals and canopies of the niches exhibits a variety of quaint figures and devices. The buttresses and pinnacles on the east and west sides of the same transept present a curious diversity of sculptured forms of plants and animals. On the south-east side are a great many musicians admirably cut. In the south wall of the nave are eight beautiful windows, each sixteen feet in height and eight in breadth, having upright mullions of stone with rich tracery. These windows light eight small square chapels of uniform dimensions, which run along the south side of the nave, and are separated from each other by thin partition walls of stone. The west end of

the nave, and five of the chapels included in it, are now
roofless.   The end next the central tower is arched over
—the side aisles and chapels with their original Gothic
roof, and the middle avenue with a plain vault thrown
over it in 1618, at which time this part of the building
was fitted up as a parish church.   The choir or chancel,
which is built in the form of half a Greek cross, displays
the finest architectural taste.   The eastern window in
particular is uncommonly elegant and beautiful.   Sir
Walter Scott, in describing this part of the building,
says—

   " The moon on the east oriel shone
     Through slender shafts of shapely stone
       By foliaged tracery combined :
     Thou would'st have thought some fairy's hand
     'Twixt poplars straight the osier wand
       In many a freakish knot had twined ;
     Then framed a spell when the work was done,
     And changed the willow wreaths to stone."

The original beautifully fretted and sculptured stone roof
of the east end of the chancel is still standing, and rises
high

     " On pillars lofty, and light, and small,
     The keystone that lock'd each ribbed aisle,
     Was a fleur-de-lys or a quatre-feuille :
     The corbells were carved grotesque and grim,
     And the pillars with cluster'd shafts so trim,
     With base and with capital flourish'd around,
     Seemed bundles of lances which garlands had bound."

The outside of the fabric is every where profusely embellished with niches having canopies of an elegant design
exquisitely carved, and some of them still containing
statues.

The cloisters formed a quadrangle on the north-west

side of the church. The door of entrance from the cloisters to the church is on the north side, close by the west wall of the transept, and is exquisitely carved. The foliage upon the capitals of the pilasters on each side is so nicely chiselled, that a straw can be made to penetrate through the interstices between the leaves and stalks. Through this door the " monk of St. Mary's aisle," in the Lay of the Last Minstrel, is said to have conducted William of Deloraine to the grave of Michael Scott, after conducting him through the cloister. The best view of the Abbey is obtained from the south-east corner of the churchyard ; but

" If thou would'st view fair Melrose aright,
  Go visit it by the pale moonlight ;
For the gay beams of lightsome day
Gild, but to flout, the ruins grey.
When the broken arches are black in night,
And each shafted oriel glimmers white ;
When the cold light's uncertain shower
Streams on the ruin'd central tower ;
When buttress and buttress, alternately,
Seem framed of ebon and ivory ;
When silver edges the imagery,
And the scrolls that teach thee to live and die ;
  When distant Tweed is heard to rave,
And the owlet to hoot o'er the dead man's grave,
Then go—but go alone the while—
Then view St. David's ruin'd pile ;
And, home returning, soothly swear,
Was never scene so sad and fair ! "

Within the Abbey lie the remains of many a gallant warrior and venerable priest. A large slab of polished marble, of a greenish-black colour, with petrified shells imbedded in it, is believed to cover the dust of Alexander II., who was interred beside the high altar under the

east window. Here, also, the heart of King Robert Bruce
is supposed to have been deposited, after Douglas had
made an unsuccessful attempt to carry it to the Holy
Land. Many of the powerful family of Douglas were
interred in this church,—among these were William Douglas, " the dark knight of Liddesdale," who tarnished his
laurels by the barbarous murder of his companion in
arms, the gallant Sir Alexander Ramsay, and was himself
killed by his godson and chief, William Earl of Douglas,
while hunting in Ettrick Forest; and James, second
Earl of Douglas, who fell at the celebrated Battle of Ot-
terburn. Their tombs, which occupied two crypts near
the high altar, were defaced by the English, under Sir
Ralph Evers and Sir Brian Latoun,—an insult which was
signally avenged by their descendant, the Earl of Angus,
at the Battle of Ancrum Moor.

Melrose Abbey was founded by David I., by whom it
was munificently endowed. The foundation was laid in
1136, but the building was not completed till 1146, when
it was dedicated to the Virgin Mary. The monks were
of the reformed class called Cistertians. They were
brought from the abbey of Rievalle, in the North-Riding
of Yorkshire, and were the first of this order who came
into Scotland. It was destroyed by the English in their
retreat under Edward II. in 1322, and, four years after,
Robert Bruce gave £2000 sterling to rebuild it. This
sum, equal to £50,000 of the money of the present day,
was raised chiefly from the baronies of Cessford and Eckford, forfeited by Sir Roger de Mowbray; and the lands
of Nesbit, Longnewton, Maxton, and Caverton, forfeited
by William Lord Soulis. The present beautiful fabric,
which is still the object of general admiration in its ruins,
was then raised in a style of graceful magnificence, that

entitles it to be classed among the most perfect works of
the best age of that description of ecclesiastical architecture to which it belongs. In 1385, it was burnt by Richard
II.; in 1545, it was despoiled by Evers and Latoun;
and again, in the same year, it was destroyed by the Earl
of Hertford. At the period of the Reformation it suffered
severely, from the misdirected zeal of the Reformers.*
The estates of the abbey were granted by Queen Mary
in 1566 to James Hepburn, Earl of Bothwell, by whose
forfeiture in 1567 they reverted again to the Crown, and
the usufruct, with the title of Commendator, was conferred, the following year, upon James Douglas, second
son to Sir William Douglas of Lochleven.† In 1609, the
abbey and its possessions were erected into a temporal
lordship for Sir John Ramsay, who had been created
Viscount Haddington, for his service in preserving James
VI. from the treasonable attempt of the Earl of Gowrie.
Lord Haddington, who was afterwards created Earl of
Holderness, appears to have disposed of the possessions
belonging to the lordship of Melrose, since we find that
they were granted by charter to Sir Thomas Hamilton,
(" Tam o' the Cowgate,") a celebrated lawyer, who was
created Earl of Melrose in 1619, and afterwards Earl of
Haddington. Part of the lands were granted to Walter
Scott, Earl of Buccleuch, and his descendants, about the
beginning of the eighteenth century, acquired by pur-

* The following verse, from a once popular ballad, shows that, at the time of
the Reformation, the inmates of this abbey shared in the general reproach of
sensuality and *irregularity* thrown upon the Romish churchmen :—

" The monks of Melrose made gude kail
        On Fridays, when they fasted;
    Nor wanted they gude beef and ale,
        As lang 's their neighbours' lasted."

† Monastic Annals of Teviotdale, p. 245.

chase the remainder of the Abbey lands included in the
lordship of Melrose, which still form a part of the extensive possessions of the same noble family.

At the abolition of heritable jurisdictions in 1747, the
Lady Isabella Scott was allowed the sum of £1200 sterling, as compensation for her right to the bailiery of Melrose.   .

When King David I. laid the foundations of Melrose
Abbey, the ground on which Melrose now stands was
occupied by a village called Fordel.   The present village
is an extremely curious and antique place, and has evidently been, in a great measure, built out of the ruins of
the abbey.   In the centre of the village stands a cross,
about twenty feet high, supposed to be coeval with the
abbey.   There is a ridge in a field near the town, called
the Corse-rig, which the proprietor of the field holds upon
the sole condition that he shall keep up the cross.

In the vicinity of Melrose are the Eildon Hills, the
Trimontium of the Romans.*   Opposite to the village,
a wire bridge leads across the Tweed, to the scattered
little village of Gattonside, with its numerous orchards.
A short way farther down the river, on a peninsula
formed by a remarkable sweep of the Tweed, stood the
ancient Monastery of Old Melrose.   The estate of Old .
Melrose was long possessed by a family of the name of
Ormestoun.   It is now the property of William Elliot
Lockhart, Esq., who has a house there delightfully situated.   Two miles below Melrose, the Leader pours its
waters from the north, through a beautiful wooded vale,
to join the Tweed.   In the immediate vicinity is Dry-

---

* It is said that Eildon hills were once an uniform cone, and that the summit
was formed into the three picturesque peaks, into which it is now divided, by
a spirit, for whom Michael Scott was under the necessity of finding constant
employment. See Lay of the Last Minstrel, Canto xi.-xiii.

grange, (John Tod, Esq.) beautifully situated. About a mile and a half from Drygrange is the house of Cowden-knows, (Dr. Home,) situated on the east bank of the Leader, at the foot of the hill of Cowdenknows, cele-brated in song for its " bonny bonny broom." A mile farther up the Leader is the village of Earlstoun, anciently Erceldoune, the dwelling of Thomas Learmont, com-monly called Thomas the Rhymer, in whom, as in the mighty men of old,

—————— the honour'd name
Of prophet and of poet was the same.

The remains of the Rhymer's Tower are still pointed out, in the midst of a beautiful haugh, on the east side of the Leader. About four miles from Melrose, on the north bank of the Tweed, within the county of Berwick, stand the picturesque ruins of

DRYBURGH ABBEY,

on a richly wooded haugh, round which the river makes a fine circuitous sweep. The situation is eminently beautiful, and both the abbey, and the modern mansion-house of the proprietor, are completely embosomed in wood. Dryburgh Abbey was founded in 1150, during the reign of David I., by Hugh de Moreville, Lord of Lauderdale, Constable of Scotland, upon a site which is supposed to have been originally a place of Druidical worship. The monks were of the Premonstratensian order, and were brought from the abbey founded at Alnwick a short time before. Edward II., in his retreat from the unsuccessful invasion of Scotland in 1322, encamped in the grounds of Dryburgh, and setting fire to the monastery, burnt it to the ground. Robert I. contributed liberally towards its repair, but it has been doubted whether it was ever fully restored to its original magnificence. In 1544, the abbey was again destroyed, by a hostile incursion of the English, under Sir George Bowes and Sir Brian Latoun. The principal remains of the building are, the western gable of the nave of the church, the ends of the transept, part of the choir, and a portion of the domestic buildings. In St. Mary's aisle, which is by far the most beautiful part of the ruin, Sir Walter Scott was buried, 26th September 1832, in the burying-ground of his ancestors, the Haliburtons of Newmains, the ancient proprietors of the abbey. Nature has been most profuse in her decorations around the Gothic walls which form the poet's grave. The chapter-house is a spacious apartment, containing a great number of plaster of Paris figures, representing the most distinguished characters of ancient and modern times. The ruins of the abbey are almost completely overgrown with foliage, and a number of fine trees have sprung up among the rubbish. In 1604, James VI. granted Dryburgh Abbey to John Earl of Mar, and he afterwards erected it into a temporal lordship and peerage, with the title of Lord Cardross, to the same Earl, who made it over to his third son, Henry, ancestor of the Earl of Buchan. The abbey was afterwards sold to the Haliburtons of Mertoun, from whom it was purchased by Colonel Tod, whose heirs sold it to the Earl of Buchan in 1786. The Earl, at his death, bequeathed it to his son, Sir David Erskine, at whose death, in 1837, it reverted to the Buchan family.

In the immediate vicinity of the abbey is the neat mansion-house of Dryburgh, surrounded by stately trees. At a short distance, is a chain suspension-bridge over the Tweed, erected in 1818, at the expense of the late Earl of Buchan ; and on a rising ground, at the end of the bridge, is a circular temple dedicated to the Muses, surmounted by a bust of Thomson, the author of the " Seasons." Farther up, on a rocky eminence over- looking the river, is a colossal statue of the Scottish patriot Wallace. The whole prospect around is emi- nently beautiful, embracing both wood and water, moun- tain and rock scenery.*

* Connected with Dryburgh is the following story, told by Sir Walter Scott in his Border Minstrelsy :—" Soon after the Rebellion in 1745, an unfortunate female wanderer took up her residence in a dark vault among the ruins of Dry- burgh Abbey, which, during the day, she never quitted. When night fell, she issued from this miserable habitation, and went to the house of Mr. Haliburton of Newmains, or to that of Mr. Erskine of Shielfield, two gentlemen of the neighbourhood. From their charity she obtained such necessaries as she could be prevailed on to accept. At twelve, each night, she lighted her candle and returned to her vault, assuring her neighbours that, during her absence, her habitation was arranged by a spirit, to whom she gave the uncouth appellation of Fatlips, and whom she described as a little man, wearing heavy iron shoes, with which he trampled the clay floor of the vault, to dispel the damps. This circumstance caused her to be regarded, by the well-informed, with compas- sion, as deranged in her understanding, and, by the vulgar, with some degree of terror. The cause of her adopting this extraordinary mode of life she would never explain. It was, however, believed to have been occasioned by a vow, that, during the absence of a man to whom she was attached, she would never look upon the sun. Her lover never returned. He fell during the civil war of 1745-6, and she never more would behold the light of day. The vault, or rather dungeon, in which this unfortunate woman lived and died, passes still by the name of the supernatural being with which its gloom was tenanted by her dis- turbed imagination."

In the vicinity of Dryburgh is the mansion of Bemerside, the lands and ba- rony of which have been in the possession of the Haigs since the time of Malcolm IV. The following rhyme respecting this family is ascribed, by tradition, to Thomas the Rhymer :—

> " Tide, tide, whate'er betide,
> There 'll ay be Haigs in Bemerside."

The above rhyme, which testifies the firm belief entertained by the country people in the perpetual lineal succession of the Haigs, is ascribed to no less vene- rable and infallible authority than that of Thomas the Rhymer, whose patri- monial territory was not far from Bemerside. " The grandfather of the present Mr. Haig had twelve daughters, before his wife brought him a male heir.* The common people trembled for the credit of their favourite soothsayer. The late Mr. Haig was at length born, and their belief in the prophecy confirmed beyond a shadow of doubt."—*Minst. Scot. Bord.*, iii., 209.

* This gentleman, being very pious, used to go out, once or twice a-day, to a retired place near his house, fall down on his knees, (placing his bonnet beneath, however,) and pray that God would send him a son. As his name was Zorobabel, we are led to suppose that he in- herited this singular degree of piety, like his name, from some ancestor contemporary with Praise God Barebones.

On the opposite bank of the Tweed lies the village of
St. Boswell's Green, or Lessuden, formerly a place of
some importance, for, when burned by the English in
1544, it contained sixteen strong towers.   On the Green
is held the fair of St. Boswell's, the principal market for
sheep and lambs in the south of Scotland.   Near this
place a bridge has lately been erected across the Tweed,
opening up a desirable communication between the north
and south sides of the river.   Two miles from St. Boswell's is the village of Maxton, and, on the opposite side
of the river, in a delightful situation, is Mertoun House,
the seat of Scott of Harden, who has lately established
his claim to the title of Lord Polwarth.   Near to Maxton, on a cliff on the south bank of the river, are the
ruins of Littledean Tower, formerly a place of great note,
and long the residence of the Kerrs of Littledean and
Nenthorn, a branch of the Cessford family.   It is now
the property of Lord Polwarth.   Six miles from St. Boswell's Green is Makerstoun, the lovely residence of Sir
Thomas Makdougal Brisbane, Bart., surrounded by luxuriant woods.   To the north, a view may be obtained of
Smailholm Tower, the scene of Sir Walter Scott's admirable ballad of the " Eve of St. John."   The poet
resided for some time, while a boy, at the neighbouring
farm-house of Sandyknowe, then inhabited by his paternal grandfather, and he has beautifully described the
scenery in one of his preliminary epistles to Marmion.*

* " It was a barren scene, and wild,
    Where naked cliffs were rudely piled ;
    But, ever and anon, between
    Lay velvet tufts of loveliest green ;
    And well the lonely infant knew
    Recesses where the wall-flower grew,
    And honeysuckle loved to crawl
    Up the low crag and ruin'd wall.
    I deem'd such nooks the sweetest shade
    The sun in all its round survey'd ;

The Tower is a high square building, surrounded by an outer wall, now ruinous. The circuit of the outer court being defended, on three sides, by a precipice and morass, is accessible only from the west by a steep and rocky path. The apartments are placed one above another, and communicate by a narrow stair. From the elevated situation of Smailholm Tower, it is seen many miles in every direction. It formerly belonged to the Pringles of Whytbank, and is now the property of Lord Polwarth. Continuing along the road, amidst the richest scenery, the tourist passes, on the right, the scanty remains of the famous CASTLE of ROXBURGH, situated near the junction of the Tweed and Teviot, which here approach so close as to form a narrow isthmus, and part of the defences of the Castle was a deep moat, filled with water from the Teviot. Roxburgh Castle was formerly a fortress of great extent and importance; but having been dismantled about 400 years ago, a few fragments of walls are all that now remain to attest its former strength. In 1460, when in possession of the English, it was besieged by James II., and, after his death, taken by his army, under the direction of his widow. The spot where James was killed, by the bursting of a cannon, is marked by a holly tree, which grows upon the opposite bank of the Tweed. Nearly opposite to the ruins of the Castle, on the left bank of the river, is FLEURS CASTLE, the seat of the Duke

> And still I thought that shatter'd tower
> The mightiest work of human power;
> And marvell'd, as the aged hind
> With some strange tale bewitch'd my mind,
> Of forayers, who, with headlong force,
> Down from that strength had spurr'd their horse,
> Their southern rapine to renew,
> Far in the distant Cheviots blue,
> And, home returning, fill'd the hall
> With revel, wassel-rout, and brawl."

I

of Roxburghe, commanding a fine view of the surrounding country.   The noble proprietor is now engaged in
making extensive alterations and repairs on this building,
which promise, when completed, to make it one of the
most stately specimens of the Tudor style in Scotland.
On the haugh, upon the south side of the river, is held,
on the 5th of August, St. James's Fair, the greatest fair,
next to St. Boswell's, in the south of Scotland.   Proceeding onward, the tourist crosses the Teviot, and,
shortly after, the Tweed, and enters the town of

KELSO,

occupying a beautiful situation on the north margin of the
Tweed. It consists of four principal streets, and a spacious
square or market-place, in which stand the town-hall,
erected in 1816, and a number of well-built houses, with
elegant shops.   Kelso is the residence of a number of
people in easy circumstances, who live in a style of considerable elegance.   It carries on a good inland trade,
and has a weekly market, and four annual fairs.*   The
most prominent object in Kelso is the venerable abbey, a
noble specimen of the solid and majestic style of architecture called the Saxon or early Norman.   The monks were
of a reformed class of the Benedictines, first established
at Tiron in France, and hence called Tironenses.   David
I., when Earl of Huntingdon, introduced the Tironenses
into Scotland, and settled them near his castle at Selkirk,
in the year 1113.   The principal residence of the kings
of Scotland, at this period, was the Castle of Roxburgh ;
and when David succeeded to the Scottish crown, after
the death of his brother, in 1124, he removed the con-

---

* Kelso is a burgh of barony, governed, under the general police act, by a
bailie and fifteen commissioners.

vent from Selkirk to Kelso, within view of his royal castle. The foundation of the church was laid on the 3d of May 1128. In consequence of its vicinity to the English border, Kelso suffered severely during the wars between the two countries, and the monastery was frequently laid waste by fire. It was reduced to its present ruinous state by the English, under the Earl of Hertford, in 1545. The only parts now remaining are the walls of the transepts, the centre tower, and west end, and a small part of the choir. After the Reformation, a low gloomy vault was thrown over the transept, to make it serve as a parish church, and it continued to be used for this purpose till 1771, when, one Sunday, during divine service, the congregation were alarmed by the falling of a piece of plaster from the roof, and hurried out in terror, believing that the vault over their heads was giving way; and this, together with an ancient prophecy attributed to Thomas the Rhymer, " that the kirk should fall when at the fullest," caused the church to be deserted, and it has never since had an opportunity of tumbling on a full congregation. The ruins were disencumbered of the rude modern masonry, by the good taste of William Duke of Roxburghe, and his successor Duke James, and, in 1823, the decayed parts were strengthened and repaired by subscription. After the Reformation, the principal part of the estates of this rich abbey were held *in commendam* by Sir John Maitland, the ancestor of the Earl of Lauderdale, who exchanged it with Francis Stewart, afterwards Earl of Bothwell, for the priory of Coldinghame. This nobleman, for his repeated treasons, was attainted in 1592, and the lands and possessions of Kelso abbey were finally conferred upon Sir Robert Kerr of Cessford, and they are still enjoyed by his descendant, the Duke of Roxburghe.

The environs of Kelso are singularly beautiful. They are thus described by Leyden, in his *Scenes of Infancy*:

" Bosom'd in woods where mighty rivers run,
Kelso's fair vale expands before the sun,
Its rising downs in vernal beauty swell,
And, fringed with hazel, winds each flowery dell,
Green spangled plains to dimpling lawns succeed,
And Tempe rises on the banks of Tweed,
Blue o'er the river Kelso's shadow lies,
And copse-clad isles amid the waters rise."

The most admired view is from the bridge, looking up the river.   In this view is comprehended the junction of the rivers—the ruins of Roxburgh Castle ; in front, the palace of Fleurs, with its lawns sloping to the margin of the Tweed, and sheltered by lofty trees behind.   On the south bank of the river are the woods and mansion of Springwood Park, with the elegant bridge of the Teviot. On the right is the town, extended along the bank of the river ; nearer is Ednam House, and immediately beyond are the lofty ruins of the abbey.   In the back ground are the hills of Stitchel and Mellerstain—the castle of Home— the picturesque summits of the Eildon Hills, Penielheugh, &c. An excellent view may also be obtained of the district around Kelso, from the top of an eminence, on the south bank of the river, called Pinnaclehill ; and a third, equally interesting, from the building appropriated as a Museum and Library, situated on an elevation termed the Terrace.*

About two miles north from Kelso, on the banks of the Eden, is the village of EDNAM, the birth-place of the poet Thomson, and near to which a monument has been

* From Kelso a road leads to Jedburgh, by the villages of Maxwellheugh and Heaton, the beautiful banks of the Kale, Grahamslaw, where there are some remarkable caves, the villages of Eckford and Crailing, Crailing House, (J. Paton, Esq.,) formerly the seat of the noble family of Cranstoun, and Bonjedward, (Archibald Jerdon, Esq.)

erected to his memory. A little to the west, is Newton-Don, the splendid seat of Sir William Don, Bart.; and two miles farther to the north is Stitchel, the fine mansion of Sir John Pringle, Bart. A short way beyond, on a considerable eminence, commanding a view of the whole Merse and a great deal of Roxburghshire, is Home Castle, once the residence of the ancient and powerful family of that name. After the battle of Pinkie, in 1547, it was taken by the English, under the Duke of Somerset, and again, during the time of the Commonwealth, it was besieged and taken by Oliver Cromwell. Three miles to the west is Mellerstain House, the seat of George Baillie, Esq., of Jerviswood, surrounded by extensive plantations.

Leaving Kelso, the road proceeds by Hendersyde Park, (John Waldie, Esq.) along the north banks of the Tweed. At the distance of two miles, is the village of Sprouston, on the south bank of the river. A mile beyond this the Eden joins the Tweed, and, half a mile farther, the tourist enters the Merse, or Berwickshire. The Tweed now forms the boundary between England and Scotland. On its south bank is Carham Church, with Carham Hall. A mile and a half farther, on the same side, are the ruins of Wark Castle, celebrated in Border history. A mile farther, on the left, is the Hirsel, the seat of the Earl of Home; the park contains some fine preserves. The road now crosses the water of Leet, and, nine miles from Kelso, enters the thriving town of

COLDSTREAM,

occupying a level and elevated situation on the north bank of the Tweed, which is here crossed by a handsome bridge. The population of the town is about 3000. In consequence of its proximity to England, Coldstream, like

Gretna Green, is celebrated for its irregular marriages. In the principal inn Lord Brougham was married. General Monk resided in Coldstream during the winter of 1659–60, before he marched into England to restore Charles II., and here he raised a horse regiment, which is still denominated the Coldstream Guards. On the bank of the Tweed, to the west of the town, is Lees, the beautiful seat of Sir William Marjoribanks, Bart. About a mile and a half to the east of the town are the ruins of the Church of Lennel, which was the name of the parish before Coldstream existed. Near it is Lennel House, (Earl of Haddington,) in which the venerable Patrick Brydone, author of "Travels in Sicily and Malta," spent the latter years of his long life.* Following the course of the river, we come to Tillmouth, where the Till, a narrow, sullen, deep, dark, and slow stream, flows into the Tweed.† On its banks stands Twisel Castle, (Sir Francis Blake, Bart.) Beneath the Castle, the ancient bridge is still standing by which the English crossed the Till, before the battle of Flodden.‡ The glen is roman-

---

* There are two roads from Coldstream to Berwick, one along the north bank and one along the south bank of the Tweed. The latter is the more interesting, and is generally preferred.

† The different characteristics of the two rivers are distinctly pointed out in the following rhyme:—

Tweed said to Till,
  "What gars ye rin sae still?"
Till said to Tweed,
  "Though ye rin wi' speed,

And I rin slaw,
Yet, where ye drown ae man
I drown twa!"

‡ ——————————— "they cross'd
  The Till, by Twisel Bridge.
High sight it is, and haughty, while
They dive into the deep defile;
Beneath the cavern'd cliff they fall,
Beneath the castle's airy wall.
  By rock, by oak, by hawthorn tree,
Troop after troop are disappearing;
Troop after troop their banners rearing,
  Upon the eastern bank you see,

Still pouring down the rocky den,
  Where flows the sullen Till,
And, rising from the dim wood glen
Standards on standards, men on men,
  In slow succession still,
And sweeping o'er the Gothic arch,
And pressing on, in ceaseless march,
  To gain the opposing hill."

                                      Marmion, c. vi.

tic and delightful, with steep banks on each side, covered
with copsewood. On the opposite bank of the Tweed is
Milne-Graden, (Admiral Sir David Milne, Bart.,) once
the seat of the Kerrs of Graden, and, at an earlier period,
the residence of the chief of a Border clan, known by
the name of Graden.* A little to the north-east is the
village of Swinton. The estate of Swinton is remarkable,
as having been, with only two very brief interruptions,
the property of one family since the days of the Anglo-
Saxon monarchy. The first of the Swintons acquired
the name and the estate, as a reward for the bravery
which he displayed in clearing the country of the wild
swine which then infested it. The family have produced
many distinguished warriors. At the battle of Beaugé,
in France, Thomas Duke of Clarence, brother to Henry
V., was unhorsed by Sir John Swinton of Swinton, who
distinguished him by a coronet of precious stones which
he wore around his helmet.† The brave conduct of
another of this warlike family, at the battle of Homildon,
Hill, in 1402, has been dramatised by Sir Walter Scott,
whose grandmother was the daughter of Sir John Swinton of Swinton. Three miles eastward is Ladykirk, nine
miles from Berwick. The church of this parish is an
ancient Gothic building, said to have been erected by
James IV., in consequence of a vow made to the Virgin,
when he found himself in great danger while crossing
the Tweed, by a ford, in the neighbourhood. By this
ford the English and Scottish armies made their mutual
invasions, before the bridge of Berwick was erected.

---

* Sir Walter Scott's *Border Antiquities*, p. 152.

† " And Swinton laid the lance in rest
  That tamed, of yore, the sparkling crest
  Of Clarence's Plantagenet."
  Lay of the Last Minstrel, c. v., s. 4.

The adjacent field, called Holywell Haugh, was the place where Edward I. met the Scottish nobility, to settle the dispute between Bruce and Baliol, relative to the crown of Scotland. On the opposite bank of the Tweed, stands the celebrated Castle of Norham. The description of this ancient fortress, in the poem of Marmion, is too well known to require to be quoted here. About four miles from Berwick, is Paxton House, the seat of Forman Home, Esq., which contains a fine collection of pictures. In the immediate neighbourhood, the Tweed is crossed by the Union Wire Suspension Bridge, constructed, in 1820, by Captain Samuel Brown. Its length is 437 feet; width, eighteen; height of piers above low water-mark, sixty-nine; and is one of the finest structures of that kind in this part of the island. Near Paxton, the Tweed is joined by the Whitadder, the principal river which flows through Berwickshire; on its banks, a few miles to the north-west, is Ninewells, the paternal seat of David Hume. Before entering Berwick, we pass Halidon Hill, the scene of a battle in 1333, between the English and the Scotch, in which the latter were defeated. The town of Berwick is more remarkable for its historical recollections than for its present importance. It is twenty-three miles distant from Kelso, and fifty-eight from Edinburgh, and is a respectable looking town, containing about 9000 or 10,000 inhabitants. It is still surrounded by its ancient walls, which only of late years ceased to be regularly fortified.

SECOND TOUR.

LEAVING Edinburgh by the great south road through the centre of Newington, the tourist passes on the right, Grange House, (Sir T. Dick Lauder, Bart.) Three miles from the city, the road passes the village and kirk of Libberton, and a mile farther, the village of Gilmerton. Six miles from Edinburgh, is the pretty village of LASSWADE, beautifully situated on the banks of the North Esk. On the right, above Lasswade, are Mavis Bank, (Mercer, Esq.,) Polton House, and Paper Mill, and the mansion of Hawthornden, and on the left MELVILLE CASTLE, (Lord Melville.) After crossing the Esk, the tourist passes on the left Eldin, (Clerk, Esq.,) formerly the residence of Mr. John Clerk, author of the well-known treatise on Naval Tactics, and father of the late Lord Eldin. Passing in succession NEWBATTLE ABBEY,* (Marquis of Lothian,) Dalhousie Castle,* (Earl of Dalhousie,) Cockpen Kirk, and Arniston, (Dundas, Esq.,) the tourist reaches Fushie Bridge Inn, eleven miles distant from Edinburgh. On the left are the oldest powder-mills in Scotland. Immediately after passing Fushie Bridge, a view is obtained of BORTHWICK CASTLE † and Borthwick Kirk, standing in the midst of a valley on the left. The father of Dr. Robertson, the historian, was minister of

---

* Described on page 99.
† For a description of this Castle, see page 100.

Borthwick, and a room in the manse is still shown as
the place where that distinguished writer was born.
Passing Middleton Inn, the road now crosses a bleak up-
land, called Heriot Muir, and a few miles farther on,
descends into the vale of Gala. Sixteen miles from Edinburgh is Heriot House, and on the right, at the distance
of a mile, Heriot Kirk. Three miles beyond, on the left,
is Crookston, (Borthwick, Esq.) A little farther on,
Pirntaiton, (Miss Innes,) on the right, Burn House,
(Thomson, Esq.,) Pirn, (Tait, Esq.,) and Torquhan, (Col-
vin, Esq.) on the left. On the right, the comfortable inn of Torsonce, and a short way beyond, the
ancient and irregular village of Stow, situated in the
middle of a district, which formerly bore the name of
We-dale, (the vale of Woe.) The whole of this territory
belonged at one time to the Bishop of St. Andrews,
and many of their charters are dated from We-dale.
Proceeding onwards, with the Gala on the right, the
tourist reaches Crosslee, on the confines of the county of
Roxburgh. The river now forms the boundary between
the counties of Roxburgh and Selkirk, and the alder,
birch, and hazel, are found in abundance on its banks.
The "braw lads of Gala water," are celebrated in Burns's
well known beautiful lyric of that name. A short way
farther on is TORWOODLEE, the fine mansion of Pringle
of Torwoodlee, situated in the midst of stately trees,
upon a fine terrace overhanging the Gala. A few hundred yards from the modern mansion are the ruins of
the old house, jutting out from the side of a hill. At a
little distance to the west of the ruin, lies the family
burying-ground, embowered in the midst of a dark grove.
The Pringles of Torwoodlee are a very old family, and
celebrated in Border story. Their representative, in the

reign of Charles II., was peculiarly obnoxious to government, on account of his exertions in the cause of the covenant, and his concern in Argyle's rebellion. Within a mile of his house, on different sides of the vale of Gala, were two old towers, called Buckholm and Blindlee, occupied by two of his inveterate enemies, who are said to have kept continual watch over his motions, in order to find occasion to accuse him to government. A short way beyond, at the distance of $30\frac{1}{2}$ miles from Edinburgh, the tourist reaches

GALASHIELS,

a thriving town, finely situated on the banks of the Gala, which joins the Tweed about a mile below. It contains about 2000 inhabitants, principally engaged in the production of woollen cloths, scarcely inferior in texture to the finest manufactured in England. The inhabitants are remarkable for their steady industry and ingenuity, combined with a strictness of morality very uncommon in manufacturing towns. The old village of Galashiels, of which hardly a vestige now remains, lay upon an eminence, a little way to the south of the present town, which was erected only about fifty or sixty years ago. Galashiels is a burgh of barony, under Scott of Gala, whose family came in place of the ancient Pringles of Gala, in the year 1623. In 1313, Mr. Richard Lees, manufacturer, assisted by a blacksmith, constructed a wire bridge over the Gala, being the first specimen of this American invention erected in the old world.

Leaving Galashiels, a fine view is obtained of the vale of the Tweed, and a passing glance of the towers of Abbotsford on the right, overtopping the surrounding trees. On the left is Langlee, (Bruce, Esq.) Farther

on is Allan Water, already described in page 124, and
soon after, the road crosses the Tweed, passes the village
of Darnick, and two miles beyond it, reaches

MELROSE,

with the magnificent ruins of its Abbey, for a full description of which the reader is referred to page 126.   Three
miles from Melrose is Newton-Dryburgh.   Half a mile
further, a beautiful view is obtained of Dryburgh Abbey
and the course of the Tweed.   A few miles farther on,
the road passes ANCRUM MOOR, where the Earl of Angus
routed the English, in 1545.   During the year 1544,
Lord Evers and Sir Brian Latoun committed the most
dreadful ravages upon the Scottish frontiers.   As a reward
for their services, the English monarch promised to the
two barons a feudal grant of the country which they had
thus reduced to a desert; upon hearing which, Archibald
Douglas, the seventh Earl of Angus, is said to have sworn
to write the deed of investiture upon their skins, with sharp
pens, and bloody ink, in resentment for their having defaced the tombs of his ancestors at Melrose.   In 1545,
Lord Evers and Latoun again entered Scotland, with an
army of upwards of 5000 men, and even exceeded their
former cruelty.   As they returned towards Jedburgh, they
were overtaken by Angus at the head of 1000 horse, who
was shortly after joined by the famous Norman Lesley
with a body of Fife-men.   While the Scottish general was
hesitating whether to advance or retire, Sir Walter Scott
of Buccleuch came up at full speed, with a small, but
chosen body of his retainers, and, by his advice, an immediate attack was made.   The battle was commenced
upon a piece of low flat ground, called Penielheugh,
and, just as it began, a heron, roused from the marshes

by the tumult, soared away betwixt the encountering
armies. " O !" exclaimed Angus, " that I had here my
white gosshawk, that we might all yoke at once !"   The
Scots obtained a complete victory, and Lord Evers and
his son, together with Sir Brian Latoun, and 800 Englishmen, many of whom were persons of rank, fell in the
engagement.   A mile beyond this, on the right, the road
passes Ancrum House, (Sir William Scott, Bart.,) and
on the opposite bank of the Ale, is the village of Ancrum.*   At the manse of Ancrum, Thomson the poet
spent much of his time with Mr. Cranstoun, the clergyman of the parish.   A short way beyond, at some distance on the left, is Mount Teviot, a seat of the Marquis
of Lothian, whose second title is Earl of Ancrum.   On the
right, two miles up the Teviot, is Chesters, (W. Ogilvie,
Esq.)   The tourist now crosses the Teviot by Ancrum
Bridge.   A short way beyond, on the right, is Tympan-
dean, and a mile farther on the left is Bonjedward, † (Jer-
dan, Esq.)   At the distance of another mile, the tourist
enters the royal burgh of

JEDBURGH, ‡

standing in a picturesque and romantic situation, on the
banks of the sylvan Jed, and surrounded by beautiful
gardens and woods.   Jedburgh is a royal burgh of very
ancient erection ; and appears from a statute of William
the Lion, to have been a place of note previous to the
year 1165.   It was one of the chief Border towns, and a
place of considerable importance before the Union.

---

* Ancrum is situated near a bend of the Ale ; and derives its name (Alncrum)
from that circumstance.

      † " Bcanjeddard, Hundlie, and Hunthill,
        Three, on they laid weel at the last."
                          Raid of Reidswire.

‡ Jedburgh is vulgarly called Jethart, a corruption of its former name Jed-
worth ; from Jed, and the Saxon " *weorth*," a hamlet.

After that period, it retrograded in prosperity for a
century and a half, but its trade has now greatly revived.   It is the county town of Roxburghshire, the
seat of the Circuit Court of Justiciary, and of a
presbytery, and contains about 5000 inhabitants.   The
remains of the ABBEY form the principal object of
curiosity in Jedburgh.   It was founded by David I.
either in 1118, or in 1147, and, after various dilapida-
tions in the course of the Border wars, was burnt by the
Earl of Hertford in 1545.   The monks were of the order
called Regular Canons, or Augustine Friars.   At the
Reformation, the lands of the Abbey were converted into
a temporal Lordship, with the title of Lord Jedburgh,
in favour of Sir Andrew Ker of Ferniehirst, and they are
now possessed by his descendant, the Marquis of Lothian.
It is a magnificent ruin, and is considered the most perfect and beautiful specimen of the Saxon and early Gothic
in Scotland.   The principal parts now remaining are, the
nave, nearly the whole of the choir, with the south aisle,
the centre tower, and the north transept, which is entire,
and has long been set apart as a burial-place for the
family of the Marquis of Lothian.   In the western gable
is a door of exceedingly beautiful workmanship.   The
west end is fitted up as a parish church, in a most barbarous and unseemly style.   It is to be hoped that this
huge mis-shapen mass will, ere long, be removed.   Some
public-spirited individuals have lately expended a considerable sum in repairing the decayed parts of the building, so as to prevent farther dilapidation.

The best view of the Abbey is obtained from the banks
of the river.   Near the Abbey formerly stood the cross,
and there also now stands the court-house.   The castle
of Jedburgh, situated on an eminence at the town head,
was a fortress of such strength, that when the Scottish

government determined to destroy it, it was meditated to impose a tax of two pennies on every hearth in Scotland, as the only means of accomplishing so arduous an undertaking. The site of this ancient fortress is now occupied by a new jail. Alexander III. was married at Jedburgh, on the 14th October 1285, to Jolande, daughter of the Count of Dreux, and here may yet be seen the old mansion in which Queen Mary lodged, after her visit to Bothwell, at Hermitage.

The inhabitants of Jedburgh, in ancient times, were a warlike race, and were celebrated for their dexterity in handling a particular sort of partisan; which, therefore, got the name of the "Jethart staff." Their timely aid is said to have turned the fortune of the day at the skirmish of Reidswire. Their proud war-cry was, "Jethart's here."* The ordinary proverb of "Jethart justice," where men were said to be hanged first, and tried afterwards, appears to have taken its rise from some instances of summary justice executed on the Border marauders. †

The environs of Jedburgh abound in rich woodland scenes, and the walk through the picturesque woods and groves which adorn the winding Jed, is especially delightful. A short distance from the town, the half ruinous castle of Ferniehirst, the ancient seat of the Kers, occupies a romantic situation on the right bank of the river. It was built by Sir Thomas Ker in 1490,

---

* Then raise the slogan with ane shout,
   "Fy, Tindaill to it! Jebrugh's here."
                    Raid of Reidswire.

† There is a similar English proverb concerning Lydford:
   "I oft have heard of Lydford law,
   Where in the morn men hang and draw,
   And sit in judgment after."
                    BROWN'S *Poems.*

and was taken by the English in 1523, and again, after the battle of Pinkie. About a mile northward from the castle grows a large oak tree, called, on account of its prodigious size, "the king of the wood," and at the foot of the bank stands another, equally large, called "the capon tree." Both trees are noticed in Gilpin's Forest Scenery.

From Jedburgh to Hawick there it a fine walk of about ten miles along the bank of the Teviot. The vale of the Rule intervenes, as also the chief hills of Teviotdale, the Dunian, and Ruberslaw. The whole course of the Teviot between these towns is studded on each side with cottages and mansions, the most distinguished of which is Minto House, the residence of the Earl of Minto. The grounds are ample and varied. In the immediate vicinity of the house are Minto crags, a romantic assemblage of cliffs which rise suddenly above the vale of Teviot. A small platform on a projecting crag, commanding a most beautiful prospect, is termed *Barnhill's Bed*. This Barnhill is said to have been a robber or outlaw. There are remains of a strong tower beneath the rocks where he is supposed to have dwelt, and from which he derived his name. On the summit of the crags are the fragments of another ancient tower in a picturesque situation.* Nearly oppo-

> * " On Minto crags the moon beams glint,
>   Where Barnhill hew'd his bed of flint,
>   Who flung his outlaw'd limbs to rest,
>   Where falcons hang their giddy nest,
>   'Mid cliffs from whence his eagle eye
>   For many a league his prey could spy,
>   Cliffs, doubling, on their echoes borne,
>   The terrors of the robber's horn;
>   Cliffs which for many a later year
>   The warbling Doric reed shall hear,
>   When some sad swain shall teach the grove,
>   Ambition is no cure for love." †
>   *Lay of the Last Minstrel.*

* Sir Gilbert Elliot, grandfather to the present Lord Minto, was the author of the beautiful pastoral song, beginning, " My sheep I neglected," &c.

site to Minto House lies the pleasant village of Denholm, the birthplace of Dr. John Leyden.

HAWICK

is a thriving town, situated upon a haugh at the junction of the Slitterick and Teviot. It is a burgh of regality, and is of considerable antiquity. Its inhabitants are principally engaged in manufactures, and are remarkable for their industry and intelligence. Hawick has made a considerable figure in Border history, and from its propinquity to the Border, has frequently suffered severely from the inroads of the English. The Slitterick is crossed by a bridge of peculiarly antique construction, and at the head of the town is a moat-hill, where the brave Sir Alexander Ramsay was acting in his capacity of Sheriff of Teviotdale, when he was seized by Sir William Douglas, the " dark knight of Liddisdale," and plunged into one of the dungeons of Hermitage Castle, where he perished of hunger. Hawick is noted among topers for its " gill." A *Hawick gill* is well known in Scotland to be half a mutchkin, equal to two gills.* On the right bank of the Teviot, about two miles above Hawick, stands the ancient tower of Goldielands, one of the most entire now extant upon the Border. The proprietors of this tower belonged to the clan of Scott. The last of them is said to have been hanged over his own gate, for march treason. About a mile farther up the river, on the opposite bank, stands the celebrated tower of Branxholm, the principal scene of the " Lay of the Last Minstrel," and during the

* " Weel she loo'ed a Hawick gill,
And leuch to see a tappit hen."
Andrew and his Cuttie Gun.

[A tappit hen is a frothing measure of claret.}

K

15th and 16th centuries the residence of the Buccleuch
family. Branxholm was famous of yore for the charms
of a *bonnie lass,* whose beauty has been celebrated by
Ramsay in a ballad beginning

> " As I came in by Teviot side,
>   And by the braes o' Branksome,
>   There first I saw my bloomin' bride,
>   Young, smiling, sweet and handsome." *

Nearly opposite Goldielands tower the Teviot is joined
by Borthwick water. In a narrow valley formed by this
stream, stands Harden Castle, an interesting specimen
of an ancient Border fortress. The carved stucco work
upon the ceiling of the old hall is well worth attention. The lobby is paved with marble ; and the man-
tle-piece of one of the rooms is surmounted with an
earl's coronet, and the letters, W. E. T. wreathed together, signifying " Walter Earl of Tarras," a title borne
in former times by the house of Harden. In front of
the house there is a dark precipitous dell covered on
both sides with beautiful trees ; in the recesses of which
the freebooting lairds of former times were said to have
kept their spoil. †

---

* The bonnie lass was daughter to a woman nicknamed Jean the Ranter, who
kept an ale-house at the hamlet, near Branxholm Castle. A young officer,
named Maitland, who happened to be quartered somewhere in the neighbourhood, saw, loved, and married her. So strange was such an alliance deemed
in those days, that it was imputed to the influence of witchcraft.

† " Where Bortho hoarse that loads the meads with sand,
    Rolls her red tide to Teviot's western strand,
    Through slaty hills whose sides are shagg'd with thorn,
    Where springs in scatter'd tufts the dark green corn,
    Towers wood-girt Harden, far above the vale,
    And clouds of ravens o'er the turrets sail ;
    A hardy race who never shrunk from war,
    The *Scott* to rival realms a mighty bar,

THIRD TOUR.

EDINBURGH—HADDINGTON—DUNBAR—BERWICK.

LEAVING Edinburgh by the Waterloo Bridge, and the south side of the Calton Hill, the tourist obtains a fine view of Salisbury Crags, Arthur's Seat, and St. Anthony's Chapel. Passing Jock's Lodge and Piershill Barracks, the road enters

PORTOBELLO,

a favourite summer residence of the citizens of Edinburgh. Tradition asserts that the first house in this village was built by a retired sailor, who had been with Admiral Vernon in his celebrated South American expedition of 1739, and therefore named it " Portobello," in commemoration of the capture of that town. A great number of elegant new streets have been built in the village, and hot and cold baths were erected in 1807.

Here fix'd his mountain home,—a wide domain,
And rich the soil had purple heath been grain;
But what the niggard ground of wealth denied
From fields more bless'd his fearless arm supplied."
LEYDEN's *Scenes of Infancy.*

" Wide lay his lands round Oakwood tower,
And wide round haunted Castle Ower;
High over Borthwick's mountain flood,
His wood-embosomed mansion stood,
In the dark glen so deep below,
The herds of plunder'd England low."
Lay of Last Minstrel, c. iii.

About two miles further, the road enters Fisherrow, and
on the opposite bank of the Esk, the town of

MUSSELBURGH,

connected with Fisherrow by three bridges, the oldest of
which is supposed to have been built by the Romans.
Musselburgh, including Fisherrow, is an ancient burgh
of regality,* and unites with Portobello, Leith, and Newhaven in returning a member to Parliament. The population of the town and parish is about 8691. The
lordship and regality of Musselburgh were granted by
James VI. to his chancellor, Lord Thirlstane, an ancestor
of the Earls of Lauderdale. From them it was purchased in 1709 by Anne, Duchess of Buccleuch and
Monmouth, and it still continues in the family of Buccleuch, along with the superiority of the burgh. The
great Randolph, Earl of Moray, the nephew of Bruce,
and regent of the kingdom, died of the stone, in Musselburgh, in 1332. On Musselburgh links, an extensive
plain between the town and the sea, the Edinburgh races,
formerly held at Leith, are run. On this plain, in 1638,
the Marquis of Hamilton, representing Charles I., met the
Covenanting party; and here Oliver Cromwell, in 1650,
quartered his infantry, while the cavalry were lodged in
the town. In a garden, at the east end of Musselburgh,
is a small cell, covered by a mound, the only remains
now existing of a religious establishment, called the
Chapel of Loretto. After the Reformation, the materials
of the ruined chapel were employed in building the pre-

* " Musselburgh was a burgh
When Edinburgh was nane,
And Musselburgh 'ill be a burgh
When Edinburgh 's gane."
                    Old Rhyme.

sent jail. For this sacrilegious act, it is said the inhabitants of Musselburgh were annually excommunicated at Rome till the end of the last century. At the east end of Musselburgh is Pinkie House, the seat of Sir John Hope, Bart., interesting for its many historical associations. It was originally a country mansion of the Abbot of Dunfermline, but was converted into its present shape at the beginning of the seventeenth century by Alexander Seton, Earl of Dunfermline. About half a mile southward of Pinkie House, on the east side of the Esk, is the spot where, in 1547, the battle of Pinkie was fought, in which the Scottish army was defeated by the English, commanded by the Duke of Somerset. Southward of Inveresk is Carbery Hill, where, in 1567, Queen Mary surrendered to the insurgent nobles.*

Leaving Musselburgh, the road passes Drummore, (W. Aitchison, Esq.) on the left; and St. Clements Wells Distillery, and Wallyford, (— Aitchison, Esq.) on the right. A short way beyond, on the left, is Preston Grange, (Sir George Suttie, Bart.) and Dolphinton village, with its castle, in ruins.

A little farther on upon the left is Preston Tower, formerly the residence of the Hamiltons of Preston. On

---

* In the year 1728, a woman named Maggy Dickson, resident in Inveresk, was tried and condemned for child murder, and duly (as was thought) executed in the Grassmarket of Edinburgh. When the dreadful ceremony was over, poor Maggy's friends put her body into a chest, and drove it away, in a cart, to Musselburgh. When about two miles from town, the cart was stopped at a place called Peffermill, and the relations adjourned to a tavern for refreshment. On coming out of the house, what was their astonishment to see Maggy sitting up in the chest, having been restored to life by the motion of the cart. They took her home to Musselburgh, and she was soon entirely recovered. Sir Walter Scott, in the "Heart of Mid-Lothian," makes Madge Wildfire speak of "half-hangit Maggie Dickson, that cried saut mony a day after she had been hangit; her voice was roupit and hoarse, and her neck was a wee agee, or ye wad hae ken'd nae odds on her frae ony ither saut-wife."—*Waverley Novels*, vol. xiii. p. 26.

the coast is the large village of Prestonpans. In this
neighbourhood, 21st September 1745, was fought the
memorable battle between the royal forces under Sir
John Cope and the Highland army under Prince Charles
Stuart. Near Tranent is Bankton House, (— M'Dowal,
Esq.,) which belonged to Colonel Gardiner, who fell
nobly fighting for his country close beside the wall of the
park attached to his own residence. Tranent is a very
ancient village, chiefly inhabited by colliers. It is mentioned in a charter of the 12th century under the name
of Travernent. A short way farther on to the left is
Seton House, which stands on the site of the once princely
palace of Seton, for many centuries the seat of the Setons
Earls of Winton.* The last Earl was attainted on ac-

* The Setons were one of the most distinguished Scottish families, whether
in respect of wealth, antiquity of descent, or splendour of alliance. They took
their original name from their habitation, Seaton, " the dwelling by the sea,"
where, it is said, their founder was settled by King David I. About the middle
of the fourteenth century, the estate descended to Margaret Seton, who married
Allan de Wyntoun, a neighbouring baron. This match was so displeasing to
her own relations, that it occasioned a deadly feud, in consequence of which,
we are assured by Fordun, no fewer than a hundred ploughs were put off work.
George Lord Seton, who lived in the time of Queen Mary, was one of her most
attached friends, and it was to his castle of Niddry that she repaired, after her
escape from Lochleven. He was grand-master of the household, in which capacity he had a picture painted of himself, with his official baton, and the following motto :—

            In adversitate patiens ;
            In prosperitate benevolus.
            Hazard, yet forward.

He declined to be promoted to an earldom, which Queen Mary offered him.
On his refusing this honour, Mary wrote, or caused to be written, the following
lines :—

            Sunt comites, ducesque, alii sunt denique reges ;
            Sethoni dominum sit satis esse mihi.

Which may be thus rendered—

            Earl, duke, or king, be thou that list to be ;
            Seton, thy lordship is enough for me.

After the battle of Langside, Lord Seton was obliged to retire abroad for safety;
and was an exile for two years, during which he was reduced to the necessity
of driving a waggon in Flanders for his subsistence. His picture in this occu-

count of his concern in the rebellion of 1715. After his attainder the furniture of the palace was sold by the Commissioners of Enquiry, and, about forty years since, the building itself was removed, and the present mansion erected on its site. At a little distance from the house stands the Collegiate Church of Seton, which is now all that remains to attest the splendour of the family. It is a handsome little Gothic edifice, still nearly entire. There are also visible some monuments of the ancient lords of Seton fast mouldering into decay. Near Seton is Long Niddry, (Lady John Campbell,) the laird of which was a zealous reformer, and had John Knox for the tutor of his children. The ruins of the family chapel, in which Knox preached, are still pointed out. Northward, near the coast, is Gosford House, a mansion of the Earl of Wemyss. About three miles from Tranent the road passes Gladsmuir, noted as the birth-place of George Heriot, founder of the Hospital at Edinburgh. Dr. Robertson was clergyman of this parish, and here he composed his History of Scotland. As the tourist leaves this hamlet, he sees a column in the distance rising conspicuously from the top of the highest of the Garleton Hills. It is a monument raised by his grateful tenantry to comme-

pation, and the garb belonging to it, was painted at the lower end of the gallery in the ancient palace of Seton. In the time of James VI. the Seton family attained the dignity of Earl of Winton, and continued to flourish until the time of George, the fifth and last who enjoyed that dignity, and the large fortune which was annexed to it. In 1715, this unfortunate nobleman entered into the rebellion, and joined the Viscount of Kenmore with a fine troop of horse. He behaved with spirit and gallantry in the affair of the barricades at Preston; and afterwards, when waiting his fate in the Tower, made his escape by sawing through, with great ingenuity, the bars of the windows. He ended his motely life at Rome, in 1749, and with him closed the long and illustrious line of Seton, whose male descendants have, by intermarriage, come to represent the great houses of Gordon, Aboyne, and Eglinton. Their estate was forfeited, and has since passed through several hands.—*Provincial Antiquities*, by SIR WALTER SCOTT, p. 97. See also *Abbot*, vol. i., p. 277.

The Earl of Eglinton was lately served heir to the title of Earl of Winton.

morate the virtues of the late Earl of Hopetoun. A
similar tribute of regret and affection, to the late Robert
Ferguson, Esq. of Raith, will soon stand near it.   Passing on the right Woodside, (— Veitch, Esq.,) and successively on the left, Elvington (— Ainslie, Esq.,) Hun-
tington, (— Ainslie,. Esq.,) and Alderston, (J, Aitchison, Esq.); and on the right, Letham, (Sir J. B. Hepburn, Bart.,) and Clerkington, (General Sir William
Houston, Bart.,) the tourist reaches

HADDINGTON,

the county town of East Lothian, distant seventeen miles
from Edinburgh. It occupies an agreeable situation on the
north bank of the Tyne, the burgh and parish containing
about 6000 inhabitants. The precise period at which Haddington became a royal burgh is unknown, its ancient records being lost, but it is known to be of very great antiquity, and is supposed to have received its name from Ada
Countess of Northumberland, who founded a nunnery here
in 1178.   It has been several times burnt by the English
or by accident, and has twice suffered greatly from an
inundation of the Tyne.   On the south side of the town
is the Franciscan Church, a noble old Gothic building,
partly in ruins.   Fordun says, that on account of its
splendour it was called the " Lamp of Lothian."   The
great tower and choir are roofless, and fast falling into
decay, but the chancel is still in repair as a parish-church.
It is alleged that the celebrated John Knox was born in
a house about a hundred feet to the east of the church.
Haddington is chiefly remarkable in the present day for
its grain market, which is accounted the most extensive
in Scotland.   About a mile to the south of Haddington
is Lennoxlove or Lethington, a seat of Lord Blantyre.
It consists of a massive old tower erected by the Giffords,

with a modern addition, and is surrounded by a grove of
lofty aged trees. Lethington came into the possession of
the Lauderdale family by purchase about the middle of
the fourteenth century, and was for some time the chief
residence of that family. It was there that the celebrated
Secretary Lethington lived, and one of its alleys, which
he frequented, is still called the Politician's Walk.* Within sight of Lethington stands the mansion-house of Coalstoun, a seat of the Earl of Dalhousie, whose mother was
the heiress of the ancient family of Broun of Coalstoun. †

To the north of Haddington lies the little village of
Athelstaneford, which, in the early part of the last century, had for its ministers successively two poets,—Robert
Blair, author of " The Grave," and John Home, the
author of " Douglas."

Resuming from Haddington the eastward course of
the London Road, and passing on the right Amisfield,
(Earl of Wemyss,) and Stevenston House, (Sir J. G.
Sinclair, Bart.,) the tourist perceives the ruins of Hailes
Castle, (Sir C. Ferguson, Bart.,) overhanging the south

---

* Lethington contains several fine portraits, particularly a full-length, by
Lely, of Frances Theresa Stuart, Duchess of Lennox, the most admired beauty
of the court of Charles II. She was a daughter of Walter Stuart, M.D., a son
of the first Lord Blantyre; and Lethington got the additional name of Lennoxlove, from being a compliment to her from her husband. It is reported by
Grammont, that the King caused this lady to be represented as the emblema-
tical figure *Britannia* on the coin of the realm.

† One of the Brouns of Coalstoun, about 300 years ago, married a daughter
of John, third Lord Yester, with whom he obtained in dowry a pear, with the
assurance that, as long as the pear was preserved, the family would be attended
with unfailing prosperity. This celebrated pear is still preserved in a silver
box. At no great distance, in the neighbourhood of Gifford, is Yester House,
the elegant seat of the Marquis of Tweeddale, the descendant of the wizard
Lord who enchanted the Coalstoun pear. The ancient Castle of Yester stood
nearer the Lammermuir Hills, and the remains of it are still to be seen on a
peninsula, formed by two streams. It contained a capacious cavern, called in
the country Bo' Hall, i. e. Hobgoblin Hall, supposed to have been formed by
magical art. The reader will not need to be reminded of the use made of the
Goblin Hall and the wizard Lord in the poem of " Marmion," Canto iii.

bank of the Tyne. It formerly belonged to the Hepburns, and was the chief residence of Queen Mary during her union with Bothwell. South of the castle rises Trapraine Law, a rocky hill anciently called Dunpender Law. The road now passes over the steep ascent of Pincraig, from which the tourist sees on his right Whittinghame, (Jas. Balfour, Esq.) ; on his left, Newbyth, (Sir D. Baird, Bart.,) and, in the distance, on the same side, North Berwick Law, North Berwick House, (Sir H. Dalrymple, Bart.,) the Bass, and Tantallon.* At

* About seven miles north-west of Dunbar, and two and a half eastward from North Berwick, are the ruins of the famous Castle of Tantallon. From the land side they are scarcely visible, till the visitor, surmounting a height which conceals them, finds himself close under the external walls. The description of this castle given in the poem of Marmion, renders any account of our own unnecessary.

———————— " Tantallon vast,
Broad, massive, high, and stretching far,
And held impregnable in war.
On a projecting rock it rose,
And round three sides the ocean flows,
The fourth did battled walls enclose,
            And double mound and fosse ;
By narrow drawbridge, outworks strong,
Through studded gates, an entrance long,
            To the main court they cross.
It was a wide and stately square,
Around were lodgings fit and fair,
            And towers of various form,
Which on the court projected far,
And broke its lines quadrangular ;
Here was square keep, there turret high,
Or pinnacle that sought the sky,
Whence oft the warder could descry
            The gathering ocean storm."
                                        c. v., st. 33.

Tantallon was a principal stronghold of the Douglas family, and when the Earl of Angus was banished in 1526, it continued to hold out against James V. The king went in person against it, and, for its reduction, borrowed from the Castle of Dunbar, then belonging to the Duke of Albany, two great cannons, whose names, Pitscottie informs us, were " Thrawn-mouth'd Mow and her Marrow ;" also " two great bocards, and two moyan, two double falcons, and four quarter-falcons," for the safe guiding and re-delivery of which three lords were laid in pawn at Dunbar. Yet, notwithstanding all this apparatus, James was forced to raise the siege, and only afterwards obtained possession of Tanthe bottom of Pincraig, the road skirts the populous village of Linton, and crosses the Tyne there by an old, narrow, and very ugly bridge. The kirk of Preston, and its village, and Smeaton House, (Sir T. B. Hepburn, Bart.) are now seen at a little distance on the left bank of the Tyne. About half a mile from Linton the road runs close past Phantassie, (—— Mitchell Innes, Esq.,) so noted in the annals of agriculture as the residence of the late Mr. Rennie. The celebrated engineer of the same name was born and educated in this neighbourhood. Tyningham House, too, the noble mansion of the Earl of Haddington, with its aged woods and spacious park,* here pre-

tallon by treaty with the governor, Simon Panango. Tantallon was at length "dung down" by the Covenanters; its lord, the Marquis of Douglas, being a favourer of the royal cause. About the beginning of the eighteenth century, the Marquis, afterwards Duke of Douglas, sold the estate of North Berwick, with the Castle of Tantallon, to Sir Hew Dalrymple, President of the Court of Session, and they now remain in the possession of his descendant, Sir Hew H. Dalrymple, Bart., of Bargeny and North Berwick.

Two miles north from Tantallon lies the Bass Island, or rather Rock, rising 400 feet sheer out of the sea. The Bass is about a mile in circumference, and is conical on the one side, presenting, on the other, an abrupt and overhanging precipice. It is remarkable for its immense quantities of sea-fowl, chiefly solan geese. Upon the top of the rock gushes out a spring of clear water, and there is verdure enough to support a few sheep. The Bass was long the stronghold of a family of the name of Lauder, one of whom distinguished himself as a compatriot of Wallace. The castle, situated on the south side of the island, is now ruinous. In 1671, it was sold by the Lauder family, for £4000, to Charles II., by whom it was converted into a royal fortress and state prison. Many of the most eminent of the Covenanters were confined here. At the Revolution, it was the last stronghold in Great Britain that held out for James VII. But, after a resistance of several months, the garrison were at last compelled to surrender, by the failure of their supplies of provisions. The Bass is now the property of Sir Hew Hamilton Dalrymple, Bart. This remarkable rock is visited in summer by numerous pleasure parties. In order to perform the visit, it is necessary to apply for a boat either at North Berwick, or at Canty Bay, near Tantallon.

* In the Tyningham grounds is a most magnificent series of holly hedges. "One of these hedges," says Mr. Miller, in his "Popular Philosophy," "is no less than twenty-five feet high and eighteen broad; and the length of what is denominated the Holly Walks, lying chiefly between two hedges of fifteen feet high and eleven broad, is no less than thirty-five chains eighty links, English measure."

sents itself as by far the finest object in that rich and
lovely country which the tourist has ever witnessed, and
which stretches for many miles before him.   To the
south of the London Road, but not seen from it, is Biel,
(Mrs. Ferguson,) with its extensive plantations and charming walks.   A beautiful sheet of water called Presmennan Lake, and just below the mansion-house, formerly
the residence of Lord Presmennan, has recently been formed in the grounds, by throwing an artificial mound across
a small rivulet which runs down from the Lammermuir
Hills.   The privilege of perambulating the grounds has
been granted by the kindness of the proprietrix, who
also allows the use of a boat upon the lake to the numerous summer parties who visit it.   Beyond, on the
right, is Belton Place, (Captain Hay, R.N.,) and on the
left, Nineware House, (James Hamilton, Esq.)   A short
way farther on is the village of Beltonford, a mile farther
West Barns, and half a mile beyond it the beautifully
situated village of Belhaven, from which Lord Belhaven
takes his title.   Near the village is excellent sea-bathing.
It is much frequented during summer by visitors from a
distance, and a sulphurous Spa lately discovered in its
neighbourhood is not the smallest of its attractions.   The
road now passes on the left Winterfield, (Colonel Anderson,) Belhaven Church, and an old tower called Knock-
enhair, used, during last war, as a signal station.   On
the right the tourist sees at a little distance Lochend
House, (Sir George Warrender, Bart.)   Still farther off,
on the same side, are seen Bower House, (General Car-
frae,) and Spott, (Jas. Sprott, Esq.,) their plantations
imparting a sylvan variety to a rich corn-field country.
Shortly after the tourist enters

DUNBAR,

a royal burgh and thriving sea-port, twenty-eight miles
distant from Edinburgh, and eleven from Haddington.
The name is supposed to be derived from two Celtic
words, signifying the Castle on the extremity. Its population is about 3000. It was created a royal burgh by
David II., ostensibly to prevent English merchants from
bringing into and carrying out of the kingdom wool, hides,
and other commodities, without the payment of custom.
The only public building worthy of notice is the church,
erected in 1819, on the site of the old collegiate church,
the first of the kind founded in Scotland. It contains a
most splendid marble monument to Sir George Home,
created Earl of Dunbar and March by James VI. There
is, at the entrance to the town from the west, the remains of a monastery of the Grey Friars. Dunbar could
also boast of a convent of the White Friars; but the
record says they were *banished to Peebles* for their *im-
morality.* The coast in the neighbourhood of Dunbar
is remarkably perilous, and the entrance to the harbour
is rocky and difficult. Oliver Cromwell contributed three
hundred pounds towards the erection of the eastern pier;
another pier on the west has been lately built, and a dry
dock has also been constructed. Arrangements are at
present in considerable progress, by which a large addition is to be made to the harbour, at the joint expense
of the town and the Fishery Board. The estimated cost
is £11,000. By this addition it is believed that Dunbar
harbour will be made the safest and the easiest of access
on this line of coast. A grain market is held every Monday, and a cattle market the first Monday of every month.
Dunbar House, the residence of the Earl of Lauderdale,
stands at the north end of the principal street. About

two hundred yards north from Dunbar House stands the
celebrated Castle of Dunbar. Its antiquity is unknown,
but so early as 1070 it was given, with the adjacent manor,
by Malcolm Canmore, to Patrick Earl of Northumberland, a princely noble, who fled from England at the
Conquest, and became the progenitor of the family of
Cospatricks, Earls of Dunbar and March.   This once
formidable fortress has passed through many varieties
of fortune, but the most memorable incident in its history was the gallant and successful defence made by
Black Agnes, Countess of March, against an English
army under the Earl of Salisbury.   When the battering
engines of the besiegers flung massive stones on the
battlements. she caused her maidens, as if in scorn,
to wipe away the dust with their handkerchiefs ; and
when the earl of Salisbury commanded a huge military engine, called a sow, to be advanced to the foot of
the walls, she, in a scoffing rhyme, advised him to
take good care of his sow, for she would make her far-
row her pigs. She then ordered an enormous rock to
be discharged on the engine, which crushed it to pieces.*
On another occasion, an arrow shot by an archer of her

* A similar story is told of Judge Banks's lady, while holding out Corffe
Castle against the Parliament forces. The incident is thus alluded to by Mr.
W. Stewart Rose, in his poem addressed to Corffe Castle :—

            " 'Twas when you rear'd, 'mid sap and siege,
          The banner of your rightful liege,
               At your she-captain's call;
        Who, miracle of womankind·!
        Lent mettle to the meanest hind
               That mann'd her castle wall.
      What time the banded zealots swore,
      Long foil'd thy banner'd towers, before
              Their fearful entrance made,
    To rase thy walls with plough and harrow,
    Yet oft the wild sow cast her farrow,
            And well the boar was bay'd."

train struck to the heart an English knight, in spite of his complete suit of armour,—" There goes one of my lady's tiring-pins," said the Earl of Salisbury,—" the Countess' love-shafts pierce to the heart." After a successful defence, which lasted six weeks, the siege was abandoned by the English troops. George, tenth Earl of Dunbar and March, on a quarrel with Alexander, Duke of Albany, brother of James III., retreated into England. His large estate was thereupon forfeited, and, with Dunbar Castle, passed into the hands of the Duke of Albany, to whom, on his memorable escape from Edinburgh Castle, it afforded shelter till he departed for France. In the year 1567, Queen Mary conferred the keeping of this important stronghold on the infamous Bothwell; and here she twice found shelter,—once, after the murder of Rizzio; and a second time, when she made her escape from Borthwick Castle, in the disguise of a page. After her surrender at Carberry Hill, Dunbar Castle was taken, and completely destroyed by the Regent Murray. It is now the property of the Earl of Lauderdale, who is also superior, in right of the Earl of March.

Near the town of Dunbar were fought two battles, in both of which the Scots were defeated,—one in 1296, when Baliol was defeated by the forces of Edward I., the other in 1650, when the Scottish army, under General Leslie, was routed with great slaughter, at Doonhill, by Cromwell. This battle is still remembered by the people of Scotland under the opprobrious epithet of " the race of Dunbar," or " the Tyesday's chase;" the engagement having taken place on a Tuesday. An eminence, lying about two miles south from the town, gives its name to the latter battle, and the former was in the same direction, but a little nearer.

Perhaps no part of the British coast affords a richer
treat to the geologist, than that lying between Belhaven
and St. Abb's Head.   Over the whole of it, Hutton and
Playfair, and Sir James Hill, have very frequently wandered; and, from its appearances, some of their favourite
theories have their clearest illustrations.   The Emperor
of Russia, when he visited Dunbar as Prince Nicholas,
was so charmed with a singularly beautiful formation of
basalt that presents itself at the entrance of the harbour,
as to direct that specimens of it should be conveyed to
Russia.

Leaving Dunbar, the tourist passes, on the left, Brox-
mouth Park, formerly the head-quarters of Cromwell at
the battle of Doonhill, but now the site of a large mansion belonging to the Duke of Roxburghe.   The stream of
Broxburn here crosses the road.   A mile and a half farther, on the right, are Barnyhill, (Sandilands, Esq.,) and
the village of East Barns.   A mile to the south is Thurs-
ton, (Hunter, Esq.)   A short way beyond, on the right,
are the ruins of Innerwick Castle, situated on the edge
of a precipitous glen; and, on the opposite side of the
glen, stands Thornton Tower: the former the fortalice
of a Hamilton, and the latter of a Hume.   Innerwick was
burnt by the English, and Thornton blown up with gunpowder, during Somerset's expedition.   Dunglas House,
the splendid mansion of Sir John Hall, embosomed amid
beautiful plantations, is well deserving the tourist's notice;* and he should alight from his carriage, and look

* Dunglas House stands on the site of the old castle, which was originally a
fortress of the Earls of Home, and still gives their second title to that family.
After the attainder of the Earl of Home, in 1516, it passed into the hands of the
Douglasses.   It was destroyed by Somerset, in 1548, but was again rebuilt and
enlarged.   It was finally destroyed in 1640, on which occasion the Earl of Had-

into that lovely glen, where the road, crossing the Dean
Burn, enters Berwickshire. A mile farther on, is the village of Cockburnspath, (a corruption of Colbrandspath.)
A mile beyond the village, and on the left, close to the
road, is the ancient tower of Cockburnspath, now the
property of Sir J. Hall of Dunglass. The tract of
country through which the road now passes is high and
flat, but broken at little distances by numerous deep and
narrow ravines, each of which has a small stream at the
bottom running towards the sea. The most remarkable
of these ravines is the Peaths, over which the celebrated
Peaths or Pease bridge was thrown in 1786, when it was
the post road. This singular structure is 123 feet in height,
300 feet in length, and sixteen feet wide. The post road
now crosses the glen, about a quarter of a mile above
the bridge. In former times, the Peaths was a most
important pass, and Oliver Cromwell describes it in his
dispatch to the Parliament, after the battle of Dunbar, as
a place " where one man to hinder, is better than twelve
to make way." The road now passes in succession,
Grant's Inn, where the Dunse road diverges to the right,
and about three miles farther, Houndwood Inn, Houndwood Church, and Houndwood House, (Mrs. Coulson.)
Two miles farther, the tourist passes, on the right, the
village of Reston, and a road turns off on the left to
the beautiful village of Coldingham, distant about three
miles.* Proceeding along the banks of the Eye, the

dington, and a number of other persons of distinction, were killed by the ex-
plosion of the powder magazine. The old parish church stands near Dunglass
House. Great good taste is displayed in the manner the ruin is preserved as the
family mausoleum.

* Coldingham is situated upon a small eminence, in the centre of a fine valley,
at a short distance from the sea. It is remarkable for the ruins of its priory,
so celebrated in Border history. The monastery was established by St. Abb, in
the seventh century, and is said to have been the first in Scotland. The build-

tourist reaches the village of Ayton, pleasantly situated on
its northern bank. Ayton House, (——Mitchell Innes, Esq.)

ings were once of great magnificence and extent, but, of late years, they have
been greatly dilapidated, by the rapacious license of the people in taking away
stones, for the purpose of building their own houses, so that only a few detached
fragments now remain. About fifty years ago, in taking down a tower at the
south-west corner, the skeleton of a nun was found standing upright in a hollow
of the wall, no doubt a victim to a breach of her vows.

North-east of Coldingham about two miles, is the celebrated promontory called
St. Abb's head. It consists of two tall hills, the western of which is occupied
by an observatory; the eastern, called the Kirkhill, still exhibits the remains
of a monastery and a church. The savage and dreary character of the scenery
is exceedingly striking. The neighbouring promontory of Fast Castle derives
its name from an ancient baronial fortress, built upon the very point of the precipitous headland. Fast Castle is the Wolf's Crag of the " Bride of Lammermuir," and is thus described in that tragic tale :—" The roar of the sea had long
announced their approach to the cliffs, on the summit of which, like the nest
of some sea-eagle, the founder of the fortalice had perched his eyry. The pale
moon, which had hitherto been contending with flitting clouds, now shone out,
and gave them a view of the solitary and naked tower, situated on a projecting
cliff, that beetled on the German Ocean. On three sides, the rock was precipitous; on the fourth, which was that towards the land, it had been originally
fenced by an artificial ditch and drawbridge, but the latter was broken down
and ruinous, and the former had been in part filled up, so as to allow passage
for a horseman into the narrow court-yard, encircled on two sides with low
offices and stables, partly ruinous, and closed on the landward front by a low
embattled wall, while the remaining side of the quadrangle was occupied by
the tower itself, which, tall and narrow, and built of a greyish stone, stood
glimmering in the moonlight, like the sheeted spectre of some huge giant. A
wilder, or more disconsolate dwelling, it was perhaps difficult to conceive. The
sombrous and heavy sound of the billows, successively dashing against the rocky
beach, at a profound distance beneath, was, to the ear, what the landscape was
to the eye,—a symbol of unvaried and monotonous melancholy, not unmingled
with horror." That castle was, in former days, a place of retreat of the great
Earls of Home. Notwithstanding its strength, it was repeatedly taken and re-
captured during the Border wars. About the close of the sixteenth century, it
became the stronghold of the celebrated Logan of Restalrig, so famous for his
share in the Gowrie Conspiracy; and it was to this place that the conspirators
intended to convey the king, after getting possession of his person. There is a
contract existing in the charter-chest of Lord Napier, between this Logan and
the celebrated Napier of Merchiston, setting forth that, as Fast Castle was supposed to contain a quantity of hidden treasure, Napier was to make search for
the same by divination, and, for his reward, was to have the third of what was
found, and to have his expenses paid in whatever event. Fast Castle now belongs to Sir J. Hall of Dunglass. The precipitous rocks on this coast are inhabited by an immense number of sea-fowl, and a number of young men in the
neighbourhood occasionally scale these dreadful and dizzy heights, in order to
steal the eggs of the birds. Strange to say, an accident does not occur among
them, perhaps, once in a century.

stands to the east of the village. The banks of the
Eye afford some fine scenery. At its confluence with
the sea, stands the sea-port and fishing town of Eyemouth. This town was formerly notorious for the
smuggling carried on by its inhabitants, but of late years
the contraband trade has been entirely destroyed.* About
two miles from Ayton, at the bottom of a deep ravine,
on the left of the road, is the romantic little fishing village
of Burnmouth, the well-situated, and formerly well-frequented haunt of the smuggler. Ten miles farther, the
tourist passes the ruins of Lamerton Kirk, where, in
1503, Margaret, daughter of Henry VII., was married
by proxy to James IV.,—a marriage which ultimately
led to the union of the crowns. Lamerton is now the
property of Colonel Renton. At Lamerton toll-bar, run-
away lovers from England are frequently united in the
bands of matrimony. At a distance of three miles, the
road enters the town of

BERWICK,

situated upon a gentle declivity close by the German
ocean, on the north side of the mouth of the river Tweed.
It is a well-built town, with spacious streets, and is surrounded by walls in a regular style of fortification. The
population amounts to about 10,000. It is governed by
a mayor, recorder, and justices, and sends two members
to Parliament. The trade of the port is considerable.

* " I stood upon Eyemouth fort,
  And guess ye what I saw ?
Fairnieside and Flemington,
  Newhouses and Cocklaw,
The fairy fouk o' Fosterland,
  The witches o' Edincraw,
The rye rigs o' Reston,
  And Dunse dings a'."
                    Old Rhyme.

Berwick occupies a prominent place in the history of the Border wars, and has been often taken and retaken both by the Scots and English. It was finally ceded to the English in 1482, and, since then, has remained subject to the laws of England, though forming, politically, a distinct territory. Its castle, so celebrated in the early history of these kingdoms, is now a shapeless ruin.

FOURTH TOUR.

EDINBURGH—LINLITHGOW—FALKIRK—STIRLING.

LEAVING Edinburgh by Princes Street, the tourist passes along the side of Corstorphine Hill, richly wooded and studded with villas, and, four miles from Edinburgh, reaches the village of Corstorphine. At the seventh milestone the road crosses Almond water, and enters Linlithgowshire. A short way farther on is the village of Kirkliston. Near the village is Newliston, (Hog, Esq.) formerly the seat of the great Earl of Stair, who is said to have caused the woods around the house to be planted so as to resemble the position of the troops at the battle of Dettingen, where he commanded under George II.*

* During the rebellion of 1745, the route of the Highland army having brought them near Newliston, an alarm arose in the Councils of Prince Charles, lest the MacDonalds of Glencoe should seize the opportunity of marking their recollection of the massacre of Glencoe, by burning or plundering the house of the descendant of their persecutor; and it was agreed that a guard should be posted, to protect the house of Lord Stair. MacDonald of Glencoe heard the resolution, and deemed his honour and that of his clan concerned. He demanded an audience of Charles Edward, and, admitting the propriety of placing a guard on a house so obnoxious to the feelings of the Highland army, and to those of his own clan in particular, he demanded, as a matter of right rather than of favour, that the protecting guard should be supplied by the MacDonalds of Glencoe. The request of the high-spirited chieftain was granted, and the MacDonalds guarded from the slightest injury the house of the cruel and crafty statesman who had devised and directed the massacre of their ancestor."—*Tales of a Grandfather*, vol. iv., p. 23.

It was in the family of the first Lord Stair, that the tragic incident occurred which forms the groundwork of Sir Walter Scott's tale of the ".Bride of Lammermuir."

A short distance beyond, to the left, are the ruins of Niddry Castle, where Queen Mary passed the first night after her escape from Lochleven. It was at that time the property of the Earl of Seton,—it now belongs to the Earl of Hopetoun. The road now passes through the village of Winchburgh, where Edward II. first halted in his flight from the battle of Bannockburn. About the sixteenth mile-stone, the road crosses the Union Canal, under an aqueduct bridge, and a short way farther on enters

LINLITHGOW,*

an ancient royal burgh, and the county town of Linlithgowshire, situated in a hollow, along the borders of a beautiful lake. So early as the beginning of the twelfth century, Linlithgow was one of the principal burghs in the kingdom. It contains a considerable number of old fashioned houses, many of which belonged of old to the knights of St. John, who had their preceptory at Torphichen, in this county.

The most interesting object in Linlithgow is the Palace, a massive quadrangular edifice, situated upon an eminence which advances a little way into the lake. It occupies about an acre of ground, and, though in ruins, is still a picturesque and beautiful object. † The inter-

---

* Popularly denominated " the faithful town of Linlithgow."

† " Of all the palaces so fair
   Built for the royal dwelling
In Scotland, far beyond compare
   Linlithgow is excelling.
And in its park, in genial June,
How sweet the merry linnet's tune,
   How blythe the blackbird's lay !
The wild buck *bells* from thorny brake,
The coot dives merry on the lake,—
The saddest heart might pleasure take
   To see a scene so gay."
                    Marmion, c. iv., st. 15.

nal architecture is extremely elegant, but the exterior
has a heavy appearance from the want of windows.
Over the interior of the grand gate is a niche which was
formerly filled by a statue of Pope Julius II., who presented James V. with the sword of state, which still
forms part of the regalia. It was destroyed during the
last century by a blacksmith, who had heard popery
inveighed against in the neighbouring church. Above
this entrance was the Parliament Hall,—once a splendid
apartment, with a beautifully ornamented chimney at one
end, and underneath it has been a magnificent piazza.
This part of the palace is understood to have been begun
by James IV., and finished and ornamented by his successor. The west side of the palace is the most ancient,
and it contains the room where the unfortunate Queen
Mary was born.*

In one of the vaults below, James III. found shelter
when he was in danger of assassination from some of his
rebellious subjects. The north side of the quadrangle is
the most modern, having been built by James VI. shortly
after his visit to Scotland in 1617. In the centre of the
court are the elaborately carved ruins of the Palace Well,
a once beautiful and ingenious work, erected by James V.
It was destroyed by the royal army in 1746.

The nucleus of the Palace seems to have been a tower
or fort, first built by Edward I., who inhabited it in person a whole winter. It was taken and demolished by
Bruce in 1307.† It appears, however, to have been

---

* Her father, who then lay on his deathbed at Falkland, on being told of her
birth, replied, "Is it so?" reflecting on the alliance which had placed the
Stewart family on the throne, "then God's will be done! It came with a lass,
and it will go with a lass." With these words he turned his face to the wall,
and died of a broken heart.

† It was taken in the following remarkable way :—The garrison was supplied
with hay by a neighbouring rustic, of the name of Binnock or Binning, who

rebuilt by the English during the minority of David II., but was again burnt down in 1424. The Palace was finally reduced to its present ruinous condition by Hawley's dragoons, who were quartered in it on the night of the 31st of January 1746. In the morning, when they were preparing to depart, the dastardly scoundrels were observed deliberately throwing the ashes of the fires into the straw on which they had lain. The whole Palace was speedily in a blaze, and it has ever since remained an empty and blackened ruin. *

favoured the interest of Bruce. " Binnock had been ordered by the English governor to furnish some cart-loads of hay, of which they were in want. He promised to bring it accordingly ; but the night before he drove the hay to the castle, he stationed a party of his friends, as well armed as possible, near the entrance, where they could not be seen by the garrison, and gave them directions that they should come to his assistance as soon as they should hear him cry a signal, which was to be,—' Call all, call all!' Then he loaded a great waggon with hay. But in the waggon he placed eight strong men, well armed, lying flat on their breasts, and covered over with hay, so that they could not be seen. He himself walked carelessly beside the waggon ; and he chose the stoutest and bravest of his servants to be the driver, who carried at his belt a strong axe or hatchet. In this way Binnock approached the castle, early in the morning ; and the watchman, who only saw two men, Binnock being one of them, with a cart of hay, which they expected, opened the gates, and raised up the portcullis, to permit them to enter the castle. But as soon as the cart had gotten under the gateway, Binnock made a sign to his servant, who, with his axe, suddenly cut asunder the *soam*, that is, the yoke which fastens the horses to the cart, and the horses, finding themselves free, naturally started forward, the cart remaining behind under the arch of the gate. At the same moment, Binnock cried, as loud as he could, ' Call all, call all !' and, drawing the sword which he had under his country habit, he killed the porter. The armed men then jumped up from under the hay where they lay concealed, and rushed on the English guard. The Englishmen tried to shut the gates, but they could not, because the cart of hay remained in the gateway, and prevented the folding-doors from being closed. The portcullis was also let fall, but the grating was caught on the cart, and so could not drop to the ground. The men who were in ambush near the gate, hearing the cry, ' Call all, call all !' ran to assist those who had leaped out from amongst the hay ; the castle was taken, and all the Englishmen killed or made prisoners. King Robert rewarded Binnock, by bestowing on him an estate, which his posterity long afterwards enjoyed." The Binnings of Wallyford, descended from that person, still bear in their coat-armorial a wain loaded with hay, with the motto, " Virtute deloquus."—*Tales of a Grandfather*, vol. i., p. 139.

* " They halted at Linlithgow, distinguished by its ancient palace, which, sixty years since, was entire and habitable, and whose venerable ruins, not

The Church, a venerable and impressive structure, stands between the Palace and the town, and may be regarded as one of the finest and most entire specimens of Gothic architecture in Scotland. It was dedicated to the archangel Michael, who was also considered the patron saint of the town. The Church was founded by David I., but was ornamented chiefly by George Crichton, bishop of Dunkeld. It is now divided by a partition-wall, and the eastern half alone is used as a place of worship. It was in an aisle in this Church, according to tradition, that James IV. was sitting when he saw the strange apparition which warned him against his fatal expedition to England.* In front of the Town-house

quite sixty years since, very narrowly escaped the unworthy fate of being converted into a barrack for French prisoners. May repose and blessings attend the ashes of the patriotic statesman (President Blair) who, amongst his last services to Scotland, interposed to prevent this profanation."—*Waverley*, vol. i., p. 92.

* The story is told by Pitscottie with characteristic simplicity :—" The king came to Lithgow, where he happened to be for the time at the Council, very sad and dolorous, making his devotion to God to send him good chance and fortune in his voyage. In this meantime, there came a man, clad in a blue gown, in at the kirk door, and belted about him in a roll of linen cloth ; a pair of brotikings (buskins) on his feet, to the great of his legs ; with all other hose and clothes conformed thereto ; but he had nothing on his head, but syde (long) red yellow hair behind, and on ¡his haffets (cheeks) which was down to his shoulders ; but his forehead was bald and bare. He seemed to be a man of two-and-fifty years, with a great pike-staff in his hand, and came first forward among the lords, crying and spiering (asking) for the king, saying, he desired to speak with him. While, at the last, he came where the king was sitting in the desk at his prayers ; but, when he saw the king, he made him little reverence or salutation, but leaned down grofling on the desk before him, and said to him in this manner, as after follows :—' Sir king, my mother hath sent me to you, desiring you not to pass, at this time, where thou art purposed ; for if thou does, thou wilt not fare well in thy journey, nor none that passeth with thee. Further, she bade thee mell (meddle) with no woman, nor use their counsel, nor let them touch thy body, nor thou theirs ; for if thou do it, thou wilt be confounded and brought to shame.'

" By this man had spoken thir words unto the king's grace, the evening song was near done, and the king paused on thir words, studying to give him an answer ; but, in the mean time, before the king's eyes, and in the presence of all the lords that were about him for the time, this man vanished away, and could no wise be seen or comprehended, but vanished away as he had been a blink of the sun, or a whip of the whirlwind, and could no more be seen. I

stands the Cross Well, a very curious and elegant erection. The present edifice was built in 1805, but it is said to be an exact facsimile of the original, erected in 1620. The sculpture is very elaborate, and the water is made to pour in great profusion from the mouths of a multitude of grotesque figures. The vast copiousness of water at Linlithgow is alluded to in the following well-known rhyme :—

> " Glasgow for bells,
> Lithgow for wells,
> Fa'kirk for beans and peas,
> Peebles for clashes and lees."

It was in Linlithgow that David Hamilton of Bothwellhaugh, on the 23d of January 1570, shot the Regent Murray, when passing through the town, in revenge for a private injury. The house from which the shot was fired belonged to the Archbishop of St. Andrews. It was taken down a number of years ago, and replaced by a modern edifice.

During the plague of 1645, Linlithgow happening to be comparatively free of the infection, the Palace and Church were used by the Courts of Justice and the members of the University of Edinburgh, as their meeting places. At the Restoration, the inhabitants of Linlithgow burned the Solemn League and Covenant amidst great rejoicing. The ringleader in this affair was one Ramsay, the minister of the parish, who had formerly

heard say, Sir David Lindesay, lyon-herauld, and John Inglis the marshal, who were, at that time, young men, and special servants to the king's grace, were standing presently beside the king, who thought to have laid hands on this man, that they might have speired further tidings at him ; but all for nought ; they could not touch him ; for he vanished away betwixt them, and was no more seen." There can be little doubt that the supposed apparition was a contrivance of the queen, to deter James from his impolitic warfare.

been a zealous supporter of the Covenant. In Linlithgow is still kept up the old custom of riding the marches. The town has derived considerable advantage from the Union Canal, which passes along the high grounds immediately to the south. Leather is the staple commodity of the place, linen and woollen manufactures are also carried on to a considerable extent. The population of the burgh and parish, in 1831, was 4874.

Proceeding westward from Linlithgow, the road crosses the Avon at Linlithgow Bridge, and enters Stirlingshire. After this nothing interesting occurs for some miles, till the tourist passes, on the left, Callander House, (W. Forbes, Esq.) formerly the seat of the Earls of Callander and Linlithgow, and a short way farther on enters the town of

FALKIRK,

delightfully situated on the face of an eminence overlooking the wide extent of country called the Carse of Falkirk. It was a town of some note in the early part of the eleventh century. The old church, which was demolished about thirty years ago, was erected in 1057. The original name of the town was *Eglishbreckk*, signifying "the speckled church," in allusion, it is supposed, to the colour of the stones. In the churchyard are shown the graves of two celebrated Scottish heroes,—Sir John Graham, the friend of Wallace, and Sir John Stewart of Bonkill, both of whom fell fighting bravely against the English at the battle of Falkirk, in 1298. Over the former a monument was erected with an inscription, which has been renewed three times since his death. It at present stands thus :—

> Mente Manuque Potens, et vallae Fidus Achates,
> conditur Hic Gramus, Bello interfectus ab Anglis.

Here lyes Sir John the Grame, baith wight ane wise,
Ane of the chiefs who rescewit Scotland thrise,
Ane better knight not to the world was lent,
Nor was gude Grame of truth and hardiment.

In the churchyard is also to be seen the monument of
two brave officers, Sir Robert Munro of Foulis, and his
brother Dr. Munro, who were killed in the second battle
of Falkirk, January 17, 1746. Falkirk is noted for its
great cattle markets or *trysts,* held thrice a-year, to which
a vast number of black cattle are brought from the Highlands and Islands.

About two miles north of the town are the celebrated
Carron Iron Works, the largest manufactory of the kind
in the world.

A short way from Falkirk is the village of Graham-
ston, near which, in 1298, was fought a battle between
the forces of Edward I. and the Scots, under Wallace
and Sir John Graham, in which the latter were defeated.
The battle of Falkirk-muir, between the Royal forces
under General Hawley, and the Highlanders, in which
the latter gained a complete victory, was fought on the
high ground lying to the south-west of the town. Hawley had suffered himself to be detained at Callander
House by the wit and gaiety of the Countess of Kilmarnock (whose husband was with the Prince's army,) until
the Highlanders had taken up an advantageous position,
and were ready to attack his army. The consequence
of his incapacity and negligence was, that his troops were
thrown into confusion, and completely routed.*

* " Hawley had not a better head, and certainly a much worse heart than
Sir John Cope, who was a humane, good-tempered man. The new general
ridiculed severely the conduct of his predecessor, and remembering that he
had seen, in 1715, the left wing of the Highlanders broken by a charge of the

The view from the eminence on which the battle was fought is remarkably extensive, varied, and beautiful.

Proceeding westward, the tourist, a short way from Falkirk, passes the village of Camelon, said to have been the situation of a Roman city built by Vespasian. A mile farther on, the road crosses the Carron. Near to this are the church and village of Larbert, and Larbert House, the seat of Sir Gilbert Stirling. In Larbert Kirk, Bruce, the famous Abyssinian traveller, lies interred. Kinnaird, his patrimonial estate, is at no great distance. A mile and a half farther on, the road passes through the remains of the Torwood Forest, where Sir William Wallace is said to have found shelter in a tree when pursued by his enemies. At Torwood-head, Mr Cargill, in 1680, excommunicated Charles II., the Duke of York, and the ministry. About four miles farther on is the village of *Bannockburn*, remarkable for its manufactories of tartans and carpets. To the left of the road,

Duke of Argyle's horse, which came upon them across a morass, he resolved to manœuvre in the same manner. He forgot, however, a material circumstance —that the morass at Sheriffmuir was hard frozen, which made some difference in favour of the cavalry. Hawley's manœuvre, as commanded and executed, plunged a great part of his dragoons up to the saddle-laps in a bog, where the Highlanders cut them to pieces with so little trouble, that, as one of the performers assured us, the feat was as easy as slicing *bacon*. The gallantry of some of the English regiments beat off the Highland charge on another point, and, amid a tempest of wind and rain which has been seldom equalled, the field presented the singular prospect of two armies flying different ways at the same moment. The king's troops, however, ran fastest and farthest, and were the last to recover their courage; indeed, they retreated that night to Falkirk leaving their guns, burning their tents, and striking a new panic into the British nation, which was but just recovering from the flutter excited by what, in olden times, would have been called the Raid of Derby. In the drawing-room, which took place at Saint James's on the day the news arrived, all countenances were marked with doubt and apprehension, excepting those of George the Second, the Earl of Stair, and Sir John Cope, who was radiant with joy at Hawley's discomfiture. Indeed, the idea of the two generals was so closely connected, that a noble peer of Scotland, upon the same day, addressed Sir John Cope by the title of General Hawley, to the no small amusement of those who heard the *quia pro quo*."—Sir Walter Scott's *Prose Works*, vol. xix., p. 303.

between Bannockburn and St. Ninians, is the scene of the famous battle, the Marathon of the North, fought June 24th, 1314, between the English army of 100,000 men, under Edward II., and the Scottish army of 30,000, commanded by Robert Bruce, in which the former were signally defeated, with the loss of 30,000 men, and 700 barons and knights. The Scottish army extended in a north-easterly direction from the brook of Bannock, which was so rugged and broken as to cover the right flank effectually, to the village of St. Ninians, probably in the line of the present road from Stirling to Kilsyth. The royal standard was pitched, according to tradition, in a stone having a round hole for its reception, and thence called the Bore-stone. It is still shewn on the top of a small eminence called Brocks Brae, to the south-west of St. Ninians. To the northward, Bruce fortified his position against cavalry by digging a number of pits so close together as to resemble the cells in a honeycomb. They were slightly covered with brushwood and green sods, so as not to be obvious to an impetuous enemy.* Two

---

* On the evening before the battle, a personal encounter took place between Bruce and Sir Henry de Bohun, a gallant English knight, the issue of which had a great effect upon the spirits of both armies. It is thus recorded by Sir Walter Scott, in "The Lord of the Isles."

> "Dash'd from the ranks Sir Henry Boune,—
> He spurr'd his steed, he couch'd his lance,
> And darted on the Bruce at once.—
> As motionless as rocks that bide
> The wrath of the advancing tide,
> The Bruce stood fast. Each heart beat high,
> And dazzled was each gazing eye.—
> The heart had hardly time to think,
> The eye-lid scarcely time to wink,
> While on the King, like flash of flame,
> Spurr'd to full speed the war-horse came!—
> The partridge may the falcon mock,
> If that slight palfrey stand the shock.—
> But, swerving from the knight's career,
> Just as they met Bruce shunn'd the spear;

large stones, erected in the lower extremity of a lawn which fronts a villa near the village of Newhouse, about a quarter of a mile from the south part of Stirling, mark the spot where a skirmish took place between Randolph Earl of Moray, and a party of English commanded by Sir Robert Clifford.* The place is still popularly called Randals-field.

> Onward the baffled warrior bore
> His course—but soon his course was o'er,—
> High in his stirrups stood the king,
> And gave his battle-axe the swing;
> Right on De Boune, the whiles he pass'd,
> Fell that stern blow—the first—the last!—
> Such strength upon the blow was put,
> The helmet crash'd like hazel-nut,
> The axe-shaft, with its brazen clasp,
> Was shiver'd to the gauntlet grasp;
> Springs from the blow the startled horse;
> Drops to the plain the lifeless corse.
> First of that fatal field, how soon,
> How sudden fell the fierce De Boune."

The Scottish leaders remonstrated with the king upon his temerity; he only answered, "I have broken my good battle-axe." The English vanguard retreated, after witnessing this single combat.

* Bruce had enjoined Randolph, who commanded the left wing of his army, to be vigilant in preventing any advanced parties of the English from throwing succours into the Castle of Stirling. Eight hundred horsemen, commanded by Sir Robert Clifford, were detached from the English army; they made a circuit by the low grounds to the east, and approached the castle. The king perceived their motion, and, coming up to Randolph, angrily exclaimed, "Thoughtless man! you have suffered the enemy to pass." Randolph hastened to repair his fault, or perish. As he advanced, the English cavalry wheeled to attack him. Randolph drew up his troops in a circular form, with their spears resting on the ground and protended on every side. At the first onset, Sir William Daynecourt, an English commander of distinguished note, was slain. The enemy, far superior in numbers to Randolph, environed him, and pressed hard on his little band; Douglas saw his jeopardy, and requested the king's permission to go and succour him. "You shall not move from your ground," cried the king; "let Randolph extricate himself as he best may, I will not alter my order of battle, and lose the advantage of my position."—"In truth," replied Douglas, "I cannot stand by and see Randolph perish, and, therefore, with your leave, I must aid him." The king unwillingly consented, and Douglas flew to the assistance of his friend. While approaching, he perceived that the English were falling into disorder, and that the perseverance of Randolph had prevailed over their impetuous courage. "Halt!" cried Douglas, "those brave men have repulsed the enemy, let us not diminish their glory by sharing it."—DALRYMPLE's *Annals of Scotland.*

About a mile from the field of battle, in another direction, is a place called the Bloody Folds, where the Earl of Gloucester is said to have made a stand and died gallantly at the head of his own military tenants and vassals. There is also a place in this neighbourhood called Ingram's Crook, which is supposed to have derived its name from Sir Ingram Umfraville, one of the English commanders. In the rear of the position occupied by the Scottish army is the Gillies' Hill, which derived its name from the following circumstance :—In a valley westward of this hill, Bruce stationed his baggage, under the charge of the gillies or servants and retainers of the camp. At the critical moment when the English line was wavering, these gillies, prompted either by the enthusiasm of the moment, or the desire of plunder, assumed, in a tumultuary manner, such arms as they found nearest, and shewed themselves on the hill like a new army advancing to battle. The English, taking these for a fresh body of troops, were seized with a panic, and fled in every direction.

About a mile westward from the field of Bannockburn, was fought, in 1488, the battle of Sauchieburn, in which James III. was defeated and slain. The Barons of Scotland, being dissatisfied with the government of the king, rose in rebellion against him, and drew into their party the king's eldest son, then a youth of fifteen, afterwards James IV. When the king saw his own banner displayed against him, and his own son in the faction of his enemies, he lost the little courage he ever possessed, fled out of the field, and fell from his horse as it started at a woman and water-pitcher near the village of Millton. He was carried into the mill in a state of insensibility by the miller and his wife, without being recognized. On recovering his senses he asked for a priest,

to whom he might make confession. One of his pursuers coming up, exclaimed, " I am a priest," and,
approaching the unfortunate monarch, who was lying in
a corner of the mill, stabbed him several times to the
heart. James IV. was seized with deep remorse for his
conduct in this affair, which manifested itself in severe
acts of penance,—among others, in wearing a heavy iron
belt, to the weight of which he added certain ounces as
long as he lived.*

St. Ninians, or, as it is commonly called, St. Ringans,
is a thriving village a short way south from Stirling. Its
steeple stands separate from the church, which is in its
immediate vicinity. The old church being used as a
powder magazine by the Highlanders in 1746, was accidentally blown up, but though the church was completely
destroyed, the steeple remained uninjured. A mile farther on, the tourist enters the royal burgh of

STIRLING,

delightfully situated on an eminence near the river Forth,
and bearing in its external appearance a considerable resemblance to Edinburgh, though on a smaller scale. The
most interesting and conspicuous object in Stirling is the
Castle, the first foundation of which is lost in the darkness
of antiquity. It was frequently taken and retaken after
protracted sieges, during the wars which were carried
on for the independence of Scotland. It became a royal
residence about the time of the accession of the house of
Stuart, and was long the favourite abode of the Scottish

* So little had the prince been accustomed to his father's company, that he
was almost a stranger to his person ; for when Sir Andrew Wood appeared before him, a few days after the battle, struck with his stately appearance, or,
perhaps, with some resemblance he bore to the late king, he asked him, " Sir,
are you my father?" To which the admiral, bursting into tears, replied, " I
am not your father, but I was your father's true servant."

M

monarchs. It was the birthplace of James II. and James
V.; and James VI. and his eldest son Prince Henry were
baptized in it.* The palace, which was built by James
V., is in the form of a quadrangle, and occupies the south-
east part of the fortress. The buildings on the south side
of the square are the oldest part of the castle. One of
the apartments is still called Douglas's Room, in consequence of the assassination of William Earl of Douglas
by James II., after he had granted him a safe-conduct.†

On the west side of the square is a long low building,
which was originally a chapel, and is now used as a store-
room and armoury. This building was erected by James
VI., and was the scene of the baptism of his son Prince
Henry. Underneath the exterior wall, on the west, a
narrow road leads from the town, and descends the precipice behind the Castle. This is called Ballangeich, a
Gaelic word signifying " windy pass," which is remark-

---

* In the autumn of 1787, Stirling was visited by Robert Burns, then on a tour
to the West Highlands. On beholding the roofless state of the Parliament
Hall of the Stuarts, his Jacobite feelings overflowed in the following lines,
which he inscribed on a pane of glass in the inn :—

> " Here Stuarts once in glory reign'd,
>   And laws for Scotia's weal ordain'd ;
>   But now unroof'd their palace stands,
>   Their sceptre's sway'd by other hands :
>   The injured Stuart line is gone,
>   A race outlandish fills their throne—
>   An idiot race, to honour lost ;
>   Who know them best, despise them most."

Upon being remonstrated with, by a friend, for his imprudence, the poet replied, " Oh, I mean to reprove myself." He then returned to the window, and
added the following lines :—

> " Rash mortal, and slanderous poet, thy name
>   Shall no longer appear in the records of fame ;
>   Dost not know that old Mansfield, who writes like the Bible,
>   Says, ' the more 'tis a truth, sir, the more 'tis a libel ? ' "

> † " Ye towers ! within whose circuit dread
>   A Douglas by his sovereign bled."
>   *Lady of the Lake.*

STIRLING CASTLE.

able as having furnished the fictitious name adopted by James V. in the various disguises which he was in the habit of assuming, for the purpose of seeing that justice was regularly administered, and frequently also from the less justifiable motive of gallantry.* To the north of the

* The two excellent comic songs, entitled "The Gaberlunzie man," and "We'll gae nae mair a roving," are said to have been founded on the success of this monarch's amorous adventures, when travelling in the disguise of a beggar. The following anecdotes respecting this frolicsome prince, are given by Sir Walter Scott :—

"Another adventure, which had nearly cost James his life, is said to have taken place at the village of Cramond, near Edinburgh, where he had rendered his addresses acceptable to a pretty girl of the lower rank. Four or five persons, whether relations or lovers of his mistress is uncertain, beset the disguised monarch, as he returned from his rendezvous. Naturally gallant, and an admirable master of his weapon, the king took post on the high and narrow bridge over the Almond river, and defended himself bravely with his sword. A peasant, who was threshing in a neighbouring barn, came out upon the noise, and, whether moved by compassion or by natural gallantry, took the weaker side, and laid about with his flail so effectually, as to disperse the assailants, well threshed, even according to the letter. He then conducted the king into his barn, where his guest requested a bason and towel, to remove the stains of the broil. This being procured with difficulty, James employed himself in learning what was the summit of his deliverer's earthly wishes, and found that they were bounded by the desire of possessing, in property, the farm of Braehead, upon which he laboured as a bondsman. The lands chanced to belong to the crown ; and James directed him to come to the palace of Holy-Rood, and inquire for the Guidman (i. e. farmer) of Ballangeich, a name by which he was known in his excursions, and which answered to *Il Bondocani* of Haroun Alraschid. He presented himself accordingly, and found, with due astonishment that he had saved his monarch's life, and that he was to be gratified with a crown-charter of the lands of Braehead, under the service of presenting an ewer, bason, and towel, for the king to wash his hands, when he shall happen to pass the Bridge of Cramond. In 1822, when George IV. came to Scotland, the descendant of this John Howison of Braehead, who still possesses the estate which was given to his ancestor, appeared at a solemn festival, and offered his Majesty water from a silver ewer."

"Another of James's frolics is thus narrated by Mr. Campbell, from the Statistical Account. 'Being once benighted when out a hunting, and separated from his attendants, he happened to enter a cottage in the midst of a moor, at the foot of the Ochil hills, near Alloa, where, unknown, he was kindly received. In order to regale their unexpected guest, the *gude-man* (i. e. landlord, farmer) desired the *gude-wife* to fetch the hen that roosted nearest the cock, which is always the plumpest, for the stranger's supper. The king, highly pleased with his night's lodging and hospitable entertainment, told mine host, at parting, that he should be glad to return his civility, and requested that, the first time he came to Stirling, he would call at the castle, and inquire for the *gude-man of Ballangeich*. Donaldson, the landlord, did not fail to call on the *gude-man*

Castle is a small mount on which executions commonly took place.* On this eminence, and within sight of their Castle of Doune and their extensive possessions, Mur-

of Ballangeich, when his astonishment, at finding that the king had been his guest, afforded no small amusement to the merry monarch and his courtiers; and, to carry on the pleasantry, he was thenceforth designated by James with the title of King of the Moors, which name and designation have descended from father to son ever since; and they have continued in possession of the identical spot, the property of Mr. Erskine of Mar, till very lately, when this gentleman, with reluctance, turned out the descendant and representative of the King of the Moors, on account of his majesty's invincible indolence, and great dislike to reform or innovation of any kind, although, from the spirited example of his neighbour tenants on the same estate, he is convinced similar exertion would promote his advantage."

The following anecdote is extracted from the genealogical work of Buchanan of Auchmar, upon Scottish surnames:—

"This John Buchanan of Auchmar and Arnpryor was afterwards termed King of Kippen,* upon the following account:—King James V., a very sociable, debonair prince, residing at Stirling, in Buchanan of Arnpryor's time, carriers were very frequently passing along the common road, being near Arnpryor's house, with necessaries for the use of the king's family, and he having some extraordinary occasion, ordered one of these carriers to leave his load at his house, and he would pay him for it; which the carrier refused to do, telling him he was the king's carrier, and his load for his majesty's use. To which Arnpryor seemed to have small regard, compelling the carrier, in the end, to leave his load; telling him, if King James was king of Scotland, he was king of Kippen, so that it was reasonable he should share with his neighbour king in some of these loads so frequently carried that road. The carrier representing this usage, and telling the story, as Arnpryor spoke it, to some of the king's servants, it came at length to his majesty's ears, who, shortly thereafter, with a few attendants, came to visit his neighbour king, who was, in the meantime, at dinner. King James having sent a servant to demand access, was denied the same by a tall fellow with a battle-axe, who stood porter at the gate, telling there could be no access till dinner was over. This answer not satisfying the king, he sent to demand access a second time; upon which he was desired by the porter to desist, otherwise he would find cause to repent his rudeness. His majesty finding this method would not do, desired the porter to tell his master that the good-man of Ballangeich desired to speak with the king of Kippen. The porter telling Arnpryor so much, he, in all humble manner, came and received the king, and having entertained him with much sumptuousness and jollity, became so agreeable to King James, that he allowed him to take so much of any provision he found carrying that road as he had occasion for; and, seeing he made the first visit, desired Arnpryor in a few days to return him a second at Stirling, which he performed, and continued in very much favour with the king, always thereafter being termed King of Kippen while he lived."

*   " Thou, O sad and fatal mound,
     That oft has heard the death-axe sound."
                                        Lady of the Lake.

---

* A small district of Perthshire.

doch Duke of Albany, Duncan Earl of Lennox, his father-in-law, and his two sons, Walter and Alexander Stuart, were beheaded in 1425. The execution of Walter Stuart is supposed, with great probability, to be the groundwork of the beautiful and pathetic ballad of " Young Waters." This " heading-hill " now commonly bears the name of Hurley-Hacket, from its being the scene of an amusement practised by James V. when a boy, and his courtiers, which consisted in sliding in some sort of chair from top to bottom of the bank. On the south side of the Castle Hill is a small piece of ground called the Valley, with a rock on the south side denominated the Ladies' Rock. On this spot tournaments used to be held. The view from the Castle Hill is remarkably magnificent. To the north and east are the Ochil Hills, and the windings of the Forth through the Carse of Stirling, with its fertile fields, luxuriant woods, and stately mansions. On the west lies the vale of Menteith, bounded by the Highland mountains. The Campsie hills close the horizon to the south, and in the foreground, on the east, are the town, the Abbey Craig, and the ruins of Cambuskenneth Abbey, and, in a clear day, the Castle of Edinburgh and Arthur's Seat are seen. Stirling Castle is one of the four fortresses of Scotland which, by the articles of the Union, are always to be kept in repair. It is now used as a barrack. South-west of the Castle lies the King's Park, and to the east of it are the King's Gardens, which, though now unenclosed, and reduced to the condition of a marshy pasture, still retain the fantastic forms into which they had been thrown by the gardeners of ancient times.

The Greyfriars or Franciscan church of Stirling was erected in 1494 by James IV., and some additions were made to it by Cardinal Beaton. It is a handsome Gothic building, and, since the Reformation, has been divided into two places of worship, called the East and West Churches. In this church the Earl of Arran, Regent of the kingdom, abjured Romanism in 1543; it was also the scene of the coronation of James VI., on the 29th July 1597, when John Knox preached the coronation sermon. The celebrated Ebenezer Erskine, founder of the Secession Church, was one of the ministers of the West Church.

To the north of the Church stands the ruins of a haggard-looking building called Mar's Work. It was built by the Earl of Mar out of the ruins of Cambuskenneth Abbey. This conduct excited a great deal of popular dissatisfaction, in allusion to which the Earl caused several inscriptions to be affixed to his house.

In the immediate neighbourhood of this building is a spacious edifice called Argyle's Lodging, which was built by Sir William Alexander, the poet, created Earl of Stirling. It afterwards passed into the hands of the Argyle family, and is now used as a military hospital.

Stirling has long been celebrated for its schools, and also for the number of its hospitals or residences for decayed persons. By an act of the Scottish Parliament in 1437, Stirling was appointed to be the place for keeping the Jug, or standard of dry measure, from which all others throughout the country were appointed to be taken, while the Firlot was given to Linlithgow, the Ell to Edinburgh, the Reel to Perth, and the Pound to Lanark. The Stirling Jug is still preserved with great care. In 1831, the population of the town and parish was 8340. Stirling Bridge was long a structure of great importance, having been, till lately, almost the only access into the

northern part of Scotland for wheeled carriages. At a
very early period there was a wooden bridge over the
Forth about half a mile above the present structure,
which was the scene of one of the most gallant
achievements of Sir William Wallace, on the 13th of
September 1297. An English army of 50,000 foot and
1000 horse, commanded by Cressingham, advanced towards Stirling in quest of Wallace, who, on his part,
having collected an army of 40,000 men, marched
southward to dispute the passage of the Forth. He
posted his army near Cambuskenneth, allowing only a
part of them to be seen. The English hurried across
the river, to attack the Scots. After a considerable
number of them had thus passed over, and the bridge
was crowded with those who were following, Wallace
charged those who had crossed with his whole strength,
slew a very great number, and drove the rest into the
river Forth, where the greater part were drowned. The
remainder of the English army, who were left on the
southern bank of the river, fled in great confusion, having
first set fire to the wooden bridge, that the Scots might
not pursue them. Cressingham himself was among the
slain, and his rapine and oppression had rendered him so
detestable to the Scots, that they flayed off his skin, and
cut it in pieces to make girths for their horses.

The view of Stirling Castle, with which our text is
illustrated, represents the scene in Waverley, where the
party of Balmawhapple, upon passing the fortress, are
saluted by a bullet from its walls. The artist has selected the moment when the valorous laird is returning the
compliment by discharging his pistol at the inhospitable
rock.

FIFTH TOUR.

LOOKING straight across the Firth, upon leaving the Chain Pier, the burgh of Burntisland may be observed directly opposite. On the same side as the Chain Pier, the Duke of Buccleuch has lately built a low-water pier, for the better accommodation of steam-boats. After passing Granton, may be seen Lauriston Castle, the residence of John Law, the projector of the Mississippi scheme. On the north shore is the town of Aberdour, and near it the seat of the Earl of Morton, who is known here by the title of " the Gudeman of Aberdour." North of the castle is the mansion-house of Hillside, and a little farther on is Dalgetty Church. Near this point is the island of Inch Colm, with the remains of a monastery, founded, in 1123, by Alexander I. On the south shore, at the mouth of the river Almond, stand the village of Cramond, and Cramond House, (Lady Torphichen,) and a little farther west is Dalmeny Park, the seat of the Earl of Rosebery. Near it are the ruins of Barnbougle Castle, an ancient seat of the family of the Moubrays, now extinct. Directly opposite is Donnibrissal, a seat of the Earl of Moray, the scene of the atrocious murder, by the Earl of Huntly, of the youthful Earl of Moray,

---

* Steam-boats sail for Alloa and Stirling every day, from Trinity Chain Pier. Coaches to the boat run from the Duty House, end of North Bridge, where correct information as to the hours of sailing may be obtained.

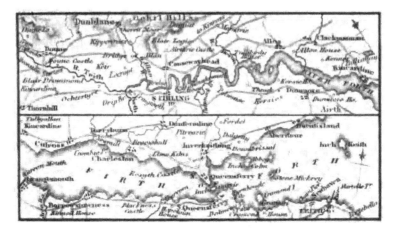

son-in-law of the celebrated Regent Murray.* A short
way to the westward lies .the ancient burgh of Inver-

* " The Earl of Huntly, head of the powerful family of Gordon, had chanced
to have some feudal differences with the Earl of Murray, in the course of which
John Gordon, a brother of Gordon of Cluny, was killed by a shot from Murray's
castle of Darnaway. This was enough to make the two families irreconcilable
enemies, even if they had been otherwise on friendly terms. About 1591-2, an
accusation was brought against Murray, for having given some countenance or
assistance to Stewart, Earl of Bothwell, in a recent treasonable exploit. King
James, without recollecting, perhaps, the hostility between the two Earls, sent
Huntly with a commission to bring the Earl of Murray to his presence. Huntly
probably rejoiced in the errand, as giving him an opportunity of revenging himself on his feudal enemy. He beset the house of Dunnibrissle, on the northern
shore of the Forth, and summoned Murray to surrender. In reply, a gun was
fired, which mortally wounded one of the Gordons. The assailants proceeded
to set fire to the house; when Dunbar, sheriff of the county of Moray, said to
the Earl, ' Let us not stay to be burnt in the flaming house : I will go out fore-
most, and the Gordons, taking me for your Lordship, will kill me, while you
escape in the confusion.' They rushed out among their enemies accordingly,
and Dunbar was slain. But his death did not save his friend, as he had generously intended. Murray, indeed, escaped for the moment, but as he fled towards the rocks of the sea-shore, he was traced by the silken tassels attached
to his head-piece, which had taken fire as he broke out among the flames. By
this means, his pursuers followed him down amongst'the cliffs, near the sea;
and Gordon of Buckie, who is said to have been the first that overtook him,
wounded him mortally. As Murray was gasping in the last agony, Huntly
came up; and it is alleged, by tradition, that Gordon pointed his dirk against
the person of his chief, saying, ' By heaven ! my Lord, you shall be as deep in
as I ;' and so he compelled him to wound Murray whilst he was dying. Huntly,
with a wavering hand, struck the expiring Earl in the face. Thinking of his

keithing.   On the two coasts are the towns of North
and South Queensferry, and, in the straits between them,
is the fortified islet of Inchgarvie.   On a rocky promontory, on the north shore, are the ruins of Rosyth Castle,
once the seat of the Stuarts of Rosyth, a branch of the
Royal House of Scotland, from whom it is said the mother
of Oliver Cromwell was descended.   Half a mile beyond
Inchgarvie is Port Edgar, where George IV. embarked,
after a visit to the Earl of Hopetoun, 29th August 1822.
On an eminence, beyond South Queensferry, is Dundas

superior beauty, even in that moment of parting life, Murray stammered out
the dying words, 'You have spoiled a better face than your own.'

   " After this deed of violence, Huntly did not choose to return to Edinburgh,
but departed for the north.   He took refuge, for the moment, in the castle of
Ravenscraig, belonging to the Lord Sinclair, who told him, with a mixture of
Scottish caution and hospitality, that he was welcome to come in, but would
have been twice as welcome to have passed by.   Gordon, when a long period
had passed by, avowed his contrition for the guilt he had incurred."—*Tales of
a Grandfather*, vol. ii., p. 191.

   Upon this tragical circumstance, the following beautiful ballad is founded :—

     " Ye Highlands, and ye Lawlands,
        Oh, where have ye been ?
     They hae slain the Earl o' Murray,
        And lain him on the green.

   ' Now, wae be to you, Huntly !
        And wherefore did ye sae ?
     I bade you bring him wi' you,
        But forbade you him to slae.'

     He was a braw gallant,
        And he rade at the ring ;
     And the bonnie Earl o' Murray,
        Oh ! he micht ha' been a king.

     He was a braw gallant,
        And he rade at the gluve ;
     And the bonnie Earl o' Murray,
        Oh ! he was the Queen's luve !

     Oh ! lang will his lady
        Look ower the Castle Doune,
     Ere she see the Earl o' Murray
        Come sounding through the toun."

Castle, the original seat of the Dundas family before the
eleventh century, and still the residence of their lineal
descendant, Dundas of that Ilk.   Farther on, upon the
same side, and about a mile from the shore, is Hopetoun
House, the splendid mansion of the Earl of Hopetoun;
and on a peninsula, to the westward, stands Blackness
Castle, one of the four fortresses which, by the articles
of the Union, are to be kept constantly garrisoned.   Close
by the village of Charleston, on the north side of the
Forth, stands Broomhall, the seat of the Earl of Elgin.
Farther on is Crombie Point and Crombie House, then
the village of Torryburn, next Torry House (Captain
Erskine Wemyss of Wemyss Castle) and Newmills village.   Returning to the south coast, and proceeding
westward, may be seen in succession Carriden House,
(James Hope, Esq.,) Kirkgrange Salt Pans, Borrowstounness, Kinneil House, the property of the Duke of
Hamilton, for some time the residence of the late Professor Dugald Stewart; and Grangemouth, situated at the
mouth of Carron Water.   On the north side is Valley-
field, (Lady Baird Preston,) and near it the ancient and
decayed burgh of Culross, (pronounced *Cooross*.)*   The
inhabitants are a remarkably primitive set of people.
Immediately behind it are the ruins of a Cistertian abbey,
founded in 1217, by Malcolm Earl of Fife.   At the Reformation, its possessions were conferred upon Sir James
Colville, who was created Lord Colville of Culross.
From the family of Colville it passed to the Earls of
Dundonald, who sold it to the late Sir Robert Preston,
Bart. A little farther on is Blair Castle, (Dundas, Esq.,)

* Culross was famous for the manufacture of *girdles*, the round iron plates
on which the people of Scotland bake their barley and oaten bread. " The
hammermen of Edinburgh are no' that bad at girdles for carcakes, neither,

and about a mile beyond this is Sands House, (Johnstone, Esq.,) after which the tourist reaches the town
and shipping-port of Kincardine.   Near it stand the
ruins of the ancient castle of Tulliallan, formerly the
property of the knights of Blackadder, and Tulliallan
Castle, the splendid residence of Baroness Keith and
Count Flahault, built by the late Admiral Lord Keith,
the father of the present proprietrix, who is also the lineal
representative of one of the most ancient families in Scotland,—the Mercers of Aldie.   On the opposite side is
Higgin's Nook, (J. Burn Murdoch, Esq.,) and beyond it,
upon a height, Airth Castle, (Graham, Esq.,) and about
a mile to the west Dunmore House, the residence of the
Earl of Dunmore.   Nearly opposite, upon the right, is
Kennet House, the seat of Robert Bruce, Esq. of Kennet.   Farther on, upon the same side, is Clackmannan,
the capital of the small county of that name ; delightfully
situated on an eminence, and to the west of the town,
is Clackmannan Tower, said to have been built by Robert Bruce.   It is now the property of the Earl of Zetland.   Close beside the tower once stood the palace of
Robert Bruce, and family house of Bruce of Clackmannan, now demolished.   This was the residence of the
old Jacobite lady, Mrs. Bruce of Clackmannan, who is
mentioned in Currie's Life of Burns as having knighted

though the Cu'ross hammermen have the gree for that."—*Heart of Mid-Lothian,*
vol. ii., 254.
    Culross was also celebrated for its salt-pans and coal-mines. In the reign of
James VI., the coal-mines were worked a great way under the bed of the Forth,
and the coals were shipped at a mound which defended from the water the
mouth of a subterraneous communication with the coal-pit. James VI., when
on a visit to the proprietor, Sir George Bruce, being conducted, by his own desire, into the coal-pit, was led to ascend from it by the mound, when it was
high tide. Seeing himself surrounded, on all sides, by water, he apprehended
a plot, and bawled out "Treason;" but Sir George soon dispelled his majesty's
fears, by handing him into an elegant pinnace that was lying alongside.

that poet with a sword which belonged to Bruce. The
sword and a helmet which had also belonged to the
hero, are now in the possession of Lord Elgin, who represents the family of Bruce, and are to be seen at Broomhall, near Dunfermline. About a mile beyond Clackmannan, is the flourishing town of Alloa, in the neighbourhood of extensive collieries and distilleries. Near
the town, and in the midst of a fine park, stands Alloa
House, the ancient seat of the family of Erskine, Earls
of Mar, and the subject of a fine Scottish air. The
principal part of the building was destroyed by fire about
twenty years ago, but there is still standing the original
tower, an erection of the thirteenth century. It is
ninety feet high, and the walls are eleven feet thick.
At Alloa commence those remarkable windings called
the " Links of Forth." These windings of the river
form a great number of beautiful peninsulas, which, being
of a very luxuriant and fertile soil, gave rise to the old
rhyme,—

> " The lairdship o' the bonnie Links o' Forth
> Is better than an earldom o' the North."

The distance by land from Alloa to Stirling Bridge is
only six miles, while by water it is fifteen and a half.
On the same side as Alloa, and a little to the westward,
is Tullibody House, a residence of the Abercromby family. The Ochil-hills, from their proximity, now assume
an air of imposing grandeur, and Stirling Castle forms
a magnificent feature in the landscape. Beyond Tullibody, on the same side, is Cambus village, at the mouth
of the Devon. The vale of the Devon is famed for its
romantic beauty, and for the striking cascades formed by

the river.   Nearly opposite Cambus is Polmaise, (Murray, Esq.)   Farther on, upon the right, are the ruins of Cambuskenneth Abbey, situated on one of the peninsular plains formed by the windings of the river.   It was founded by David I., in 1147, for canons regular of the order of St. Augustine.   It was one of the richest and most extensive abbeys in Scotland.   At the Reformation, its possessions were bestowed by James VI. on the Earl of Mar, but about the year 1737 it was purchased by the Town Council of Stirling, for the benefit of Cowan's Hospital.   Of the once extensive fabric of the Abbey, nothing now exists except a few broken walls and a tower, which was the belfrey.   On the right is seen the Abbey Craig, and soon after the tourist reaches Stirling.

From Stirling a pleasant episodical tour may be made to Castle Campbell, the Rumbling Brig, and the Devil's Caldron.

Leaving Stirling, the tourist has on his left the soft green pastoral yet lofty hills of the Ochil range, with their magnificent wooded glades and warm sunward slopes, consisting of intermingling copse, cornfields, and meadows, while on the right is a rich and level country, bounded by the Forth, now entwining its silver links and spreading into a noble estuary.   The most southerly of the Ochil-hills is Damyat, famous for the extensive and splendid view obtained from its summit.   In its neighbourhood is Bencleuch, which shoots up into a tall rocky point, called Craigleith, remarkable in ancient times for the production of falcons.   In a hollow near this the snow often lies far into the summer.   The people give it the picturesque name of Lady Alva's Web.   Three miles from Stirling the tourist reaches the beautiful village of Blairlogie, and four miles beyond it the village of Alva, which was formerly remarkable for its silver mines. Alva House, the residence of Johnstone of Alva, stands on an eminence projecting from the base of the Woodhill.* Three miles from Alva is Tillicoultry, and at the distance of other three miles is the village of Dollar, about thirteen miles from Stirling, and seven from Alva. At Dollar there is an extensive academy, founded by a person of the name of Macnab, a native of the parish, who had realized a large fortune in London. It is a handsome Grecian building, and is furnished with good masters for the various branches of education. In the neighbourhood is the remarkable ruin of Castle Campbell, occupying a wild and romantic situation on the top of a high and almost insulated rock. The only access to the castle is by an isthmus connecting the mount with the hill behind. The mount on which it is situated is nearly encompassed on all sides by thick bosky woods, and mountain rivulets descending on either side, unite at the base. Immediately behind rises a vast amphitheatre of wooded hills. Castle Campbell is a place of great antiquity. The precise period at which it came into the possession of the Argyle family is not certainly known. In 1493 an act of Parliament was passed for changing the name of " the castle called the Gloume,"† to Castle Campbell, and it continued to be a possession of the great clan family of Argyle, till about thirty years ago, upon the death of the late Duke, it was sold to the late Mr. Tait of Harvieston. It is said that John Knox resided in Castle Campbell, under the protection of Archibald, the fourth Earl, who was the first of the Scottish

---

* " Oh, Alva woods are bonnie,
    Tillicoultry hills are fair,
    But when I think o' the bonnie braes e' Menstrie,
    It mak's my heart aye sair."

Fairy Rhyme.

The village of Menstrie lies two miles west of Alva. Menstrie House was the seat of the Earl of Stirling.

† The ancient name of the castle, it is often said, was the Castle of Gloom. The mountain streams that flow on the different sides are still called, the one the Water of Care, the other the Burn of Sorrow; and, after the junction in front of the castle, they traverse the valley of Dollar, or Dolour. The proper etymologists, however, tell a different tale. The old Gaelic name of the stronghold was *Cock Leum*, or Mad Leap. The glen of Care, was the glen of *Caer* or castle, a British word; and Dollar is simply *Dalor*, the high field.—CHAMBERS's *Gazetteer*, vol. i., 191.

nobility that publicly embraced the Protestant religion. Castle Campbell was destroyed in 1645. " The feudal hatred of Montrose, and of the clans composing the strength of his army, the vindictive resentment also of the Ogilvies for the destruction of " the bonnie House of Airlie," and that of the Stirlingshire cavaliers for that of Menstrie, doomed this magnificent pile to flames and ruin. The destruction of many a meaner habitation by the same unscrupulous and unsparing spirit of vengeance has been long forgotten, but the majestic remains of Castle Campbell still excite a sigh in those that view them, over the miseries of civil war."* About two miles above Dollar is an interesting spot where the Devon forms a series of cascades, one of which is called the Caldron Linn.† The river here suddenly enters a deep gulf, where, finding itself confined, it has, by continual efforts against the sides, worked out a cavity resembling a large caldron. From this gulf the water works its way through an aperture beneath the surface into a lower cavity, where it is covered with a constant foam. The water then works its way into a third caldron, out of which it is precipitated by a sheer fall of forty-four feet. The best view of this magnificent scene is from the bottom of the fall. About a mile farther up the vale, the rocks on each side rise to the height of eighty-six feet, and the banks of the stream are contracted in such a manner, that a bridge of twenty-five feet span connects them. A handsome new bridge has lately been erected above the old one, and a hundred and twenty feet from the bed of the stream. On account of the rocky nature of the channel, the river here makes a violent noise, hence the name of the Rumbling Bridge.‡ A few hundred yards farther up, there

* Tales of a Grandfather, vol. iii., p. 12.

† Instead of the usual route, pedestrians, in coming from Dollar, should strike off the high road soon after they get above *Vicar's Bridge*, and take along a path to the right, leading to *Cowden* and *Muckart Mill*, and from thence, by the *Blair Hill*, to the Caldron Linn. This is a short *cut*, which keeps near the river by a far more romantic line than the turnpike road.

‡ A short distance from the Rumbling Bridge is Aldie Castle, the ancient seat of the Mercers of Aldie, now represented by Baroness Keith. At Aldie, a man, on being hanged for the slight offence of stealing a *caup fu' o' corn*, is said to have uttered a malediction upon the family, to the effect that the estate of Aldie should never be inherited by a male heir for nineteen generations. It is a somewhat singular coincidence, that this has already so far taken effect,— Lady Keith being the daughter of an heiress, who was the grand-daughter and

is another cascade, called the Devil's Mill, where the water, vibrating from one side to another of the pool, and constantly beating against the sides of the rock, produces an intermittent noise like that of a mill in motion. The whole of the scenes around these remarkable cascades are of the most romantic kind, and strikingly different from all other Scottish scenery. " The clear, winding Devon," as almost every reader will recollect, has been celebrated by Burns in his beautiful lyric, " The banks of the Devon." Miss Charlotte Hamilton, (afterwards Mrs. Adair,) the lady on whom this song was composed, was at that time residing at Harvieston, near Dollar.

The tourist may, if he choose, proceed by the Crook of Devon to Kinross, and thence to Edinburgh,—a route which he will find described in the tour from Edinburgh to Perth, or he may proceed to Dunfermline, and thence to North Queensferry, by a route much more agreeable, and only two miles longer.

A short but pleasant excursion may also be made from Stirling to Dunblane, distant six miles, and to the Roman Camp at Ardoch, twelve miles distant.

Leaving Stirling, the tourist crosses the Forth by Stirling Bridge. A short way farther up the river is the Old Bridge, a very antique structure, narrow, and high in the centre. General Blakeney, the governor of the Castle, in 1745, caused the south arch to be destroyed, to interrupt the march of the Highlanders. On this bridge Archbishop Hamilton of St. Andrews, the last Roman Catholic Archbishop of Scotland, was hanged in 1571, in full pontificals, for his alleged accession to the assassination of Regent Murray. The tourist now passes, on the right, Airthrey Castle, (Lord Abercromby,) and afterwards the pretty little village of the Bridge of Allan, much resorted to in summer on account of a mineral well in the neighbourhood. In the vicinity is Keir, the seat of Archibald Stirling, Esq., and a mile and a half beyond it, the road passes Kippenross, the seat of Stirling of Kippendavie. In the lawn there is a remarkable plane-tree, supposed to be the largest in the kingdom. It is twenty-seven feet in circumference at the ground, and thirty where the branches shoot out. A little beyond Kippenross is

successor of another heiress, and being herself the mother of an only daughter. The slogan, or war-cry, of the Mercers of Aldie, was " The grit pule."

DUNBLANE,*

an ancient cathedral city, situated on the banks of the beautiful
little river Allan. The cathedral, which was founded in 1142, and
richly endowed by David I., is still tolerably entire. The east end
is fitted up, in an elegant style, as a parish church. The prebendal
stalls of richly carved dark oak, have fortunately been preserved.
Several of the Bishops of Dunblane were distinguished persons, but
the most celebrated of them was the good Bishop Leighton, afterwards Archbishop of Glasgow, who founded a library here, which
has been greatly increased by subsequent literary donations. The
mineral spring at Cromlix, in the vicinity of Dunblane, is greatly
frequented.

About two miles east by north of Dunblane is Sheriffmuir, the
scene of the battle which was fought in 1715 between the Earl of
Mar and the royal forces under the Duke of Argyle. In this engagement the left wing of each army was defeated, and the right
of each was victorious, but the fruits of the victory remained with
the Duke of Argyle.† Near the western extremity of the muir is
Kippendavie, (— Stirling, Esq.,) and four miles beyond is Greenloaning. A mile and a half farther on, the tourist reaches Ardoch
House, the seat of Major William Moray Stirling. Within his
parks is the celebrated Roman Camp of Ardoch, esteemed the
most entire in the kingdom. General Wade's military road passes
over one of its sides. The measure of the whole area is 1060 feet

* Popularly characterized as "drucken Dumblane."
† Some person having remarked to the Duke of Argyle, that the rebels would
probably claim the victory, his Grace replied,

" If it wasna weel bobbit, weel bobbit, weel bobbit,
If it wasna weel bobbit, we 'll bobb it again ; "

alluding to the well known old song, called "The Bob of Dunblane."

A number of noblemen and gentlemen, on both sides, were slain in this engagement ; among others, the Earls of Forfar and Strathmore, the chieftain of
Clanranald, &c. The body of the gallant young Earl of Strathmore was
found on the field, watched by a faithful old domestic, who, being asked the
name of the person whose body he waited upon with so much care, made this
striking reply, " He was a man yesterday." " There was mair *tint* (lost) at
Sheriffmuir," is a common proverb in Scotland. It is told, that a Highlander
lamented that, at the battle of Sheriffmuir, he had " lost his father and his
mother, and a gude buff belt, weel worth them baith." Burns has made this
battle the subject of a song, replete with humour.

by 900, and it is calculated to have contained no fewer than 20,000 men. There appear to have been three or four ditches, and as many rampart walls surrounding the camp. The prætorium, which rises above the level of the camp, but is not precisely in the centre, forms a regular square, each side being exactly twenty yards. The camp is defended on the south-east side by a deep morass, and on the west side by the banks of the water of Knaick, which rises perpendicularly to the height of about fifty feet. In the immediate vicinity there are two other encampments more slightly fortified.

The tourist may proceed from Greenloaning to Perth, by Blackford, Auchterarder, and Dalraich Bridge, passing on the road Braco Castle, Orchill, Gleneagles, Kincardine Castle, Strathallan Castle, Gask, and Dupplin Castle.

SIXTH TOUR.

THERE are two roads which lead from Stirling to Doune, the first stage on the way to Loch Katrine: one crosses the Forth by Stirling Bridge, and proceeds along the east bank of the Teith, passing, in succession, the beautiful village of Bridge of Allan, and the neat parish church o Lecropt, built in the Gothic style; the other, proceeding up the valley of the Forth, passes the House of Craigforth, (Callander, Esq.,) and, two miles from Stirling, crosses the river at the Bridge of Drip. At the distance of about four miles from Stirling, the road passes Ochtertyre, (Dundas, Esq.,) once the residence of Mr. J. Ramsay, the friend of Blacklock, of Burns, and of Scott; a mile and a half farther on, the road passes the mansion of Blair Drummond, (Home Drummond, Esq.,) embosomed in fine woods and plantations. About sixty or seventy years ago, the late Lord Kames became proprietor of this estate, and commenced that series of operations, by which what was once a bleak marsh has been turned into rich corn fields. The road now crosses the Teith, by a fine old bridge built by Robert Spittal, tailor to Queen Margaret, widow of James IV., and, about nine miles from Stirling, enters the village of

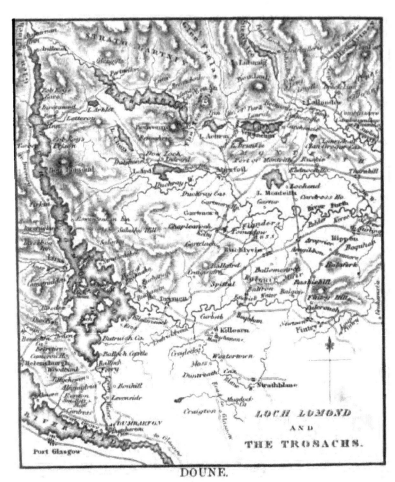

DOUNE.

Just before crossing the bridge, and on the left hand, are Deanston Works, one of the most extensive cotton factories in Scotland. The village of Doune was, in former times, celebrated for the manufacture of Highland pistols. The ruins of Doune Castle, a massive and extensive fortress, supposed to have been built about the fourteenth century, are situated on the point of a steep and narrow green bank, washed on one side by the Teith, and on the other by the Ardoch. It was anciently the seat of the Earls of Menteith, but, about the beginning of the fifteenth century, it was forfeited to the Crown, and became the favourite residence of the two successive Dukes of Albany, who governed Scotland during the captivity of James I.; Queen Margaret, and the unfortunate Queen Mary, are also said frequently to have resided in this fortress. It was held for Prince Charles during the rebellion of 745, and here he disposed his prisoners taken at Falkirk, and, among the rest, the author of the tragedy of Douglas.* Doune Castle has long been the

* " This noble ruin," says Sir Walter Scott, " holds a commanding station on the banks of the river Teith, and has been one of the largest castles in Scotland. Murdock, Duke of Albany, the founder of this stately pile, was beheaded on the Castlehill of Stirling, from which he might see the towers of Doune, the monument of his fallen greatness. In 1745-6, a garrison, on the part of the Chevalier, was put into the castle, then less ruinous than at present. It was commanded by Mr. Stewart of Balloch, as governor for Prince Charles; he was a man of property, near Callander. This castle became, at that time, the actual scene of a romantic escape made by John Home, the author of Douglas, and some other prisoners, who, having been taken at the battle of Falkirk, were confined there by the insurgents. The poet, who had, in his own mind, a large stock of that romantic and enthusiastic spirit of adventure which he has described as animating the youthful hero of his drama, devised and undertook the perilous enterprise of escaping from his prison. He inspired his companions with his sentiments, and when every attempt at open force was deemed hopeless, they resolved to twist their bed-clothes into ropes, and thus to descend. Four persons, with Home himself, reached the ground in safety. But the rope broke with the fifth, who was a tall, lusty man. The sixth was Thomas Barrow, a brave young Englishman, a particular friend of Home's. Determined to take the risk, even in such unfavourable circumstances, Barrow committed himself to the broken rope, slid down on it as far as it could assist him, and then let himself drop. His friends beneath succeeded in breaking his fall. Nevertheless, he dislocated his ankle, and had several of his ribs broken. His companions, however, were able to bear him off in safety. The Highlanders next morning sought for their prisoners with great activity. An old gentleman told the author, he remembered seeing the commander Stewart,

'Bloody with spurring, fiery red with haste,'

riding furiously through the country in quest of the fugitives."—*Note, Waverley,* vol. ii., pp. 81, 82.

property of the Earls of Moray, who derive from it their second title of Lord Doune. About a mile to the north-west, the Earl of Moray has a mansion named Doune Lodge, formerly designated Cambus--Wallace, when it was the property of the Edmonstones. At the distance of three miles from Doune, on the opposite side of the river, is Lanrick Castle, the seat of Sir Evan Murray M'Gregor, chieftain of Clan-Gregor, and three miles far-ther on is Cambusmore, (A. Buchanan, Esq.,) where Sir Walter Scott, in his juvenile days, spent some months, for several summers.* The village of

CALLANDER,

sixteen miles from Stirling, is situated at the foot of the chain of mountains which forms the Highland boundary. It is a neat and regular modern village, with a comfort-able inn. Although not within the boundary of the Highlands, " yet, from having been so long in the near

---

* He has given a striking sketch of the most interesting objects on this route, in his description of Fitz-James's ride, after the combat with Roderick Dhu :—

" They dash'd that rapid torrent through,
    And up Carhonie's hill they flew ;
    Still at the gallop prick'd the knight,
    His merry-men follow'd as they might.
    Along thy banks, swift Teith ! they ride,
    And in the race they mock thy tide ;
    Torry and Lendrick now are past,
    And Deanstown lies behind them cast ;
    They rise, the banner'd towers of Doune,
    They sink in distant woodland soon ;
    Blair-Drummond sees the hoofs strike fire,
    They sweep like breeze through Ochtertyre ;
    They mark just glance and disappear
    The lofty brow of ancient Kier ;
    They bathe their courser's sweltering sides,
    Dark Forth ! amid thy sluggish tides,
    And on the opposing shore take ground,
    With plash, with scramble, and with bound.
    Right-hand they leave thy cliffs, Craig-Forth !
    And soon the bulwark of the North,
    Grey Stirling, with her towers and town,
    Upon their fleet career look'd down."
                        Lady of the Lake, c. v., st. 18.

neighbourhood, it has caught much of the very best part
of the Highland character.   Few hills out of the Highlands—if, indeed, they be out of it—exhibit bolder
bosoms of wooded crag and pastoral enclosure, than
those which overhang the village, securing it from the
blasts of the east and the north, and receding in grand per-
spective far back in the sky."*   To the westward two
little rivers, issuing respectively from Loch Lubnaig and
Loch Venachar, unite and form the Teith.   At the east
end of the village there is a neat villa, the property of
Lady Willoughby D'Eresby.   The Falls of Bracklinn,

* Christopher North, in Blackwood's Magazine.   Vol. xx., p. 402.

about a mile to the north of the village, form one of the most attractive objects in this vicinity. They consist in a series of short falls, shelving rapids, and dark linns, formed by the Keltie Burn. Above a chasm where the brook precipitates itself from a height of at least fifty feet, there is thrown a rustic foot-bridge, of about three feet in breadth, which is scarcely to be crossed by a stranger without awe and apprehension. The magnificent mountain, Benledi, 3000 feet in height, which closes the prospect towards the west, forms the most striking feature of the scenery in this neighbourhood.*

* At Callander a road, much frequented by tourists, leads, in a northerly direction, to Loch-Earn-head, (fourteen miles,) by the beautiful Pass of Leny, Loch Lubnaig, and Balquidder. The Pass of Leny is thus described, in the opening scene of the Legend of Montrose :—" Their course had been, for some time, along the banks of a lake, whose deep waters reflected the crimson beams of the western sun. The broken path, which they pursued with some difficulty, was, in some places, shaded by ancient birches and oak-trees, and, in others, overhung by fragments of huge rock. Elsewhere, the hill, which formed the northern side of this beautiful sheet of water, arose in steep, but less precipitous acclivity, and was arrayed in heath of the darkest purple." The scenery in this district has been celebrated by Sir Walter Scott, in the Lady of the Lake. It was up the Pass of Leny that the cross of fire was carried by young Angus of Duncraggan.

> " Benledi saw the Cross of Fire ;
> It glanced like lightning up Strath-Ire ;
> O'er hill and dale the summons flew,
> Nor rest, nor pause young Angus knew ;
> The tear that gather'd in his eye
> He left the mountain breeze to dry ;
> Until, where Teith's young waters roll,
> Betwixt him and a wooded knoll,
> That graced the sable strath with green,
> The chapel of St. Bride was seen."

Here the cross is delivered to Norman of Armandave, who starts off with it along the shores of Loch Lubnaig, and away towards the distant district of Balquidder. The chapel of St. Bride stood on a small romantic knoll, between the opening of the Pass of Leny and Loch Lubnaig, and Strath-Ire is situated at the south end, and along the eastern side of Loch Lubnaig ; Armandave is on the west side of the loch. By the side of Lubnaig is Ardhullary, a house built for a Highland retreat by Bruce the Abyssinian traveller, in which it is said he wrote the account of his travels. In the churchyard of Balquidder Rob Roy was interred, beneath a stone, marked only with a fir-tree crossed by a sword, supporting a crown. "The braes of Balquither" have been celebrated in song.

N

There are two roads which lead from Callander to the Trosachs, the north and south roads; of these, the former is the more picturesque. Passing the valley of Bo-chastle, the House of Leny, (Hamilton Buchannan, Esq.) and the waterfalls of Carchonzie, the tourist reaches " Coilantogle Ford," about two and a half miles from Callander. This is the scene of the combat between Fitz-James and Roderick Dhu. Loch Venachar is four miles long, Loch Achray a mile and a half, the space between the lochs about half a mile, and from the western extre-mity of the latter to Loch Katrine, one mile, making the whole distance between Callander and Loch Katrine from nine to ten miles. Lanrick Mead, the mustering-place of Clan Alpin, lies on the north side of Loch Venachar. Soon after the tourist passes the hamlet of Duncraggan, the huts of which

> " Peep like moss-grown rocks half seen,
> Half hidden in the copse so green."

The Bridge of Turk* crosses the water, which, de-scending from Glenfinlas, joins the Teith between Lochs Venachar and Achray; and a mile and a half further on, is the inn of Ardcheanochrochan, beautifully situa-ted on the side of Loch Achray.† The tourist is now in

* Here a road strikes off, on the right, to Glenfinlas, once a royal hunting forest; it is now the property of the Earl of Moray, and is inhabited by a primi-tive race of small farmers, all Stewarts. In times of yore, it was chiefly inha-bited by the Macgregors. Glenfinlas is the scene of Sir Walter Scott's ballad, entitled " Glenfinlas ; or, Lord Ronald's Coronach."

† The crowds of tourists visiting the Trosachs, during the summer months, make it a matter of great uncertainty whether accommodation can be obtained at the inn. The usual effects of monopoly will also be experienced, and the civilities are nicely proportioned to the means the tourist is supposed to possess for compensating them. The boats upon Loch Katrine belong to the inn, and, after paying the regular fare, (2s. 6d.,) the boatmen proceed to extort gratuities from the passengers, which they state (with what truth we know not) to be the only remuneration they receive for their services. The charge of these High-land gillies, for conveying luggage from the inn to the loch, is also most extra-

the Trosachs, (etymologically, bristled territory,) the road which traverses them is rather more than a mile in length. The opening into the pass is flanked on the left by Benvenue, 2800 feet high, and on the right by Benan.

> " High on the south, huge Benvenue
> Down on the lake in masses threw
> Crags, knolls, and mounds confusedly hurl'd,
> The fragments of an earlier world;
> A wildering forest, feather'd o'er
> His ruin'd sides and summit hoar;
> While on the north, through middle air,
> Benan heaved high his forehead bare."[*]

In the defile of Beal-an-Duine, (where Fitz-James lost his " gallant grey,") we are in the heart of the great gorge.[†] Then appears a narrow inlet, and a moment

vagant. The distance is about a mile, and three shillings have been occasionally extorted for carrying a small parcel this trifling distance. These practices, it must be admitted, are calculated, in a high degree, to uphold the ancient reputation of Loch Katrine, or, with more correctness of etymology, Loch Kateran, which, being interpreted, signifieth *The Loch of the Robbers.*

[*] Lady of the Lake.

[†] " A skirmish actually took place at a pass thus called, in the Trosachs, and closed with the remarkable incident mentioned in the ' Lady of the Lake.' It was greatly posterior in date to the reign of James V.

" In this roughly wooded island,[*] the country people secreted their wives and children, and their most valuable effects, from the rapacity of Cromwell's soldiers, during their inroad into this country in the time of the Republic. These invaders, not venturing to ascend by the ladders, along the side of the lake, took a more circuitous road, through the heart of the Trosachs, the most frequented path at that time, which penetrated the wilderness about half way between Binean and the lake, by a tract called Yea-chailleach, or the Old Wife's Bog.

" In one of the defiles of this by-road, the men of the country at that time hung upon the rear of the invading enemy, and shot one of Cromwell's men, whose grave marks the scene of action, and gives name to that pass.[†] In revenge of this insult, the soldiers resolved to plunder the island, to violate the women, and put the children to death. With this brutal intention, one of the party, more expert than the rest, swam towards the island, to fetch the boat to his comrades, which had carried the women to their asylum, and lay moored

[*] That at the eastern extremity of Loch Katrine, called " Ellen's Isle."
[†] Beallach-an-duine.

afterwards, Loch Katrine itself bursts upon our view, the Alps of Arroquhar towering in the distance. Loch Katrine is of a serpentine form, encircled by lofty moun-

in one of the creeks. His companions stood on the shore of the mainland, in full view of all that was to pass, waiting anxiously for his return with the boat. But, just as the swimmer had got to the nearest point of the island, and was laying hold of a black rock to get on shore, a heroine, who stood on the very point where he meant to land, hastily snatching a dagger from below her apron, with one stroke severed his head from the body. His party seeing this disaster, and relinquishing all future hope of revenge or conquest, made the best of their way out of their perilous situation. This amazon's great-grandson lives at Bridge of Turk, who, besides others, attests the anecdote."—*Sketch of the Scenery near Callander*. Stirling, 1806, p. 90. I have only to add to this account, that the heroine's name was Helen Stuart.—*Notes to the Lady of the Lake*, p. 53.

The following striking description of the Trosachs is given by Sir Walter Scott, in the Lady of the Lake :—

> " The western waves of ebbing day
> Roll'd o'er the glen their level way ;
> Each purple peak, each flinty spire,
> Was bathed in floods of living fire.
> But not a setting beam could glow
> Within the dark ravines below,
> Where twined the path, in shadow hid,
> Round many a rocky pyramid,
> Shooting abruptly from the dell
> Its thunder-splinter'd pinnacle ;
> Round many an insulated mass,
> The native bulwarks of the pass,
> Huge as the tower which builders vain
> Presumptuous piled on Shinar's plain.
> The rocky summits, split and rent,
> Form'd turret, dome, or battlement,
> Or seem'd fantastically set
> With cupola or minaret,
> Wild crests as pagod ever deck'd,
> Or mosque of Eastern architect.
> Nor were these earth-born castles bare,
> Nor lack'd they many a banner fair ;
> For, from their shiver'd brows display'd,
> Far o'er the unfathomable glade,
> All twinkling with the dew-drops sheen,
> The briar-rose fell in streamers green,
> And creeping shrubs, of thousand dyes,
> Waved in the west wind's summer sighs.

> " Boon nature scatter'd free and wild,
> Each plant or flower, the mountain's child.
> Here eglantine embalm'd the air,
> Hawthorn and hazel mingled there ;

LAKE GEORGE.

tains, and is ten miles in length, attaining, in some places, a breadth of two miles. The scenery which fringes it at its eastern extremity is precisely of the same wild character as the Trosachs. Near the eastern shore there is an island exactly corresponding with the description of the residence of Douglas, in the Lady of the Lake. A cottage was erected upon it by Lady Willoughby D'Eresby, which, a few years ago, was accidentally burnt down. Coir-nan-Uriskin, " the Den of the Goblin," is marked by a deep vertical gash in the face of one of the extensive ramifications of Benvenue, overhanging the lake. It is surrounded with stupendous rocks, and overshaded by birch trees, mingled with oaks, the spontaneous production of the mountain, even where its cliffs appear denuded of soil. Above the eastern hollow, is the pass of Beal-ach-nam-Bo, a magnificent glade overhung with birch trees. By this pass, in the days of blackmail and reivers, cattle were driven across the shoulder of the hill.

The primrose pale, and violet flower,
Found in each cliff a narrow bower;
Foxglove and nightshade, side by side,
Emblems of punishment and pride,
Group'd their dark hues with every stain
The weather-beaten crags retain.
With boughs that quaked at every breath,
Grey birch and aspen wept beneath;
Aloft, the ash and warrior oak
Cast anchor in the rifted rock;
And, higher yet, the pine-tree hung
His shatter'd trunk, and frequent flung,
Where seem'd the cliffs to meet on high,
His boughs athwart the narrow'd sky.
Highest of all, where white peaks glanced,
Where glist'ning streamers waved and danced,
The wanderer's eye could barely view
The summer heaven's delicious blue;
So wondrous wild, the whole might seem
The scenery of a fairy dream."

The district of Menteith, only a few miles to the south of the Trosachs, comprehends a range of scenery little inferior in beauty. It contains the Lake of Menteith, Aberfoyle, Loch Ard, and Loch Chon, and is approached from Stirling by Ochtertyre, Kincardine, and Ruskie. The lake of Menteith is a beautiful circular sheet of water, about five miles in circumference, and adorned with ancient woods. There are two small islands in the centre, called Inchmachome, or the Isle of Rest,* and Talla, or the Earl's Isle. The former, which is the larger and more easterly island, consists of about five acres, and contains the ruins of a Priory, where Queen Mary resided during the invasion of the English in 1547, before she was removed to France. This priory was founded, about the year 1238, by Walter Cumming, second son of William Cumming, Earl of Buchan. He obtained, by grant from the Crown, the extensive district of Badenoch, and, by marriage with the Countess of Menteith, he became Earl of Menteith. After his death, Walter Stewart, brother of Alexander, High-Steward of Scotland, obtained a grant of the title and estates of Menteith, in right of his wife, the younger sister of the Countess of Menteith. His second son was Sir John of Ruskie, properly called Stewart, but usually Menteith, the betrayer of the patriot Wallace. In the choir of the church is an ancient tombstone, supposed to be that of Walter Stewart. A writ granted by Robert Bruce, at this place, in April 1310, is recorded in the Chartulary of Arbroath. The buildings connected with this monastery are supposed to have been destroyed at the Reformation. The island of Inchmachome is now the property of his Grace the Duke of Montrose. The principal proprietors around the lake are his Grace, General Graham Stirling, and Mr. Erskine of Cardross. The smaller island contains the remains of the Castle of the Grahams, Earls of Menteith, a race long extinct.†

* " The world's gay scenes thou must resign,
    Stranger, when youth has past;
  Oh! were such bless'd asylum thine,
    As this—*The Isle of Rest!*"

† " The Earls of Monteith, you must know, had a castle, situated upon an island in the lake, or loch, as it is called, of the same name. But though this residence, which occupied almost the whole of the islet, upon which its ruins still exist, was a strong and safe place of abode, and adapted accordingly to such perilous times, it had this inconvenience, that the stables and other domestic offices were constructed on the banks of the lake, and were, therefore, in some sort defenceless.

They had their garden on the isle of the Priory, and their pleasure-grounds on the neighbouring shore, which is still beautifully adorned with oak, Spanish chestnut, and plane trees of ancient growth. Some of the chestnuts are seventeen feet in circumference at six feet above the ground, and must be above three centuries old. Gartmore House, (Graham, Esq.) lies to the west, and Rednock House, the east of General Graham Stirling, to the east of the lake. Callander is distant seven miles. Proceeding westward, at the distance of four miles, the traveller reaches Aberfoyle, the scene of so many of the incidents in the novel of Rob Roy.* At the Clachan of Aberfoyle is the junction of the Duchray and Forth, here called Avondhu, or the Black River.. Under the rocky precipice on the north, lies the pass of Aberfoyle, the scene of the defeat of a party

"It happened upon a time that there was to be a great entertainment in the castle, and a number of the Grahams were assembled. The occasion, it is said, was a marriage in the family. To prepare for this feast, much provision was got ready, and, in particular, a great deal of poultry had been collected. While the feast was preparing, an unhappy chance brought Donald of the Hammer to the side of the lake, returning at the head of a band of hungry followers, whom he was conducting homewards to the West Highlands, after some of his usual excursions into Stirlingshire. Seeing so much good victuals ready, and being possessed of an excellent appetite, the Western Highlanders neither asked questions, nor waited for an invitation, but devoured all the provisions that had been prepared for the Grahams, and then went on their way rejoicing, through the difficult and dangerous path which leads from the banks of the Loch of Monteith, through the mountains, to the side of Loch Katrine.

"The Grahams were filled with the highest indignation. The company who were assembled at the castle of Monteith, headed by the earl himself, hastily took to their boats, and, disembarking on the northern side of the lake, pursued with all speed the marauders and their leader. They came up with Donald's party in the gorge of a pass, near a rock, called Craig-Vad, or the Wolf's Cliff. The battle then began, and was continued with much fury till night. The Earl of Monteith, and many of his noble kinsmen, fell, while Donald, favoured by darkness, escaped with a single attendant. The Grahams obtained, from the cause of the quarrel, the nickname of Gramoch-an-Garrigh, or Grahams of the Hens."—*Tales of a Grandfather*, vol. ii., p. 317-19.

* "To the left lay the valley, down which the Forth wandered on its easterly course, surrounding the beautiful detached hill, with all its garland of woods. On the right, amid a profusion of thickets, knolls, and crags, lay the bed of a broad mountain lake, lightly curled into tiny waves by the breath of the morning breeze, each glittering in its course under the influence of the sunbeams. High hills, rocks, and banks, waving with natural forests of birch and oak, formed the borders of this enchanting sheet of water; and, as their leaves rustled to the wind and twinkled in the sun, gave to the depth of solitude a sort of life and vivacity."—*Rob Roy*, vol. ii., p. 202.

of Cromwell's troops, by Graham of Duchray.* Loch Ard is a
small lake, or rather two lakes connected by a stream of 200 yards
in length, beautifully situated in the middle of a fertile valley.
A delightful view of the upper loch.is obtained from a rising ground
near its lower extremity. Looking westward, Ben Lomond is seen
in the back-ground. On the right is the lofty mountain of Benogh-
rie. In the fore-ground is Loch Ard itself, three miles in length,
and one and an eighth in breadth. The traveller passes along the
verge of the lake, under a ledge of rock from thirty to fifty feet high.
If a person standing immediately under this rock, towards its western extremity, pronounces with a firm voice a line of ten syllables,
it is returned first from the opposite side of the lake, and then with
equal distinctness from the wood on the east. But the day must
be perfectly calm, and the lake as smooth as glass. In the upper
loch is a rocky islet, on which are the mouldering ruins of a stronghold of Murdoch, Duke of Albany. Near the head of the lake, on
the northern side, behind the House of Ledeard, is the romantic
waterfall, thus described in Waverley :†—" It was not so remarkable either for great height or quantity of water, as for the beautiful
accompaniments which made the spot interesting. After a broken
cataract of about twenty feet, the stream was received in a large
natural basin filled to the brim with water, which, where the bubbles
of the fall subsided, was so exquisitely clear, that although it was of
great depth, the eye could discern each pebble at the bottom. Eddy-
ing round this reservoir, the brook found its way as if over a broken
part of the ledge, and formed a second fall, which seemed to seek
the very abyss ; then, wheeling out beneath from among the smooth

* " Our route, though leading towards the lake, had hitherto been so much
shaded by wood, that we only from time to time obtained a glimpse of that
beautiful sheet of water. But the road now suddenly emerged from the forest
ground, and, winding close by the margin of the loch, afforded us a full view of
its spacious mirror, which now, the breeze having totally subsided, reflected in
still magnificence the high, dark, heathy mountains, huge grey rocks, and
shaggy banks, by which it is encircled. The hills now sunk on its margin so
closely, and were so broken and precipitous, as to afford no passage except just
upon the narrow line of the track which we occupied, and which was overhung with rocks, from which we might have been destroyed merely by rolling
down stones, without much possibility of offering resistance."—Rob Roy, vol. ii.,
p. 208. An excellent road has now been formed, along the northern margin of
the lake.

† Vol. i., p. 234.

dark rocks, which it had polished for ages, it wandered murmuring down the glen, forming the stream up which Waverley had just ascended." A footpath strikes off towards Ben Lomond, by which the tourist may cross the hill and reach Rowardennan, on the banks of Loch Lomond ; or he may proceed from Aberfoyle Inn, by Gartmore and Drymen, to Dumbarton, a distance of twenty-two miles. Loch Chon is a secluded sheet of water, three miles in length. The scenery around these lakes is eminently beautiful ; but it is customary for travellers to visit only the former of the two, and then to cross over the hill from Aberfoyle to the Trosachs, a distance of only five miles.

During the summer and autumn, a boat sails every forenoon from the east to the west end of Loch Katrine, pausing at all the places in which strangers are supposed to take an interest.*

" In sailing along you discover many arms of the lake—here a bold headland, where black rocks dip in unfathomable water—there the white sand in the bottom of a bay, bleached for ages by the waves. In walking on the north side, the road is sometimes cut through the face of the solid rock, which rises upwards of 200 feet perpendicular above the lake, which, before the rock was cut, had to be mounted by a kind of natural ladder. Every rock has its echo, every grove is vocal with the

* The same boat returns in the afternoon, with those tourists who have crossed from Loch Lomond. Between the time when the passengers arrive, and the sailing of the boat from the western extremity of the loch, there is often a very long delay, and, as the shores of the loch at this end are flat and uninteresting, the patience of the tourist is very severely tried. A row of mean and dirty cottages affords the only shelter to be obtained, and the manners of the inhabitants are not more inviting than the aspect of their dwellings. The tide of strangers that annually sweeps past them, has worn off the primitive simplicity which might be expected to distinguish the inhabitants of such a spot ; and, while the untutored hospitality of rustic life has thus been obliterated, there have not been substituted any of those artificial courtesies attendant on a more refined state of society.

harmony of birds, or by the airs of women and children gathering nuts in their season.   Down the side of the opposite mountain, after a shower of rain, flow an hundred white streams, which rush with incredible noise and velocity into the lake.   On one side, the water-eagle sits in majesty, undisturbed on his well-known rock, in sight of his nest on the top of Benvenue, the heron stalks among the reeds in search of his prey, and the sportive ducks gambol in the waters or dive below.   On the other, the wild goats climb where they have scarce room for the soles of their feet, and the wild birds, perched on exalted trees and pinnacles, look down with composed indifference on man.   The scene is closed by a west view of the lake, which is ten miles long, having its sides lined with alternate clumps of wood and ample fields, and the smoke rising in spiral columns through the air from farm-houses, which are concealed by intervening woods, and the prospect is bounded by the towering Alps of Arrochar." *

Those conversant with the writings of Sir Walter Scott, will remember the spirited song sung by the retainers of Roderick Dhu, while rowing down Loch Katrine :—

" Hail to the Chief, who in triumph advances !
    Honour'd and bless'd be the ever-green Pine !
Long may the Tree, in his banner that glances,
    Flourish, the shelter and grace of our line !
            Heaven send it happy dew,
            Earth lend it sap anew,
    Gaily to bourgeon, and broadly to grow,
            While every Highland glen
            Sends our shout back agen,
' Roderigh Vich Alpine dhu, ho ! ieroe ! '

* Statistical Account of Scotland.

" Ours is no sapling, chance-sown by the fountain,
   Blooming at Beltane, in winter to fade ;
When the whirlwind has stripp'd every leaf on the mountain,
   The more shall Clan-Alpine exult in her shade.
      Moor'd in the rifted rock,
      Proof to the tempest's shock,
   Firmer he roots him the ruder it blow ;
      Menteith and Breadalbane, then,
      Echo his praise agen,
  ' Roderigh Vich Alpine dhu, ho ! ieroe ! '

" Proudly our pibroch has thrill'd in Glen Fruin,
   And Bannochar's groans to our slogan replied :
Glen Luss and Ross-dhu, they are smoking in ruin,
   And the best of Loch-Lomond lie dead on her side.
      Widow and Saxon maid,
      Long shall lament our raid,
   Think of Clan-Alpine with fear and with woe ;
      Lennox and Leven-glen
      Shake when they hear agen,
  ' Roderigh Vich Alpine dhu, ho ! ieroe ! '

" Row, vassals, row, for the pride of the Highlands,
   Stretch to your oars, for the ever-green Pine !
O ! that the rose-bud that graces yon islands
   Were wreathed in a garland around him to twine !
      O that some seedling gem,
      Worthy such noble stem,
   Honour'd and bless'd in their shadow might grow !
      Loud should Clan-Alpine then
      Ring from the deepmost glen,
  ' Roderigh Vich Alpine dhu, ho ! ieroe ! ' "

From the west end of the lake, a wild valley, traversed
by a pathway about five miles long, affords a communication with Loch Lomond, upon which it opens at Inversnaid
Mill, where the steam-boat, which every day plies along
Loch Lomond, takes in the Loch Katrine tourists.* The

* A flock of shaggy Highland ponies is in attendance, to convey travellers
across this moorland region, and a pony cart to carry their luggage. The ex-

small lake, Arklet, lies in the hollow near this pathway.
In one of the smoky huts in the valley between Loch
Katrine and Loch Lomond may be seen a long Spanish
musket, once the property of Rob Roy, whose original
residence was in this lone vale.   Beside the way are the
ruins of Inversnaid Fort, erected in 1713 to check the
MacGregors.   While the tourist is in the midst of the
country of the MacGregors, he may be gratified by the
perusal of Sir Walter Scott's splendid lyric, " The Gathering of Clan-Gregor :"

> " The moon 's on the lake, and the mist 's on the brae,
> And the clan has a name that is nameless by day ;
> Then gather, gather, gather, Gregalich !
>
> Our signal for fight, that from monarchs we drew,
> Must be heard but by night in our vengeful haloo !
> Then haloo, Gregalich ! haloo, Gregalich !

tortion and incivility to which tourists are subjected, at this stage of their progress, are a reproach to Scotland. A recent sufferer thus addresses the editor
of a Glasgow paper on the subject :—

" On being landed at the hill of Inversnaid, we as usual took our departure for Loch
Katrine, mounted on the Highland ponies which awaited us. I shall say nothing of the
charge, (four shillings each,) which certainly appeared rather high for a ride of five miles on
the back of such cattle; but I feel bound to mention the conduct of the boatmen, and
others, who formed an escort to our party. They came provided with a small pony cart,
which carries the luggage across, and here their extortion began. On reaching the margin
of Loch Katrine, one gentleman, who had not the precaution to make a bargain with them,
was charged eight shillings for the carriage of a few articles; another party five shillings;
and so on in proportion. The sun was fast sinking, and, under the pretence of refreshing
themselves, the whole party sat smoking and drinking for above an hour, deaf to all the
entreaties which were made to them, and at length, with rudeness and extreme reluctance,
at half-past five o'clock set out; so that by the time we reached the Trosachs, it was quite
dark, and we reached the crowded inn, only to be obliged to take horses and hurry away ten
miles to Callander. The consequence of this was, that we not only lost the view of the
lovely scenery through which we passed, but the comfort, and even the health of our party,
were endangered, by night travelling and its accompaniments."

Were this a solitary instance, we should not have quoted it here; but having
personally experienced the annoyance, and many of our friends having suffered
in the same way, we have no hesitation in cautioning travellers to make an ex-
press bargain, before they avail themselves of either ponies or cart. For a pony,
we regard 2s. 6d. a moderate, and 3s. 6d. a liberal hire.

Glen Orchy's proud mountains, Coalchuirn and her towers,
Glenstrae and Glenlyon no longer are ours;
   We 're landless, landless, landless, Gregalich !

But, doom'd and devoted by vassal and lord,
Macgregor has still both his heart and his sword !
   Then courage, courage, courage, Gregalich !

If they rob us of name, and pursue us with beagles,
Give their roofs to the flame, and their flesh to the eagles !
   Then vengeance, vengeance, vengeance, Gregalich !

While there 's leaves on the forest, or foam on the river,
Macgregor, despite them, shall flourish for ever !
   Come then, Gregalich ! come then, Gregalich !

Through the depths of Loch Katrine the steed shall career,
O'er the peak of Ben Lomond the galley shall steer ;
And the rocks of Craig-Royston like icicles melt,
Ere our wrongs be forgot, or our vengeance unfelt !
   Then gather, gather, gather, Gregalich ! "

It is said that General Wolfe once resided in Inversnaid
Fort. At Inversnaid Mill there is a little rivulet and a
cataract, the scene of Wordsworth's beautiful poem to
the " Highland Girl."

Loch Lomond,* (" the lake full of islands,") is unquestionably the pride of Scottish lakes. " This noble
lake, boasting innumerable beautiful islands of every
varying form and outline which fancy can frame,—its
northern extremity narrowing until it is lost among
dusky and retreating mountains, while, gradually widening as it extends to the southward, it spreads its base
around the indentures and promontories of a fair and
fertile land, affords one of the most surprising, beautiful,

---

* The tourist may proceed from the head of Loch Lomond, by Glenfalloch,
Crianlaroch, Tyndrum, and Glencoe, to Fort-William, (see Itinerary,) or by
Arroquhar, Glencroe, and Cairndow, to Inverary.

and sublime spectacles in nature." *   Its upper extremity is not unworthy of comparison with the finest
views on Loch Awe, while there are points in the same
division not dissimilar to the more striking parts of the
Trosachs, and fully equal to them in wild grandeur. Its
length is about twenty-three miles, its breadth, where
greatest, at the southern extremity, is five miles, from
which it gradually grows narrower, till it terminates in a
narrow prolonged stripe of water. The depth varies considerably; south of Luss it is rarely more than twenty
fathoms, in the northern part it ranges from sixty to
100, and in the places where deepest, never freezes.
The total superficies of the lake is about 20,000 acres.
About two-thirds of the loch, and most of the islands,
are in the county of Dumbarton, the rest, with the right
bank, are in the county of Stirling. After taking on
board the tourists from Loch Katrine, the steam-boat
visits the upper part of the lake, which is there narrowed
and hemmed in by the neighbouring mountains. At the
northern extremity of the lake is a wide elevated valley
called Glenfalloch. Sailing southwards, three miles from
the upper end, is a small wooded island called Eilan
Vhou, and two miles farther, another called Inveruglas,
on each of which are the ruins of a stronghold of the
family of Macfarlane. The slogan of this clan was
" Loch Sloy," a small lake between Loch Long and Loch
Lomond. At the distance of other three miles, Tarbet
Inn is passed on the right, where there is a ferry by
which Ben Lomond may be approached. Farther south,
a projecting headland is seen on the right, where is the
ferry of Inveruglas to Rowardennan Inn, the usual starting point for those who desire to ascend to the top of

* Rob Roy, vol. ii., p. 317.

Ben Lomond. This mountain is 3210 feet above the level of the lake, which is thirty-two feet above the level of the sea. The distance from the inn to the top of the mountain is six miles of continued ascent. The view from the summit is varied and most extensive, comprehending the counties of Lanark, Renfrew, and Ayr, the Firth of Clyde, and the islands of Arran and Bute, to the south, and the counties of Stirling and the Lothians, with the windings of the Forth, and the Castles of Stirling and Edinburgh, to the east. About three and a half miles from Inveruglas, is Luss, a delightful little village, situated on a promontory which juts into the lake. One of the finest points for enjoying the scenery of Loch Lomond and the environs of Luss, is Stonehill, to the north of the village. Near Luss is Rossdow, the splendid residence of Sir James Colquhoun, Bart. In the vicinity of the mansion is a tower of the ancient castle of the family of Luss, the last heiress of which married Colquhoun of Colquhoun. A short way farther on are the ruins of the Castle of Banachra, overhanging the entrance to Glen Fruin.* This castle was anciently the residence of the Colquhouns, and here the chief of that clan was basely murdered, in 1640, by one of the Macfarlanes. Near it is the lofty hill of Dunfion, or the hill of Fingal, according to tradition one of the hunting-

* It was in Glen Fruin, or the Glen of Sorrow, that the celebrated battle took place between the Macgregors and Colquhouns, fraught with such fatal consequences to both parties. There had been a long and deadly feud between the Macgregors and the Laird of Luss, head of the family of Colquhoun. At length the parties met in the vale of Glenfruin. The battle was obstinately contested, but in the end the Macgregors came off victorious, slaying two hundred of the Colquhouns and making many prisoners. It is said that, after the battle, the Macgregors murdered about eighty youths, who had been led by curiosity to view the fight. A partial representation of these transactions having been made to James VI., letters of fire and sword were issued against the Clan-Gregor. Their lands were confiscated, their very name proscribed, and, being driven to such extremity, they became notorious for acts of daring reprisal. Their legal rights were restored to them in 1755.

seats of that hero. From Luss southward, the breadth
of the lake expands rapidly, and the surface of the water
is studded with islands of many sizes, and various aspects.
The islands of Loch Lomond are about thirty in number,
and ten of these are of considerable size.

> " All the fairy crowds
> Of islands, which together lie
> As quietly as the spots of sky
> Among the evening clouds."

After leaving Luss, the boat passes, in succession, Inch-
Cruin, or the Round Island, (formerly a retreat for lunatics,) Inch Moan, or the Peat Island, and Inch Fad,
and, on the right, Inch Tavanagh, (to the south of
which the ruins of Galbraith Castle start up from the
water,) Inch Lonaig, (used as a deer-park by the family of
Luss,) Inch Carachan, Buck Inch, and Inch Cardach. The
steamer now skirts Inch Cailliach, the Island of Women,
so called from its having been the site of a nunnery. Inch
Cailliach formerly gave name to the parish of Buchannan.
The church belonging to the nunnery was long used as
the place of worship for the parish of Buchannan, but
scarcely any vestiges of it now remain ; the burial ground,
which contains the family places of sepulture of several
neighbouring clans, still continues to be used ; the monuments of the Lairds of Macgregor, and of other families
claiming a descent from the old Scottish King Alpine
are most remarkable.

> " The shafts and limbs were rods of yew,
> Whose parents, in Inch Cailliach, wave
> Their shadows o'er Clan-Alpine's grave,
> And, answering Lomond's breezes deep,
> Soothe many a chieftain's endless sleep."
> *Lady of the Lake*, c. iii., *and notes.*

At the north-east corner of Inch Cailliach, passengers are

often landed at Bealach-nam-bo, a celebrated Highland pass.* Here some tourists choose to land, to pursue their journey through the pass, and along the banks of the loch to Rowardennan. The steam-boat next approaches the little island of Clar Inch, from which the Buchannans took their slogan or war-cry. The last island is a long narrow one, named Inch Murrin, the largest island in Loch Lomond. It is finely clothed with wood, and is employed as a deer-park by the Duke of Montrose. At its southern extremity there is an old ruined fortalice, called Lennox Castle, formerly a residence of the Earls of Lennox. Here Isabel Duchess of Albany, daughter of Duncan Earl of Lennox, resided after the death of her husband, Murdoch Duke of Albany, and of her two sons, and her father, who were executed after the restoration of James I., in 1424. See ante, p. 206. On the east side of the lake are the ruins of Butruich Castle, farther south is Balloch Castle, (Buchannan, Esq.) and near it, on the margin of the lake, stood the ancient castle of Balloch, a stronghold of the once powerful family of Lennox; its site and moat are still visible. The steam-boat now returns to Balloch, where a coach is waiting to convey the passengers to Dumbarton, and from thence a steam-boat lands them in Glasgow the same evening.

* See Lady of the Lake, canto iii., st. 27.

GLASGOW.

GLASGOW, the commercial metropolis of Scotland, and
the third city in the United Kingdom in wealth, population, and manufacturing and commercial importance, is
situate in Lanarkshire, in the lower part of the basin of
the Clyde; about twenty miles from the Atlantic Ocean,
and nearly double that distance from the German Sea.
The fine range of the Campsie and Kilpatrick hills,
forms a screen around it, from north-east to north-west,
at the distance of eight to ten miles, and the uplands of
Lanarkshire and Renfrewshire swell beautifully up on
the east, south, and south-west. The climate is tem-
erate, but, from its vicinity to the sea, and the high,
grounds in the neighbourhood, it is much subject to hu-
midity. St. Mungo, or, as he has also been styled, St.
Kentigern, is the reputed founder of the city. Somewhere about the year 560, he is supposed to have founded
the bishoprick of Glasgow, where the older and upper
part of the town still remains. In those rude times, the
vicinity of churches and churchmen was eagerly desired
from the comparative security they afforded; and thus,
the nascent elements of the future city, under the pastoral protection of the good saint and his pious successors

had leisure afforded them to extend and mature their natural capacities for improvement. The annals of Glasgow, from the period above mentioned to the early part of the twelfth century, are involved in the obscurity which overshadows nearly the whole contemporary history of those rude ages, a fact we are disposed to acquiesce in rather cheerfully, as, where little is known, little probably exists that it would be useful to know. The first fact of any importance which emerges from the clouds of its earlier history, is the erection of its noble Cathedral, which, for so many centuries, has witnessed the growing prosperity and enlargement of the city, forming a fine link between the past and the present, and throwing the shadow of its venerable magnificence upon scenes memorable in Scottish history, but upon which modern civilization has impressed an entirely new character. This fine old Minster* was erected by John Achaius,

* This venerable building contained formerly three churches, one of which, the Old Barony, was situated in a vault,† but now there is only one, a new church having recently been erected, in a different part of the city, in place of the second, the space occupied by which has been thrown into the choir, or central part of the fabric. Having fallen, of late years, much into decay, the Government, the custodiers of the cathedral, have agreed to repair and renew certain parts of the building; and plans for its renovation having been prepared by an eminent architect, the Corporation of Glasgow has granted a thousand pounds towards the object; other public bodies are expected also to contribute, and a private subscription is in flourishing progress, whilst we write, for the same landable purpose. The revenues of the see of Glasgow were at one time very considerable, as, besides the royalty and baronies of Glasgow, eighteen baronies of land, in various parts of the kingdom, belonged to it, besides a large estate in Cumberland, denominated the spiritual dukedom. Part of these revenues have fallen into the University of Glasgow, and part to the crown.

† " Conceive, an extensive range of low-browed, dark, and twilight vaults, such as are used for sepulchres in other countries, and had long been dedicated to the same purpose in this, a portion of which was seated with pews, and used as a church. The part of the vaults thus occupied, though capable of containing a congregation of many hundreds, bore a small proportion to the darker and more extensive caverns which yawned around what may be termed the inhabited space. In those waste regions of oblivion, dusky banners and tattered escutcheons indicated the graves of those who were once, doubtless, 'princes in Israel.' Inscriptions, which could only be read by the painful antiquary, in language as obsolete as the act of devotional charity which they implored, invited the passengers to pray for the souls of those whose bodies rested beneath."—*Rob Roy*, vol. ii., p. 267.

Bishop of Glasgow, in 1133, or, according to M'Ure, in
1136, in the reign of David the First, whose pious lar-
gesses to the clergy obtained for him the name and
honours of a saint, but drew from one of his impoverished
successors the splenetic remark, that " he had been a sair
saunct for the crown."

About forty years after the building of the Cathedral,
William the Lion granted a charter to the bishop, to hold
" a weekly mercat" in Glasgow, and a few weeks after,
another was obtained for an annual fair.   In these con-
cessions of a despotic sovereign, we behold the rude and
early germs of the future wealth and commercial greatness of Glasgow.   The same indulgent sovereign completed the emancipation of the city, by erecting it into
a burgh of regality, and thus placing its rights of independent traffic upon a broad and liberal basis.   The new
burgh was, however, unfortunately situated betwixt the
more ancient royal burghs of Rutherglen and Renfrew,
who beheld, with a jealous eye, its growing prosperity ;
and their rival exactions, and prescriptive immunities, for
a time impeded the progress of the infant community,
until the city obtained a charter of relief and independence, in 1242, from Alexander the Second.*

Some of the details of the early history of Glasgow,
after it had fairly started on its career as an independent
community, are not a little curious and instructive, from
their graphic simplicity and statistical interest, but there
is little to interest the general reader, till we turn the

---

* It is not a little curious to contemplate the "revenges which the restless
whirligig of time" is sure to bring about. Whilst Glasgow has shot up into the
third city of the British empire, Rutherglen and Renfrew, whose ancient importance is only to be traced in a few pages of Scottish history, have dwindled
into absolute insignificance under the overshadowing influence of their ancient
rival, whose commercial relations are now commensurate with the limits of
civilization and commerce.

corner of the seventeenth century. It was ravished by the plague no less than four times during the fourteenth, and five times during the seventeenth century. The loathsome disease of leprosy prevailed also for a long time, and, as late as 1589, some lepers were confined in a house in the suburbs of Gorbals. It is no wonder, indeed; for, whatever might be the virtues of the citizens of Glasgow in these primitive times, cleanliness certainly was not one of them, as appears from sundry curious enough enactments by the city authorities. Previous to the seventeenth century, the principal part of the houses were built of wood, and the inhabitants lived chiefly in narrow lanes or closes, leading from the main streets. The population, in 1651, was about 14,000; in 1831, when the last census was taken, it amounted to 202,426; and it was recently estimated by Dr. Cleland, an able statistical writer, to be 271,656.

Previous to 1775, the mercantile capital and enterprise of Glasgow were almost wholly employed in the tobacco trade. Large fortunes were made, and the city still exhibits evidences of the wealth and social importance of the " Tobacco Lords," as they were termed; some of the finest private dwellings in the city, and several elegant streets, being the splendid relics of their former civic grandeur and importance. The interruption which the war of the American Revolution gave to this traffic, turned the attention* of the citizens to the manufacture of cot-

---

* For more than forty years, however, previous to this period, there existed in Glasgow a considerable manufacture of linen, lawns, and cambrics, which ultimately merged in the cotton manufacture. Its progress was not very rapid till towards the close of the last century, when the wars which sprung out of the French Revolution, by suspending and limiting for a time the manufactures of the continental nations, gave a new impetus to this manufacture in Great Britain, in which impetus Glasgow largely partook. Of the extent of that branch of the cotton manufacture in which hand-loom weavers are employed,

ton goods, then feebly developing its latent energies in Lancashire, and to this branch of manufacture Glasgow

It is impossible to form any thing like an accurate estimate, from the absence of any ascertained data. It is supposed, but the calculation is necessarily loose and imperfect, that 40,000 hand-loom weavers are employed by Glasgow manufacturers, the produce of whose labour, including the additional value appended to it before it is brought to market, has been assumed to be about three millions sterling.

Power-loom weaving was introduced into Glasgow as far back as 1792, but, until 1801, it may be considered as having been merely experimental. At present, there are from sixteen to seventeen thousand steam-looms set in motion by Glasgow capital. Each loom, on an average of the different kinds of work, produces about twenty-one yards daily, or 336,000 yards in all; and, in a year of 300 working days, 100,800,000 yards. Assuming sixpence per yard as the average value, this branch of the cotton manufacture in Glasgow amounts to £2,520,000,—a stupendous result, when it is considered that it is not quite forty years since its introduction.

The spinning of cotton yarn was begun in Glasgow in 1792, and has gradually and, of late years, rapidly increased. The total number of spindles in motion in Glasgow, and belonging to Glasgow capitalists, has been calculated, by experienced persons, to be about 1,100,000 at present. Of the value of the products, no estimate can be attempted with any certainty, but from three to four millions sterling have been assumed as the probable amount. In 1818, only 46,565 bales of cotton were consumed, and, in 1834, the consumption was 95,603 bales; since which it has considerably increased. Besides the spinning and weaving of cotton, the staple manufactures of Glasgow, silk has also become an extensive article of commerce and manufacture. This article, with various rich foreign wools, are now woven into cotton fabrics with the most brilliant success. Calico printing is also carried on to a vast extent, especially since the abolition of the duty on printed goods. It was first attempted, in 1742, on a small scale, at Pollockshaws, in the neighbourhood of Glasgow, and now there are few streams, in a vicinity of ten miles round the city, the waters of which do not carry abundant evidence of the printing establishments on their banks. The works of Henry Monteith and Company at Barrowfield, those on the Leven, lately the property of Messrs. Kibble, and of Messrs. Crum at Thornly Bank, are amongst the most noted and extensive. The establishment of the first mentioned house, from the perfection of their machinery and its close vicinity to Glasgow, has long been a point of interest to intelligent strangers.

Glasgow is the seat of various other extensive trades and manufactures, such as dying, bleaching, calendering, &c. The smelting of iron is also carried on to a vast extent in its neighbourhood, owing, in a great degree, to the adoption of the hot blast, an improvement which, with less than one-half of fuel, produces one-third more of iron. In 1834, the whole produce of the iron-works of Scotland, (of which at least from two-thirds to three-fourths are carried on by Glasgow capital,) was 110,240 tons; and, although no accurate data are to be obtained as to the present amount of production, it cannot be far short of 150,000 tons. The coal trade is carried on, to an enormous extent, in the neighbourhood of Glasgow, chiefly for home consumption, though a considerable exportation takes place. In 1831, 561,049 tons passed into and through the city, of which 124,000 were exported, principally coastwise, since which a very large

chiefly owes her pre-eminence as a commercial and manufacturing city.

In 1451, application was made to the Pope for a bull to establish a university, and eight years afterwards a member of the illustrious house of Hamilton bequeathed four acres of ground, with a tenement of houses, for the same purpose. And thus this noble educational institution was established, and after encountering many difficulties, arising from the unsettled character of the times, from its origin to near the end of the seventeenth century, rose into fame, importance, and utility. It is unnecessary here to state the many eminent names which adorn its annals, and which have shed a lustre over the literary and civil history of Scotland. It is a corporate body, and is governed by a chancellor, rector, and dean. The number of students is seldom less than 1000, and generally considerably more. The Hunterian Museum, attached to the College, is one of the chastest buildings in Scotland, and is rich in various departments of natural history, particularly in anatomical preparations, and in coins and medals. The whole has been valued at £70,000. The Grammar, or High School, for elementary classical education, is supported by the Corporation, on whom its su-

increase has taken place. The manufacture of machinery employs also a large capital and numerous work-people, especially the making of marine steam-engines. Ship-building has been recently established in the vicinity, on the banks of the river Clyde, and is reported to be in a highly flourishing state, especially the building of steam-vessels, for which Glasgow and Greenock are celebrated all over the kingdom ; as the deepening and improvement of the river and harbour proceed, the two latter branches of trade may be expected largely to increase. In this rough outline of the trade and manufactures of Glasgow, it would be unpardonable to omit the extensive chemical manufactory of Messrs. Charles Tennant and Company, at St. Rollox, near Glasgow, considered to be the largest in Europe, and containing four acres under roof. As the situation is high, on the north side of the city, the numerous chimneys form a prominent feature in the general view of Glasgow. The bleaching powder, sulphuric acid, and other chemical compounds, are manufactured to a large extent, and of the best quality, besides there being an extensive manufactory of soap.

perintendence devolves. It costs the city about £1000 per annum. Of late years the range of elementary instruction has been extended, and various modern languages, besides drawing and mathematics, are taught. The number of scholars is considerable.

Anderson's University was founded about the middle of last century by Professor Anderson, chiefly for the promotion of physical science ; its lectures, particularly on medical and anatomical subjects, are well attended, and its professors are considered highly respectable. Its winter soirées have attracted much attention. There is an excellent museum attached to this institution. In Hanover Street, running from George's Square to the north, stands the Mechanic's Institution, the lectures of which are numerously attended ; attached to it is an excellent library, with a valuable scientific apparatus ; and they have, together with the Mechanic's class in Anderson's University, perhaps the most beautiful and extensive series of models of steam-engines and machinery of various kinds to be found in any similar institution in the country. Besides these principal educational establishments, there are several others of an inferior, but respectable description in the suburbs, which are well attended. Lectures upon a variety of important subjects, scientific, educational, and economical, are also delivered by various scientific and philanthropic individuals, at which great numbers attend. There is a Philosophical Society, two Statistical Societies, a Literary and Commercial Society, and various other societies for mutual instruction, indicating the intelligent activity of mind and thirst for knowledge of the good citizens of Glasgow. The elementary schools are numerous, and are attended by great numbers of children, but no certain data exist from which to estimate the entire number of scholars. Nearly £30,000 sterling have been mortified by various worthy individuals, at different times, for educational purposes, in Glasgow. A normal seminary, the first of the kind in Scotland, and a handsome building, has recently been erected to the north of the city, and is reported to be in a flourishing condition. So that, on the whole, either in the amount or quality of its educational means, Glasgow is behind no city in the kingdom. In 1763, the illustrious James Watt began that memorable series of experiments in mechanical science which issued in the successful application of steam as a great motive power, and about fifty years after, Mr. Henry Bell launched on the Clyde the first steam vessel ever seen in this country. To the labours and discoveries of these eminent men, Glasgow may be said to owe her present prominent position as a manufacturing and commercial community. Monuments, to perpetuate their memory, have been erected by their grateful fellow-citizens. That of the former is placed in George's Square, in the centre of the city, and the latter at Dunglass, on the Clyde, eleven miles below the town, in a fine commanding situation.

Glasgow is also rich in religious, charitable, and philanthropic institutions of every variety of description, which are supported by annual donations to the extent of £50,000. To particularise these, would occupy far too much space, but two of the most recent establishments deserve especial notice, the Asylum for the Houseless Poor, and the House of Refuge for Indigent and Orphan Boys. A similar institution to the latter, for the reception of Destitute Young Females, is also soon to be erected. The former of these affords shelter during the night to about a hundred houseless creatures, who must other-

wise lie in the streets, and the latter has from one hundred and thirty to one hundred and forty boys within its
walls, learning some trade, and receiving the elements of
a useful education. It is a fine building, in a prominent
situation to the north-east of the city.

In a commercial community like that of Glasgow, where
the learned professions bear a small proportion to those
engaged in the pursuits of trade and commerce, comparatively few individuals, not professional, are to be found
of a purely literary character. Yet no city in the kingdom, the society of which is composed of similar elements, can exhibit a larger number of enlightened and
well-educated mercantile men ; and it may be said generally, that whilst the chief springs of action are to be found
in the stimulants of commercial and manufacturing enterprise, the general character of the population is that of
intellectual activity, and eagerness for the acquisition of
general and available knowledge.

WALK FIRST.

GEORGE'S SQUARE—STATUES OF SIR JOHN MOORE—JAMES WATT—
MONUMENT TO SIR WALTER SCOTT—ROYAL EXCHANGE—ROYAL BANK
—QUEEN STREET—ARGYLE STREET—ARCADE—DUNLOP STREET—
THEATRE ROYAL—MILLER STREET—GLASSFORD STREET—STOCK-
WELL—HUTCHESON'S HOSPITAL—CANDLERIGGS, AND BAZAAR—TRON
STEEPLE—CROSS—TONTINE BUILDINGS—EQUESTRIAN STATUE OF
WILLIAM THE THIRD—TOWN HALL—CROSS STEEPLE—SALTMARKET
—ST. ANDREW'S SQUARE, AND CHURCH—BRIDGEGATE—COURT-
HOUSES, AND JAIL—HUTCHESON'S BRIDGE—GREEN—NELSON'S MO-
NUMENT—LONDON STREET—HIGH STREET—COLLEGE BUILDINGS—
BRIDEWELL—BELL OF THE BRAE—INFIRMARY—CATHEDRAL—
NECROPOLIS—ASYLUM FOR THE BLIND—GEORGE'S STREET.

GLASGOW is far inferior in point of picturesque situation
to Edinburgh. Whilst the latter stands upon a suc-

cession of bold ridges, sloping finely down to the Firth
of Forth ; with the rich indented coast of Fife, and the
noble range of the Ochils in the distance, to the north,
and on the south and west, the green swelling outlines
of the Pentlands—Glasgow is situate in the valley of
the Clyde, and chiefly on the levels along its banks,
although some portions of the city are located on acclivities to the north, which, by their commanding position,
vary and enliven the monotony of an otherwise nearly
unbroken level. Neither can Glasgow exhibit the same
rich and picturesque variety of surface · within its limits
proper, which Edinburgh presents. There is no Castlehill, with its summit bristling with the rude fortifications
of the middle ages, and an abrupt and lofty mass of
rock, sinking suddenly down into the bed of an ancient
lake, now transformed into pleasure-gardens; or a Calton-
hill, rising boldly in the centre of the city, gorgeous with
splendid mansions, noble public buildings, and monuments
to the illustrious dead ; nor has it the bold and rough ridge
of Salisbury Crags, diversifying the landscape, and carrying the mind of the spectator away from the busy hum
and haunts of man, to the more still retreats, and the
solitary grandeur of nature. So far, therefore, Glasgow
must suffer in the eye of the tourist, on a comparison of
its natural advantages with those of Edinburgh, and not
less so, perhaps, when the general character and appearance of the two cities are compared. Edinburgh, with
its Old Town, still exhibiting in whole streets and divisions, the irregular but striking style of architecture
patronized by our fathers, and teeming at every step
with ancient buildings, associated with numberless historical reminiscences ; and opposite to this, her New
Town, with its splendid architectural vistas, and the

chaste elegance of its general exterior. Glasgow has no
such glowing and startling contrasts to present; yet, if
the tourist will put himself under our guidance for a
short time, we promise to shew him one of the finest
cities in the British dominions, and even in a mere landscape point of view, presenting a series of pictures of equal
beauty and interest. We shall adopt the same method
we have found so convenient in perambulating Edinburgh,
and conduct the stranger in a succession of walks through
the busy city.

Suppose the tourist then snugly deposited in one of·
the excellent hotels in George's Square, one of the most
central places in the city, and from which, as from a
common centre, we shall commence our examination of
the memorabilia of this great commercial emporium of
the west.

Sallying from any of the various respectable hotels* in
this spacious and handsome square—which of itself, from
the elegance and agreeable bustle of its area, attracts
attention from a stranger—the first object which strikes
the eye, is the monument recently erected to Sir Walter
Scott. It is in the form of a fluted Doric column, about
eighty feet in height, with a colossal statue of the great
Minstrel on the top. The figure is half enveloped in a
shepherd's plaid,† and the expression of the countenance is
characterised by that air of *bonhommie* and shrewd sense
which distinguished that illustrious individual. Directly
in front of Sir Walter's pillar, there is a fine pedestrian
statue, in bronze, by Flaxman, of the lamented Sir John
Moore, who was a native of Glasgow. To the right of

* There are four excellent hotels in George's Square,—the George Hotel,
Comrie's, Grimshaw's, and the Royal Hotel; at any of which the stranger is
sure of the best entertainment, as the old sign hath it, for "man and horse."
† It is somewhat unfortunate, that the plaid is placed on the wrong arm.

Sir John Moore's statue, in the south-west angle of the square, there is also a noble figure of James Watt, in bronze, and of colossal magnitude. It is intended, as opportunity offers, to place the statues and monuments of other eminent men around the inclosed area of this handsome square, which is ornamented with shrubberies and walks, so that in process of time it will become a sort of open Pantheon, dedicated to the illustrious dead. Standing on the north side of the square, the spectator has before him one of the finest architectural vistas in the city. On the right, the bold spire of St. George's Church, 162 feet in height, catches the eye, surmounting a building, obviously too small for such a vast superstructure. Somewhat nearer, on the same side, is the Dissenting Chapel in which the celebrated Dr. Wardlaw officiates,—an elegant building, of Grecian chasteness of conception. To the right and left a noble street, George Street, extends for about half-a-mile, without presenting any other objects of especial interest. Looking to the south, the lofty colonnade of the Royal Exchange* appears, towards which imposing mass of building we shall now conduct the tourist. It stands in Queen Street, at the termination of Ingram Street, one of the finest openings in the city. This splendid fabric is built in the florid Corinthian style of architecture, and is surmounted by a lantern, which forms one of the most conspicuous objects in the city. The News Room is one of the most striking apartments in the kingdom, about 100 feet long, by 40 broad, with a richly ornamented oval roof, supported by

* The colonnade of the Royal Exchange is one of the boldest and most imposing architectural objects in the kingdom ; and consists of a double range of fluted Corinthian pillars of great height. As a whole, the Royal Exchange of Glasgow is one of the most striking edifices in the empire, the general effect of which is grand and impressive, though some of the details may be liable to the objections of a refined criticism.

fluted Corinthian columns.   The Royal Exchange is
placed in the centre of a noble area, two sides of which
are lined with splendid and uniform ranges of buildings,
but simpler in design than the Exchange, and occupied
as warehouses, shops, and counting-houses.   Behind it is
the Royal Bank, which is much admired by good judges,
for the elegant simplicity and chasteness of its design.
It is built after the model of a celebrated Greek temple.
On each side of the Bank, two superb Doric arches, of
bold and imposing character, afford access to Buchanan
Street, also one of the principal streets in the city, in
fact, the Regent Street of Glasgow.

Proceeding down Queen Street, one of the great
thoroughfares and most animated avenues in the city, at
the northern extremity of which, in the north-west corner of George's Square, is the terminus of the Edinburgh and Glasgow Railway, the stranger emerges into
the principal street, the main artery of Glasgow, here
called Argyle Street, but which bears the names of the
Trongate and Gallowgate, towards its eastern extremities.
Taking in the whole extent of this noble avenue, from
east to west, it exhibits a continuation of street of at least
three miles in length.   .

Turning towards the east, the stranger finds himself
involved in the bustle and animation of one of the most
crowded thoroughfares in Europe, through which the
stream of human existence flows at all hours of the day,
and in all seasons, with undiminished volume and velocity.   The general character of the buildings is plain,
and there is no attempt at plan or uniformity of arrangement.   An ancient tenement or two, with its narrow
pointed gables and steep roofs, occasionally attracts the
eye, and forms a fine contrast to the modern elegance of

the shops below. On the left, a handsome entrance
gives access to a covered arcade, extending from this
point to Buchanan Street, and containing numerous handsome shops, with a gay crowd of pedestrians at all hours.
On the right, the first opening is Dunlop Street, containing the Theatre-Royal, a recent erection, but by no means
very chaste or happy in its style.   There was formerly
a handsome theatre in Queen Street, which was destroyed by fire about ten years ago.   Opposite is Miller
Street, in which were formerly the stately mansions of
the old Virginian merchants, but which are now occupied as places of business.   Virginia Street, on the same
side, is a narrow but handsome thoroughfare, in which
the new Glasgow Union Bank is the most conspicuous
building.   It is built after the model of the Temple of
Jupiter Stator at Rome, and is one of the chastest and
most elegant buildings in the city.   On the left, the next
opening of any importance is Glassford Street, broad, and
handsome in the style of its buildings, especially an edifice lately occupied as the Ship Bank.   Here the new
Post-Office is located, a plain but handsome structure,
with no architectural pretensions.   Opposite Glassford
Street, and running to the right towards the river, is the
Stockwell, one of the oldest streets in the city.   A few
old tenements still show their venerable front here, but
the remorseless march of improvement has recently swept
away some of the finest.   Sixty years ago, this was one
of the chief avenues of the city, and the principal approach from the south, by the old bridge of Glasgow.
Passing several other streets of no great importance, with
the exception of Hutcheson Street, with its fine hospital
of that name, at the upper end, surmounted by an ele-

gant tapering spire,* and Candleriggs Street, terminated
by St. David's Church and tower, and containing the
Bazaar, a large general market, and also the Corn Exchange, covered in, and containing extensive accommodation, the stranger will observe, on the right, a rather
puny but venerable-looking spire, which is the Tron
Steeple, and which finely breaks the monotony of the
long line of street which he has just traversed.   On the
right side, opposite the Candleriggs, is King Street, an
old and well-frequented opening, containing the public
markets for beef, mutton, fish, and vegetables.   It terminates in the Bridgegate, a fine old street, irregular in
its appearance, and of considerable breadth in some parts.
An old steeple, of remarkably good proportions, rises up
behind it, which anciently formed part of the building
used as a hall for the merchants of Glasgow, but which
has long ago been pulled down.   Seventy years ago, this
street was inhabited by the most respectable classes of
citizens, and contained many handsome buildings.   Many
lanes or closes run off from it on either side, inhabited
by a numerous and rather turbulent population, of the
poorest classes.   Some very old buildings are still to be
found in these closes, whose appearance tells a tale of
other times, but the dun and squalid character of its
present occupants, does not invite to a lengthened examination of these remnants of antiquity.   Returning to the

---

* This building is erected on the site of the old hospital, founded by two
brothers, whose statues are placed in the front of the edifice, and who left
considerable property for its support, chiefly in ground on the south side of the
river, and on which the extensive suburb of Hutchesontown is built. A number of poor boys receive a gratis education from its funds, besides being supported otherwise. In Candleriggs Street are situate also the extensive wholesale
and retail warehouses of the Messrs. Campbells, said to be one of the largest
commercial establishments in the kingdom, and worthy of a visit, from the excellence of its interior arrangements.

Trongate, a little further on is the Cross of Glasgow, forming a centre, and termination to the Trongate, the Gallowgate, (a continuation of this street,) the High Street, and the Saltmarket. There is an equestrian statue of William the Third placed here, of no great merit as a work of art. A noble range of building, with a superb piazza under it, extends in front, denominated the Tontine, from having been built upon that principle. There is a fine large News Room here, which was formerly known by the appellation of the Coffee-Room, and, until the New Exchange was erected, was the great focus of business and politics. The ancient jail of the burgh stood exactly at the corner of the High Street and Trongate. Criminals were executed formerly in front of this building. On its site a heavy, tasteless pile of building has been erected, occupied by shops and warehouses. The old Court-houses also stood here, but they have been removed to the New Jail buildings, at the foot of the Saltmarket. The Town-Hall, however, still remains,—a fine apartment, containing portraits of some of the Scottish and English sovereigns, besides a very fine marble statue of William Pitt, by Chantrey. The Cross Steeple, too, survives still, a relic of the ancient civic splendour of this part of the city, and in itself an interesting object. Leaving the ancient Cross of Glasgow, we next enter the Saltmarket, not now, alas! as in the palmy days of Bailie Nicol Jarvie, the domicile of bailies, and other civic dignitaries, but occupied with a busy population of inferior shopkeepers and trades people. The lower part, and some portions of the neighbourhood, form the Monmouth Street and Rag Fair of Glasgow, being chiefly occupied with furniture brokers and old clothes dealers. On the left is St.

Andrew's Square, the buildings of which are characterised by an elegant simplicity and chaste regularity of architecture. The greater part of the area of this square is occupied with St. Andrew's Church, the largest, and, in many respects, the ne st church in the city, the portico of which, for lightness and elevation, is much admired. On the right is the Bridgegate, of which notice has already been taken. Here stood anciently several fine old buildings of some historical note,—in one of which Cromwell is said to have lodged when in Glasgow,—but, with many other ancient tenements in this street, they have long since fallen victims to the progress of time and improvement. The stranger now emerges into a fine broad esplanade, with the Public Park or Green stretching away to the left, and the imposing pile of buildings forming the Court-houses and Jail, on the right. These elegant buildings are in the Grecian style of architecture. The front is chaste and simple, but thought to be rather low for its length. From the vast increase of the city and its population, these buildings are now found to be deficient in accommodation, and, it is probable, new Court-houses will soon be erected, and the whole of the present edifice used as a prison. An act for this purpose was obtained two years ago, but, from some unfortunate mistakes and local jarrings, has never been acted upon. On the right of the Court-houses is the river Clyde, crossed at this point by Hutcheson's Bridge, a recently built, but heavy and tasteless erection. A carriage drive extends around the Green, which is about two miles and a quarter in circumference. Passing up the green, on the left, is the fine column erected to the memory of Nelson, 143 feet in height, and modelled on the Trajan Pillar at Rome. When the tide is at the full, the brimming waters of the Clyde appear at this point to great advantage, and there is a fine landscape view down the river, with the four bridges in the distance, and the variety of buildings, public and private, on the opposite banks. On the south side, vast ranges of chimneys appear, indicating the *locale* of some of the largest spinning and weaving factories in the city. The same appearances are beheld to the north-east, whilst, on the south and south-east appear, at a few miles distance; the beautiful slopes of the Cathkin Braes, adorned with fine plantations, and gentlemen's seats. The Green is diversified with walks, some of which are shaded by noble rows of trees, and there are several fountains of fine spring water, round which abundance of damsels may be seen clustering with their *boynes* and pitchers,—the Green being the common property of the inhabitants, and much used for the washing and bleaching of clothes. The north side of this fine pleasure-ground rises a little, and is termed the Calton Green, and has a handsome row of dwelling-houses lining one side of it, called Monteith Row, which, from their elevation and beauty of situation, are amongst the pleasantest in the city. Leaving the Green by the North-west Gate, (on the west and north it is surrounded, for most of its length, by an iron railing,) and crossing Charlotte Street, a quiet, dull-looking street, with some fine old mansions in it, we enter London Street, a broad and handsome avenue, but sorely bungled, and in a half-built and disgraceful state of dilapidation, considering its immediate vicinity to the Cross, the centre of the city. Arrived again at the Cross, let us take a passing glance at the Gallowgate, the name of the eastern section of the main street of the city, and which begins at this point. It is irregular, both in the

appearance of its buildings and in its width, sometimes
steep and narrow, then broad and winding.   It contains
large barracks for foot soldiers, and, near its easterly extremity, the Cattle-market, one of the most interesting
sights of Glasgow.   It occupies 30,000 square yards,
and is admirably, and even elegantly laid out, for its
especial objects.   The tower of St. John's Church is the
most prominent feature in this part of the city, which,
exhibiting no other objects of peculiar interest to a
stranger, we shall return from this hasty sally, and proceed due north, up the High Street, which ancient avenue may be considered as the back-bone of the skeleton
of the old city.

The buildings in this fine old street are many of them
venerable from their antiquity; but the presence of new
ones on every side, indicates the rapid disappearance of
the ancient characteristics of this part of the city.   On
every side, numerous *closes*, or narrow lanes, appear,
teeming with population, and alive with the hum and stir
of active life.   They are inhabited chiefly by the lower
classes, and, in many of them, as well as in those in the
Saltmarket and Bridgegate, the inmates are so densely
wedged together, that this, co-operating with other fatal
causes, has tended to foster the elements of contagious
diseases, and greatly to lower the average duration of
life in the city.   Proceeding up the street, and passing
one or two inferior streets, on the right, is a long range
of venerable monastic-looking buildings, with a fine stone
balcony in the front.   These are the buildings of the
University, the external aspect of which harmonizes well
with the grave purposes to which they are devoted.
There are three inner courts; and, in the first, there is a
fine old staircase, much admired for its stately elegance.

The buildings are old, and imposing in their appearance, but some of the older portions, having been taken down a few years ago, have been replaced by others of a character wholly foreign to the original style, thus marring the harmony, and disturbing the uniformity and propriety of the structure. Behind is the Hunterian Museum, a splendid edifice of the Grecian character.

A little above the College is Duke Street, a fine opening to the east, and containing the City and County Bridewell, a large and striking mass of buildings in the old Saxon style of architecture.* The High Street becomes here rather steep and narrow, with a considerable curve, and is called the Bell of the Brae. Here, in the year 1300, a severe action took place betwixt the English and Scots; the former commanded by Percy and Bishop Beik, and the latter by the Scottish champion—Wallace. The English were defeated with the loss of their commander. Within these twenty-five years, this part of the High Street contained the oldest and most curious-looking buildings in the city, but almost the whole of these ancient tenements have been pulled down, and replaced by others of the most ordinary character. At the top of this ascent, on the right, is the Drygate, and on the left, the Rottenrow; both of them very old streets, and still exhibiting sundry venerable-looking buildings, the relics of their ancient grandeur and importance. A few yards further we reach a large open space, containing in front, the Infirmary, a large and elegant building, of a

* This establishment is justly celebrated for the superior excellence and economy of its arrangements and management. It contains ample accommodation and means of classification for nearly 300 prisoners, by whose labour its expenses are almost wholly defrayed. Each prisoner, it is calculated, costs the community no more than £1, 10s. per annum, so judicious is the system pursued.

P

composite character of architecture, and light and airy in
appearance; and a little to the right, the huge mass of
the Cathedral at once arrests and detains the eye of the
stranger. Having already, in the historical and introductory matter, briefly noticed this noble relic of antiquity, we shall merely observe farther, that it is surrounded by a vast churchyard, in which the bones of
many generations rest from their labours; besides which,
it contains a great many rich and ancient monumental
tombs of the worthies of the old city, and the grave dignitaries of church and state in the days of other times.—
The Glasgow Infirmary is a very large building, including the recent additions made to it for a Fever Hospital. The extent of its accommodation may be inferred from the fact, that 6272 patients were admitted during the year 1837–1838. It bears a high character,
not merely for the matured excellence of its arrangements, but the superior character of its medical school.*
A building in the worst possible taste, stands a little to
the right of these two fine specimens of ancient and modern architecture, which is the Barony Church. Betwixt
this eye-sore and the wall of the Cathedral burying-ground,
which is lined with ancient sepulchral monuments, a narrow path conducts to the Bridge of Sighs, so called from
its affording access to the new Glasgow Necropolis,
anciently called the Fir Park, and believed to have been
one of the dark retreats of the Druids. With a fine bold
arch, the bridge spans the brawling waters of a rivulet,
called the Molendinar Burn, which, after being collected

* Its affairs are managed by twenty-five Directors, ten of whom are elected
by the subscribers of two guineas a-year, the others are elected by the various
public bodies of the city; the Members for the city are also *ex officio* Directors.

into a small dam or lake, dash briskly over an artificial cascade down a steep ravine, imparting a character of life and cheerfulness to a spot consecrated to the most solemn associations. The bold and rocky eminence which forms the Necropolis, shoots suddenly up to the height of from 200 to 300 feet, forming, with its fine shrubberies, a noble back-ground to the Cathedral. A splendid gate-way, in the Italian style, appears in front, and the entire surface of the rock is divided into walks, and bristling with columns, and every variety of monumental erec-tion, some of them peculiarly happy and chaste in style. The fine statue of Knox on the summit, and one erected to the memory of Mr. William M'Gavin, with the monument to the late Rev. Dr. Dick of Glasgow, are particularly conspicuous, and will instantly attract the eye of the stranger. It is proposed to carry a tunnel through the hill from south to north, and to form galle-ries and chambers in the solid rock, so as to form a vast crypt, in addition to the cemetery above. From the sum-mit, 250 feet above the level of the Clyde, the Great Reformer just mentioned looks grimly down on one of the most striking scenes that can well be imagined. The huge mass of the venerable Cathedral, surrounded by the crumbling remains and memorials of twenty-five generations, stands still and solemn at your feet, like the awful Genius of the Past; the vast city stretches away in long lines and perspectives before you in every direction, intersected by the broad and brimming Clyde, while the uplands of Lanarkshire and Renfrewshire, with the Dumbartonshire and Argyleshire hills, form a noble frame to the picture.* Descending from this elevated

* A little to the west of the Cathedral is the asylum for the blind, (an esta-blishment of great merit in its arrangements,) the appearance of which is rather

site, we shall retrace our steps down the High Street,
and, striking to the right, enter George Street, a broad
and handsome opening, but, with the exception of the
buildings of Anderson's University, which are respectable
but plain in appearance, and the New High School behind them, a large building, and equally devoid of architectural attraction, it offers no particular inducement to
the tourist to linger on its pavements, and he now finds
himself again in George's Square, ready, after a brief repose, for

WALK SECOND.

BUCHANAN STREET—VIEW FROM THE TOP OF ST. VINCENT STREET—
   WEST GEORGE STREET—REGENT STREET—BATH STREET—CLELAND
   TESTIMONIAL—LUNATIC ASYLUM—SAUCHIEHALL ROAD—GARNET
   HILL—FINE VIEW FROM THE TOP—WOODSIDE CRESCENT—BOTANIC
   GARDEN—ELMBANK CRESCENT—INDIA STREET—ST. VINCENT STREET
   —BLYTHSWOOD SQUARE.

TURNING to the right, and still continuing in George
Street, now called West George Street, and which,
after passing round St. George's Church, continues its
course for nearly half a mile further, till it is lost in
Blythswood Square, the tourist enters Buchanan Street.
Here it may be proper to observe, that four great lines
of street run west from Buchanan Street, parallel to
each other, two of them for nearly a mile in length,—
St. Vincent Street, West George Street, Regent Street,

quaint, but in very good taste. The inmates are employed in various ways,
and manufacture articles of use or ornament to a considerable extent, which
are disposed of for the benefit of the institution. The new method of printing
for the blind has been carried here to great perfection. Generally speaking,
any respectable inn-keeper knows how to procure an order of admission for
this and any other public institution in Glasgow.

and Bath Street. The first and last named are the longest and finest. Turning north, we shall follow the easy ascent of Buchanan Street, and when at the top, we recommend a brief pause, to take a hasty look behind. The eye courses down the long vista of a spacious street, lined with handsome buildings, and in the lower half crowded with a gay population, for we have already mentioned that this is the Regent Street (London) of Glasgow. It is finely terminated by St. Enoch's Church, standing in the Square of that name; and beyond, in the distance, the green slopes of the Renfrewshire uplands appear above the houses, giving a rich and half rural character to the view. A few yards further on, we reach Sauchiehall Street, or road, at the corner of which stands a handsome pile of buildings, denominated the Cleland Testimonial, from having been built and presented to the eminent statist of that name, by his friends in Glasgow, on his retirement from the public service of the city, after having been for many years superintendent of public works. From this point, the lofty dome of the Lunatic Asylum meets the eye. This is one of the largest and finest buildings belonging to the city of Glasgow. From an octagonal centre four wings diverge, of three storeys in height, and the style of the whole building is impressive and striking. Its accommodation is very extensive, and the grounds contain about four acres. As a medical and restorative establishment, it ranks very high, for the excellence of its management and arrangements.* Sauchiehall Road is lined with handsome rows

---

* This building has lately been purchased by the directors of the Town's Hospital, for the accommodation of the poor of the city. A new Lunatic Asylum is about to be erected far to the west of the city, for which purpose sixty-six acres of land have been obtained, to meet the fast-growing popularity of this estimable institution.

of houses, and is very broad for the first half of its length. As the tourist proceeds, he finds, on the left, various handsome streets, opening into it from the south, forming part of the new town, and chiefly occupied by the wealthier classes. On the right, an elevated ridge accompanies him, containing many handsome villas, and intersected with streets. This is called Garnet Hill, and should be specially visited by the picturesque tourist, as it commands a noble view from its summit. To the north and north-west, bold ranges of hills appear at a few miles' distance; and, faintly looming on the horizon, the lofty peaks of the Argyleshire and Perthshire mountains are seen; nearer, the masts of vessels on the Forth and Clyde Canal appear, in the basin at Port-Dundas, with a rich undulating surface, crowded with villas, private dwellings, and the tall chimneys of numerous public works. Returning to Sauchiehall Street, the tourist arrives at Woodside Crescent, and is struck with surprise at the number and elegance of the fine streets, rows, and terraces, intermixed with ornamental shrubberies, which attract his eye. This part of the suburbs is the most recently built, and is at present the most fashionable quarter for what are called self-contained houses. A quarter of a mile further on, is the Botanic Garden, which, under the able superintendence of Sir William Jackson Hooker and Mr. Murray, the curator, has obtained an extensive celebrity. Lectures are delivered here, during the summer, by the Professor of botany in the University, and strangers obtain admission to the garden, on payment of a shilling. The collection of foreign plants is considered to be very complete, and, in some departments, unrivalled, and the plan of the garden is good. It is soon to be removed, however, to a site about a mile more to the north-west, on the fine slope of a gentle elevation, which will add to the general effect very considerably.

Retracing our steps, we shall strike down the first opening on the right, into Elmbank Crescent, a very handsome row of houses, but only half built. Passing through a new street just begun, and containing a few very handsome buildings, in the stately but somewhat stiff style of Louis the Fourteenth's time, and called India Street, the stranger finds himself at the western extremity of St. Vincent Street, here called Greenhill Place. Proceeding citywards, along this noble street, and ascending gradually, on the right is Blythswood Square, the buildings of which, from their lofty position and elegant exterior, form one of the finest and most prominent objects to the stranger approaching Glasgow from the west. The view from this square, to the south and west, is very fine, but, on the north, it is intercepted by the more commanding ridge of Garnet Hill. Returning to St. Vincent Street, the stranger finds himself descending gradually, with elegant masses of building on each side, and a noble and lengthy street vista before him. On the left is a handsome building, recently fitted up as a club-house, but there being no particular object to detain the eye, we shall suppose the tourist once more deposited in George's Square, in the north-west angle of which this noble opening has its termination.

WALK THIRD.

LEAVING George Square again, and proceeding down
Queen Street on the left, the eye glancing along Ingram
Street, rests on the fine portico of the Assembly Rooms,*
standing boldly forward, with the grave old College
steeple in the distance, looking demurely down on the
bustle and animation of this great business thoroughfare. A splendid pile of building is at present erecting
at the west end of this street, opposite to the Exchange,
intended for the British Linen Company's Bank. This
range of building promises to be one of the most striking
in the city. Entering Argyle Street once more, and
threading our way eastward, through its busy crowd, to
the Stockwell, we request the stranger to dash with us
down this avenue towards the river, and there being no
objects of any note on the route, but those which have
been already seen and commented on, we find ourselves
on the Old Bridge of Glasgow. This bridge was built
in 1345, and is the first stone bridge erected in Glasgow.

---

* The Assembly Rooms is one of the finest edifices in the city, taken in con-
nexion with the buildings on each side, which are built on a plan connected
with it. The principal room is 80 feet long, 35 feet wide, and 27 in height, with
a tastefully painted ceiling.

It has been twice widened, and the last time in a very elegant and ingenious manner, by adding footpaths, supported by cast-iron frames of a tasteful character, from a design by the late Mr. Telford. Looking up the stream, the back and one side of the Jail buildings are seen on the left, with the Green sloping beautifully down to the river. The view downwards is still finer; two bridges—the nearest, a very fine and perfectly level one, of wood—span the glittering waters of the river. On the right is a plain respectable-looking building, the Poors' House.* Next to it, the Catholic Chapel, one of the most striking modern buildings in the Gothic style of architecture in the kingdom. It is very large, and elegantly fitted up, and is officiated in by Bishop Murdoch, and several Catholic clergymen. Beyond it a little way is the New Custom House, a respectable-looking building. On the left bank of the river, the spire of the Gorbals Church breaks the uniformity of the outline in a pleasing manner, and two fine masses of buildings, East and West Carleton Place, from their simplicity, good taste, and happy elevation, confer a peculiar dignity upon this part of the river vista. Proceeding along this noble street, Glasgow or Broomielaw Bridge next demands the attention of the tasteful stranger. It is one of the finest bridges in Europe—500 feet in length, and sixty feet wide, being seven feet wider than London Bridge. It is cased with Aberdeen granite, and consists of seven arches, whilst the curve is so slight as scarcely to be observed. It forms a superb entrance to the city from the south, and from it one of the finest river harbour views in the United Kingdom may be obtained.

* As previously observed, the present Lunatic Asylum is about to be converted into a receptacle for the poor of the city.

To the south, a fine broad avenue stretches away, till it is lost in the country. On the right, the Broomielaw Street extends for nearly a mile, with a fine ample mar-gin to the river, and long ranges of covered sheds, and other harbour appurtenances. A noble basin, from three to four hundred feet wide, and about three-quarters of a mile in length, with its range of quays, is before the eye, crowded with vessels of every description, from four hundred tons burden to the smallest coasting craft, whilst steam-vessels are perpetually sending up clouds of smoke or steam, and dashing in or out with a startling velocity and noise.*

Crossing the river, the stranger will admire the spacious and elegant streets which, as he walks along, strike his eye. Portland Street is nearly a mile in length, very broad, and lined with handsome buildings. The population, on this side of the river, is understood to be about 60,000, located in Laurieston, Tradeston, and Hutcheson-town, all in the Barony of Gorbals, which is a depen-

---

* There are always several steam-vessels of the largest class lying in the river to get in their machinery, and there is a powerful crane, capable of raising thirty tons, for lifting the heavy boilers, &c., on board; a much larger one is preparing, expected to be the most powerful in Britain. Glasgow has attained great celebrity as a manufactory of marine steam-engines, and, indeed, of ma-chinery of every description. The depth of water at the Broomielaw at spring tides is now from 14 to 16 feet, and it is proposed by the Trustees of the harbour and river, to deepen to the extent of 20 feet at neap tides, no obstacles existing, according to the report of the engineer, to prevent such a result being obtained. It is also intended to widen the river, for ten or twelve miles down, to from 300 to 400 feet wide, the width to increase downwards; to bevel off the banks on either side, and to remove every other obstacle to the freedom of the naviga-tion; so that, in a few years, with wet docks, for which a large space of ground on the south side, immediately below the suburb of Tradeston, has recently been purchased, Glasgow will possess one of the most spacious and convenient harbours in the kingdom. From July 1837 to July 1838, 4600 sailing vessels, of every description, arrived and departed from the harbour, with a tonnage of 214,471 tons; and the steam tonnage on the river during the same period was 731,028 tons; these latter vessels made 7850 trips in the same time. The reve-nue from the harbour and river last year was £43,287, 16s. 10d.; customs levied in 1839, £468,974, 12s. 2d.; and post-office revenue, £47,597, 7s. 7d.

dency of Glasgow. The parliamentary constituency elect their own magistrates, by poll election, who must, however, be approved of by the Town Council of Glasgow. The terminus of the Ayr, Paisley, and Greenock Railway is on this side, close to Glasgow Bridge, and, half a mile to the south, is the basin of the Johnston and Paisley Canal; to which places light and swift passage-boats depart, almost every hour, during the summer. Arrived at the Old Bridge of Glasgow again, the stranger, before crossing, will probably cast one lingering look on the river, and noble view on either side, after which, retracing his steps up Stockwell Street, he may, if he pleases, return to George Square, by Glassford Street, Ingram Street, and the Royal Exchange, thus passing through the most crowded and interesting business thoroughfares of the city.

SEVENTH TOUR.

GLASGOW—BOTHWELL CASTLE AND BRIDGE—HAMILTON—LANARK—
FALLS OF CLYDE.

LEAVING Glasgow,* the tourist proceeds eastward, and
passes Camlachie and Tollcross, where there are extensive coal and iron works. On the opposite side of the
Clyde is the ancient royal burgh of Rutherglen, formerly
a place of some importance, but now much reduced. In
the church of Rutherglen, a peace was concluded between the Scotch and English, 8th February 1297. All
along the sides of the road are numerous elegant villas.
Five miles from Glasgow is Broomhouse. At this point,
a new line of road has lately been opened up as far as
the village of Uddingston, where the old road, which
passes near the banks of the river, again joins it. A
quarter of a mile beyond Broomhouse, the road crosses
the North Calder Water by a new bridge. Half way
between Broomhouse and Uddingston, the Edinburgh
road, by Holytown and Whitburn, branches off to the
left. A little to the right from this point, a bridge has
lately been thrown across the Clyde, uniting the parishes
of Bothwell and Blantyre. A little farther on is the
village of Uddingston, situated on an eminence, com-

* There is another road from Glasgow to Hamilton on the other side of the
Clyde, by Rutherglen, but it is by no means so interesting as the route described.

SEVENTH TOUR.
GLASGOW to HAMILTON, LANARK,
& THE FALLS OF CLYDE.

EIGHTH TOUR.
GLASGOW, DUMBARTON, HELENSBURGH,
GREENOCK, DUNOON, ROTHSAY.

Edinburgh: Published July 1, 1841 by Adam & Charles Black, 27 North Bridge

manding a delightful view. A short way beyond, on the right, are the magnificent ruins of

BOTHWELL CASTLE.

This noble structure is built of red freestone, and consists of a large oblong quadrangle, flanked, towards the south, by two huge circular towers, and covering an area of 234 feet in length and ninety-nine feet in breadth. The origin of the castle is unknown, but, in the wars between Bruce and Baliol, Edward I. made a grant of it to Aymer de Valence, whom he had appointed governor of Scotland. In this fortress a number of the English nobility took refuge, after the battle of Bannockburn, but were speedily obliged to surrender. Bruce bestowed Bothwell Castle

BOTHWELL CASTLE.

on Andrew Murray, who had married that monarch's sister. It next came into the possession of Archibald the Grim, Earl of Douglas, who married the grand-daughter of Andrew Murray. After the forfeiture of the Douglasses, in 1445, it was successively possessed by the Crichtons, John Ramsay, a favourite of James III., and the Hepburns, Earls of Bothwell. After the forfeiture of the infamous nobleman of that name, it passed through

several hands, till it at last reverted to the noble family
of Douglas.* The present residence of Lord Douglas is
a plain mansion, standing on a beautiful lawn, near the

* The following beautiful description of Bothwell Castle and the surrounding
scenery is given in the notes to Wordsworth's Poems, vol. v., p. 379:—"It was
exceedingly delightful to enter thus unexpectedly upon such a beautiful region.
The Castle stands nobly, overlooking the Clyde. When we came up to it, I was
hurt to see that flower-borders had taken place of the natural overgrowings of
the ruin, the scattered stones and wild plants. It is a large and grand pile of
red freestone, harmonizing perfectly with the rocks of the river, from which, no
doubt, it has been hewn. When I was a little accustomed to the unnaturalness
of a modern garden, I could not help admiring the excessive beauty and luxuriance of some of the plants, particularly the purple-flowered clematis, and a
broad-leafed creeping plant without flowers, which scrambled up the castle
wall, along with the ivy, and spread its vine-like branches so lavishly that it
seemed to be in its natural situation, and one could not help thinking that,
though not self-planted among the ruins of this country, it must somewhere
have its native abode in such places. If Bothwell Castle had not been close to
the Douglas mansion, we should have been disgusted with the possessor's miserable conception of *adorning* such a venerable ruin; but it is so very near to
the house, that of necessity the pleasure-grounds must have extended beyond
it, and perhaps the neatness of a shaven lawn, and the complete desolation
natural to a ruin might have made an unpleasant contrast; and, besides being
within the precincts of the pleasure-grounds, and so very near to the dwelling
of a noble family, it has forfeited, in some degree, its independent majesty, and
becomes a tributary to the mansion; its solitude being interrupted, it has no
longer the command over the mind in sending it back into past times, or exclud-
ing the ordinary feelings which we bear about us in daily life. We had then
only to regret that the castle and the house were so near to each other; and it
was impossible *not* to regret it; for the ruin presides in state over the river, far
from city or town, as if it might have a peculiar privilege to preserve its memorials of past ages, and maintain its own character for centuries to come. We
sat upon a bench, under the high trees, and had beautiful views of the different
reaches of the river, above and below. On the opposite bank, which is finely
wooded with elms and other trees, are the remains of a priory built upon a rock;
and rock and ruin are so blended, that it is impossible to separate the one from
the other. Nothing can be more beautiful than the little remnant of this holy
place: elm trees (for we were near enough to distinguish them by their branches,)
grow out of the walls, and overshadow a small, but very elegant window. It
can scarcely be conceived what a grace the castle and priory impart to each
other; and the river Clyde flows on, smooth and unruffled below, seeming to
my thoughts more in harmony with the sober and stately images of former times,
than if it had roared over a rocky channel, forcing its sound upon the ear. It
blended gently with the warbling of the smaller birds, and the chattering of the
larger ones, that had made their nests in the ruins. In this fortress the chief
of the English nobility were confined after the battle of Bannockburn. If a
man *is* to be a prisoner, he scarcely could have a more pleasant place to solace
his captivity; but I thought that, for close confinement, I should prefer the
banks of a lake, or the seaside. The greatest charm of a brook or river is in the

old castle. It was built by the young Earl of Forfar,
who was killed at the battle of Sheriffmuir. The scenery
around Bothwell Castle is remarkably splendid, and is
adorned with luxuriant natural wood. The Clyde here
makes a beautiful sweep, and forms the fine semicircular
declivity called Bothwell Bank, celebrated in Scottish
song. The following interesting anecdote, quoted from
a work entitled " Verstegan's Restitution of Decayed Intelligence," printed at Antwerp in 1605, is a proof of the
antiquity of at least the air to which the song of " Bothwell Bank" is sung :—" So fell it out of late years, that
an English gentleman, travelling in Palestine, not far
from Jerusalem, as he passed through a country town, he
heard, by chance, a woman sitting at her door dandling
her child, to sing, *Bothwel Bank, thou blumest fair.* The
gentleman hereat wondered, and forthwith, in English,
saluted the woman, who joyfully answered him, and
said, she was right glad there to see a gentleman of our
isle ; and told him that she was a Scottish woman, and
came first from Scotland to Venice, and from Venice
thither, where her fortune was to be the wife of an officer
under the Turk ; who being at that instant absent, and
very soon to return, she entreated the gentleman to stay
there until his return. The which he did ; and she, for
country sake, to show herself the more kind and boun-
tiful unto him, told her husband, at his home-coming,

liberty to pursue it through its windings ; you can then take it in whatever mood
you like ; silent or noisy, sportive or quiet. The beauties of a brook or river
must be sought, and the pleasure is in going in search of them ; those of a lake
or of the sea come to you of themselves. These rude warriors cared little, perhaps, about either ; and yet, if one may judge from the writings of Chaucer, and
from the old romances, more interesting passions were connected with natural
objects in the days of chivalry than now ; though going in search of scenery, as
it is called, had not then been thought of. I had previously heard nothing of
Bothwell Castle, at least nothing that I remembered ; therefore, perhaps my
pleasure was greater, compared with what I received elsewhere, than others
might feel."

that the gentleman was her kinsman ; whereupon her husband entertained him very kindly, and, at his departure, gave him divers things of good value." Leyden makes the following allusion to this story, in his Ode on Scottish music :—

> " And thus the exiled Scotian maid,
>   By fond alluring love betray'd,
>   To visit Syria's date-crown'd shore,
>   In plaintive strains that soothed despair,
>   Did ' Bothwell's Banks, that bloom so fair,'
>   And scenes of earlier youth deplore."

Directly opposite to Bothwell Castle, on the south bank of the Clyde, are the ruins of Blantyre Priory, situated on the brink of a perpendicular rock.

Proceeding onwards, at the distance of a mile and a half, the tourist reaches Bothwell village and church. The old church, part of which is still standing, is the remains of an ancient Gothic fabric, cased all over with a thin coating of stone. Within its walls, the unfortunate Robert Duke of Rothsay, who was starved to death by his uncle the Duke of Albany, in Falkland Palace, was married to a daughter of Archibald the Grim, Earl of Douglas.

At a little distance in front, the tourist crosses the Clyde by Bothwell Bridge, the scene of the famous battle which took place in 1679, between the royal forces, under the Duke of Monmouth, and the Covenanters. The royal army moved towards Hamilton, and reached Bothwell-moor on the 22d of June. The insurgents were encamped chiefly in the Duke of Hamilton's park, along the Clyde, which separated the two armies. Bothwell Bridge was then long and narrow, having a portal in the middle, with gates, which the Covenanters shut and barricadoed with stones and loads of timber. This important post was defended by 300 of their best men, under Hackston of Rathillet and Hall of Haughhead. The more moderate of the insurgents waited upon Monmouth, to offer terms, and obtained a promise that he would interpose with his Majesty on their behalf, on condition of their immediately dispersing themselves, and yielding up their arms. The Cameronian party, however, would accede to no terms with an uncovenanted king, and, while they were debating on the Duke's proposal, his fieldpieces were already planted on the eastern side of the river, to cover the attack of the foot-guards, who were led on by Lord Livingstone, to force the bridge. Here Hackston maintained his post with zeal and courage, nor was it until all his ammunition was expended, and every support denied him by the general, that he reluctantly abandoned the important pass. When his party were drawn back, the Duke's army slowly, and with their cannon in front, defiled along the bridge, and formed in line of battle as they came over the river. The Duke commanded the foot, and Claverhouse the cavalry. It would seem that these movements could not have been performed without at least some loss, had the enemy been serious in opposing them. But the insurgents were otherwise employed. With the strangest delusion that ever fell upon devoted beings, they chose these precious moments to cashier their officers, and elect others in their room. In this important operation, they were at length disturbed by the Duke's cannon, at the very first discharge of which, the horse of the Covenanters wheeled and rode off, breaking and trampling down the ranks of the infantry in their flight. Monmouth humanely issued orders to stop the effusion of blood, but Claverhouse,

burning to avenge his defeat, and the death of his cornet
and kinsman, at Drumclog, made great slaughter among
the fugitives, of whom 400 were slain. These events
are thus described in *Clyde*, a poem by Wilson, reprinted
in *Scottish Descriptive Poems*, edited by Dr. Leyden,
Edinburgh, 1803:—

> " Where Bothwell's Bridge connects the margin steep,
> And Clyde below runs silent, strong, and deep,
> The hardy peasant by oppression driven
> To battle, deem'd his cause the cause of Heaven ;
> Unskill'd in arms, with useless courage stood,
> While gentle Monmouth grieved to shed his blood ;
> But fierce Dundee, inflamed with deadly hate,
> In vengeance for the great Montrose's fate,
> Set loose the sword, and to the hero's shade
> A barbarous hetacomb of victims paid." *

Many of the fugitives found shelter in the wooded parks
around Hamilton Palace.

Great changes have now been made on the scene of
the engagement. The gateway, gate, and house of the
bridge-ward were long ago removed. The original breadth
of the bridge was twelve feet ; but, in 1826, twenty-two
feet were added to its breadth, the hollow which once lay
at the Hamilton extremity was filled up, and an alteration was also made in the road, at the other end. The
open park in which the Covenanters were posted, is now
changed into enclosed fields and plantations, and the
moor upon which the royal army advanced to the engagement, is now a cultivated and beautiful region.

The level grounds, which stretch away from Bothwell
Bridge along the north-east bank of the river, once

* See notes to the ballad of " The Battle of Bothwell Bridge," in the Border
Minstrelsy. The reader cannot but remember the spirited description given of
this engagement in the novel of Old Mortality.

formed the patrimonial estate of Hamilton of Bothwell-haugh, the assassin of the Regent Murray.

A mile and a half beyond Bothwell Bridge, and ten miles and a half from Glasgow, the tourist enters the town of

HAMILTON,

the capital of the Middle Ward of Lanarkshire. Hamilton is a burgh of regality, dependent on the Duke of Hamilton; it contains about 6000 inhabitants, of whom a considerable number are engaged in weaving. The town has been much improved, by the recent erection of a new bridge, called Cadzow Bridge, opening into a street of the same name. The principal object of attraction, in this vicinity, is Hamilton Palace, the seat of the Duke of Hamilton, which stands on a plain between the town and the river. It is a magnificent structure, and has been greatly enlarged and improved by the present Duke. Its interior is extremely splendid, and it contains a magnificent collection of paintings, supposed to be the best in Scotland. The most celebrated of these is *Daniel in the Lion's Den,* by Rubens.* Among other curiosities, Hamilton Palace contains the carbine with which Both-wellhaugh shot the Regent Murray.

---

* On this splendid picture Wordsworth has composed the following sonnet:
　　"Amid a fertile region green with wood
　　And fresh with rivers, well doth it become
　　The ducal Owner, in his palace-home
　　To naturalise this tawny Lion brood:
　　Children of Art, that claim strange brotherhood
　　(Couched in their den) with those that roam at large
　　Over the burning wilderness, and charge
　　The wind with terror while they roar for food.
　　Satiate are *these;* and still—to eye and ear;
　　Hence, while we gaze, a more enduring fear!
　　Yet is the Prophet calm, nor would the cave
　　Daunt him—if his Companions, now be-drowsed,
　　Outstretched and listless, were by hunger roused:
　　Man placed him here, and God, he knows, can save."

Near Hamilton is the river Avon, a tributary of the Clyde. The vale which this stream waters is adorned with gorgeous old wood, and several ancient and modern mansions, the most famous of which is Cadyow or Cadzow Castle, the ancient baronial residence of the family of Hamilton, situated upon the precipitous banks of the Avon, about two miles above its junction with the Clyde. It was dismantled in the conclusion of the civil wars, during the reign of the unfortunate Mary. The situation of the ruins, embossed in wood, darkened by ivy and creeping shrubs, and overhanging the brawling torrent, is romantic in the highest degree. In the immediate vicinity of Cadyow is a grove of immense oaks, the remains of the Caledonian forest, which anciently extended through the south of Scotland, from the Eastern to the Atlantic Ocean. Some of these trees measure twenty-five feet and upwards in circumference, and the state of decay in which they now appear, shows that they may have witnessed the rites of the Druids. The whole scenery is included in the magnificent park of the Duke of Hamilton. The famous breed of Scottish wild cattle, milk-white in colour, with black muzzles, horns, and hoofs, are still preserved in this forest. They were expelled about 1760, on account of their ferocity, but have since been restored.* The following description of their habits is abridged from an article, by the Rev. W. Patrick, in the Quarterly Journal of Agriculture :—

"I am inclined to believe that the Hamilton breed of cattle is the oldest in Scotland, or perhaps in Britain. Although Lord Tankerville has said they have 'no wild habits,' I am convinced, from personal observation, that this is one of their peculiar features. In browsing their extensive pasture, they always keep close

* See notes to the ballad of Cadyow Castle, in the Border Minstrelsy.

together, never scattering or straggling over it, a peculiarity which does not belong to the Kyloe, or any other breed, from the wildest or most inhospitable regions of the Highlands. The white cows are also remarkable for their systematic manner of feeding. At different periods of the year their tactics are different, but by those acquainted with their habits they are always found about the same part of the forest at the same hour of the day. In the height of summer, they always bivouac for the night towards the northern extremity of the forest; from this point they start in the morning, and browse to the southern extremity, and return at sunset to their old rendezvous; and during these perambulations they always feed *en masse*.

SCOTTISH WILD OX.

" The bulls are seldom ill-natured, but when they are so, they display a disposition more than ordinarily savage, cunning, pertinacious, and revengeful. A poor bird-catcher, when exercising his vocation among the ' Old Oaks,' as the park is familiarly called, chanced to be attacked by a savage bull. By great exertion he gained a tree before his assailant made up to him. Here he had occasion to observe the habits of the animal. It did not roar or bellow, but merely grunted, the whole body quivered with passion and savage rage, and he frequently attacked the tree with his head and hoofs. Finding all to no purpose, he left off the vain attempt, began to browse, and removed to some distance from the tree. The bird-catcher tried to descend, but this watchful Cerberus was again instantly at his post, and it was not till after six hour's imprisonment, and various bouts at ' bo-peep' as above, that the unfortunate man was relieved by some shepherds with their dogs. A writer's apprentice, who had been at the village of Quarter on business, and who returned by the 'Oaks' as a 'near-hand cut,' was also attacked by one of these savage brutes, near the northern extremity of the forest. He was fortunate, however, in getting into a tree, but was watched by the bull, and kept there during the whole of the night, and till near two o'clock next day.

"These animals are never taken and killed like other cattle, but are always shot in the field. I once went to see a bull and some cows destroyed in this manner—not by any means for the sake of the sight—but to observe the manner and habits of the animal under peculiar circumstances. When the shooters approached, they, as usual, scampered off in a body, then stood still, tossed their heads on high, and seemed to snuff the wind; the manœuvre was often repeated, till they got so hard pressed, (and seemingly having a sort of half-idea of the tragedy which was to be performed,) they at length ran furiously in a mass, always preferring the sides of the fence and sheltered situations, and dexterously taking advantage of any inequality in the ground, or other circumstances, to conceal themselves from the assailing foe. In their flight, the bulls, or stronger of the flock, always took the lead; a smoke ascended from them which could be seen at a great distance; and they were often so close together, like sheep, that a carpet would have covered them. The cows which had young, on the first 'tug of war,' all retreated to the thickets where their calves were concealed; from prudential motives, they are never, if possible, molested. These and other wild habits I can testify to be inherent in the race, and are well-known to all who have an opportunity of acquainting themselves with them."

Sir Walter Scott has made Cadyow Castle the subject of the following magnificent ballad, the perusal of which must gratify every lover of poetry and of historical recollections :—

> " 'Tis night—the shade of keep and spire
> Obscurely dance on Evan's stream ;
> And on the wave the warder's fire
> Is chequering the moon-light beam.

Fades slow their light; the east is grey;
  The weary warder leaves his tower;
Steeds snort; uncoupled stag-hounds bay,
  And merry hunters quit the bower.

The draw-bridge falls—they hurry out—
  Clatters each plank and swinging chain,
As, dashing o'er, the jovial rout
  Urge the shy steed, and slack the rein.

First of his troop, the chief rode on;
  His shouting merry-men throng behind;
The steed of princely Hamilton
  Was fleeter than the mountain wind.

From the thick copse the roe-bucks bound,
  The startled red-deer scuds the plain,
For the hoarse bugle's warrior-sound
  Has roused their mountain haunts again.

Through the huge oaks of Evandale,
  Whose limbs a thousand years have worn,
What sullen roar comes down the gale,
  And drowns the hunter's pealing horn?

Mightiest of all the beasts of chase,
  That roam in woody Caledon,
Crashing the forest in his race,
  The Mountain Bull comes thundering on!

Fierce, on the hunters' quiver'd band,
  He rolls his eyes of swarthy glow,
Spurns, with black hoof and horn, the sand,
  And tosses high his mane of snow.

Aim'd well, the chieftain's lance has flown;
  Struggling in blood, the savage lies;
His roar is sunk in hollow groan—
  Sound, merry huntsmen! sound the *pryse!* *

    * The note blown at the death of the game.

'Tis noon—against the knotted oak
   The hunters rest the idle spear;
Curls through the trees the slender smoke,
   Where yeoman dight the woodland cheer.

Proudly the chieftain mark'd his clan,
   On greenwood lap all careless thrown,
Yet miss'd his eye the boldest man,
   That bore the name of Hamilton.

' Why fills not Bothwellhaugh his place,
   Still wont our weal and woe to share?
Why comes he not our sport to grace?
   Why shares he not our hunter's fare? '—

Stern Claud replied, with darkening face,
   (Grey Paisley's haughty lord was he)
' At merry feast, or buxom chace,
   No more the warrior wilt thou see.

' Few suns have set since Woodhouselee
   Saw Bothwellhaugh's bright goblets foam,
When to his hearths, in social glee,
   The war-worn soldier turn'd him home.

' There, wan from her maternal throes,
   His Margaret, beautiful and mild,
Sate in her bower, a pallid rose,
   And peaceful nursed her new-born child.

' O change accursed ! past are those days;
   False Murray's ruthless spoilers came,
And, for the hearth's domestic blaze,
   Ascends destruction's volumed flame.

' What sheeted phantom wanders wild,
   Where mountain Eske through woodland flows,
Her arms enfold a shadowy child—
   Oh is it she, the pallid rose?

' The wilder'd traveller sees her glide,
  And hears her feeble voice with awe—
" Revenge," she cries, " on Murray's pride !
  And woe for injured Bothwellhaugh ! " '

He ceased—and cries of rage and grief
  Burst mingling from the kindred band,
And half arose the kindling chief,
  And half unsheathed his Arran brand.

But who, o'er bush, o'er stream and rock,
  Rides headlong with resistless speed,
Whose bloody poniard's frantic stroke
  Drives to the leap his jaded steed ?

Whose cheek is pale, whose eye-balls glare,
  As one some vision'd sight that saw ;
Whose hands are bloody, loose his hair ?—
  'Tis he ! 'tis he ! 'tis Bothwellhaugh !

From gory selle,* and reeling steed,
  Sprung the fierce horseman with a bound,
And, reeking from the recent deed,
  He dash'd his carbine on the ground.

Sternly he spoke—' 'Tis sweet to hear
  In good greenwood the bugle blown,
But sweeter to Revenge's ear,
  To drink a tyrant's dying groan.

' Your slaughter'd quarry proudly trode,
  At dawning morn, o'er dale and down,
But prouder base-born Murray rode
  Through old Linlithgow's crowded town.

' From the wild Border's humbled side,
  In haughty triumph, marched he,
While Knox relax'd his bigot pride,
  And smiled the traitorous pomp to see.

* Saddle. A word used by Spencer, and other ancient authors.

‘ But can stern Power, with all his vaunt,
　Or Pomp, with all her courtly glare,
The settled heart of Vengeance daunt,
　Or change the purpose of Despair?

‘ With hackbut bent,* my secret stand,
　Dark as the purposed deed, I chose,
And marked, where, mingling in his band,
　Troop’d Scottish pikes, and English bows.

‘ Dark Morton, girt with many a spear,
　Murder’s foul minion, led the van ;
And clash’d their broad-swords in the rear,
　The wild Macfarlanes’ plaided clan.

‘ Glencairn and stout Parkhead were nigh,
　Obsequious at their regent’s rein,
And haggard Lindesay’s iron eye,
　That saw fair Mary weep in vain.

‘ Mid pennon’d spears, a steely grove,
　Proud Murray’s plumage floated high ;
Scarce could his trampling charger move,
　So close the minions crowded nigh.

‘ From the raised visor’s shade his eye,
　Dark-rolling, glanced the ranks along,
And his steel truncheon, waved on high,
　Seem’d marshalling the iron throng.

‘ But yet his sadden’d brow confess’d
　A passing shade of doubt and awe ;
Some fiend was whispering in his breast,
　“ Beware of injured Bothwellhaugh ! ”

‘ The death-shot parts—the charger springs—
　Wild rises tumult’s startling roar !
And Murray’s plumy helmet rings—
　Rings on the ground to rise no more.
　　　　　* Gun cock’d.

' What joy the raptured youth can feel,
    To hear her love the loved one tell,—
Or he who broaches on his steel
    The wolf, by whom his infant well !

' But dearer to my injured eye,
    To see in dust proud Murray roll ;
And mine was ten times trebled joy,
    To hear him groan his felon soul.

' My Margaret's spectre glided near :
    With pride her bleeding victim saw ;
And shriek'd in his death-deafen'd ear,
    " Remember injured Bothwellhaugh ! "

' Then speed thee, noble Chatlerault !
    Spread to the wind thy banner'd tree ;
Each warrior bend his Clydesdale bow—
    Murray is fallen, and Scotland free.'

Vaults every warrior to his steed ;
    Loud bugles join their wild acclaim—
' Murray is fallen, and Scotland freed !
    Couch Arran ! couch thy spear of flame ! ' "

Opposite Cadyow is Chatelherault, a summer residence of the Duke of Hamilton, so called from the estate and dukedom in France, anciently possessed by his Grace's ancestors.*

Leaving Hamilton, the tourist proceeds in a southeasterly direction, and, at the distance of half a mile, crosses the Avon. On the opposite bank of the Clyde is Dalziel House, (General Hamilton,) surrounded by fine plantations, giving an imposing effect to the land-

* The banks of the South Calder, which lie at no great distance from Hamilton, are extremely romantic, and adorned with a number of fine seats, the most remarkable of which are Wishaw Castle (Lord Belhaven,) Coltness, (Henry Holdsworth, Esq.,) Murdieston, (Admiral Sir A. Inglis Cochrane,) Allanton, (Sir Henry Steuart, Bart.) &c.

scape. The views now obtained of the river and the surrounding scenery are extremely fine. About a mile beyond Avon Bridge, the road strikes off the Carlisle road, leading towards Douglasdale, and gradually descending towards the margin of the river. On the opposite bank is Cambusnethan, (R. Lockhart, Esq.,) a fine castellated mansion, seated on a beautiful lawn, partly shaded by splendid lime trees. This district, which has earned the name of " The Orchard of Scotland," or " The Fruit Lands," is eminently worthy of its appellation, presenting, as it does, "one uninterrupted series of grove, garden, and orchard,—a billowy ocean of foliage, waving in the summer wind, and glowing under the summer sun." During spring, the luxuriance of the blossom, and during autumn, the teeming abundance of the fruit, contribute to render this one of the most delightful drives in Scotland. Six miles from Hamilton, the Edinburgh road to Ayr crosses the Clyde at Garrion Bridge, which derives its name from a seat of Lord Belhaven's, in the immediate vicinity. A mile beyond, is the delightful bower-like village of Dalserf, celebrated for its excellent orchards. On the left is Dalserf House, (Campbell, Esq.,) and, on the right, Millburn House, (Brown, Esq.) On the opposite bank of the river is Brownlee, (Harvie, Esq.,) and the stately mansion of Mauldslie Castle, the seat of the last Earl of Hyndford, now the property of Nisbet of Carfin.* A little farther on is Milton-Lockhart, (Captain Lockhart,) a handsome edifice in the Tudor style, standing on a fine promontory, with delightful sloping banks and gardens; and Waygateshaw, (Steel, Esq.,)

* Robert Bruce granted ten merks sterling out of his mills at Mauldslie for the purpose of keeping a lamp constantly burning upon St. Machute's tomb at Lesmahago. The lamp was kept burning till the Reformation.

FALL OF THE CLYDE AT STONEBYRES.

once the residence of the notorious Major Weir and his sister, condemned for witchcraft in the seventeenth century. Two miles and a half beyond Dalserf, the tourist crosses the river Nethan, at Nethanfoot, by a bridge. On the right, near the junction of the Nethan and the Clyde, are the ruins of the Castle of Craignethan, or Draphane, situated on a single rock, overhanging the former stream. Craignethan appears to have been, at one time, a most extensive and important fortress. It was the seat of Sir James Hamilton, called the Bastard of Arran, a man noted for his sanguinary character, in the reign of James V.; and here Queen Mary lodged for a few days, after her escape from Lochleven. Craignethan has furnished the author of " Old Mortality" with his description of Tillietudlem. It is now the property of Lord Douglas. The scenery around the castle exhibits a striking mixture of the sublime and beautiful. A short way beyond, on the north bank of the river, is Carfin House, (Nisbet, Esq.,) and, soon after, the road enters the plantations of Stonebyres, (Vere, Esq.) The channel of the river now becomes rugged and confined, and the banks more precipitous, and, in a short time, the tourist reaches the first of the Falls of the Clyde, as he approaches from the west,*

THE FALL OF STONEBYRES.

The river here makes three distinct falls, being broken by two projecting rocks. The scene is uncommonly magnificent.

Passing, on the left, Sunnyside Lodge, (A. Gillespie, Esq.,) and, on the right, Kirkfield, (Steel, Esq.,) and other elegant villas, the tourist, at the distance of a mile

* The approach is by a path laid out by the celebrated Robert Owen.

from the Fall of Stonebyres, crosses the Clyde by an
ancient bridge of three arches, and soon after reaches

LANARK,

a royal burgh, and the county town of Lanarkshire, situated at the distance of twenty-five miles from Glasgow,
and thirty-two from Edinburgh. Lanark is a town of no
great importance in itself; till lately, it was extremely
dull, but the extension of the cotton-works in its neighbourhood, and the erection of several good public buildings, have considerably improved its appearance;* while
its vicinity to the Falls of Clyde, makes it a favourite
place of resort for strangers during the summer months.
The principal inn, the Clydesdale Hotel, is equal, in point
of accommodation, to any provincial establishment in
Scotland. It was in Lanark that the Scottish hero Wallace commenced his glorious exertions to free his country
from a foreign yoke, and tradition points out a number
of localities in the vicinity, identified with his name and

---

* It is said that the burgh of Lanark was till very recent times so poor that
the single butcher of the town, who also exercised the calling of a weaver in order to fill up his spare time, would never venture upon the speculation of kill-
ing a sheep till every part of the animal was ordered beforehand. When he
felt disposed to engage in such an enterprise, he usually prevailed upon the
minister, the provost and the town-council, to take shares; but when no person
came forward to bespeak the fourth quarter, the sheep received a respite till
better times should cast up. The bellman or *skellyman*, as he is there called,
used often to go through the streets of Lanark with advertisements such as
are embodied in the following popular rhyme:—

> Bell-ell-ell!
> There's a fat sheep to kill!
> A leg for the provost,
>   Another for the priest,
> The bailies and deacons
>   They'll tak the neist;
> And if the fourth leg we cannot sell,
> The sheep it maun leeve and gae back to the hill!
> 　　　　　CHAMBERS' *Rhymes of Scotland*, p. 140.

exploits. A statue of the hero is placed in a niche, above the principal entrance to the parish church.

About a quarter of a mile to the east of the town, are the ruins of the very ancient church of Lanark, surrounded by the parish burying-ground.

There are a number of handsome seats in the neighbourhood of Lanark, the most splendid of which is Carstairs House, the seat of Henry Monteith, Esq.

In visiting the Falls of Clyde from Lanark, the tourist should at once proceed to the uppermost, called Bonnington Linn, two miles from Lanark. A romantic path leads to it, through the grounds of Bonnington House, (Lady Mary Ross.) Above this cataract the river moves very slowly, but all at once it bends towards the northeast, and throws itself over a perpendicular rock of about thirty feet. Immediately below the first fall, the river hurries along with prodigious rapidity, boiling and foaming over its narrow and rocky channel. The banks are very steep, and, at one point, the river struggles through a chasm of not more than four feet, where it may be stepped over. Half a mile below Bonnington Linn is

CORRA LINN,

where the river takes three distinct leaps, making altogether a height of about eighty-four feet. The best view of this magnificent fall, is from the semicircular seat on the verge of the cliff opposite. There is also a rustic staircase, leading to the bottom of the Falls, partly formed of wood, and partly cut out of the solid rock, from which the cataract has a very magnificent effect. Above is a pavilion, erected, in 1708, by Sir James Carmichael, then of Bonnington, which commands a fine view, and which is filled up with mirrors, so arranged as

to give the cataract the appearance of being precipitated
upon the spectator. Upon a rock above the fall, on the
opposite side of the river, is the old castle of Corra; and,
to the right of this castle, is Corra House, the seat of
George Cranston, Esq., half hid by trees.

About half a mile below Corra Linn is the celebrated
village of New Lanark, originally established in the year
1783 by the benevolent David Dale of Glasgow, father-
in-law of the famous Robert Owen. The inhabitants,
who amount to about 2500, are exclusively engaged in
cotton-spinning.

In Bonnington House are preserved two relics of Sir
William Wallace, a portrait of the hero, and a very curious chair on which he is said to have sat.

No traveller should leave this district without visiting
Cartland Crags on Mouse Water, about a mile west from
Lanark. The stream flows through a deep chasm, apparently formed by an earthquake, instead of following
what seems a much more natural channel a little farther
to the east. The rocky banks on both sides rise to the
height of about 400 feet. A few years ago a bridge was
thrown across this narrow chasm, consisting of three
arches of the height of 128 feet. At a little distance
below is a narrow old bridge, supposed to be of Roman
origin. On the north side of the stream, a few yards
above the new bridge, is a cave in the face of the rock,
termed "Wallace's Cave," which is pointed out by tradition as the hiding-place of that hero after he had slain
Haselrig the English sheriff.

About a mile and a half westward from Lanark, on
the south side of the Mouse, is the ancient house of
Jerviswood, the seat of the illustrious patriot who was
murdered under the forms of law during the infamous

government of Charles II. The attainder of Jerviswood was reversed by the Convention Parliament at the Revolution. On the opposite bank of the stream, situated amidst extensive plantations, is Cleghorn, the seat of Allan Elliot Lockhart, Esq. of Borthwickbrae.

About three miles below Lanark, on the north bank of the Clyde, is Lee House, the seat of Sir Norman Macdonald Lockhart, Bart. It is a fine mansion, lately modernized in the castellated style, and contains a good collection of pictures. Here is kept the famous Lee Penny, the use made of which by Sir Walter Scott, in his splendid tale of " The Talisman," must be familiar to every reader. The following curious extract is given in the introduction to that tale:—" Quhilk day, amongest the referries of the Brethren of the Ministry of Lanark, it was proponed to the Synod that Gavin Hamilton of Raploch had pursueit an Complaint before them against Sir James Lockhart of Lee, anent the superstitious using of an Stone, set in silver, for the curing of deseased Cattle, q^{lk} the said Gavin affirmed could not be lawfully usit, and that they had deferrit to give ony decisionne thairin till the advice of the Assemblie might be had concerning the same. The Assemblie having inquirit of the manner of using thereof, and particularly understood, be examination of the said Laird of Lee, and otherwise, that the custom is only to cast the stone in some water, and give the deceasit Cattle thereof to drink, and that the same is done without using any words, such as Charmers and Sorcereirs use in thair unlawfull practices; and considering that in nature thair are many things seen to work strange effects, whereof no human wit can give a reason, it having pleast God to give to stones and herbs a speciall vertue for healing of many infirmities in man and beast,

R

advises the Brethren to surcease thair process, as therein they perceive no ground of Offence, and admonishes the said Laird of Lee, in using of the said stone, to take heid that it be usit hereafter with the least scandle that possibly maybe. Extract out of the Books of the Assemblie, holden at Glasgow, and subscribed at thair command.— M. ROBERT YOUNG, Clerk to the Assemblie at Glasgow."

In the grounds of Lee there is a huge oak tree, which is so completely hollowed out by age that it can hold half a dozen individuals standing upright.

The tourist may proceed from Lanark to Edinburgh (32 miles) by West Calder, Calder House, (Lord Torphichen,) Mid-Calder, Dalmahoy, (Earl of Morton,) &c. For a description of this route see Itinerary.

EIGHTH TOUR.

GLASGOW — DUMBARTON — PORT-GLASGOW — HELENSBURGH — GREENOCK — GOUROCK — DUNOON — ROTHSAY.

*** A Chart of this Tour will be found facing page 257.

STARTING from Broomielaw in one of the steam-boats which ply on the river,* a few minutes' sail brings the passengers to the mouth of the Kelvin, a stream celebrated in Scottish song. The village on the left is Govan. On both sides of the river there is a series of pleasant suburban villas. About two miles below Govan, on the same side of the river, is Shieldhall, A. Johnston, Esq. On the right, Jordanhill, James Smith, Esq. A little farther down the river, and on the same side, is Scotstoun, the seat of Miss Oswald. On the left is Elderslie House, the seat of Alexander Spiers, Esq.; and about a mile farther down is Blythswood House, the seat of Archibald Campbell, Esq. Between the two last mentioned places is Renfrew Ferry, where a near view may be obtained of the ancient burgh of Renfrew. The appearance of the town is mean and antiquated. In the neighbourhood, Somerled, Thane of Argyle and Lord of the Isles, who had rebelled against Malcolm IV., was defeated and slain in the year 1164. The barony of Renfrew was the first possession of the Stuart family in Scotland. It gives the title of Baron to the Prince of

---

* The railway to Greenock affords the means of reaching that town with greater rapidity than by water, but tourists are recommended to take the steamer throughout, as a better prospect of the country is thereby attained.

Wales.   The collected waters of the two Carts and the
Gryfe flow into the Clyde at Inchinnan, about a mile
below Renfrew.   Near Inchinnan Bridge, the Earl of
Argyle was taken prisoner in 1685.   On the left, and a
little above Erskine Ferry, stands Northbarr, a plain and
now dilapidated mansion, formerly the seat of Lord Sempill.   Near the river, on the left, is the old mansion-
house of Erskine, anciently the seat of the Earls of Mar,
and latterly of the Blantyre family.   Robert, eleventh
Lord Blantyre, who perished accidentally in the commo-
tions at Brussels, in 1830, erected the new princely mansion which crowns the rising ground a little farther down.
The tourist is now half-way between Glasgow and
Greenock.   The river has expanded greatly, and assumed
the appearance of a lake, apparently closed in front.   The
lofty heights on the right are the Kilpatrick Hills, and the
village in the narrow plain between them and the river
is Kilpatrick, supposed to have been the birth-place of
St. Patrick, the tutelar saint of Ireland.   The little bay
in front of Kilpatrick is Bowling Bay.   Opposite Bowling
Inn may be perceived the mouth of the Great Junction
Canal, which unites the east and west coasts of Scotland,
by means of the Firths of Forth and Clyde.   At a short
distance below, on the right, is the little promontory of
Dunglass Point, the western termination of Antoninus'
Wall or Graham's Dyke, with the ruins of Dunglass Castle, formerly the property of the Colquhouns of Luss, but
now belonging to Buchanan of Auchintorlie.   On this
spot a statue has lately been erected of the late Henry
Bell, the first person who applied the steam-engine to
river navigation.   On the left, in the distance, are seen
the church and manse of Erskine; Bishopton House,
(Lord Blantyre); Drums, (Captain Darroch.)   On the

opposite side are Milton Island, Milton House, and Printworks, (Mitchell, Esq.) ; Dumbuck House, (Colonel Geils) ; at the foot of Dumbuck Hill (*Hill of Roes*) Garshake, (Dixon, Esq.) ; Chapel Green and Silverton Hill. But by far the most prominent object is the rock of

DUMBARTON,

which rises suddenly from the point of junction of the Leven and Clyde, to the height of 560 feet, measuring a mile in circumference, terminating in two sharp points, one higher than the other, and studded over with houses and batteries. Previous to his being sent to England, Wallace was confined for some time in this castle, the governor of which was the infamous Sir John Menteith, who betrayed him. The highest peak of the rock is still denominated " Wallace's Seat," and a part of the castle " Wallace's Tower." In one of the apartments, a huge two-handed sword, said to have belonged to that hero, is still shown. At the union of Scotland with England, this was one of the four fortresses stipulated to be kept up ; and, accordingly, it is still in repair, and occupied by a garrison.* Opposite to Dumbarton Castle, on the

* During the wars which desolated Scotland in the reign of Queen Mary, this formidable fortress was taken in the following remarkable way, by Captain Crawford of Jordanhill, a distinguished adherent of the King's party :—"He took advantage of a misty and moonless night to bring to the foot of the castle-rock the scaling-ladders which he had provided, choosing for his terrible experiment the place where the rock was highest, and where, of course, less pains were taken to keep a regular guard. This choice was fortunate ; for the first ladder broke with the weight of the men who attempted to mount, and the noise of the fall must have betrayed them, had there been any sentinel within hearing. Crawford, assisted by a soldier who had deserted from the castle, and was acting as his guide, renewed the attempt in person, and having scrambled up to a projecting ledge of rock where there was some footing, contrived to make fast the ladder, by tying it to the roots of a tree, which grew about midway up the rock. Here they found a small flat surface, sufficient, however, to afford footing to the whole party, which was, of course, very few in number. In scaling the second precipice, another accident took place :—One of the party,

left, is West Sea Bank; and beyond the Leven, on the
right, is Leven Grove, the seat of the Dixons of Dumbarton.   Two miles farther, on the left, is Finlayston, formerly the family mansion of the Earls of Glencairn, now
the seat of Graham of Gartmore; on the right are Clyde
Bank and Clyde Cottage.   Approaching Port-Glasgow,
we reach the Castle of Newark, which, after having
belonged, in succession, to a branch of the Maxwells and
to the Belhaven family, is now the property of Lady
Shaw Stewart.   PORT-GLASGOW was founded, in 1668,
by the merchants of Glasgow, for the embarkation and
disembarkation of goods.   Since the river was deepened,
Port-Glasgow has lost much of the consequence which it
originally possessed.   On the opposite shore of the Clyde
are the remains of an ancient castle, believed to have
been that of Cardross, in which Robert Bruce breathed
his last.   For several miles the shore is thickly studded
with villas, among which are Ardarden House, Ardmore
House, Cames-Eskan, Kilmahew Castle, and Drumfork
House, all on the right side of the Firth.   Three and a
half miles from Dumbarton is the Kirk of Cardross, with
its little attendant village.   Five miles further along the
shore, the beautiful sea-bathing village of HELENSBURGH
occupies a sheltered situation at the opening of the Gare
Loch.   It was founded about fifty years ago by Sir James

subject to epileptic fits, was seized by one of these attacks, brought on perhaps
by terror, while he was in the act of climbing up the ladder.   His illness made
it impossible for him either to ascend or descend.   To have slain the man would
have been a cruel expedient, besides that the fall of his body from the ladder
might have alarmed the garrison.   Crawford caused him, therefore, to be tied
to the ladder; then all the rest descending, they turned the ladder, and thus
mounted with ease over the belly of the epileptic person.   When the party
gained the summit, they slew the sentinel ere he had time to give the alarm,
and easily surprised the slumbering garrison, who had trusted too much to the
security of their castle to keep good watch.   This exploit of Crawford may
compare with any thing of the kind which we read of in history."

Colquhoun. A mile to the westward is the pleasant inn
of Ardincaple; and a mile and a half further are the village and kirk of Row, which is the parish church of
Helensburgh. The promontory opposite to Helensburgh,
between the Gare Loch and Loch Long, is occupied by
the mansion and beautiful grounds of Roseneath, a seat
of the Argyle family. This palace, built in the Italian
style, occupies the site of a fine old castle, which was
burnt down in 1802. After a sail from Glasgow of about
two hours and a half, the steamer reaches the large and
populous seaport of

GREENOCK,

which occupies part of a narrow stripe of level ground
stretching along the shore. Close upon the quay stands
the Custom-house, the finest public building in Greenock.
It is a remarkable proof of the opulence of the inhabitants, that the sum of £10,000, required for the erection
of this building, was subscribed in two days. This
town was the birth-place of Watt. The situation of
Greenock, with the mountains of Argyleshire and Dumbartonshire rising on the opposite side, is very fine.
The view from the quay is perhaps the finest commanded
by any seaport in the kingdom. Leaving Greenock,
the steamer makes direct for Kempock Point. The principal villas on the shore, to the left, are Rosebank, Sea-
bank, Glenpark, Finnart, Ladyburn House, and Bridgend.
About three miles below Greenock, at the bottom of a
little bay, is situated the pretty village of GOUROCK. It
commands a noble sea-view, and the walks along the
shore towards the Cloch are very beautiful. About a
quarter of a mile off Kempock Point, a promontory which
forms the western boundary of Gourock Bay, the Comet

steam-boat was run down by the Ayr steam-packet,
October 21, 1825, when upwards of fifty individuals
found a watery grave. A mile further along this coast,
is the old ruin of Leven Tower, crowning a fine eminence. About three miles below Gourock, the coast
bends to the south at the Cloch Light-house, one of the
most important beacons on the Clyde. A little below
stands Ardgowan, the seat of Sir R. M. Shaw Stewart,
Bart. A short way farther on, at the bottom of a small
bay, is the little sequestered village of Innerkip, one of
the most delightful watering-places on the west coast.
In the neighbourhood is Kelly House, the seat of Robert
Wallace, Esq. M.P. The counties of Renfrew and Ayr
are here divided by Kellyburn. The next promontory is
Knock Point, on rounding which we come in sight of the
beautiful picturesque village of Largs. The battle of
Largs, between the Scottish army and that of Haco, King
of Norway, in which the latter was defeated with great
slaughter, took place in 1263, on a large plain upon the
sea-shore to the south of the village.

Returning to Cloch Point, straight opposite on the
coast of Argyle, stands DUNOON, a sea-bathing village,
which commands several fine and diversified seaward
views. The Castle of Dunoon is an interesting relic of
antiquity. It was once a royal residence, and a strong
fortress. The hereditary keepership of this castle was
conferred by Robert Bruce on the family of Sir Colin
Campbell of Loch Awe, an ancestor of the Duke of
Argyle. It was the residence of the Argyle family in
1673, but from the commencement of the eighteenth
century was allowed to fall into a state of ruin. At a
short distance from Dunoon, is the Holy Loch, surrounded by steep and picturesque hills. On its eastern

shore is situated the little village of Kilmun, where may
be still seen the ruins of the Collegiate Church, founded,
in 1442, by Sir Duncan Campbell of Loch Awe, ancestor of the Argyle family.   Here the Argyle family have
their burying-place.   On leaving Dunoon, the steamer
skirts along Bawkie Bay.   The peninsula of Cowal ends
a few miles lower at Toward Point, where there is a
light-house, besides a large modern edifice, Toward
Castle, the seat of Kirkman Finlay, Esq.   On the neighbouring height, on the right, are seen the venerable
ruins of Toward Castle, the ancient seat of the Lamonts.
Turning Toward Point, we enter the Kyles of Bute, the
crooked strait which divides Argyleshire from Bute, and
in a short time reach the pleasant town of ROTHSAY.
The town consists of several neat streets, and the views
to be obtained of the neighbouring coasts, from various
elevated points around it, are extremely beautiful.   The
ancient royal castle of Rothsay, the favourite residence
of Robert III., is one of the finest ruins in Scotland.   It
was burned down by the Earl of Argyle in 1685.   The
closet in which Robert III. died is still pointed out.
Rothsay gave the title of Duke to the eldest son of the
Scottish kings, as it still does to the heir-apparent of the
British crown.   The western side of the Bay of Rothsay
commands a noble view of the entrance to the Kyles,
and the mouth of Loch Strevin, with the shores of
Cowal.   About two miles from Rothsay, the steam-boat
passes Port Bannatyne, a beautiful village encircling the
bottom of Kames Bay.   In the immediate vicinity stands
Kames Castle, an old fortified mansion still inhabited.
Between Rothsay and Kilchattan Bay stands Mount
Stewart, the seat of the Marquis of Bute, surrounded by

fine woods. Etterick Bay, on the west side of the island, is often visited on account of its picturesque scenery. After passing the mouth of Loch Strevin, the channel rapidly narrows. Between the ferry and the entrance of Loch Ridden, it is contracted by four islands. The passage, though narrow and intricate, is exceedingly interesting. Leaving the entrance to Loch Ridden on the right, the steamer emerges into the open space between Ard Lamont Point on the mainland, and Etterick Bay in Bute. The heights of Arran are seen here to great advantage. On rounding, the steamer enters Loch Fyne. On the left is the islet of Inchmarnock, with the ruins of a chapel, and soon after we pass another islet, called Slate Island. On the left is the wild and rugged coast of Kintyre. The harbour of East Tarbet, however, into which the steamer now enters, is remarkably secure. East Tarbet is a picturesque fishing village, situated upon a very narrow isthmus, uniting Kintyre to Knapdale. In the immediate vicinity is the Castle of Tarbet, now in ruins. Here the Earl of Argyle kept his troops previous to his unsuccessful descent upon the Lowlands in 1685. Leaving Tarbet, and pursuing our course northward, we pass Barmore Island, and shortly after come in sight of the village of Lochgilphead, and the extremity of the Crinan Canal. This canal, which was formed to save doubling the Mull of Kintyre, is only nine miles in length, but has no fewer than fifteen locks. On entering the canal, a good view is obtained of Lochgilphead and Kilmory, the seat of Sir John Ord. Two miles from the sea-lock, on the left, is Oakfield. The canal here passes through an extensive tract of marshy uninteresting country. Passing the village of

Bellanach, we enter the Bay of Crinan. Upon the right
is the modernized Castle of Duntroon, (Malcolm, Esq.,)
and northward, on the same side, Loch Craignish, a fine
arm of the sea, intersected by a chain of beautiful little
islands, covered with ancient oak-trees. The steam-boat
proceeds through the Dorishmore, or Great Gate, between
the point of Craignish and one of the chain of islets just
mentioned. Iona and Islay are now in sight. On the
south are the shores of Knapdale, and to the north the
islands of Shuna and Luing, with Loch Melfort opening
to the right. Two miles from the Point of Luing is
Blackmill Bay, opposite to which is the Island of Lunga.
Three miles farther north is the slate islet of Balnahuay,
and farther to the west the Garveloch Isles. The Sound
of Cuan runs between the northern extremity of Luing
and the Island of Seil. The length of this beautiful and
diversified passage is about three miles. On the west
side of Seil is the circular islet of Easdale, celebrated for
its slate quarries. After passing Easdale and the Point
of Ardincaple, Loch Feochan opens on the right, and a
distinct view of the broad-shouldered and double-peaked
Ben Cruachan is obtained. To the north is the island
of Kerrera, with the ruins of Gylen Castle occupying its
southern point. This island forms a natural break-water
to the Bay of Oban. At the head of this bay is situated
the pleasant and thriving village of Oban. The high
cliffs on the north side of the bay command one of the
finest views in Scotland. They terminate in a rocky
promontory, surmounted by Dunolly Castle, an ivy-clad
square keep, the ancient seat of the M'Dougals of Lorn,
whose representative resides here in Dunolly House. A
little to the north of Dunolly stands the Castle of Dun-

staffnage, which is ranked as one of the royal palaces of
Scotland, in consequence of its having been occasionally
possessed by the early Scottish kings.   From this ancient seat of royalty, it is said, the coronation stone, now
in Westminster Abbey, was transferred by Kenneth II.
to Scone.

NINTH TOUR.

GLASGOW—INVERARY—LOCH AWE—DALMELLY—TAYNUILT—OBAN.

THE tourist has his choice of several different routes to Inverary. He may proceed by Loch Lomond, or by Loch Long, to Arroquhar, and thence, by Cairndow, to Inverary,—or by Loch Goil and St. Catharine's,—or by the Holy Loch, Loch Eck, and Strachur,—or by Rothsay, Tarbet, and Lochgilphead.

Supposing him to take the first route, he proceeds by steam-boat to Dumbarton, and thence to the foot of Loch Lomond, where he embarks in a steam-boat, and sails fourteen miles northward, to Tarbet, on its west side. From this point to Arroquhar, on the shores of Loch Long, is a delightful walk of about half an hour, across the isthmus which lies between Loch Lomond and Loch Long. The inn of Arroquhar is twenty-two miles from Dumbarton. Loch Long is an arm of the sea, about twenty-four miles in length. In 1263, the Norwegians, who invaded Scotland, and were ultimately defeated at Largs, sailed up this loch with a fleet of sixty vessels, ravaging the country on all sides, and, on reaching the head of the loch, they drew their boats across the isthmus into Loch Lomond, and committed the same depredations on its shores. Near the head of Loch Long is a fantastic peak, called Ben Arthur or the Cobbler, from its grotesque resemblance to a shoemaker at work. Arroquhar was formerly the seat of the chief of the clan Macfarlane,—it is now the property of Sir James Colquhoun of Luss. Starting from the inn at this spot, the tourist winds round the head of Loch Long, and crossing the water of Taing, enters Argyleshire. The road now skirts the western shore of Loch Long, till, within a few yards of Ardgarten House, (Campbell, Esq.) where it turns to the right, and enters the vale of Glencroe,—a desolate but magnificent glen about six miles in length, guarded on the right by the bold and fantastic peak of Ben Arthur. A steep path conducts the traveller to the summit of the pass, where there is a stone seat, with the inscription, "Rest and be thankful."* The road now gradually descends, passing, on the left, a small sheet of water, called Loch Restal, and enters the lonely valley of Glenkinglas. Passing through this solitary vale, at the distance of about three miles, the tourist is gladdened with a view of Loch Fyne. The road now passes, on the right, the farm-house of Strowan, and, on the left, Ardkinglass, (Campbell, Bart.) and shortly after reaches the inn of Cairndow, (thirty-six miles from Dumbarton,) where there is a ferry across Loch Fyne to Inverary; or, if the tourist should prefer another route, there is a road of nine and a half miles round the head of the loch.

* On this Wordsworth has composed the following sonnet :—

"Doubling and doubling with laborious walk,
   Who, that has gain'd at length the wish'd-for Height,
   This brief, this simple way-side Call can slight,
   And rest not thankful? Whether cheer'd by talk
With some loved friend, or by the unseen hawk
   Whistling to clouds and sky-born streams, that shine
   At the sun's outbreak, as, with light divine,
   Ere they descend to nourish root and stalk
Of valley flowers. Nor, while the limbs repose,
   Will we forget that, as the fowl can keep
   Absolute stillness, poised aloft in air,
   And fishes front, unmoved, the torrent's sweep,—
So may the Soul, through powers that Faith bestows,
   Win rest, and ease, and peace, with bliss that angels share."

The second route to Inverary leads the tourist up Loch Goil, which branches off from Loch Long. The peninsular group of rugged mountains which separate them is called Argyle's Bowling Green. The shores are bold and magnificent. Near Loch Goil are the ruins of Carrick Castle, an ancient seat of the Dunmore family, situated on a high and nearly insulated rock. From Loch Goil head an excellent road leads through a wild valley, called Hell's Glen, to St. Catharine's, a distance of seven miles, whence the tourist may proceed across Loch Fyne (four miles) to Inverary.

By the third route, the tourist sails from Glasgow up the small arm of the sea called the Holy Loch, and disembarks at Kilmun; from thence he may walk, or take a coach provided for the purpose, through a wild vale of four or five miles in length, to Loch Eck, where he embarks on board a steam-boat, by which he is carried to the head of that beautiful lake. Loch Eck is about six miles long and only half a mile broad. It occupies the centre of the peninsula formed by the approach of Loch Long and Loch Fyne to each other. The scenery around the lake is very fine. At its southern extremity it discharges its waters by the river Eachaig, which, after a course of about two miles, falls into the Holy Loch. At the head of Loch Eck a coach is provided, which carries the tourist a distance of seven miles to the village of Strachur, on the banks of Loch Fyne, where a steamboat carries him across that loch to Inverary.

By the fourth, and much the longest route, the tourist proceeds to Rothsay, then through the Kyles of Bute, and into the long arm of the sea called Loch Fyne.

INVERARY,

the county town of Argyleshire, stands at the lower end

of a small bay, where the river Aray falls into Loch Fyne.
It was erected into a royal burgh in 1648 by Charles I.
while he was a prisoner in Carisbrook Castle. An obelisk
has been erected in a garden beside the church, to commemorate the execution of several gentlemen of the name
of Campbell, who suffered here in 1615, for their oppo-
sition to Popery. The population of Inverary is about
1000 or 1100. Its staple trade is the herring fishery,—
the herrings of Loch Fyne being celebrated for their superior excellence. Large sums of money have been laid
out by the Dukes of Argyle in improving and adorning
the town and neighbourhood. Inverary unites with Oban,
Campbelton, Irvine, and Ayr, in electing a member of
Parliament.

The most interesting object in this vicinity is Inverary
Castle, the seat of the Duke of Argyle. Both the inter-

INVERARY CASTLE.

nal decorations and the scenery around the mansion, are
remarkably splendid. The Castle was begun by Duke
Archibald in 1748, after a plan by Adam. It is built of
blue granite, and consists of two storeys and a sunk floor,
flanked with round overtopping towers, and surmounted
with a square-winged pavilion. There is an interesting
collection of old Highland armour in the saloon. The
view from the hill of Duniquoich is very fine, and the

rides and the walks through the grounds are remarkably extensive and picturesque.*

From Inverary a road leads through Glen Aray, to Loch Awe, distant about twelve miles. After leaving the pleasure-grounds round Inverary Castle, the tourist will find little to attract his attention till he reaches the head of the glen, and begins to descend towards Cladich, when the beautiful expanse of Loch Awe breaks upon his view. Loch Awe is about twenty-four miles in length, and varies from one and a half to two and a half in breadth. The mingled grandeur and beauty of the scenery are scarcely equalled in Britain.

Loch Awe is surrounded by lofty mountains of a rude and savage aspect, the highest of which (Ben Cruachan) rises to the height of 3400 feet, while its base, which reaches to Loch Etive, occupies an area of twenty square miles. Its towering proportions give a striking character to the scenery at the eastern extremity of Loch Awe. The sloping banks of the lake are well cultivated and wooded. The river Awe flows from its northern side, and pours its waters into Loch Etive at Bunawe. The gully or hollow, known by the name of the *Brender*, through which the river flows, is of the most frightful description. There are about twenty-four little islands

* " Embarked on the bosom of Loch Fyne, Captain Dalgetty might have admired one of the grandest scenes which nature affords. He might have noticed the rival rivers Aray and Shiray, which pay tribute to the lake, each issuing from its own dark and wooded retreat. He might have marked, on the soft and gentle slope that ascends from the shores, the noble old Gothic castle, with its varied outline, embattled walls, towers, and outer and inner courts, which, so far as the picturesque is concerned, presented an aspect much more striking than the present massive and uniform mansion. He might have admired those dark woods which, for many a mile, surrounded this strong and princely dwelling, and his eye might have dwelt on the picturesque peak of Duniquoich, starting abruptly from the lake, and raising its scathed brow into the mists of middle sky, while a solitary watch-tower, perched on its top like an eagle's nest, gave dignity to the scene by awakening a sense of possible danger."—*Legend of Montrose.*

s

in Loch Awe, some of them beautifully crowned with trees. On one of these islets, (Inishail, or the Beautiful Isle,) which has been happily described as " Beauty sleeping in the lap of Horror," are the ruins of a small nunnery of the Cistertian order. It was suppressed at the Reformation, and its possessions were erected into a temporal lordship in favour of Hay, Abbot of Inch-affray, who abjured the Roman Catholic faith. The old churchyard in this island contains a number of ancient tomb-stones, curiously carved. The MacArthurs for-merly inhabited the shores of Loch Awe, opposite the island, and numerous stones in the churchyard bear the names of individuals of that ancient race. On Innes Fraoch, or the Heather Isle, are the ruins of an ancient castle of the chief of the MacNaughtons. This isle was the Hesperides of the Highlands, and is said to have derived its name from Fraoch, an adventurous lover, who, attempting to gratify the longing of the fair Meyo for the delicious fruit of the isle, encountered and destroyed the serpent by which it was guarded, but perished himself in the conflict. The point of land which runs into the lake immediately beyond the village of Cladich, is called In-nistrynich, or the Island of the Druids, and is the pro-perty of Mr. M'Allister of Innistrynich, who is an ex-tensive proprietor on the opposite shore of the lake. The island of Fraoch, with the contiguous lands, were granted, in 1267, to Gilbert MacNaughton, by Alexander III. The MacNaughtons formed part of the force of MacDougal, Lord of Lorn, when he attacked Robert Bruce at Dal-righ, near Tyndrum. It is stated by Barbour that Mac-Naughton pointed out to the Lord of Lorn the deeds of valour which Bruce performed in this memorable retreat, with the highest expressions of admiration. " It seems to give thee pleasure," said Lorn, "that he makes such havoc among our friends."—"Not so, by my faith," replied MacNaughton; "but be he friend or foe who achieves high deeds of chivalry, men should bear faithful witness to his valour; and never have I heard of one who, by his knightly feats, has extricated himself from such dangers as have this day surrounded Bruce." The Mac-Naughtons, an ancient Highland tribe, are supposed to have derived their origin from one Naughton, a distinguished warrior in the reign of Malcolm IV., who received various grants of lands from the Lord of Lochers, as a reward for the services which he rendered to him in his wars with the M'Dougals of Lorn. It is said by Buchannan of Auchmar, that "the ancestors or chiefs of this sirname are reported to have been, for some ages, thanes of Loch Tay, and also to be possessed of a great estate betwixt the south side of Loch Fine and Lochers, parts of which are Glenera, Glenshira, and Glenfine." The chief of the clan, in the reign of Charles I. and II., was Sir Alexander MacNaughton, a stanch royalist. At the Reformation, he was knighted, and received a liberal pension, as a reward for his services. His circumstances, however, became embarrassed, and the family estates were seized by his creditors for debts, it is said, no way equivalent to their value. His great-grandson was a custom-house officer on the east coast.

At the eastern extremity of Loch Awe, at the base of Ben Cruachan, the conjoined waters of two rivers, the Strae and the Orchy, descend from their respective glens, and empty themselves into the lake. On a rocky elevation at the head of the lake, where the Orchy flows into it, stand the ruins of the celebrated castle of KILCHURN, or more properly Coalchuirn. The great tower is said to have been erected, in 1440, by the lady of Sir Colin Campbell, the Black Knight of Rhodes, second son of Sir Duncan Campbell of Loch Awe, ancestor of the Argyle family. Sir Colin acquired by marriage a considerable portion of the estates of the family of Lorn, and was the founder of the powerful family of Breadalbane. Sir Colin was absent on a crusade when his lady erected this noble pile, which (says Macculloch), "in the Western Highlands at least, claims the pre-eminence, no less from its magnitude and the integrity of its ruins, than from the very picturesque arrangements of the building." So late as 1745, Kilchurn was garrisoned by the King's troops, and all the exterior and greater part of the interior walls are still entire.*

* Our space will not admit of our quoting the whole of Wordsworth's fine Address to Kilchurn Castle, but we give the introductory part of the Poem and the prose extract with which it is prefaced.

"From the top of the hill a most impressive scene opened upon our view, —a ruined castle on an island, (for an island the flood had made it,) at some distance from the shore, backed by a cove of the mountain Cruachan, down which came a foaming stream. The castle occupied every foot of the island that was visible to us, appearing to rise out of the water,—mists rested upon the mountain side, with spots of sunshine ; there was a mild desolation in the low grounds, a solemn grandeur in the mountains, and the castle was wild, yet stately—not dismantled of turrets—nor the walls broken down, though obviously a ruin."—*Extract from the Journal of my Companion.*

"Child of loud-throated War ! the mountain stream
Roars in thy hearing ; but thy hour of rest
Is come, and thou art silent in thy age ;
Save when the winds sweeps by, and sounds are caught
Ambiguous, neither wholly thine nor theirs.
Oh ! there is life that breathes not : powers there are
That touch each other to the quick in modes
Which the gross world no sense hath to perceive,
No soul to dream of. What art thou, from care
Cast off—abandon'd by thy rugged Sire,
Nor by soft Peace adopted ; though, in place
And in dimension, such that thou might'st seem
But a mere footstool to yon sovereign Lord,
Huge Cruachan, (a thing that meaner hills
Might crush, nor know that it had suffer'd harm ;)
Yet he, not loth, in favour of thy claims
To reverence, suspends his own ; submitting

There is a good inn at Dalmally, near the head of the
lake, and from it there is a beautiful view of the vale of
Glenorchy. The old church of Glenorchy is of great
antiquity, and the churchyard contains many ancient
gravestones. The road from Dalmally to Taynuilt passes
the new church of Glenorchy, and makes a long circuit
round the head of the lake. Two miles from Dalmally,
we cross the river Strae, which descends from Glenstrae
on the right. The whole of this district was at one time
possessed by the Clan-Gregor, but they have long ago
been deprived of all their possessions around Loch Awe,
and may now say, in the words of the poet—

" Glenorchy's proud mountains, Coalchuirn and her towers,
Glenstrae and Glenlyon no longer are ours,
We're landless, landless, Gregalich !" *

" In a wild hollow or *corrie* of Ben Cruachan, is pointed
out a huge stone, from behind which a MacGregor, no
longer able to continue his flight, shot a bloodhound
which had been set upon his track, and from which he
found it impossible otherwise to make his escape. This

All that the God of Nature hath conferr'd,
All that he holds in common with the stars,
To the memorial majesty of Time
Impersonated in thy calm decay ! "

* " In the early part of the 17th century, a young man of the name of Lamont, travelling from Cowal, in Argyleshire, to Fort-William, fell in with the
son of a chieftain of the clan Macgregor, resident in Glenstrae, while on a shooting excursion. Having adjourned to a public-house, a dispute arose, which
terminated in a scuffle, in which Macgregor was mortally stabbed. Lamont
instantly escaping, was closely pursued. Descrying a house, he sped thither
for shelter : unquestioned, the host assured him of protection. Those in pursuit coming up, communicated the startling intelligence that the fugitive was
the murderer of the eldest son of the family. Macgregor, however, faithful to
his word, conducted the young man to Loch Fyne, and saw him safe across.
His clemency and magnanimity were not without their recompense. Not long
after, the Clan-Gregor were proscribed ; when Lamont received the aged chieftain to his house, and, by every act of kindness to him and his relatives, sought
to supply the place of him of whose support he had been the means of bereav-
ing them."—*Anderson's Guide to the Highlands.*

is alleged to have been the last instance in which any of the outlawed Clan-Alpine were chased as beasts of prey." *

In later times, this district fell into the hands of the Campbells, and often afforded them shelter in times of danger. " It's a far cry to Lochow," was the slogan of the clan, indicating the impossibility of reaching them in these remote fastnesses. Passing the farm-house of Corry, the road now skirts the tremendous base of Ben Crua-chan, and leaving behind the majestic lake, descends the course of the foaming and rapid river Awe. The rocks and precipices which stoop down perpendicularly on the path, exhibit some remains of the wood which once clothed them, but which has, in later times, been felled to supply the iron foundries at Bunawe. The whole of this pass is singularly wild, particularly near the bridge which has been thrown across the impetuous river. Here was fought the celebrated battle between Robert Bruce and John of Lorn, chief of the MacDougals, in which that warlike clan were almost destroyed. The Bridge of Awe is the scene of Sir Walter Scott's beautiful tale of the Highland Widow.† Proceeding onwards about two miles, a view is obtained of Loch Etive, and the little village of Bunawe. Crossing an old bridge, and

* Swan's Views of the Lakes of Scotland, with descriptive letterpress by J. M. Leighton, Esq.

† The following description is given of the spot where her cottage stood:— " We fixed our eyes with interest on one large oak, which grew on the left hand towards the river. It seemed a tree of extraordinary magnitude and picturesque beauty, and stood just where there appeared to be a few roods of open ground lying among huge stones, which had rolled down from the mountain. To add to the romance of the situation, the spot of clear ground extended round the foot of a proud-browed rock, from the summit of which leaped a mountain stream in a fall of sixty feet, in which it was dissolved into foam and dew. At the bottom of the fall, the rivulet with difficulty collected, like a routed general, its dispersed forces, and, as if tamed by its descent, found a noiseless passage through the heath to join the Awe."

passing the church on the right, the tourist reaches the Inn of Taynuilt, on the south side of Loch Etive, twelve miles distant from Dalmally. About a mile to the north is the village of Bunawe, where there is a ferry across Loch Etive, and an extensive iron furnace, which has been wrought, since the middle of last century, by a Lancashire company. The portion of Loch Etive above' Bunawe possesses a high degree of simple and sequestered grandeur. Bunawe is the point from which the ascent of Ben Cruachan can be best effected. The prospect from the top of the mountain is remarkably extensive and interesting. Leaving Taynuilt, the road, at the distance of four miles, descends to the shore of Loch Etive, beautifully fringed with wood. On the north side of the loch, about three miles from Taynuilt, are seen the ruins of Ardchattan Priory and Ardchattan House, covered with luxuriant ivy, and o'ercanopied by trees. The Priory was built by John MacDougal in the thirteenth century, and was burnt by Colkitto during Montrose's wars. Robert Bruce held a Parliament here. In the distance are seen the dark mountains of Mull and Morven, and the green island of Lismore. Three miles farther is Connel Ferry, where, from the narrowness of the passage, and a reef of sunken rocks, a very turbulent rapid is occasioned at particular states of the tide. In the immediate vicinity, antiquaries have placed the Pictish capital of Beregonium. There is also a vitrified fort. Three miles beyond Connel Ferry, are the ruins of Dunstaffnage Castle, at the entrance of Loch Etive. They occupy the summit of a perpendicular rock near the extremity of a low peninsular flat projection from the southern shore. Dunstaffnage was inhabited by the MacDougals till 1448, when it was taken by Bruce after his victory at the Pass of Awe. It is now a royal castle, the Duke of Argyle being hereditary keeper. From Dunstaffnage, the celebrated stone on which our Scottish monarchs used to be crowned, was transported to Scone, whence it was removed to England by Edward I., and it is now deposited beneath the coronation chair in the chapel of Edward the Confessor, in Westminster Abbey. At a little distance from the castle is a small roofless chapel, where one of the Scottish kings is said to have been buried. Three miles from Dunstaffnage is the pleasant thriving village of OBAN, situated at the head of a fine bay. The scenery in its neighbourhood is very romantic. In the vicinity is Dunolly Castle, the ancient fortress of the MacDougals of Lorn, situated on the point of a rocky promontory. Near it is Dunolly House, inhabited by the representative of that once powerful family.*

* "Nothing can be more wildly beautiful than the situation of Dunolly. The ruins are situated upon a bold and precipitous promontory overhanging Loch Etive, and distant about a mile from the village and port of Oban. The principal part which remains is the donjon or keep; but fragments of other buildings, overgrown with ivy, attest that it had been once a place of importance, as large apparently as Ardtornish or Dunstaffnage. These fragments enclose a court-yard, of which the keep probably formed one side ; the entrance being by a steep ascent from the neck of the isthmus, formerly cut across by a moat, and defended, doubtless, by outworks and a drawbridge. Beneath the castle stands the present mansion of the family, having on the one hand Loch Etive, with its islands and mountains, on the other two romantic eminences tufted with copsewood. There are other accompaniments suited to the scene ; in particular, a huge upright pillar, or detached fragment of that sort of rock called plum-pudding stone, upon the shore, about a quarter of a mile from the castle. It is called *Clachna-cau*, or the Dog's Pillar, because Fingal is said to have used it as a stake to which he bound his celebrated dog, Bran. Others say, that when the Lord of the Isles came upon a visit to the Lord of Lorn, the dogs brought for his sport were kept beside this pillar. Upon the whole, a more delightful and romantic spot can scarce be conceived ; and it receives a moral interest from the considerations attached to the residence of a family once powerful enough to confront and defeat Robert Bruce, and now sunk into the shade of private life. It is at present possessed by Patrick MacDougal, Esq., the lineal and undisputed representative of the ancient Lords of Lorn. The heir of Dunolly fell in Spain, fighting under the Duke of Wellington,—a death well becoming his ancestry."—*Lord of the Isles.*

TENTH TOUR.

GLASGOW TO INVERNESS, BY THE CALEDONIAN CANAL.

TOURISTS generally proceed to Oban by Lochgilphead and the Crinan Canal. There are two routes by land from Oban to Fort-William; the coast line, by Connel Ferry and Appin, which is the shorter of the two, and the other by Taynuilt, Dalmally, and Glencoe. Loch Linnhe, bounded on the one hand by the craggy knolls of Appin, and on the other by the purple hills of Morven, is the commencement of that chain of salt and fresh water lakes formed into the Caledonian Canal, and presents on both sides scenery of a most romantic character. Opposite to the upper extremity of the island of Lismore, Loch Creran branches off into Lorn. The first mansion to the north of this loch is Airds, the seat of Sir John Campbell; next is the ruin of Castle Stalker, Appin House, (Downie of Appin,) next occurs, and after that, at the mouth of Loch Leven, Ardshiel, (Stewart, Esq.) From Ballachulish Ferry on Loch Leven, noted for its slate quarry, the West Highland road penetrates the savage vale of Glencoe. Coran Ferry, nine miles from Fort-William, divides Loch Linnhe from Loch Eil. Fort-William, and the contiguous village of Maryburgh, stand on a bend of Loch Eil, near the confluence of the river Lochy. The fort was erected in the reign of William III. It is provided with a bomb-proof magazine, and its barracks accommodate about 100 men. Maryburgh

is a village of about 1500 inhabitants, and contains two respectable inns. BEN NEVIS, which till lately was considered the highest mountain in Scotland, is one of the most striking features of this neighbourhood.   It rises 4358 feet above the level of the sea, and its circumference at the base, which, upon one side, is almost washed by the sea, is supposed to exceed twenty-four miles. "Its northern front consists of two grand distinct ascents, or terraces, the level top of the lowest of which, at an elevation of about 1700 feet, contains a wild tarn or mountain lake. The outer acclivities of this the lower part of the mountain are very steep, although covered with a short grassy sward, intermixed with heath ; but at the lake this general vegetable clothing ceases. Here a strange scene of desolation presents itself. The upper and higher portion seems to meet us, as a new mountain, shooting up its black porphyritic rocks through the granitic masses, along which we have hitherto made our way, and, where not absolutely precipitous, its surface is strewed with angular fragments of stone of various sizes, wedged together, and forming a singularly rugged covering, among which we look in vain for any symptoms of vegetable life, except where round some pellucid spring

the rare little Alpine plants, such as Epilobium alpinum,
Silene acaulis, Saxifraga stellaris and nivalis, which live
only in such deserts wild, are to be found putting forth
their modest blossoms, amid the encircling moss. The
eagle, sallying from his eyry, may greet the approach of
the wanderer, or the mournful plover with plaintive note
salute his ear; but for those birds of the mountain, the
rocky wilderness were lifeless and silent as the grave;
its only tenants the lightnings and the mists of heaven,
and its language the voice of the storm." * A terrific
precipice on the north-eastern side makes a sheer descent
from the snow-capt summit of not less than 1500 feet.
The tourist who is so fortunate as to ascend the mountain in a favourable state of the atmosphere, is rewarded
with a prospect of remarkable extent and grandeur.
Ben Lomond, Ben Cruachan, Ben More, Ben Lawers,
Schehallion, and Cairngorm, rear their gigantic heads
around, while other peaks, scarcely less aspiring, extend
in countless number and infinite variety of form and
character, to the extreme verge of the horizon.† Two
miles from Fort-William stands the old Castle of Inver-

* Guide to the Highlands and Islands of Scotland, by George Anderson and
Peter Anderson, Esquires. London, 1834.

† "The ascent of Ben Nevis usually occupies three hours and a half from
the base of the mountain, and the descent rather more than half that time.
Some travellers go up at night, that they may enjoy the sunrise: by doing so,
they run a great risk of being disappointed, as in the morning the view is generally obscured by mists, and only occasional glimpses can be caught of the
glorious prospect, which is generally clearest from mid-day to six o'clock in
the evening. It is imprudent for a stranger to undertake the ascent without a
guide, and one can always be procured about Fort-William for seven or eight
shillings. The inexperienced traveller, also, may be the better of being reminded to carry with him some wine or spirits, (which, however, should be
used with caution,) wherewith to qualify the spring water, which is, fortunately,
abundant, and to which he will be fain to have frequent recourse, ere he attain
the object of his labours. It is customary to ascend the hill on the northern
side. By making a circuit to the eastward beyond Inverlochy Castle, the traveller can proceed as far as the lake on the back of a Highland pony."—Anderson's Guide to the Highlands, p. 268.

lochy, and (lately enclosed and ornamented with evergreens and shrubs) near which Montrose, in 1645,
achieved one of his most easy and decisive victories. He
attacked the Campbells by surprise, and with a sacrifice
of only three of his men, slaughtered or drowned upwards of 1500 of Argyll's forces. A few years since, a
quantity of bones were dug up on the scene of this sanguinary rout, where so many fell to deck a single name.
Between Inverlochy and Fort-William, the country has
an aspect of stern and rugged sublimity. Hills rise over
hills, of all shapes and sizes, and of various hues, from
the deep distant blue to the hard weather-beaten grey
and dark-wooded green. A high range of limestone
rocks in Glen Nevis (where there is some splendid
scenery) forms a magnificent panorama of mountains,
especially when lighted up by the setting sun. About
three miles from the sea, on the river Lochy, are the
ruinous walls of Tor Castle, the ancient seat of the clan
Chattan. From Loch Eil to Loch Lochy the distance is
eight miles. At Corpach are three locks, and, a mile
beyond, a series of eight locks called Neptune's Staircase. Each lock is 180 feet long, 40 broad, and 20
deep. Passing the villages of West and East Moy, the
steamer, two miles farther, enters Loch Lochy, which is
ten miles in length by about one in breadth ; near the
west end there is a fine bay, called the Bay of Arkaig,
at a short distance from which is the mansion of Cameron of Lochiel, chief of that clan.

Between Loch Lochy and Loch Oich is the village of
Laggan. The distance between the two lochs is nearly
two miles. Loch Oich is about three and a half miles
long by half a mile broad, and forms the summit level
of the Caledonian Canal. Near the mouth of the river

Garry, which discharges itself into this loch, are the ruins of Invergarry Castle, the ancient gathering-place of the clan Macdonell, with a small islet and green trees in front, and a high mountain behind, called *Craig an phi-tich*, or the Rock of the Raven, an appellation which formed the war-cry, and is still the motto of the chiefs of Glengarry. A solitary wild swan may be seen on Loch Oich, which has sailed there for above thirty years.

From Loch Oich, the steam-boat descends to Loch Ness, by six locks; the distance between the locks being five and a half miles. At the south-western extremity of the latter and close upon the edge of the water, stands Fort Augustus. It was built shortly after the rebellion of 1715. In form it is quadrangular, with four bastions at the corners. The barracks contain accommodation for about 300 men, but only six privates and a sergeant are now kept in the place.

Loch Ness is nearly twenty-four miles in length, and averages a mile and quarter in breadth. In many places it is of great depth—about 140 fathoms—and, from the uniformity of temperature maintained by this depth of water, the lake never freezes. The character of its scenery, though highly interesting, is not so varied and striking as that through which we have already conducted our tourist.

A short distance from Fort Augustus, we pass the mouth of Glenmoriston, and the mansion of James Murray Grant, Esquire, the proprietor, beautifully situated. A few miles farther on the right are Foyers House and the mouth of the river Foyers, where the steamer stops to afford passengers an opportunity of viewing the celebrated fall.

This famous cataract consists in reality of two falls, of which the lower is by far the more imposing. The upper fall is about thirty feet high, twice broken in its descent; a bridge of one arch—an aerial-looking structure —being thrown over the chasm. It is seen to the best advantage from the channel of the river below the bridge.

FALL OF FOYERS.

After pursuing its impetuous course for about a quarter of a mile, the stream makes its second descent in a sheet of spray of dazzling whiteness, into a deep and spacious linn, surrounded by gigantic rocks. The cavity of the fall is lined with a profusion of shrubs and plants, nursed by the perpetual spray. The height of this fall is variously stated, but it cannot be less than ninety feet. The banks on either side are diversified with the birch and the ash, and an undergrowth of copsewood, with those stupendous chasms and rocky eminences which confer additional grandeur on such a scene.* About two and a

* Dr. E. D. Clarke, who visited this fall, declared it to be a finer cascade than

half miles from this, on the left, are seen the ruins of
Castle Urquhart, often noticed in the annals of the earlier
Scottish monarchs, and which was the last to surrender
to Edward the First. Further notice of this fine ruin
will be found in our Thirteenth Tour. Glen Urquhart,
which recedes behind the castle, is a beautiful Highland
vale, containing many gentlemen's seats; and, at the
mouth of the glen, there is a good inn called Drumindrochet. Glen Urquhart chiefly belongs to Grant of Grant.
At the Ferry of Bona, eight and a half miles from Drumindrochet, the steamer enters Loch Dochfour by a narrow channel about a quarter of a mile in length. At
Lochend the steamer again enters the canal, and proceeds
to Muirton, where it descends by four locks to the level
of Loch Beauly, an arm of the Murray Frith.

The Caledonian Canal was finally opened in October
1822. The whole distance from the Atlantic to the German Ocean is sixty and a half miles, of which thirty-seven
are through natural sheets of water, and twenty-three
cut as a canal. The present depth of water is fifteen
feet, but it is proposed to deepen it to twenty feet, according to the original plan; also to increase the effi-
ciency of the works, and to place steam-tugs on the lakes.

Tivoli, and, of all he had seen, inferior only to Terni. The following lines were
written by Burns upon the spot on September 5, 1787.

> " Among the heathy hills and ragged woods,
> The roaring Foyers pours his mossy floods,
> Till full he dashes on the rocky mounds,
> Where through a shapeless breach his stream resounds.
> As high in air the bursting torrents flow,
> As deep recoiling surges foam below,
> Prone down the rock the whitening sheet descends,
> And viewless echo's ear, astonish'd, rends.
> Dim-seen, through rising mists and ceaseless show'rs,
> The hoary cavern, wide-surrounding, low'rs;
> Still thro' the gap the struggling river toils,
> And still below the horrid caldron boils."

These improvements have been suggested to the Lords
of the Treasury by Mr. Walker, engineer, and, if carried
into effect, there can be little doubt that this magnificent
public work would be more productive to the Government, as well as more advantageous to the country.   The
total expenditure of the Caledonian Canal, up to May
1840, was £1,029,040, 8s. 6¾d.

For a description of Inverness, we refer to the Thirteenth Tour.

ELEVENTH TOUR.

STAFFA AND IONA.

TOURISTS wishing to proceed to Staffa usually leave Glasgow in a steam-boat for Oban, where, in the summer and autumn months, a vessel is kept for the accommodation of strangers wishing to visit this far-famed spot.

After leaving Oban, the steamer passes Kerrera, a narrow rugged island, forming a natural breakwater to the bay of Oban. It was here that Alexander II. died on his expedition in 1249, and here Haco, king of Norway, met the island chieftains, who assisted him in his ill-fated descent on the coasts of Scotland. Upon the south point of the island are the ruins of the Danish fort, Gylen. The boat now approaches Lismore,* a fertile island, about nine miles in length and two in breadth. In ancient times it was the residence of the bishops of Argyle, who were frequently styled " Episcopi Lismorienses." Leaving. Lismore on the right, the steamer enters the Sound of Mull, and passes the Lady Rock, visible only at low water, on which Maclean of Duart exposed his wife, a daughter of the second Earl of Argyle, intending that she should be swept away by the returning tide ; but she was fortunately rescued by some of her father's people, who were passing in a boat. Maclean gave out that she had died suddenly, and was allowed to go through the ceremonial of a mock funeral, but was shortly afterwards put

* *Leosmore*, that is, " the Great Garden."

to death by the relations of his injured wife.   This incident has been made the subject of one of Joanna Baillie's
dramas—the "Family Legend."   On the brink of a high
cliff, on the shore of Mull, is Duart Castle, formerly the
seat of the chief of the warlike and powerful clan of the
Macleans.   The steamer now sails along through a narrow but deep channel.   On the left are the bold and
mountainous shores of Mull, on the right those of that
district of Argyleshire called Morven, successively indented by deep salt water lochs running up many miles
inland.   To the south-eastward, arise a prodigious range
of mountains, among which Ben Cruachan is pre-eminent,
and to the north-east is the no less huge and picturesque
range of the Ardnamurchan Hills.   Many ruinous castles,
situated generally upon cliffs overhanging the ocean, add
interest to the scene.   In fine weather a grander and
more impressive scene, both from its natural beauties, and
associations with ancient history and tradition, can hardly
be imagined.   When the weather is rough, the passage
is both difficult and dangerous, from the narrowness of
the channel, and in part from the number of inland lakes,
out of which sally forth a number of conflicting and
thwarting tides, making the navigation perilous to open
boats.   The sudden flaws and gusts of wind which issue,
without a moment's warning, from the mountain glens,
are equally formidable ; so that, in unsettled weather, a
stranger, if not much accustomed to the sea, may sometimes add to the other sublime sensations excited by the
scene, that feeling of dignity which arises from a sense of
danger.*   Opposite to Duart, on the coast of Morven,

* Notes to the Lord of the Isles. The following sonnet was composed by
Wordsworth in the Sound of Mull:
           "Tradition be thou mute! Oblivion, throw
            Thy veil in mercy o'er the records, hung
            Round strath and mountain, stamp'd by the ancient tongue

are the ruins of Ardtornish Castle, the scene of the opening canto of the "Lord of the Isles." "The situation is
wild and romantic in the highest degree, having on the
one hand a high and precipitous chain of rocks overhanging the sea, and, on the other, the narrow entrance to the
beautiful salt water lake, called Loch Aline, which is in
many places finely fringed with copsewood. The ruins
of Ardtornish are not now very considerable, consisting
chiefly of the remains of an old keep or tower, with fragments of outward defences. But, in former days, it was
a place of great consequence, being one of the principal
strongholds which the Lords of the Isles, during the period
of their stormy independence, possessed upon the mainland
of Argyleshire." Above the castle of Ardtornish, is
Ardtornish House, (Gregorson, Esq.) Another residence
of the Island Kings next meets the eye in the Castle of
Aros, in Mull, a powerful rock-built fortress, situated
about half-way from either end of the Sound.* A short
way beyond, on the Morven coast, is Killundine Castle.
Holding on towards the head of the Sound, the steamer,
seven miles beyond Aros, reaches Tobermory, (the well
of our Lady St. Mary,) the only village of any note in
Mull. It was founded, in 1788, by the British Fishery

On rock and ruin darkening as we go,—
Spots where a word, ghost-like, survives to show
What crimes from hate, or desperate love, have sprung :
From honour misconceived, or fancied wrong,
What feuds, not quench'd, but fed, by mutual woe.
Yet though a wild vindictive Race, untamed
By civil arts and labours of the pen,
Could gentleness be scorn'd by those fierce Men,
Who, to spread wide the reverence they claim'd
For patriarchal occupations, named
Yon towering Peaks, 'Shepherds of Etive Glen?'" †

* From the village of Aros there is a road which leads across the island to
Loch-na-Keal, and thence to Laggan Ulva, where there is a place of embarkation for Staffa and Iona.

† In Gaelic, *Buachaill Elte.*

Company, and is finely situated at the head of the inner
recess of a well protected bay. In the immediate vicinity is Drimfin, the splendid mansion of Maclean of Coll.
This romantic spot is well worthy the notice of the tourist.
Quiting Tobermory, we enter Loch Sunart. Seven miles
from Tobermory, on the Ardnamurchan coast, is the castle of Mingarry, which

> sternly placed,
> O'erawes the woodland and the waste.

The ruins, which are tolerably entire, are surrounded by
a very high wall, forming a kind of polygon, for the purpose of adapting itself to the projecting angles of a precipice overhanging the sea, on which the castle stands.
It was anciently the residence of the MacIans, a clan of
Macdonalds, descended from Ian or John, a grandson of
Angus Og, Lord of the Isles. Rounding the point of
Cullich, the last promontory of Mull, we find ourselves
moving freely on the bosom of the Atlantic, and at the
same moment, if the weather is fine, the islands of Mull,
including the Trishnish Isles, Tiree, Coll, Muck, Eig, and
Rum, burst on the view, and, far to the north-west, the
faint outlines of South Uist and Barra.

Staffa is about eight miles distant from the western
coast of Mull. It is of an irregular oval shape, and about
three-fourths of a mile in length by half a mile in breadth.
The most elevated point is toward the south-west, where
the rock attains an elevation of about 144 feet. The first
cave approached is the Clam or Scallop-shell Cave, on one
side of which the basaltic columns appear bent like the
ribs of a ship, while the opposite wall is made up of the
ends of horizontal columns, resembling the surface of a
honeycomb. This cave is 30 feet in height, and 16 or
18 in breadth at the entrance, its length being 130

FINGAL'S CAVE, STAFFA.

feet. Next occurs the noted rock Buachaille, or the Herdsman, a conoidal pile of columns about 30 feet high. From this spot the pillars extend in one continued colonnade along the whole face of the cliff to the entrance of Fingal's Cave, by far the most impressive and interesting object in the island. The height from the water at mean tide to the top of the arch at the entrance is 66, its breadth 42, and its whole length is 227 feet. The sides within are columnar, and for the most part perpendicular, the columns being broken and grouped in many different ways. As the sea never entirely ebbs from this cave, the beautiful green water forms the only flooring, along which a boat may be pushed. Nothing can surpass the beautiful symmetry and grandeur of this wondrous pile. In the language of Sir Walter Scott:—

> " Where, as to shame the temples deck'd
> By skill of earthly architect,

T

Nature herself, it seem'd, would raise
A Minster to her Maker's praise !
Not for a meaner use ascend
Her columns, or her arches bend ;
Nor of a theme less solemn tells
That mighty surge that ebbs and swells,
And still, between each awful pause,
From the high vault an answer draws,
In varied tone prolong'd and high,
That mocks the organ's melody.
Nor doth its entrance front in vain
To old Iona's holy fane,
That Nature's voice might seem to say,
' Well hast thou done, frail Child of clay !
Thy humble powers that stately shrine
Task'd high and hard—but witness mine ! ' "

"'This palace of Neptune," the Poet adds in a note to
these noble lines, "·is even grander upon a second than
the first view.   The stupendous columns which form the
sides of the cave, the depth and strength of the tide
which rolls its deep and heavy swell up to the extremity
of the vault—the variety of tints formed by white, crimson, and yellow stalactites, or petrifactions, which occupy
the vacancies between the base of the broken pillars
which form the roof, and intersect them with a rich,
curious, and variegated chasing, occupying each inter-
stice—the corresponding variety below water, where the
ocean rolls over a dark-red or violet-coloured rock, from
which, as from a base, the basaltic columns arise—the
tremendous noise of the swelling tide, mingling with the
deep-toned echoes of the vault,—are circumstances elsewhere unparalleled." *   The Boat Cave, and Mackin-

---

* On this cave Wordsworth has composed the following sonnet :—

    " Thanks for the lessons of this spot—fit school
    For the presumptuous thoughts that would assign
    Mechanic laws to agency divine ;

non's, or the Cormorant's Cave, are two of less extent
and beauty, which are usually visited after Fingal's Cave.

IONA.

Iona or Icolmkill, celebrated as an early seat of Chris-
tianity, is about nine miles to the south of Staffa. "In
any other situation," says Dr. Macculloch, "the remains
of Iona would be consigned to neglect and oblivion; but,
connected as they are with an age distinguished by the
ferocity of its manners and its independence of regular
government; standing a solitary monument of religion
and literature, such as religion and literature then were,
the mind imperceptibly recurs to the time when this
island was ' the light of the western world,' ' a gem in
the ocean,' and is led to contemplate with veneration its
silent and ruined structures. Even at a distance, the

> And, measuring heaven by earth, would overrule
> Infinite power. The pillared vestibule,
> Expanding, yet precise, the roof embowed,
> Might seem designed to humble man, when proud
> Of his best workmanship by plan and tool.
> Down-bearing with his whole Atlantic weight
> Of tide and tempest on the Structure's base,
> And flashing to that Structure's topmost height,
> Ocean has proved its strength, and of its grace
> In calms is conscious, finding for his freight
> Of softest music some responsive place."

aspect of the cathedral, insignificant as its dimensions
are, produces a strong feeling of delight in him who,
long coasting the rugged and barren rocks of Mull, or
buffeted by turbulent waves, beholds its tower first rising
out of the deep, giving to this desolate region an air of
civilization, and recalling the consciousness of that human
society, which, presenting elsewhere no visible traces,
seems to have abandoned these rocky shores to the cormorant and the sea-gull." Iona is nearly three miles in
length, and one in breadth. The origin of the celebrity
of this island* is to be traced to its having become, about
the year 565, the residence of Columba, an Irish Christian
preacher. The monastery became, in subsequent years,

---

* The following splendid and well-known passage records the emotions excited in the breast of Dr. Johnson by the prospect of Iona. "We were now
treading that illustrious island which was once the luminary of the Caledonian
regions, whence savage clans and roving barbarians derived the benefits of
knowledge, and the blessings of religion. To abstract the mind from all local
emotion would be impossible, if it were endeavoured, and would be foolish if it
were possible. Whatever withdraws us from the power of our senses—whatever makes the past, the distant, or the future predominate over the present,
advances us in the dignity of thinking beings. Far from me and from my
friends be such frigid philosophy as may conduct us indifferent and unmoved
over any ground which has been dignified by wisdom, bravery, or virtue. That
man is little to be envied whose patriotism would not gain force upon the plains
of Marathon, or whose piety would not grow warm among the ruins of Iona."
Wordsworth has composed the following sonnet upon landing at Iona :—

> " How sad a welcome ! To each voyager
> Some ragged child holds up for sale a store
> Of wave-worn pebbles, pleading on the shore
> Where once came monk and nun with gentle stir,
> Blessings to give, news ask, or suit prefer.
> Yet is yon neat trim church a grateful speck
> Of novelty amid the sacred wreck
> Strewn far and wide. Think, proud Philosopher !
> Fallen though she be, this Glory of the west,
> Still on her sons the beams of mercy shine ;
> And ' hopes, perhaps more heavenly bright than thine,
> A grace by thee unsought and unpossest,
> A faith more fixed, a rapture more divine
> Shall gild their passage to eternal rest.'"

the dwelling of the Cluniacenses, a class of monks who followed the rule of St. Bennet. At the Reformation, Iona, with its abbey, was annexed to the bishopric of Argyle by James VI. in the year 1617. The celebrated ruins consist of a cathedral, a nunnery, and St. Oran's Chapel. The latter, which appears to be the oldest building now standing, is of small extent (60 feet by 20) and rude architectural style, and was probably built by the Norwegians. It contains some tombs of different dates, and there are many carved stones in the pavement. The chapel of the nunnery is the next in the order of antiquity; it is in good preservation; the roof has been vaulted, and part of it still remains. The nuns were not displaced at the Reformation, but continued, a long time after that event, to live together. They followed the rule of St. Augustine. The Cathedral Church of St. Mary is the principal edifice; it has obviously been erected at two distinct periods. Its present form is that of a cross, the length being about 160 feet; the breadth 24; the tower is about 70 feet high, divided into three stories. " In the different cemeteries are the tombs of forty-eight Scottish kings, four kings of Ireland, eight Norwegian monarchs, and one king of France, perhaps the most extensive holy alliance or congress of sovereigns in Europe."* Most families of distinction in the Highlands had burying-places here, and many erected votive chapels in different parts of the island. On the west side of Martyrs' Street is Maclean's Cross, a beautifully carved pillar, and one of the 360 stone crosses which once adorned the island; but about the year 1560, they were thrown into the sea by order

* Music and Friends. By W. Gardiner. Lond. 1838.

of the Synod of Argyle.   Iona contains 450 inhabitants,
and is the property of the Duke of Argyle.

   " Homeward we turn.   Isle of Columba's Cell,
     Where Christian piety's soul-cheering spark
     (Kindled from Heaven between the light and dark
     Of time) shone like the morning-star, farewell!—
     And fare thee well, to Fancy visible,
     Remote St. Kilda, lone and loved sea-mark
     For many a voyage made in her swift bark,
     When, with more hues than in the rainbow dwell,
     Thou a mysterious intercourse dost hold ;
     Extracting from clear skies and air serene,
     And out of sun-bright waves, a lucid veil,
     That thickens, spreads, and, mingling fold with fold,
     Makes known, when thou no longer canst be seen,
     Thy whereabout to warn the approaching sail."

TWELFTH TOUR.

GLASGOW—PAISLEY—AYR—AND THE LAND OF BURNS, BY THE
GLASGOW AND AYRSHIRE RAILWAY.

THE prospectus of the railway between Glasgow and
Ayrshire was issued in the spring of 1836; operations
were commenced about the middle of May 1838; several
portions of the line were opened at different periods;
and the entire line between Glasgow and Ayr was opened
on the 12th of August 1840.

The station-house at Glasgow is situate on the west
side of Bridge Street, Tradeston, and very near the
" Glasgow Bridge." On leaving Glasgow, the tourist
passes an immense number of cotton and silk manufactories, iron-works, and other establishments of a similar
kind, together with a succession of elegant villas, belonging to the wealthy merchants and manufacturers connected
with the city. About half way between Glasgow and
Paisley the ruins of Crookston Castle are to be seen on
an eminence overhanging the south bank of the White
Cart. This castle was at one time the property of the
Stewarts of Lennox, and here Queen Mary resided, when
receiving the addresses of Darnley. It is now the property of Sir John Maxwell of Pollock. Proceeding onward, the tourist, at the distance of seven miles from
Glasgow, reaches the large manufacturing town of

PAISLEY,

situate on the banks of the White Cart. Paisley is a

place of great antiquity, and owes its first existence to a
religious establishment founded here, about the year 1160,
by Walter Stewart, the ancestor of the royal family of
Scotland.   The progress of the town was slow, and it
was not until towards the close of last century that it
assumed any appearance of importance.   The original
manufactures of Paisley were coarse checked linen cloth,
and checked linen handkerchiefs, and these were succeeded by fabrics of a lighter and more fanciful kind.
About the year 1760, the manufacture of gauze was introduced into Paisley, in imitation of the manufactures of
Spitalfields.   The experiment met with remarkable success, and the immense variety of elegant and richly ornamented fabrics which were issued from this place, surpassed all competition.   The gauze trade now employs
but few hands, and shawls of silk and cotton, plaids,
scarfs, chenille and Canton crape shawls and handkerchiefs, silks, and Persian velvets, are at present the staple
manufactures of this town.

Among the most interesting objects in Paisley, the
Abbey Church occupies a prominent place.   This magnificent building, which was dedicated to St. James and
St. Mirren, suffered severely at the Reformation, and its
immense revenues became the prey of several of the
nobility.   The chancel, which is now used as a parish
church, still remains entire, along with the window of
the northern transept.   Attached to its south side is a
small but lofty chapel, which possesses a remarkably fine
echo, and contains a tomb, surmounted by a recumbent
female figure, usually supposed to represent Marjory,
daughter of Robert Bruce, and wife of Walter Stewart,
founder of the abbey.   This lady, who was mother of
Robert Second, the first of the Stewart sovereigns, was

killed by a fall from her horse, at a place in the neighbourhood of Paisley. The buildings connected with the
abbey are the property of the Marquis of Abercorn, the
representative of Claud Hamilton, the last abbot, and
first temporal superior of Paisley, referred to in Sir Walter Scott's ballad of Cadyow Castle, as

> " Stern Claud ——————
> Grey Paisley's haughty lord."

The population of the town and parish of Paisley
amounted, in 1831, to 57,466. It returns one member
to the House of Commons. A short distance from Paisley, the line passes on the left the straggling village of
Elderslie. Here, near the turnpike-road, is the oak in
which, according to tradition, Sir William Wallace, the
" Knight of Elderslie," concealed himself from the English troops. Elderslie House, which stands at a short
distance, appears to be of later erection than the era of
the hero. About three miles from Paisley is the town
of JOHNSTONE, situate on the banks of the Black Cart. It
is a thriving seat of the cotton manufacture, and contains a population of about 5900. In the vicinity of the
town, to the west, is Milliken House, the seat of Sir
W. M. Napier, Bart. Farther, to the north-west, is
Houston House, A. Spiers, Esq., M.P., Lord-Lieutenant
of the county of Renfrew. A short way farther on is
the village of Kilbarchan, containing a population of
3612. The superiors of this village, in ancient times,
were the Sempills of Beltrees, a family in which poetical
talent was long hereditary. Sir James Sempill, ambas-
sador to England in 1599, wrote the satire of " The
Packman and the Priest." His son, Robert Sempill,
was the author of the poem entitled " The Life and

Death of the Piper of Kilbarchan." Francis, the son of this poet, wrote the well-known songs, " Maggie Lauder, and " She rose and loot me in." A few years ago a statue of Habbie Simpson, the piper above mentioned, was affixed to the steeple of the Town Hall. After leaving the Howood station, the line runs through a rich strath, celebrated for its beautiful scenery. On the right are the extensive and highly ornamented pleasure-grounds of Castle Semple, the seat of Colonel Harvey. On the left, above the public road to Beith, are the ruins of Elliston Tower, formerly the seat of the Sempill family. At the distance of about sixteen miles from Glasgow, the tourist sees the village of Lochwinnoch, situate on the side of Castle Semple Loch, near the bottom of a range of Hills. The population amounts to about 3000. At a short distance to the west of the village is Barr Castle, supposed to have been built in the fifteenth century. In the vicinity is Barr House, (W. M'Dowell, Esq.) Castle Semple Loch, which is about a mile in length, contains three wooded islets, on one of which are the remains of a fortalice erected, in ancient times, by Lord Sempill. About two and a quarter miles from Lochwinnoch, the tourist passes the town of BEITH, containing a population of about 6000. In the vicinity of the town are the ruins of Giffen Castle, formerly a possession of the Eglinton family. A little farther on we perceive, near the river Garnock, the remains of the ancient castle of Glengarnock, the property of the Earl of Glasgow, and the beautiful sheet of water called Kilbirnie Loch, extending about two miles in length, and half a mile in breadth. Twenty miles from Glasgow we pass the village of Kilbirnie, situate on the banks of the Garnock, at the distance of about a mile and a half to the right.

Two miles farther on, the tourist reaches the thriving village of DALRY, situate on an eminence, and nearly surrounded with the waters of the Garnock, Rye, and Caaf. It contains 4326 inhabitants, who are chiefly employed in weaving. Proceeding onwards, we reach the point where, on the right, a branch of the railway leads off to the towns of SALTCOATS and ARDROSSAN, the former being about four miles distant, and the latter about five and a half miles. About two hundred years ago, Saltcoats was inhabited by only four families, who gained their livelihood by making salt. It now contains 4000 inhabitants, including seamen. The town of Ardrossan is of recent origin, and its rise is owing chiefly to the public-spirited exertions of the Eglinton family. It possesses an excellent harbour, for which it was indebted to the late Earl of Eglinton, who laid out an enormous sum of money on the undertaking, without the satisfaction of having completed what had been so much an object of his solicitude. Ardrossan of late has attained great celebrity as a watering place.* At the distance of about twenty-six miles from Glasgow, four miles from Dalry, and fourteen miles from Ayr, the tourist reaches KILWINNING.†

* Steam-boats ply regularly between this town and Glasgow. Communication by the railways to and from Glasgow and Ayr, and the intermediate towns, takes place five times a day.

† At the distance of about a mile from Kilwinning stands Eglinton Castle, the splendid mansion of the Earl of Eglinton and Wintoun, towards which public attention was recently directed by the tournament which was held in its vicinity in September 1839. The castle was built about forty years ago, and is surrounded by extensive pleasure-grounds. The family of Montgomeryfis of Norman origin, and the first of the name that settled in Scotland was Robert de Montgomerie, who obtained from Walter, the High Steward of Scotland, a grant of the barony of Eaglesham, in the county of Renfrew. In the fourteenth century Alexander de Montgomerie acquired the baronies of Eglinton and Ardrossan, by marriage with Elisabeth, daughter and sole heiress of Sir Hugh de Eglinton. At the famous battle of Otterbourne, fought in 1387, Henry Percy, the renowned Hotspur, was taken prisoner by Sir Hugh Montgomery, and, for his ransom, built the castle of Penoon or Polnoon, in Renfrewshire, which is still the property

Kilwinning signifies the cell of Winning, and derives
its name from the circumstance of a saint named Winning having resided here in the eighth century. Hugh de
Moreville, lord of Cunningham, in 1107, founded here
an abbey for monks of the Tyronensian order, dedicated to Saint Winning, the ruins of which still exist.
The greater part of this splendid edifice was destroyed
at the Reformation, and a grant of it was made to the
Earl of Glencairn ; but the temporalities were erected,
in 1603, into a lordship in favour of Lord Eglinton.   A
party of freemasons, who came from the continent to
assist in the building of this monastery, were the first to
introduce freemasonry into Scotland, and, by means of
the establishment of lodges, the knowledge of their mysteries was diffused over the rest of the country.   Kilwinning is also distinguished as a seat of archery, a company of archers having been organized here in 1488.
They have a custom of shooting annually for a prize at
the popinjay or popingo, a practice described in the tale
of Old Mortality.   The population of Kilwinning is
3772.   Proceeding onward, should the atmosphere be
clear, the tourist will obtain, on the right, a view of the
Island of Arran, with its lofty and precipitous mountains.
The line next crosses the Garnoch, which here forms the

of the Eglinton family. In 1488, the representative of the family was raised
to the peerage, by the title of Lord Montgomery, and, in 1507-8, Hugh, the
third baron, was created Earl of Eglinton. In 1582, Robert, the first Earl of
Wintoun, married Lady Margaret Montgomery, eldest daughter of Hugh, third
Earl of Eglinton, and the third son of that marriage, Sir Alexander Seton of
Foulstruther, was adopted into the family, and became sixth Earl of Eglinton.
The direct line of the Wintoun family having failed, the present Earl of Eglinton
was, in January 1841, served heir to the title of Earl of Wintoun. The late Earl,
Hugh, was created a British peer, by the title of Baron Ardrossan. Archibald
William, the present and thirteenth Earl, was born 29th September 1812, and
succeeded to the titles and estates on the death of his grandfather Hugh, 14th
December 1819.

boundary betwixt the parishes of Kilwinning and Irvine.
A little farther on, it crosses the river Irvine by an elegant bridge of six arches, and reaches the town of IRVINE
29½ miles distant from Glasgow, and 10¼ miles from
Ayr. Irvine is a royal burgh of considerable antiquity;
and a monastery of Carmelite or White Friars was
founded here in 1412. There are 124 vessels belonging to the port, which employ 1000 seamen. Irvine
unites with Ayr, Campbelton, Inverary, and Oban, in
returning a member to Parliament. The population in
1840 was 10,779. Irvine is remarkable for having been
the temporary residence of Burns, and the birth-place of
James Montgomery the poet, and John Galt the novelist. After leaving Irvine, a view is obtained, on the
left, of the remains of the ancient castle of Dundonald,
standing on an elevated position, about two miles distant. The situation of this castle, on the top of a beautiful hill, is singularly noble. It was the property of
Robert Stewart, who, in right of his mother, Marjory
Bruce, succeeded to the Scottish throne under the title
of Robert II. Here he wooed and married his first
wife, the beautiful Elizabeth Mure of Rowallan, and
here he died in 1390. This castle gives the title of
earl to the noble family of Cochrane. The estate passed
into the hands of the Earl of Eglinton in the beginning
of last century; but the castle, along with the hill on
which it stands, and five roods of adjoining land, still
belongs to the Earl of Dundonald. In the vicinity of
Dundonald Castle are the remains of an ancient church,
dedicated to the Virgin, called Our Lady's Kirk. James
IV., in passing through this part of his kingdom, uniformly made an offering at this Kirk, generally giving
fourteen shillings at a time. About four and a half

miles from Irvine, and six miles from Ayr, the tourist passes the village of Troon, situate on the right, at the distance of about half a mile. The Duke of Portland is superior of this place, and under his patronage it has attained to considerable importance. It is a well-frequented watering-place, and carries on a large coasting trade. The line now passes very near the sea ; and in the course of a short time we observe, on the left, Fullarton House, a seat of the Duke of Portland, situate on a spacious lawn, and surrounded, except in front, with extensive woods. Proceeding onward, the tourist passes the village of Monkton ; a mile farther on the small burgh of Prestwick ; a little beyond it, the ruins of Kingscase, a charitable institution, endowed by King Robert Bruce ; and, at the distance of forty miles from Glasgow, reaches the town of

AYR,

the county town and a royal burgh, situate at the mouth of the river of the same name. Ayr is a very ancient town, and was erected into a royal burgh by William the Lion. It contains a number of handsome public buildings, and many of its shops and dwelling-houses may vie in elegance with those of the metropolis. The river Ayr divides Ayr Proper from Newton and Wallacetown. This river rises on the border of the county, at the eastern extremity of the parish of Muirkirk, and, after a course of about thirty miles, falls into the sea at this place. It is crossed here by two bridges, respectively, termed the Auld and New Brigs, which are noticed under these denominations by Burns, in his poem of " The Twa Brigs." The Auld Brig was said to have been built in the reign of Alexander III, (1249–1285) by two maiden sisters of the name of Lowe, whose effigies

were consequently carved upon a stone in the eastern
parapet, near the south end of the fabric. It is stated
by tradition, that before the erection of this bridge, a
ford, about two hundred yards farther up, called the
Doocote Stream, afforded the best passage which is to
be had across the river in this quarter. The new bridge
was erected in 1788, chiefly through the exertions of
Provost Ballantyne, the gentleman to whom Burns dedicated the poem of "The Twa Brigs." The "Dungeon Clock," alluded to in the poem, was placed at the
top of an old steeple in the Sandgate, which was taken
down in 1826. The "Wallace Tower" was a rude old
building, which stood in the eastern part of the High-
Street, at the head of a lane named the Mill Vennel. It
was in this tower, according to tradition, that Wallace
was confined. Having become ruinous, it was taken
down in 1835, and a Gothic structure erected on its site,
containing at the top the clock and bells of the dungeon
steeple, and ornamented in front by a statue of Wallace,
executed by Mr. Thom, the well-known self-taught
sculptor. Another statue of "Scotia's ill-requited chief"
was placed about thirty years ago by a citizen of Ayr,
on the front of a dwelling-house, which occupies the
site of the ancient court-house of Ayr, supposed to have
been that in which, according to Blind Harry, the Scottish lords were treacherously hanged. The Fort of Ayr
was built by Oliver Cromwell, in 1652, upon a level
piece of ground between the town and the sea. A few
fragments of the ramparts still remain, together with an
old tower, which formed part of St. John's Church,
founded in the twelfth century. Cromwell inclosed this
church within the walls of his citadel, and turned it into
an armoury, but, as a compensation to the inhabitants,

he gave £150 towards the erection of the present Old
Church of Ayr, on the site of a Dominican monastery,
remarkable in history as the place where Robert Bruce
held the Parliament which settled his succession.   The
only memorial now existing of this monastery, is in the
name of a spring called the Friar's Well, which runs
through the church-yard into the river.   The Old Church
still contains the same seats and galleries with which it
was originally fitted up.

At the north-eastern angle of the fort, close upon the
harbour, is supposed to have stood the ancient Castle of
Ayr, built by William the Lion.   The Cross of Ayr, an
elegant structure in the form of a hexagon, which stood
where Sandgate Street meets High Street, was removed
when the New Bridge was built in 1788.

The population of the burgh and parish of Ayr amounted, in 1831, to 7606.

About two and a-half miles to the south of Ayr, overhanging the sea, is the old castle of Greenan, of which
mention is made in a charter granted towards the end of
the twelfth century, in the reign of King William the
Lion.

DUNURE CASTLE stands about five miles farther along
the coast, round the Heads of Ayr, and not far from the
mouth of the Doon.   Dunure is now a tall empty tower,
occupying a commanding situation on this rugged coast.
It appears to have been the first mansion of any consequence possessed by the family of Kennedy, and was
the place where, in 1570, Gilbert fourth Earl of Cassillis
confined Allen Stewart, Commendator of the Abbey of
Crossraguel ; and, in order to prevail upon him to surrender his lands, roasted him before a slow fire, till pain
obliged him to comply.   This castle, which has been in

ruins since the seventeenth century, now gives a territorial designation to a branch of the family of Kennedy, the present representative of which is T. F. Kennedy, Esq., formerly Member of Parliament for the Ayr district of burghs.

COLZEAN, or COLYEAN CASTLE, the principal seat of Archibald Marquis of Ailsa, and twelfth Earl of Cassillis, is situate about three miles farther along the Carrick coast, and about two miles from the village of Kirkoswald. This magnificent and picturesque mansion was built in 1777 by David, tenth Earl, on the site of the old House of the Cove, erected about the middle of the sixteenth century by Sir Thomas Kennedy, second son of Gilbert Earl of Cassillis. It stands upon the verge of a great basaltic cliff, overhanging the sea, and presents along the verge of a precipice " a range of lofty castellated masses, with windows in a Gothic taste, a splendid terraced garden in front, a bridge of approach, and offices in corresponding style at a little distance to the left, the whole covering an area of four acres," and conveying a most imposing impression of " baronial dignity, affluence, and taste." The interior of the castle contains an extensive and valuable collection of arms and armour.

The Kennedys have long held a prominent place among the aristocracy of Ayrshire. According to the old rhyme,

> " 'Twixt Wigton and the town o' Ayr,
>   Port-Patrick and the Cruives of Cree,
> Nae men need think for to bide there,
>   Unless he court wi' Kenedie."

This powerful race was first ennobled, in 1466, by the title of Lord Kennedy; in 1510 they attained the dignity of Earls of Cassillis; and, in 1831, Archibald, the twelfth and present Earl, was created Marquis of Ailsa.

U

The main line of the Cassillis family became extinct in
1759, and the title and family estates became the inheritance of Sir Thomas Kennedy of Colzean, who accordingly became ninth Earl of Cassillis. He was assassinated near the town of Ayr, May 12th, 1602, by Kennedy of Bargeny, at the instigation of Mure of Auchin-
drane, a deed which has been made the subject of a drama
by Sir Walter Scott.

Directly underneath the castle are the Coves of Colzean, six in number. According to popular report, they
are a favourite haunt of fairies, and are known to have
afforded shelter, after the Revolution, to Sir Archibald
Kennedy of Colzean, who acquired an unenviable noto-
riety as a *persecutor*, during the reigns of Charles II. and
James VII.

Colzean and the Cove are thus alluded to by Burns,
in his " Halloween" :

> " Upon that night when fairies light,
>   On Cassillis Downan's dance,
> Or owre the lays in splendid blaze,
>   On sprightly coursers prance,
> Or for *Colzean* the route is ta'en,
>   Beneath the moon's pale beams,
> There up the *Cove*, to stray and rove,
>   Among the rocks and streams,
>   To sport that night."

TURNBERRY CASTLE,

> " Where Bruce once rul'd the martial ranks,
>   And shook the Carrick spear,

stands a few miles to the south of Colzean. It was
in the twelfth and thirteenth centuries " the principal
house in Carrick, and the seat of a powerful race of
native chiefs, derived from Fergus, Lord of Galloway,

and designated Earls of Carrick, who possessed the supreme influence in this mountainous region previous to the rise of the Kennedies." In 1271, Robert Bruce, son of the Lord of Annandale, married the widowed Countess of Carrick, to whom the earldom had descended. From this union sprung Robert Bruce, King of Scotland, who, if not born in Turnberry Castle, must have spent many of his youthful years in it. It was in the neighbourhood of this place that a fire, accidentally kindled, was mistaken by the hero for an appointed signal, and caused him to cross the sea from Arran to Carrick, to attempt the deliverance of his country. On landing, the mistake was discovered, but he nevertheless determined to proceed with the enterprise; and though he was not immediately successful in his exertions for the liberation of Scotland from the English yoke, he was never again forced to leave the country till this object was attained. This incident has been related both by Barbour, and by Sir Walter Scott, in the "Lord of the Isles." The latter thus describes the appearance of the "ruddy signal" kindled on Carrick shore:

" As less and less the distance grows,
  High and more high the beacon rose;
  The light that seemed a twinkling star,
  Now blazed portentous, fierce, and far.
  Dark-red the heaven above it glow'd,
  Dark-red the sea beneath it flow'd;
  Red rose the rocks on ocean's brim,
  In blood-red light her islets swim,
  Wild scream the dazzled sea-fowl gave,
  Dropp'd from their crags on plashing wave.
  The deer to distant covert drew,
  The black-cock deem'd it day, and crew.
  Like some tall castle given to flame,
  O'er half the land the lustre came.

*   *   *   *   *

> Wide o'er the sky the splendour glows,
> As that portentous meteor rose;
> Helm, axe, and falchion glitter'd bright,
> And in the red and dusky light,
> His comrade's face each warrior saw,
> Nor marvell'd it was pale with awe,
> Then high in air the beams were lost,
> And darkness sunk upon the coast."*

" The only tradition now remembered of the landing of Robert Bruce in Carrick, relates to the fire seen by him from the Isle of Arran. It is still generally reported and religiously believed by many, that this fire was really the work of supernatural power, unassisted by the hand of any mortal being; and it is said, that for several centuries the flame rose yearly on the same hour of the same night of the year on which the king first saw it from the turrets of Brodick Castle; and some go so far as to say, that if the exact time were known it would be still seen. That this superstitious notion is very ancient, is evident from the place where the fire is said to have appeared being called the Bogle's Brae, beyond the remembrance of man.

" The top of the rock on which Turnberry is built is about eighteen feet above high-water mark. The ruin rising between forty and fifty feet above the water, has a majestic appearance from the sea. Around the Castle of Turnberry was a level plain of about two miles in extent, forming the Castle Park. There could be nothing more beautiful than the copsewood and verdure of this extensive meadow before it was invaded by the ploughshare." †

---

* Lord of the Isles, c. v., s. 13, 14.
† Notes to Canto v. of the Lord of the Isles.

Turnberry is still enumerated (under the denomination of Carrick), among the royal palaces of Scotland. It is now the property of the Marquis of Ailsa.

Within sight of Turnberry, and not more than a mile from it, is the farm of Shanter, formerly the residence of Douglas Graham, the original of " Tam o' Shanter."

At a short distance is the village of Kirkoswald, at which Burns attended school for some months, in the nineteenth year of his age. In the church-yard of this village two of his characters, Tam o'Shanter and Souter Johnny, are interred.

AILSA CRAIG, a huge rock, which rises sheer out of the sea, presents a striking appearance from this shore. Its nearest distance to land is about ten miles from the coast near Girvan. It is 1103 feet in height, and about two miles in circumference at the base. The ruins of a tower, of three storeys, are to be seen perched upon it. It is the property of the Marquis of Ailsa, who takes his title as a British Peer from it. Its principal productions are solan geese, goats, and rabbits, and it is let at £30 per annum. Ailsa Craig is noticed by Burns, in his song of " Duncan Gray."

BURNS' MONUMENT & COTTAGE, ALLOWAY KIRK, AND THE BRIG OF DOON.

Burns' Monument is 2¾ miles south of Ayr, 5¼ miles from Maybole, 36¼ miles from Glasgow by the Turnpike, and 42¼ by the Railway. Following the road from Ayr, a short distance from the town, there is a hill called Barnweil, which is said to have derived its name from the circumstance, that Wallace, on leaving Ayr, after having, in revenge for the treacherous slaughter of his friend, set on fire the barns in which the English

soldiery were inclosed, paused on this spot to look back
upon the conflagration, and remarked, " The Barns o'
Ayr burn well." There is good reason, however, to
doubt the accuracy of this traditionary etymology, and
it is more likely that the name is of Celtic origin, and is
descriptive of the nature of the ground. In the neighbourhood of Kirk Alloway are the various localities mentioned in " Tam O' Shanter's" route. At the distance
of about one hundred and fifty yards from a bridge, called
Slaphouse Bridge, is

> " The Ford,
> Where in the snaw the chapman smoor'd."

About one hundred yards from the " Ford," and about
twenty from the road, in the plot of ground behind the
house occupied by Roselle gamekeeper, is

> " The meikle stane,
> Whare drunken Charlie brak 's neck-bane."

Passing on the left the beautiful mansion of Roselle,
(Archibald Hamilton, Esq. of Carcluie), the tourist, at
the distance of about two miles from Ayr, reaches the
cottage where Burns was born on the 25th of January
1759. The original erection was a *Clay Bigging*, consisting of two apartments, the kitchen and the *spence*, or
sitting-room. The cottage was built on part of seven
acres of ground, of which Burns' father took a perpetual
lease from Dr. Campbell, physician in Ayr, with the view
of commencing business as nurseryman and gardener.
Having built this house with his own hands, he married,
in December 1757, Agnes Brown, the mother of the
Poet; and, having been engaged by Mr. Ferguson of
Doonholm, as his gardener and overseer, he abandoned
his design of forming a nursery, but continued to reside

in the cottage till 1766. On removing to Lochlea, he sold his leasehold to the Corporation of Shoemakers in Ayr, to whom the house and ground still belong. The house is now occupied as an ale-house. In the interior of the kitchen is shewn a recess, where stood the bed in which the Poet was born. This bedstead may now be seen at Brownhill Inn, near Thornhill, Dumfries-shire.

About a mile and a half to the south-east of the cottage, on an eminence, stands the farm of Mount Oliphant, which William Burns rented on leaving the Cottage at Whitsuntide 1766.

Proceeding towards Burns' Monument, we perceive in a field a single tree, enclosed with a paling, the last remnant of a group which covered

> " The cairn
> Where hunters fand the murder'd bairn.''

The position of the " cairn " and also of the " ford," at a distance from the highway, is accounted for by the fact, that the old road from Ayr, by which the poet supposed his hero to have approached Alloway Kirk, was to the west of the present line. We now reach

> " Alloway's auld haunted kirk."

This interesting building has long been roofless, but the walls are pretty well preserved, and it still retains its bell at the east end. The wood-work has all been taken away to form-snuff-boxes and other memorials of this celebrated spot.

In the area of the kirk, the late Lord Alloway, one of the Judges of the Court of Session, was interred; and near the gate of the churchyard is the grave of Burns' father, marked by a plain tombstone, a renewal of the original stone, which had been demolished and carried

away in fragments. "The churchyard of Alloway,"
says Mr. Robert Chambers, "has now become fashionable with the dead as well as the living. Its little area
is absolutely crowded with modern monuments, referring
to persons, many of whom have been brought from considerable distances to take their rest in this doubly consecrated ground."

A few yards to the west of Alloway Kirk, a well
trinkles down into the Doon, where formerly stood the
thorn on which

> " Mungo's mither hang'd hersel'."

A few hundred yards from the kirk is the "Auld
Brig" of Doon, which figures so conspicuously in the
tale of Tam o'Shanter. The age of the structure is unknown, but it is evidently of great antiquity. The "New
Bridge," which has been built since the time of Burns,
stands about a hundred yards below the Old. The
tasteful cottage between the Kirk and the Bridge belongs
to Mr. David Auld, to whom the admirers of the Ayrshire bard are deeply indebted for the unwearied zeal
and fine taste which he has displayed in adorning the
grounds of the Monument. Close beside the end of the
bridge is a neat inn for the accommodation of tourists.
Directly over the bridge stands the beautiful monument
to Burns, the foundation stone of which was laid on
25th January 1820. The project of erecting this monument originated with the late Sir Alexander Boswell of
Auchinleck. It was designed by Thomas Hamilton,
Esq., architect, Edinburgh, and cost upwards of L.3300.
The grounds around it measure about an acre and a
rood, and are very tastefully laid out. In a circular
apartment on the ground-floor there are exhibited seve-

ral articles appropriate to the place,—various editions of
the poet's works, a snuff-box made from the woodwork
of Alloway Kirk, a copy of the original portraits of Burns
by Naysmith, &c., and the Bibles given by Burns to his
Highland Mary. The possessor of these interesting
relics having emigrated to Canada in 1834, they were
purchased by a party of gentlemen in Montreal for £25,
and forwarded to the Provost of Ayr, to be presented in
their name to the trustees for the Monument. This
was accordingly done on the 25th of January 1841, the
anniversary of the poet's birth-day. From the base of
the columns, a remarkably splendid view is obtained of
the surrounding scenery. In a small grotto at the south
side of the enclosed ground are shown the two far-famed
statues of Tam o'Shanter and Souter Johnnie by Mr.
Thom of Ayr.

The Doon, to which the writings of Burns have given
such celebrity, takes its rise in a lake of the same name,
about eight miles in length, which is situated at the junction of the counties of Ayr and Kirkcudbright. The
Doon has a course of eighteen miles, throughout which
it forms the boundary between the districts of Carrick
and Kyle. The scenery of the Ness Glen, through
which the river runs immediately after issuing from the
lake, is remarkably woody and picturesque, and is a
favourite resort of *picnic* parties. Colonel M'Adam of
Craigengillan, with a praiseworthy liberality, allows visi-
ters to pass through his grounds on their way to the
Loch from Dalmellington. On a small island near the
upper extremity of Loch Doon are the ruins of an ancient castle of considerable strength, which figured in the
wars between England and Scotland during the time of
Robert Bruce. Sir Chrystal Seton, that hero's brother-

in-law, took refuge in this fortress after the defeat at
Methven, June 1306.   When the castle was surrendered
to the English, Sir Chrystal was taken, and barbarously
put to death at Dumfries, by command of King Edward.

TARBOLTON, COILSFIELD, &c.

William Burns, on the death of his landlord, Provost Ferguson, removed from Mount Oliphant, in 1777, to Lochlee,
situate in the parish of Tarbolton, and about three miles
from the village of that name. While residing in this farm,
Burns established a Bachelor's Club in Tarbolton, in the
latter part of the year 1780; and here, in 1783, he was
initiated into the mysteries of free-masonry. About two
hundred yards north of the village, on the road leading
to Galston, lies the scene of " Death and Dr. Hornbook."
" Willie's Mill," alluded to in the poem, was the Mill of
Tarbolton, situated on the Faile, about two hundred
yards east of the village, and was called by the name used
in the poem, in consequence of its being then occupied
by William Muir, a friend of the Burns family.

About half a mile from Tarbolton stands the mansion-
house of Coilsfield, designated by Burns " the Castle o'
Montgomery," from its being in his time the residence
of Colonel Hugh Montgomery, afterwards Earl of Eglinton.   Here Mary Campbell, Burns' " Highland Mary,"
lived in the humble capacity of a dairymaid. In this
neighbourhood, near the junction of the rivulet Faile with
the Ayr, was the scene of the parting which the poet has
described in such exquisite terms.   In the anticipation
of her marriage with Burns, Mary resolved to pay a visit
to her relations in Argyleshire.   Previous to her departure, she met her lover on a Sunday in May, and at their
parting, " standing one on each side of a small brook,
they laved their hands in the stream, and, holding a

Bible between them, pronounced a vow of eternal constancy." This was their last meeting. In returning from her visit of filial duty, Mary Campbell fell sick, and died at Greenock. This event produced an indelible impression on the mind of Burns, and he has given utterance to his feelings in some of the finest and most touching verses he has ever written. That " noblest of all his ballads," as the Address to " *Mary in Heaven*" has justly been designated, was composed at Ellisland, in 1789, on the anniversary of the day on which he heard of the death of his early love. According to the account given by Mrs. Burns to Mr. Lockhart, " Burns spent that day, though labouring under a cold, in the usual work of his harvest, and apparently in excellent spirits. But as the twilight deepened, he appeared to grow ' very sad about something,' and at length wandered out into the barn-yard, to which his wife, in her anxiety for his health, followed him, entreating him in vain to observe that frost had set in, and to return to the fireside. On being again and again requested to do so, he always promised compliance—but still remained where he was, striding up and down slowly, and contemplating the sky, which was singularly clear and starry. At last Mrs. Burns found him stretched on a mass of straw, with his eyes fixed on a beautiful planet, ' that shone like another moon ;' and prevailed on him to come in. He immediately, on entering the house, called for his desk, and wrote, exactly as they now stand, with all the ease of one copying from memory, the sublime and pathetic verses—

" Thou lingering star, with lessening ray,
 That lovest to greet the early morn,
Again thou usherest in the day
 My Mary from my soul was torn.

O, Mary ! dear departed shade,
   Where is thy place of blissful rest ?
See'st thou thy lover lowly laid,
   Hear'st thou the groans that rend his breast ?" &c.

According to unvarying tradition, Coilsfield derives its name from " Auld King Coil," who is supposed to have left his name to this whole district of Ayrshire, as well as to the rivulet of Coyl and the parish of Coylton.   He is said to have been overthrown and slain in this neighbourhood, in a bloody battle with Fergus King of Scots. This statement receives some countenance from the fact, that in May 1837, several urns, and a stone grave containing some bones, were dug up in a circular mound near Coilsfield, where, according to unvarying tradition, the remains of " Auld King Coil" were deposited.   Burns alludes to this tradition in his poem of " The Vision."

   " There where a scepter'd Pictish shade,"
   Stalk'd round his ashes lowly laid,
   I mark'd a martial race portray'd
      In colours strong ;
   Bold, soldier-featured, undismay'd,
      They strode alone.

The " martial race," here referred to, are the Montgomerys. Coilsfield is now the property of the Earl of Eglinton, grandson of the gentleman who possessed it in Burns' time.

MAUCHLINE, MOSSGIEL, &c.

On the death of William Burns, his widow and family removed to Mossgiel, a farm about a mile north of Mauchline, which the poet and his brother Gilbert had taken some months before the death of their father. Here Burns lived during the period of his life extending from his 25th to his 28th year, and here he wrote his principal poems. The *spence* of this farm-house is the scene described in the opening of *The Vision*, and in the *stable-loft*, where he slept, many of his most admired poems were written. Mauchline, which " appropriated a large share of the notice of the poet during his residence at Mossgiel," lies about nine miles from Kilmarnock, and eleven from Ayr. It is situated on the face of a slope, about a mile from the river Ayr, and contains upwards of 1300 inhabitants. Mauchline was the scene of the *Holy Fair*, and of the *Jolly Beggars*, and here dwelt John Dow, Nanse Tinnock, " Daddy Auld," and other characters who figure conspicuously in the poet's writings. The churchyard was the scene of the *Holy Fair*, but the present church is a recent substitute for the old barn-like edifice which existed in Burns's time. Near the church is the *Whitefoord Arms* Inn, where Burns wrote, on a pane of glass, the well-known amusing epitaph on the landlord, John Dow. Nearly opposite the churchyard gate is the house of " Auld Nanse Tinnock," bearing over the door the date 1744. " It is remembered," says Mr. Chambers, " that Nanse never could undersand how the poet should have talked of enjoying himself in her house three times a-week.—" The lad," she said, " hardly ever drank three half-mutchkins under her roof in his life." The cottage of *Poosie Nansie*, the scene of the " Jolly Beggars," is also pointed out. Close behind the churchyard is the house in which Mr. Gavin Hamilton, the early friend of Burns, lived. In this house is shewn the room in which Burns composed the satirical poem entitled " The Calf." This room is farther remarkable as the one in which the poet was married.

The scenes of some of Burns's most admired lyrics are to be found on the banks of the Ayr, at a short distance

from Mauchline.   The " Braes of Ballochmyle," the
scene of his beautiful song entitled " The Lass o' Ballochmyle," are situated at the distance of about two miles
from Mossgiel, and extend along the north bank of the
Ayr, between the village of Catrine and Howford Bridge.
They form part of the pleasure-grounds connected with
Ballochmyle House, the seat of Claud Alexander, Esq.
Ballochmyle was at one time the property of the White-
foords, an old and once powerful Ayrshire family. Colonel
Allen Whitefoord, one of the members of this family,
was the original of the character of Colonel Talbot, described in the novel of Waverley.   Another of them,
Caleb Whitefoord, " the best natured man, with the
worst natured muse," has been immortalized by Goldsmith
in a postscript to his witty poem entitled " Retaliation."
Sir John Whitefoord, the representative of the family in
the time of Burns, having been forced to part with his
estate in consequence of declining circumstances, Burns
wrote some plaintive verses on the occasion, referring to
the grief of Maria Whitefoord, now Mrs. Cranstoun, on
leaving the family inheritance:

> " Through faded groves Maria sang,
>   Hersel' in beauty's bloom the while,
> And aye the wild-wood echoes rang,
>   Fareweel the braes of Ballochmyle.
> Low in your wintry beds, ye flowers,
>   Again ye'll flourish fresh and fair;
> Ye burdies dumb in withering bowers,
>   Again ye 'll charm the vocal air;
> But here, alas! for me nae mair
>   Shall birdie charm or floweret smile;
> Fareweel the bonnie banks of Ayr—
>   Farweel, fareweel, sweet Ballochmyle."

Ballochmyle was purchased by Claud Alexander, Esq.;

. and shortly after that gentleman had taken possession of the mansion, his sister, Miss Wilhelmina Alexander, a famed beauty, walking out along the braes one evening in July 1786, encountered Burns, with his shoulder placed against one of the trees. The result was, that the poet, during his homeward walk, composed the well-known song entitled " The Lass of Ballochmyle." The spot where Miss Alexander met the poet is now distinguished by a rustic grotto or moss-house, ornamented with appropriate devices; and on a tablet in the back there is inscribed a fac simile of two of the verses of the poem, as it appeared in the holograph of the author. Near Ballochmyle is the manufacturing village of Catrine, at one time the seat of Dr. Stewart, and of his son, the celebrated Professor Dugald Stewart. To them Burns alludes in the following stanza in " The Vision : "

> " With deep-struck reverential awe,
>   The learned sire and son I saw,
>   To Nature's God and Nature's law
>   They gave their lore ;
>   This all its source and end to draw,
>   That to adore."

Between the villages of Tarbolton and Mauchline stands the mansion of Barskimming, occupying a romantic situation on the banks of the Ayr. The scenery of the river at this spot is remarkably beautiful. Barskimming, and its late proprietor, Lord Justice-Clerk Miller, are thus alluded to in the above-mentioned poem :—

> " Through many a wild romantic grove,
>   Near many a hermit-fancied cove,
>   Fit haunts for friendship or for love ;
>   In musing mood,
> An aged judge I saw him rove,
>   Dispensing good.

Barskimming is now the property of Sir William Miller of Glenlee, Bart., only son of Lord Justice-Clerk Miller, and a retired Judge of the Court of Session.

A short distance farther up the river, at the point where the Lugar joins the Ayr, is the spot where Burns composed the poem entitled " Man was made to mourn."

EDINBURGH, KINROSS, PERTH, DUNKELD, BLAIR ATHOLL.

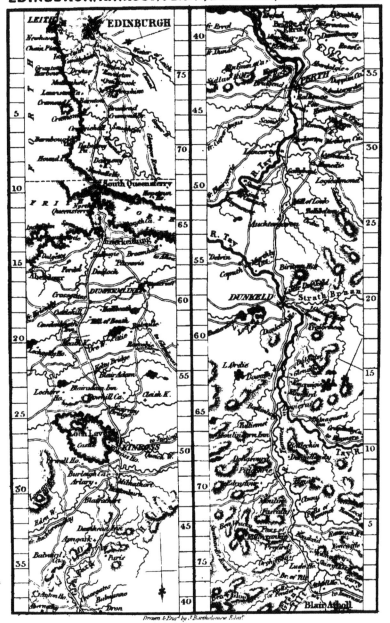

Drawn & Engd by J. Bartholomew Edinr

Edinburgh, Published July 1 1841 by Adam & Charles Black, 7 North Bridge.

THIRTEENTH TOUR.

EDINBURGH TO INVERNESS BY KINROSS—PERTH—DUNKELD—BLAIR ATHOLL.

LEAVING Edinburgh by the Queensferry Road, the tourist crosses the Water of Leith by Dean Bridge, a superb edifice of four arches, each ninety feet in span. Below, on the right, is St. Bernard's Well. On the left stands the village of the Water of Leith; and at a short distance are two buildings of great elegance—the Hospital endowed by John Watson, W.S. for the maintenance and education of destitute children, and the new Orphan Hospital, opened in 1833. The road now passes the new Episcopal Chapel, and on the right Dean House, (Sir J. Nisbet,) Craigleith, (Bonar, Esq.,) and Craigleith Quarry, from which the stone employed in building the New Town of Edinburgh was chiefly procured. At a short distance to the left is Ravelston, (Lady Murray Keith,) and Craigcrook, (Lord Jeffrey.) About four miles from Edinburgh stands Barnton House, (W. R. Ramsay, Esq.) A mile farther on, the tourist crosses the Almond by Cramond Bridge, and passes, on the left, Craigiehall, (Hope Vere, Esq.,) and on the right Newhall, (Scott Moncrieff, Esq.) On the shore is the village of Cramond, and the entrance to Dalmeny Park, (Earl Rosebery.) The banks of the river Almond in this neighbourhood are very beautiful, and the scenery about the old bridge of Craigiehall is very romantic. Passing in succession

x

Dalmeny Kirk, a little to the left, 7½ miles, and Ha's
Inn, 8 miles from Edinburgh, you enter South Queensferry, which was erected into a royal borough by Malcolm Canmore, and derived its name from Margaret his
queen.   Here are some ruins of a monastery of Carmelite Friars, founded in 1330.   On the left is Dudding-
stone House, (G. H. Dundas, Esq.,) and a little to the
south, the ruins of Dundas Castle, a building of great
antiquity, which has been in the Dundas family upwards
of 700 years.   The ferry across the Forth belonged, before the Reformation, to the Abbot of Dunfermline, and
was at that period sold by his orders to a joint stock
company.*   Three miles west from Queensferry stands
HOPETOUN HOUSE, a building of great splendour, and
possessing a delightful prospect.   In the narrow strait at
Queensferry, there is the little island of Inch Garvie, on
which a fort was established during the last war.   On
this island, previous to the reign of Charles II., the principal state prison was placed.   Upon a promontory, on
the northern coast, stands the small village of North
Queensferry.   It is remarkable as the place where Oliver
Cromwell first encamped on crossing the Forth, in 1651.
On this promontory, which is called the Cruicks, there is
a lazaretto, where goods landed on this part of the coast,
from tropical climates, have to pass quarantine.   In the
immediate neighbourhood is Rosyth Castle, a huge square
tower, situated close by the sea.   It was the ancient seat
of the Stuarts of Rosyth, a branch of the royal family,

----

* The agent appointed to dispose of the ferry divided it into sixteen shares,
and offered the same for sale. The project was immediately successful; the
shares were eagerly purchased; the agent continued to sell as long as he found
persons willing to buy; and, scandalous to relate, there is evidence still in existence that he actually sold eighteen sixteenth shares of the Queensferry passage.

from which Oliver Cromwell is said to have descended. The bay between the Cruicks and Rosyth Castle is called St. Margaret's Hope, from the circumstance of the Princess Margaret, sister of Edgar Atheling, afterwards consort of Malcolm Canmore, having been wrecked there in her flight from England, immediately after the Norman conquest.

Two miles beyond North Queensferry, the road enters
INVERKEITHING,
a royal burgh of very great antiquity. By its first existing charter, which it received from William the Lion, the town obtained jurisdiction over a very extensive tract of country, but its importance is now greatly reduced. It was frequently the residence of David I. and of Queen Annabella Drummond, wife of Robert III., and an antique house is yet pointed out, which she is said to have inhabited. Great quantities of coal and salt are annually exported here. In the neighbourhood of Inverkeithing, a body of Scottish loyalists were defeated with great slaughter by a superior force under the command of Lambert, the English Parliamentary general. In this engagement a foster father and seven sons sacrificed themselves for Sir Hector M'Lean of Duart; the old man, whenever one of his boys fell, thrusting forward another to fill his place, at the right hand of the beloved chief, with the words, " Another for Hector." This incident has been introduced with great effect by Sir Walter Scott, in his description of the combat between the Clan Kay and Clan Chattan, in the Fair Maid of Perth.*

* At the distance of three miles from this part of the coast stands the ancient town of DUNFERMLINE, which, about the time of Malcolm Canmore, became the seat of government, and continued to be a favourite residence of the Scottish kings down to the Union of the crowns.
   " The king sits in Dunfermline town,
      Drinking the blude-red wine."—*Ballad of Sir Patrick Spens.*
The most ancient of the antiquities of Dunfermline is the castle of Malcolm Canmore, the remains of which are still visible on a peninsular eminence jutting into

A short distance to the east of Inverkeithing, and close upon the shore, stands Donnibrissel House, a seat of the Earl of Moray. (See Fifth Tour, p. 192.) The tourist now passes in succession, on the right, Fordel (Sir J. Henderson, Bart.), Lochgelly (Earl of Minto), and Lochore (Sir W. Scott). A short way to the left, on the old road, is the Kirk of Beath, six miles from Inverkeithing; two and a-half miles beyond that, Maryburgh, the birth-place of the two brothers Adam, the celebrated architects, and, farther on, Blair-Adam, (Sir Charles Adam.) The road crosses the Kelty Water, and shortly after the Gairney at Gairney Bridge, where the poet, Michael Bruce once

a ravine near to the town. South-east of the town are the ruins of the later palace, which seems to have been a building of great magnificence. The south-west wall is all that remains of it. This palace was the birth-place of Charles I. The bed in which he was born is preserved in Broomhall, the seat of the Earl of Elgin, two miles from the town. The last monarch who occupied this palace was Charles II., who lived in it for some time during his campaign in 1650-51. The Abbey of Dunfermline was founded by Malcolm III. It was burned down, excepting the church and cells, by Edward I., in 1303. The parts thus spared were much injured at the Reformation. The founder, his queen, and seven other monarchs, were interred within its precincts. The nave of the church, which is the only part that has been entire for a long time, has been used as a parish church ever since the Reformation. In 1818 it was judged expedient to abandon this part of the building, and it was resolved to provide a new parish church by rebuilding the chancel and transepts, which was accordingly done. It is to be regretted that the bad taste displayed in the erection has, in a great measure, marred the beauty of the design. In clearing away the ruins of the ancient choir, the tomb of Robert Bruce, who was buried here in 1329, was discovered. The skeleton of the illustrious monarch was found entire, together with the lead in which his body was wrapt, and even some fragments of his shroud. He was reinterred with much state by the Barons of the Exchequer, immediately under the pulpit of the new church. In the area of the church is shewn a large marble slab, broken into three pieces, said to be the tombstone of Queen Margaret; also six large flat stones, affirmed to mark the graves of as many kings. The remains of the Abbey are very extensive, but it is generally asserted that the original buildings were much more so. The Fratery still retains an entire window, much admired for its elegant and complicated workmanship. Beneath the Fratery there were six and twenty cells, many of which still remain. The celebrated Ralph Erskine, one of the founders of the Secession Church, was, for a number of years, minister of Dunfermline. The tourist ought to ascend the old steeple of the church, from which a very extensive and magnificent prospect may be obtained. Dunfermline has greatly increased within the last thirty years, and is now distinguished by its activity in the manufacture of linen.

taught a small school; and, twenty-seven miles from Edinburgh, the tourist enters

KINROSS,

the capital of the county of that name, pleasantly situated on the banks of Loch Leven. Kinross House (Sir J. Graham Montgomery of Stanhope), erected in 1685, stands on the edge of the lake. The promontory on which it stands was once occupied by a stronghold, long the residence of the Earls of Morton. By far the most interesting object in the neighbourhood of Kinross is the lake, on the banks of which the town is situated. Loch Leven is well worthy of a visit from tourists, not only on account of the beautiful scenery with which it is surrounded, but especially on account of the historical associations with which it abounds. This lake is of an irregular oval figure, and extends from ten to eleven miles in circumference. It contains four islands, the chief of which are St. Serf's Isle, near the east end, so named from its having been the site of a priory dedicated to St. Serf; and another, about two acres in extent, situated near the shore opposite Kinross, on which are the picturesque ruins of LOCH LEVEN CASTLE, celebrated from its being the prison-house of the unfortunate Queen Mary.* Loch Leven Castle is of unknown antiquity; but it is noticed in history as early as 1334, when an unsuccess-

* " Gothic the pile, and high the solid walls,
　With warlike ramparts, and the stong defence
　Of jutting battlements: an age's toil!
　No more its arches echo to the noise
　Of joy and festive mirth. No more the glance
　Of blazing taper through its windows beams,
　And quivers on the undulating wave;
　But naked stand the melancholy walls,
　Lash'd by the wintry tempest, cold and bleak,
　That whistle mournful through the empty halls,
　And piecemeal crumble down the towers to dust."
　　　　　Loch Leven, a Poem, by Michael Bruce.

ful siege was laid to it by an English army, commanded
by John de Strevelin. It was anciently a royal castle,
and was for some time the residence of Alexander III.
It has been repeatedly used as a state prison. Patrick
Graham, Archbishop of St. Andrews, and grandson of
Robert III., after an unsuccessful attempt to reform the
lives of the Catholic clergy, was, through their influence
at Court, arrested, confined in different monasteries, and
at last died a prisoner in Loch Leven Castle in 1478. In
1542 Loch Leven Castle was granted by James V. to Sir
Robert Douglas, stepfather to the famous Earl of Murray; and in 1567, Queen Mary was imprisoned there
after her surrender at Carberry Hill. The view with
which our text is illustrated, represents Lord Lindsay
and his party on the occasion of that memorable visit to
Queen Mary, which terminated in her abdication of the
crown. The pennon of the ruthless baron is displayed
by one of his attendants, as a signal for the boat, while
he himself blows "a clamorous blast on his bugle."
Queen Mary escaped from the castle, May 2, 1568,
through the aid of young Douglas, and is said, by general
tradition, to have landed at a place called Balbinny, at
the south side of the lake, whence she was conducted,
by Lord Seton, to Niddry Castle in West Lothian. The
keys of the castle, which were thrown into the lake at
the time of her escape, were recently found by a young
man belonging to Kinross, who presented them to the
Earl of Morton. Between the castle island and the
nearest point of land at the churchyard, a causeway
runs along the bottom of the water, which is here so
shallow, that in dry seasons it is possible to wade to the
isle upon this strange pavement. Loch Leven is celebrated for the excellence of its trout. The rich taste
and bright red colour are derived from a small red shell-

LOCHLEVEN CASTLE.

fish upon which they feed. The silver grey trout is apparently the original native of the loch, and, in many respects, the finest fish of the whole. At the eastern extremity of the loch, there are some remains of the monasteries of Portmoak and Scotland's Well. The little sequestered village of Kinneswood, situated on the north-east shore of Loch Leven, was the birth-place of Michael Bruce, the poet. The house in which he first saw the light is still pointed out. His poem on Loch Leven Castle, his ballad of Sir James the Rose, and his verses in anticipation of his own death, are much admired. He died at the early age of twenty-one, before his poetical genius arrived at maturity.* The river Leven flows from the lake on the east side, and pursues an easterly course to the Firth of Forth. The vale of the Leven is beautiful, and is ornamented with the woods around Leslie, the seat of the Earl of Rothes. About two miles from Kinross, is the village of Milnathort, or Mills of Forth ; and to the right, at some distance, are the ruins of Burleigh Castle, which gave title to Lord Burleigh, attainted in 1716. The road now enters Glenfarg, a romantic little valley, enclosed by the Ochils, which are clothed to their summits with verdure.

At the northern extremity of the glen is Ayton House (Murray,) and a short distance to the right the ancient village of Abernethy, once the capital of the Pictish kingdom, and a most extensive Culdee establishment, consisting of a university and a monastery, besides a church. Abernethy still contains a round tower similar to that of Brechin, supposed to have been erected by the

---

* A most interesting biography of Bruce has lately been published by the Rev. Mr. M'Kelvie of Balgedie, who has satisfactorily proved that the Ode to the Cuckoo, and several of the paraphrases, published by Logan in his own name, were in reality written by Bruce.

Picts.   Passing some hamlets, the tourist reaches the BRIDGE OF EARN, a village which affords accommodation to the strangers who resort in great numbers to Pitcaithly Wells in the neighbourhood.   There is a ball-room and a library, with every other requisite convenience.   The rules by which the society of this watering-place is regulated are of a peculiar, but very judicious kind.   Shortly after passing Pitcaithly, the tourist reaches the hill of Moncreiff, from which he will obtain the first view of Perth.*   The prospect from this hill has been much and deservedly admired.   The fertile Carse of Gowrie,—the Firth of Tay, with the populous town of Dundee,—the city of Perth, and the beautiful valley of Strathearn, bounded by the hills of Menteith, are all distinctly seen from this eminence.   Pennant calls this view " the Glory of Scotland."

PERTH,

An ancient royal burgh, and one of the handsomest towns in Scotland, is beautifully situated on the west bank of the Tay, at the distance of forty-four miles from

* One of the most beautiful points of view which Britain, or perhaps the world, can afford, is, or rather we may say was, the prospect from a spot called the Wicks of Baiglie, being a species of niche at which the traveller arrived, after a long stage from Kinross, through a waste and uninteresting country, and from which, as forming a pass over the summit of a ridgy eminence which he had gradually surmounted, he beheld stretching beneath him, the valley of the Tay, traversed by its ample and lordly stream; the town of Perth, with its two large meadows, or Inches, its steeples, and its towers; the hills of Moncreiff and Kinnoul faintly rising into picturesque rocks, partly clothed with woods; the rich margin of the river, studded with elegant mansions; and the distant view of the huge Grampian mountains, the northern screen of this exquisite landscape. The alteration of the road, greatly, it must be owned, to the improvement of general intercourse, avoids this magnificent point of view, and the landscape is introduced more gradually and partially to the eye, though the approach. must be still considered as extremely beautiful. There is still, we believe, a footpath left open by which the station at the Wicks of Baiglie may be approached; and the traveller, by quitting his horse or equipage, and walking a few hundred yards, may still compare the real landscape with the sketch which we have attempted to give."—*Fair Maid of Perth*, vol. i., p. 21.

Edinburgh. It occupies the centre of a spacious plain, having two beautiful pieces of public ground called the North and South Inches extending on each side of it.

A splendid bridge of ten arches and 900 feet in length, built in 1772, leads across the Tay to the north. Perth, or, as it used to be called from its church, St. Johnstoun, boasts of the most remote antiquity, and has been the scene of many interesting events. On account of its importance and its vicinity to the royal palace of Scone, it was long the metropolis of the kingdom before Edinburgh obtained that distinction. Here, too, the Parliaments and national assemblies were held, and many of the nobility took up their residence. Perth contains several beautiful streets and terraces, and a number of fine public buildings. The oldest of these is St. John's Church, the precise origin of which is unknown. It has undergone various modifications, and is now divided into the East, West, and Middle Churches. The demolition of ecclesiastical architecture which accompanied the Reformation commenced in this church, in consequence of a sermon preached by John Knox against idolatry. At the south end of the Watergate stood Gowrie House, the scene of the mysterious incident in Scottish history, called the Gowrie Conspiracy. The whole of that fine old building has unfortunately been removed, and the site is now occupied by the County Hall, a splendid structure in the Grecian style. In George Street stands a fine building, erected in 1823 in honour of Provost Marshall, in the lower part of which is the Public Library, and in the upper part the Museum of the Literary and Antiquarian Society, founded in 1784, and probably the finest provincial collection of the kind in Scotland. Perth also contains an excellent Academy, a Gas-work of large dimensions, a Water-house of excellent architecture, and an Infirmary equally handsome. The Depot, erected for the reception of prisoners during the French war, is being converted into a Penitentiary for the West of Scotland. Previous to the Reformation, Perth contained an immense number of religious houses. One of these, the Monastery of Greyfriars, stood at the end of the Speygate. In Blackfriars monastery, which was situated at the north side of the town, James I. was assassinated by a band of conspirators. But of these and many other interesting buildings not a vestige now remains. Perth has been the scene of many important historical events. It was occupied by the English during the reign of Edward I., but was besieged and taken by Robert Bruce. In the time of the great civil war it was taken by the Marquis of Montrose after the Battle of Tippermuir. In 1715, and again in 1745, it was occupied by the rebel Highland army, who there proclaimed the Pretender as king. The Inches are two beautiful pieces of ground, each about a mile and a-half in circumference, affording agreeable and healthy walks to the inhabitants, and delightfully variegated with trees. On the North Inch there took place, in the reign of Robert III., that singular combat between the Clan Kay and Clan Chattan, which Sir Walter Scott has introduced with so much effect into his novel of the Fair Maid of Perth. The town is surrounded on all sides with the most beautiful and picturesque scenery, and the interesting objects in the neighbourhood are so numerous, that it would require a volume to notice them all. The views from the tops of the hills of Moncreiffe and Kinnoull are well worthy of a visit,—the latter, in particular, no tourist should omit seeing, as it is one of the

finest prospects in Scotland. At the foot of Kinnoull
Hill, lies Kinfauns Castle, from which every visitor
returns delighted with the natural and artificial beauties both in and around it. Scone Palace (noticed below) will amply repay the trouble of a visit; and so
will Dupplin Castle, the seat of the Earl of Kinnoull,
situated about five miles west of Perth. The Dupplin
Library is well known for its collection of rare and valuable editions of the classics, and the woods around the
castle are magnificent. Lynedoch, also, is a favourite
excursion, chiefly on account of the graves of Bessy Bell
and Mary Gray, which are situate on the romantic
banks of the Almond. The population of Perth is about
25,000.

Leaving Perth by the North Inch, the tourist passes
on the left, Tulloch Printfield and Few House, (Nicol,
Esq.,) and at the distance of two and a half miles from
Perth, on the opposite side of the Tay, sees Scone Palace, the seat of the Earl of Mansfield, who represents
the old family of Stormont. It is a modern building,
occupying the site of the ancient palace of the kings of
Scotland. Much of the old furniture has been preserved
in the modern house. Among other relics are a bed
used by James VI., and another of a flowered crimson
velvet, said to have been wrought by Queen Mary when
imprisoned in Loch Leven Castle. The gallery, which is
160 feet long, occupies the site of the old hall in which
the coronations were celebrated. The situation of the
palace is highly picturesque, and the view from the windows of the drawing-room is most splendid. At the
north side of the house is a *tumulus*, termed the Moat
Hill, said to have been composed of earth from the estates of the different proprietors who here attended on

the kings. The famous stone on which the Scottish monarchs were crowned was brought from Dunstaffnage to this Abbey. It was removed by Edward I. to Westminster Abbey, where it still remains, forming part of the coronation chair of the British monarchs. The Abbey of Scone was destroyed at the time of the Reformation by a mob from Dundee, and the only part now remaining is an old aisle, containing a magnificent marble monument to the memory of the first Viscount Stormont. The old market-cross of Scone still remains, surrounded by the pleasure grounds which have been substituted in the place of the ancient village. Two and a half miles from Perth, the road crosses the Almond near its junction with the Tay, and winds among plantations chiefly on Lord Lynedoch's estate. About two miles in advance a road leads off from the left to Redgorton and Monedie, and a few paces farther on a road upon the right conducts to the field of Luncarty, situated on the west bank of the Tay, about four miles from Perth, the scene of a decisive battle between the Scots and Danes in the reign of Kenneth III. The Scots were at first forced to retreat, but were rallied by a peasant of the name of Hay, and his two sons, who were ploughing in the neighbourhood. By the aid of these courageous peasants, who were armed only with a yoke, the Scots obtained a complete victory. In commemoration of this circumstance, the crest of the Hays has for many centuries been a peasant carrying a yoke over his shoulder. The plain on which the battle was fought is now used as a bleachfield. A mile in advance the road crosses the fine trouting streams of Ordie and Shochie.* A

* Perth suffered from a nocturnal inundation of the Tay in the year 1210, and it is predicted that it will again be destroyed in a similar manner :—

little farther on, a road turns off to the right to the Linn of Campsie, where the Tay forms a magnificent cascade, and the village of Stanley, famous for its extensive spinning-mills. The tourist next passes on the left the ruins of a residence of the family of Nairn, and the Mill of Loak; and nine miles from Perth, enters the village of Auchtergaven. Three miles farther on the tourist passes Murthly Castle, (Stewart, Bart.,) and a short way north of it, the old Castle of Murthly. In the immediate neighbourhood is Birnam Hill, 1580 feet above the level of the sea, and Birnam Wood, so famous for its connection with the fate of Macbeth. The ancient forest has now disappeared, and been replaced by trees of modern growth. The traveller now passes the village of Little Dunkeld,* crosses the river Tay, and enters

DUNKELD.

" There are few places," says Dr. Macculloch, " of which the effect is so striking as Dunkeld, when first seen on emerging from this pass, (a pass formed by the Tay, by which the traveller enters the Highlands,) nor does it owe this more to the suddenness of the view, or to its contrast with the long preceding blank, than to its own intrinsic beauty; to its magnificent bridge and its cathe-

" Says the Shochie to the Ordie,
   ' Where shall we meet?'
  ' At the cross o' Perth,
    When a' men are fast asleep.' "
Popular Rhyme.

* " O what a parish, what a terrible parish,
   O what a parish is that of Dunkell!
  They hae hangit the minister, drown'd the precentor,
   Dung down the steeple, and drucken the bell!
  Though the steeple was down, the kirk was still stannin'
   They biggit a burn where the bell used to hang;
  A stell-pat they gat, and they brewed Hieland whisky,
   On Sundays they drank it, and rantit and sang."
Old Song.

dral nestling among its dark woody hills; to its noble
river, and to the brilliant profusion of rich ornament.
The leading object in the landscape is the noble bridge
standing high above the Tay. The cathedral seen above
it, and relieved by the dark woods by which it is embosomed, and the town, with its congregated grey houses,
add to the general mass of architecture, and thus enhance
its effect in the landscape. Beyond, rise the round and
rich swelling woods that skirt the river, stretching away
in a long vista to the foot of Craiginean, which, with all
its forests of fir, rises a broad shadowy mass against the
sky. The varied outline of Craig-y-Barns, one continuous range of darkly-wooded hill, now swelling to the
light, and again subsiding in deep shadowy recesses, forms
the remainder of the splendid distance. The Duke of
Atholl's grounds present a succession of walks and rides
in every style of beauty that can be imagined, but they
will not be seen in the few hours usually allotted to
them, as the extent of the walks is fifty miles, and of the
rides thirty. It is the property of few places, perhaps
of no one in all Britain, to admit, within such a space, of
such a prolongation of lines of access, and everywhere
with so much variety of character, such frequent changes
of scene, and so much beauty." The most interesting
object in the town of Dunkeld, is the ancient and venerable cathedral. The great aisle measures 120 by 60
feet, the walls are 40 feet high, and the side aisles 12
feet wide. It is now roofless, but the choir was rebuilt
and converted into a place of worship by the late Duke
of Atholl, at an expense of £5000. The new church
is handsomely fitted up. In the vestry there is a statue
in armour, of somewhat rude workmanship, which was
formerly placed at the grave of the notorious *Wolf of*

Badenoch, who burned the cathedral of Elgin. The early history of this establishment is obscure, but it is understood that there was a monastery of the Culdees here, which David I. converted into a bishoprick, A.D. 1127. Among its bishops were Gawin Douglas, famous for his poetical talents, and Bishop Sinclair, celebrated for his patriotic exertions in the reign of Robert Bruce. Immediately behind the cathedral, stands the ancient mansion of the Dukes of Atholl. A magnificent new mansion was commenced by the late Duke, but his death, in 1830, has suspended the progress of the building, the expense of which was estimated at half a million. At the end of the cathedral are the first two larches introduced into Britain. They were originally brought from Switzerland 103 years ago, and placed in flower-pots in a green-house, but are now ninety feet high, one of them measuring fifteen feet in circumference, at two feet from the ground. The walks through the policies of Dunkeld have been pronounced, by the late Dr. E. Clarke, to be almost without a rival. The larch woods alone cover an extent of 11,000 square acres; the number of these trees planted by the late Duke of Atholl being about twenty-seven millions, besides several millions of other sorts of trees. The tourist returns from the policies to Dunkeld by the village of Inver, in which the small thatched house long occupied by Neil Gow, the celebrated musician, may be seen. An old wooden press, said to have belonged to him, forms part of the furniture of the present tenant.

From the base of Craigvignan, a long wooded eminence projects, across which a path leads to Ossian's Hall, situated beside a cataract formed by a fall of the Braan. This is generally esteemed the greatest curiosity of Dunkeld. A hermitage or summer-house is placed

forty feet from the bottom of the fall, and is constructed
in such a manner that the cascade is entirely concealed
by the walls of the edifice.   Opposite to the entrance is
a picture of Ossian playing upon his harp, and singing
the songs of other times.   At the touch of the guide, the
picture suddenly disappears with a loud noise, and the
whole cataract foams at once before the visitor, reflected
in several mirrors, and roaring with the noise of thunder.
The spectacle is exceedingly striking.   About a mile
higher up the Braan, is the Rumbling Bridge, which is
thrown across a narrow chasm, eighty feet above the
waterway.   Into this gulf the Braan pours itself with
great fury, foaming and roaring over the massive fragments of rock which have fallen into the stream, and
casting a thick cloud of spray high above the bridge.

" The most perfect and extensive view," says Dr.
Macculloch, " of the grounds of Dunkeld, is to be obtained opposite to the village of Inver, and at a considerable elevation above the bridge of the Braan ; it affords
a better conception of the collected magnificence and
grandeur of the whole than any other place." *

* From Dunkeld the tourist may go off to the east by Cluny to Blairgowrie,
distant twelve miles ; a route which comprises some exquisitely beautiful scenery.   The road winds along the foot of the Grampians, and passes in succession the Loch of Lowe, Butterstone Loch, the Loch of Cluny, with the ancient
castle of Cluny, a seat of the Earl of Airlie, on a small island near the southern shore, Forneth, (Binny, Esq.,) the Loch of Marlie, Kinloch, (Hog, Esq.)
Baleid, (Campbell, Esq.) ; the House of Marlie, (Farquharson, Esq.,) and the
church and inn of Marlie or Kinloch, much resorted to by parties from Perth
and Dunkeld, and two miles farther, Blairgowrie, situated on the west bank of
the Ericht, containing a population of 1500.   Near Blairgowrie is Craighall-
Rattray, one of the most picturesquely situate mansions in Scotland, being built
on the top of a perpendicular rock of great height on the banks of the Ericht. .

ABERFELDY — KENMORE — TAYMOUTH CASTLE — KILLIN — LOCHEARN-
HEAD — COMRIE — CRIEFF.

THE tourist who wishes to survey the beautiful scenery of Kenmore and Killin, may either proceed to Blair Atholl, and thence
to Kenmore, distant, by the common road, twenty-eight miles—
over the hills, twenty miles—or he may adopt the route by Logierait and Aberfeldy. If he prefers the former, shortly after leaving
Blair Atholl he reaches a chasm in the hill on the right hand,
through which the little river Bruar falls over a series of beautiful
cascades. These falls were formerly unadorned by wood, but, in
consequence of the poetical address, written by Burns, entitled
"Humble petition of Bruar Water," the Duke of Atholl has
formed a plantation along the chasm. The river makes three distinct falls, the lowest of which forms an unbroken descent of 100
feet. The shelving rocks on both banks—the depth of the chasm
—and the roughness of the channel through which the stream
rushes, add greatly to the sublimity and interest of the scene.
From these falls, the tourist may either proceed by the common
road, or over the hill on the south side of the vale, to Tummel
Bridge and Inn. The scenery around this spot is extremely beautiful. In the midst of it stands Foss, the seat of — Stewart, Esq.
From the Bridge of Tummel there is a road which leads through
a gloomy and mountainous country to Loch Rannoch. This
lake is about ten or eleven miles in length and two and a half in
breadth, and is surrounded by lofty mountains covered with forests.
In the neighbourhood is the steep mountain Schehallion, 3550 feet
high, which afforded shelter to Robert Bruce after the battle of
Methven. Leaving the Bridge of Tummel, an Alpine road of seven
or eight miles in length leads to Strath Tay. The ruins of a high
square keep, called Garth Castle, occupying a narrow rocky promontory at the confluence of two rivulets, form a prominent object
in the landscape. The stream runs in deep perpendicular chan-
nels, and the dell is richly wooded, and so deep that the roaring of
the waters can scarcely be heard. The view from the confined
channel of the burn, over-canopied by slanting trees, is peculiarly
striking; and the whole scene presents an exquisite combination of
beauty and terror. The tourist now descends along the edge of a
deep and wooded dell, bordered by sloping cultivated ground, and

Y

passing Coshieville Inn, reaches Fortingal, as the lower part of Glen Lyon is called, and, crossing the Lyon by a boat, he turns the corner of a hill, and all at once alights upon the lovely village of Kenmore.

If, however, as is usually the case, the tourist should prefer the route by Logierait and Aberfeldy, on leaving Dunkeld he crosses the Tay by a magnificent bridge of seven arches, and a little farther on, reaches the village of Inver, where the Braan is crossed by a bridge, and a road strikes off upon the left to Amulree. Three miles beyond this, the road enters the village of Dalmarnock, then the village of Ballalachan, and a mile and a half beyond, passes Dalguise, (Stewart, Esq.) on the left. The road now leads along a wide cultivated valley, through which flow the combined waters of the Tay and Tummel. It abounds in the finest scenery, and extensive masses of larch and pine skirt the edges of the hills above. Six and a half miles from Dunkeld we pass Kinnaird House, (Duke of Atholl,) and one mile further, the village of Balmacneil,—opposite this spot the Tummel falls into the Tay. On a tongue of land, formed by the confluence of these rivers, stands the village of Logierait, (eight and a half miles from Dunkeld.) One mile from Balmacneil is Port village, and one mile further, Balnaguard Inn,—the opening scene of Mrs. Brunton's novel, entitled "Self Control." On the right, is Eastertyre, (Major M'Glashan.) Across the Tay is Ballechin, (Hope Stuart, Esq.) which appears to have been the scene of the slaughter of Sir James the Rose, in the original ballad of that name. A mile and a half beyond is Eastmill, and opposite, across the Tay, Fyndynet. After passing some Highland villages, the venerable Castle of Grandtully (Stewart, Bart.) appears on the left, surrounded by rows of stately elms. It is an old structure, but kept in a habitable condition, and is said by Sir Walter Scott to bear a great resemblance to the mansion of Tullyveolan in Waverley. One of the square wings is completely encompassed with ivy. Three miles from Grandtully is the village of Aberfeldy, near which are the beautiful falls of Moness, said by Pennant to be an epitome of everything desirable in a waterfall. The description which Burns has given of these falls is not only beautiful in itself, but strikingly accurate:

> " The braes ascend like lofty wa's,
> · The foaming stream deep roarin fa's,
> O'erhung wi' fragrant spreading shaws,
>   The birks of Aberfeldy.

> The hoary cliffs are crown'd wi' flowers,
> White o'er the linn the burnie pours,
> And rising, weets wi' misty showers,
>   The birks of Aberfeldy."

The falls are three in number; the lowest is a mile from the village, the upper, half a mile beyond it. The glen is deep, and so exceedingly confined, that the trees in some places almost meet from the opposite sides. The lowest fall consists chiefly of a series of cascades formed by a small tributary rivulet pouring down the east side of the dell. The next series consists of a succession of falls, comprising a perpendicular height of not less than a hundred feet. The last and highest cascade is a perpendicular fall of about fifty feet. Here the traveller may cross the dell by means of a rustic bridge, and return to the inn by a varied route. Opposite Aberfeldy the Tay is crossed by one of General Wade's bridges. About a mile in advance, on the north side, stands Castle Menzies, the seat of Sir Neil Menzies, the chief of that name, erected in the sixteenth century. It stands at the foot of a lofty range of rocky hills, and is surrounded by a park filled with aged trees. Weem Castle, the former seat of the family, was burnt by Montrose. About a mile farther is Balfrax, (Sir Neil Menzies, Bart.) and about a mile beyond, the Lyon water joins the Tay. Six miles from Aberfeldy the tourist reaches the beautiful little village of Kenmore, situated at the north-east extremity of Loch Tay. It consists of an inn and fifteen or sixteen houses, neatly whitewashed, and some of them embowered in ivy, honeysuckle, and sweet-briar. The most remarkable object in the vicinity of Kenmore, is TAY-MOUTH CASTLE, the princely mansion of the Marquis of Breadal-bane, with its much admired environs. The castle is a magnificent dark-grey pile of four stories, with round corner towers, and terminating in an airy central pavilion. Its interior is splendidly fitted up, and it contains one of the best collections of paintings in Scotland. The pleasure-grounds are laid out with great taste, and possess a striking combination of beauty and grandeur. The hills which confine them are luxuriantly wooded and picturesque in their outlines, and the plain below is richly adorned with old gigantic trees. The view from the hill in front of the castle is reckoned one of the finest in Scotland. On the right is Drummond Hill, and behind it the lofty Ben Lawers, with Ben More in the remote distance. On the left, two hills, partially wooded, rise from the water, one above another. In the foreground, a portion of the lake is seen, and the village and church of Kenmore, and to the north of them, the bridge across the Tay, immediately behind which is the little wooded island of Loch Tay, with the ruins of a priory founded by Alexander I., whose Queen, Sybilla, lies interred here.* The scene is thus described in an impromptu of Robert Burns, who visited the spot in August 1787.

> " The outstretching lake, embosom'd 'mong the hills,
> The eye with wonder and amasement fills;
> The Tay, meandering sweet in infant pride;
> The palace rising by his verdant side;
> The lawns, wood-fringed, in nature's native taste,
> The hillocks dropt in nature's careless haste;
> The arches striding o'er the new-born stream,
> The village glittering in the noon-tide beam."

Along the north bank of the river, there is a terrace sixteen yards wide and three miles in length, overshadowed by a row of stately beech trees, and, on the opposite side, there is a similar walk extending a mile from Kenmore. These promenades are connected by a light cast-iron bridge. Taymouth Castle was first built by Sir Colin Campbell, sixth knight of Lochaw, in the year 1580. It was then, and until lately, called Balloch, from the Gaelic *bealach*, a word signifying the outlet of a lake or glen. The builder being asked why he had placed his house at the extremity of his estate, replied, " *We'll brizz yont*," (press onward,) adding, that *he intended Balloch should in time be in the middle of it*. The possessions of the family have, however, extended in the opposite direction. They now reach from Aberfeldy, four miles eastward, to the Atlantic Ocean, a space upwards of one hundred miles, and are said to be the *longest* in Britain.

Leaving Kenmore and Taymouth, the tourist proceeds along the shores of the Loch to Killin, which is sixteen miles distant at the opposite extremity. Both shores abound in beautiful scenery, but the southern is preferable, on account of the view which it commands of the gigantic Ben Lawers, which borders the other side of the loch.† This road, however, is unfortunately impassable

---

* The last residents in this priory were three nuns who, once a-year, visited a fair in Kenmore, which, owing to that circumstance, is still called " Holy Women's Market."

† " The northern shore of the lake presented a far more Alpine prospect than that upon which the Glover was stationed. Woods and thickets ran up the

LOCH ASSYNT— BEN MORE IN THE DISTANCE.

for a carriage. There is a good deal of cultivated ground on either
side, with a prodigious number of rude and picturesque cottages.
Two miles from Kenmore, on the south side of the lake, is the fine
waterfall of Acharn, half a mile off the road. The cascade appears
to be about eighty or ninety feet high, and a neat hermitage has
been formed, commanding an excellent view of the fall. Killin is
a straggling little village on the banks of the Dochart, near its
junction with the Lochy. Fingal's grave in a field immediately to
the north of the village, is indicated by a stone about two feet in
height. The village is much admired for the varied beauty of its
landscapes. The vale of the Dochart is stern and wild, but that
of the Lochy is peculiarly beautiful. At the village, the Dochart
rushes over a strange expanse of rock, and encircles two islands,
one covered with magnificent pines, on one of which is the tomb
of the Macnabs. From the upper end of the lower island there
are three bridges across the stream. " Killin," says Dr. Macculloch,
" is the most extraordinary collection of extraordinary scenery in
Scotland—unlike every thing else in the country, and perhaps on
earth, and a perfect picture gallery in itself, since you cannot move
three yards without meeting a new landscape. A busy artist might

sides of the mountains, and disappeared among the sinuosities formed by the
winding ravines which separated them from each other; but far above these
specimens of a tolerable natural soil, arose the swart and bare mountains
themselves, in the dark grey desolation proper to the season. Some were
peaked, some broad-crested, some rocky and precipitous, others of a tamer
outline; and the clan of Titans seemed to be commanded by their appropriate
chieftains—the frowning mountain of Ben Lawers, and the still more lofty eminence of Ben Mohr, arising high above the rest, whose peaks retain a dazzling
helmet of snow far into the summer season, and sometimes during the whole
year. Yet the borders of this wild and silvan region, where the mountains descended upon the lake, intimated, even at that early period, many traces of human habitation. Hamlets were seen, especially on the northern margin of the
lake, half hid among the little glens that poured their tributary streams into Loch
Tay, which, like many earthly things, made a fair show at a distance, but,
when more closely approached, were disgustful and repulsive, from their squalid
want of the conveniences which even attend Indian wigwams. The magnificent
bosom of the lake itself was a scene to gaze on with delight. Its noble breadth,
with its termination in a full and beautiful run, was rendered yet more picturesque by one of those islets which are often happily situated in Scottish
lakes. The ruins upon that isle, now almost shapeless, being overgrown with
wood, rose, at the time we speak of, into the towers and pinnacles of a priory,
where slumbered the remains of Sibilla, daughter of Henry I. of England, and
consort of Alexander the First of Scotland."—*Fair Maid of Perth.*

here draw a month and not exhaust it. * * * Fir-trees, rocks,
torrents, mills, bridges, houses, these produce the great bulk of the
middle landscape, under endless combinations, while the distances
more constantly are found in the surrounding hills, in their varied
woods, in the bright expanse of the lake, and the minute ornaments
of the distant valley, in the rocks, and bold summit of Cailleach,
and in the lofty vision of Ben Lawers, which towers, like a huge
giant, to the clouds—the monarch of the scene." On the north
side of Loch Tay, and about a mile and a half from the village of
Killin, stand the picturesque ruins of Finlarig Castle, an ancient
seat of the Breadalbane family. The castle is a narrow building
of three storeys, entirely overgrown with ivy, and surrounded by
venerable trees. Immediately adjoining is the family vault. The
following anecdote of the olden times is related by the Messrs. Anderson in their excellent Guide to the Highlands : "On the occasion
of a marriage festival at Finlarig, in years gone by, when occupied
by the heir apparent, intelligence was given to the company, which
comprised the principal youth of the clan, that a party of the
Macdonalds of Keppoch, who had just passed with a drove of
lifted cattle, had refused to pay the accustomed *road* collop. Flushed
with revelry, the guests indignantly sallied out and attacked the
Macdonalds on the adjoining hill of Stronoclachan, but, from their
irregular impetuosity, they were repulsed, and twenty young gentlemen left dead on the spot. Tidings of the affray were conveyed
to Taymouth, and a reinforcement arriving, the victors were overtaken in Glenorchy, and routed, and their leader slain."

On leaving Killin the tourist proceeds up Glen Dochart, and
passes, on the right, the mansion house of Achlyne, a seat of the
Marquis of Breadalbane. A little beyond, at a place called Leeks,
a road strikes off to Crianlarich Inn, from which the tourist may
either go by Tyndrum and Dalmally to Inverary, or he may descend Glenfalloch till he reach the head of Loch Lomond. The
traveller now enters Glen Ogle, a narrow and gloomy defile, hemmed in by the rocky sides of the mountains, which are here strikingly grand, rising on the one side in a succession of terraces, and
on the other, in a steep acclivity, surmounted by perpendicular precipices. At the distance of eight miles from Killin, is the little
village of Lochearnhead, with a good inn. From this point the
tourist may turn southward by Balquhidder, the burial place of

Rob Roy, and through the wild pass of Loch Lubnaig and Lenny to Callander, a distance of thirteen miles. Loch Earn is about seven miles in length, and about one mile in breadth. " Limited as are the dimensions of Loch Earn," says Dr. Macculloch, " it is exceeded in beauty by few of our lakes, as far as it is possible for many beauties to exist in so small a space. Its style is that of a lake of far greater dimensions,—the hills which bound it being lofty, and bold, and rugged, with a variety of character not found in many of even far greater magnitude and extent. It is a miniature and model of scenery that might well occupy ten times the space. Yet the eye does not feel this. There is nothing trifling or small in the details,—nothing to diminish its grandeur of style, and tell us we are contemplating a reduced copy. On the contrary, there is a perpetual contest between our impressions and our reasonings ; we know that a few short miles comprehend the whole, and yet we feel as if it was a landscape of many miles,—a lake to be ranked among those of first order and dimensions."

" While its mountains thus rise in majestic simplicity to the sky, terminating in bold, and various, and rocky outlines, the surfaces of the declivities are equally bold and various, enriched with precipices and masses of protruding rock, with deep hollows and ravines, and with the courses of innumerable torrents, which pour from above, and, as they descend, become skirted with trees, till they lose themselves in the waters of the lake. Wild woods also ascend along their surface in all that irregularity of distribution so peculiar to these rocky mountains, less solid and continuous than at Loch Lomond, less scattered and romantic than at Loch Katrine, but from these very causes, aiding to confer upon Loch Earn a character entirely its own."

There is a road on each side of the lake, but the southern route is to be preferred. About a mile and a half from the inn, we come to Edinample, an ancient castellated mansion belonging to the Marquis of Breadalbane. There is also a beautiful waterfall here, immediately below the road. The Ample, a mountain rivulet, pours in two perpendicular streams over a broad rugged rock, and uniting about midway, is precipitated again over a second precipice. The road now passes through continuous woods of oak, larch, ash, and birch. The view to the south is closed up by the huge Ben Voirlich, (*i. e.* the Great Mountain of the Lake,) which rises to the height of 3300 feet. About midway between Lochearnhead

and the east end of the lake is Ardvoirlich, (William Stewart, Esq.),
the Darlinvaroch of the *Legend of Montrose*.* The landscapes to

* " During the reign of James IV., a great feud between the powerful families
of Drummond and Murray divided Perthshire. The former, being the most
numerous and powerful, cooped up eight score of the Murrays in the kirk of
Monivaird, and set fire to it. The wives and children of the ill-fated men, who
had also found shelter in the church, perished by the same conflagration. One
man, named David Murray, escaped by the humanity of one of the Drum-
monds, who received him in his arms as he leaped from amongst the flames.
As King James IV. ruled with more activity than most of his predecessors, this
cruel deed was severely revenged, and several of the perpetrators were beheaded
at Stirling. In consequence of the prosecution against his clan, the Drummond,
by whose assistance David Murray had escaped, fled to Ireland, until, by means
of the person whose life he had saved, he was permitted to return to Scotland,
where he and his descendants were distinguished by the name of Drummond,
Eirinich, or Ernoch, that is, Drummond of Ireland ; and the same title was
bestowed on their estate.

" The Drummond-Ernoch of James the Sixth's time was a king's forester in
the forest of Glenartney, and chanced to be employed there in search of venison about the year 1588, or early in 1589. The forest was adjacent to the chief
haunts of the MacGregors, or a particular race of them, known by the title of
MacEagh, or Children of the Mist. They considered the forester's hunting in
their vicinity as an aggression, or perhaps they had him at feud, for the apprehension or slaughter of some of their own name, or for some similar reason.
This tribe of MacGregors were outlawed and persecuted, as the reader may see
in the Introduction to Rob Roy; and every man's hand being against them,
their hand was of course directed against every man. In short, they surprised
and slew Drummond-Ernoch, cut off his head, and carried it with them, wrapt
in the corner of one of their plaids.

" In the full exultation of vengeance, they stopped at the house of Ardvoirlich, and demanded refreshment, which the lady, a sister of the murdered
Drummond-Ernoch, (her husband being absent,) was afraid or unwilling to refuse. She caused bread and cheese to be placed before them, and gave directions for more substantial refreshments to be prepared. While she was absent
with this hospitable intention, the barbarians placed the head of her brother
on the table, filling the mouth with bread and cheese, and bidding him eat, for
many a merry meal he had eaten in that house.

" The poor woman returning, and beholding this dreadful sight, shrieked
aloud, and fled into the woods, where, as described in the romance, she roamed
a raving maniac, and for some time secreted herself from all living society.
Some remaining instinctive feeling brought her at length to steal a glance from
a distance at the maidens while they milked the cows, which, being observed,
her husband, Ardvoirlich, had her conveyed back to her home, and detained
her there until she gave birth to a child, of whom she had been pregnant ; after
which she was observed gradually to recover her mental faculties.

" Meanwhile the outlaws had carried to the utmost their insults against the
regal authority, which, indeed, as exercised, they had little reason for respecting. They bore the same bloody trophy, which they had so savagely exhibited
to the lady of Ardvoirlich, into the old church of Balquhidder, nearly in the
centre of their country, where the Laird of MacGregor and all his clan being

the east of the house are peculiarly beautiful. At the foot of Loch Earn, there is a small artificial islet covered with wood, which was

convened for the purpose, laid their hands successively on the dead man's head, and swore, in heathenish and barbarous manner, to defend the author of the deed. This fierce and vindictive combination gave the late lamented Si Alexander Boswell, Bart., subject for a spirited poem, entitled " Clan-Alpin's Vow," which was printed, but not published, in 1811."

We give the spirited conclusion of the poem :—" The Clan-Gregor has met in the ancient church of Balquhidder. The head of Drummond-Ernoch is placed on the altar, covered for a time with the banner of the tribe. The Chief of the tribe advances to the altar:—

> " And pausing, on the banner gazed ;
> Then cried in scorn, his finger raised,
> ' This was the boon of Scotland's king ; '
> And, with a quick and angry fling,
> Tossing the pageant screen away,
> The dead man's head before him lay.
> Unmoved he scann'd the visage o'er,
> The clotted locks were dark with gore,
> The features with convulsion grim,
> The eyes contorted, sunk, and dim.
> But unappall'd, in angry mood,
> With lowering brow, unmov'd he stood.
> Upon the head his bared right hand
> He laid, the other grasp'd his brand ;
> Then kneeling, cried, " To Heaven I swear
> This deed of death I own, and share ;
> As truly, fully mine, as though
> This my right hand had dealt the blow ;
> Come then, our foemen, one, come all;
> If to revenge this caitiff's fall
> One blade is bared, one bow is drawn,
> Mine everlasting peace I pawn,
> To claim from them, or claim from him,
> In retribution, limb for limb.
> In sudden fray, or open strife,
> This steel shall render life for life.'
> He ceased ; and at his beckoning nod,
> The clansmen to the altar trod ;
> And not a whisper breath'd around,
> And nought was heard of mortal sound,
> Save from the clanking arms they bore,
> That rattled on the marble floor;
> And each, as he approach'd in haste,
> Upon the scalp his right hand placed ;
> With livid lip, and gather'd brow,
> Each uttered, in his turn, the vow.
> Fierce Malcolm watch'd the passing scene,
> And search'd them through with glances keen ;

at one time the retreat of a bandit sept of the name of Neish. Having on one occasion plundered some of the Macnabs, a party of that clan, commanded by the chieftain's son, carried a boat from Loch Tay to Loch Earn, surprised the banditti by night, and put them all to the sword. In commemoration of this event, the Macnabs assumed for their crest a man's head, with the motto " Dreadnought."

At the east end of Loch Earn stands the neat little village of St. Fillans. It was formerly a wretched hamlet, known by the name of Portmore, but through the exertions of Lord and Lady Willoughby de Eresby, on whose ground it stands, it has become one of the sweetest spots in Scotland. It derived its name from St. Fillan, a celebrated saint who resided in this place. He was the favourite saint of Robert Bruce, and one of his arms was borne in a shrine by the Abbot of Inchaffray at the battle of Bannockburn. On the summit of a hill in this neighbourhood, called Dun Fillan, there is a well consecrated by him, which even to this day is supposed to be efficacious for the cure of many disorders. The St. Fillan's Society, formed in 1819, holds an annual meeting in this place for athletic sports and performances on the bagpipe, and confers prizes on the successful competitors. These games are usually attended by great numbers of persons of condition, male and female, from all parts of the Highlands. The valley of Strathearn, which extends from this place nearly to Perth, contains many fine villas and wooded parks, and is celebrated for its beauty and fertility. Leaving St. Fillans, the road winds along the banks of the Earn, through groves of lofty trees, presenting here and there broken glimpses of the ridges of the neighbouring mountains. About two miles and a half from Loch Earn, we pass the mansion of Duneira, the favourite seat of the late Lord Melville, with its picturesque grounds and delightful pleasure walks. It is now the property of Sir David Dundas, Bart. A little farther on, Dalchonzie (Skene,

> Then dash'd a tear-drop from his eye;
> Unbid it came—he knew not why.
> Exulting high, he towering stood;
> ' Kinsmen,' he cried, ' of Alpin's blood,
> And worthy of Clan-Alpin's name,
> Unstain'd by cowardice and shame,
> E'en do, spare nocht, in time of ill
> Shall be Clan-Alpin's legend still!' "
>
>   *Introduction to Legend of Montrose.*

Esq.) and Aberuchill Castle* (Drummond, Esq.) are seen on the right ; and, five miles and a half from St. Fillans, the tourist enters the village of Comrie, pleasantly situated on the north bank of the Earn, at its confluence with the Ruchill. Comrie is remarkable for the earthquakes with which it has occasionally been visited for a number of years. It is by many supposed to have been the scene of the dreadful battle between Galgacus and Agricola. Half a mile south of the village are the remains of a Roman camp. Close to the village stands Comrie House, (Dundas, Bart.,) on the east side of which the Lednock Water flows into the Earn. On the summit of a hill called Dunmore, a monument seventy-two feet in height has been erected to the memory of the late Lord Melville, overhanging a turbulent little stream called the " Humble Bumble." At the foot of Dunmore, there is a place called the " Devil's Caldron," where the Lednock, at the farther extremity of a long, deep, and narrow chasm, is precipitated into a dark and dismal gulf. From the monument there is an extensive and interesting view of the adjacent country.

Leaving Comrie, we descend towards Crieff, through a scene of the most enchanting beauty. A mile and a half beyond Comrie, we pass, on the left, Lawers' House, (the mansion of the late Lord Balgray,) the parks of which contain some of the largest pine-trees in Scotland. A mile farther on is Clathick, (Colquhoun, Esq.,) and half a mile beyond the road passes Monivaird Kirk. On an eminence to the south of this place there is an obelisk, erected to Sir David Baird, Bart. A mile and a half beyond is Ochtertyre, (Sir William Murray,) celebrated for the romantic beauty of its situation. The adjacent vale of the Turit exhibits a variety of romantic scenery, which has been rendered classical by the pen of Burns.† The road now winds along the brow of a wooded hill, and, about six and a half miles from Comrie, enters the thriving town of Crieff, delightfully situated on a slope above the river Earn, backed by hills and crags, and the Knock of Crieff, all of considerable altitude. It contains about 5000 inhabitants, who are principally engaged in the manufacture of cotton goods. The

* Aberuchill was built in 1602, and was the scene of many sanguinary battles between the Campbells and Macgregors.

† While on a visit to Sir William Murray at Ochtertyre, he wrote the beautiful song, " Blythe was she," on Miss Euphemia Murray of Lintrose, a lady whose beauty had acquired for her the name of " The Flower of Strathmore."

environs of Crieff are exquisitely beautful, and will amply repay
the visit of the tourist. Three miles south from the town is the
delightful little village of Muthil, with its new church, a pleasing
specimen of the Gothic style. In the same direction, on the road
to Dumblane, is Drummond Castle, the ancient residence of the
noble family of Perth, now represented by Lady Willoughby
d'Eresby. " If Drummond Castle," says Macculloch, " is not all
that it might be rendered, it is still absolutely unrivalled in the
low country, and only exceeded in the Highlands by Dunkeld and
Blair. Placed in the most advantageous position to enjoy the
magnificent and various expanse around, it looks over scenery
scarcely any where equalled. With ground of the most commanding and varied forms, including water and rock, and abrupt hill
and dell, and gentle undulations, its extent is princely, and its
aspect that of ancient wealth and ancient power. Noble avenues,
profuse woods, a waste of lawn and pasture, an unrestrained scope,
everything bespeaks the carelessness of liberality and extensive
possessions, while the ancient castle, its earliest part belonging to
1500, stamps on it that air of high and distant opulence which adds
so deep a moral interest to the rural beauties of baronial Britain."

North from Crieff, on the road to Amulree, is Monzie Castle,
(pronounced *Monée*,) Campbell, Esq., situated amid splendid scenery. The paintings and armoury are well worthy of attention.
Leaving Crieff for Perth, we pass in succession Fernton, (Lady
Baird ;) a mile beyond this Cultoquhey, (Maxton, Esq.,) then
Inchbrakie, (Græme, Esq.,) and next on the right, Abercairney,
(Moray, Esq.) Farther on is the village of Foulis, and a mile beyond this are the ruins of the Abbey of Inchaffray, founded in
1200 by an Earl of Strathearn and his Countess, and the abbot of
which carried the arm of St. Fillans at the battle of Bannockburn.
A mile farther on, the road passes Gorthy, (Mercer, Esq.,) and
shortly after enters the plantations of Balgowan, the seat of Lord
Lynedoch. A little farther, the road passes on the right Tipper-
malloch, (Moncrief, Esq.,) and, between six and seven miles from
Perth, enters the village of Methven, containing a population of
about 2000. In the immediate neighbourhood stands Methven
Castle, (Smythe, Esq.) Near Methven, Robert Bruce was defeated, June 19, 1306, by the English, under the command of
Aymer de Valence, Earl of Pembroke. About two miles and a
half from Perth, the road passes the ancient castle of Ruthven,

the scene of the memorable incident known in Scottish history by the name of the *Raid of Ruthven*. The building has now been converted into a residence for workmen, and its name changed to Huntingtower. A short distance to the north is Lynedoch Cottage, within the grounds of which is Burn Braes, a spot on the banks of Brauchieburn, where Bessy Bell and Mary Gray

> ———— " biggit a bower
> And theekit it ower wi' rashes.

Dronach Haugh, where these unfortunate beauties were buried, is about half a mile west from Lynedoch Cottage, on the banks of the river Almond.* Over their supposed grave is placed a stone with the following inscription, "they lived—they loved—they died." The road now passes Tulloch bleachfield and printfield, and shortly after enters the town of Perth.

* The common tradition is, that Bessie Bell and Mary Gray were the daughters of two country gentlemen in the neighbourhood of Perth, and an intimate friendship subsisted between them. Bessie Bell, daughter of the Laird of Kinnaird, happening to be on a visit to Mary Gray, at her father's house of Lynedoch, when the plague of 1666 broke out. To avoid the infection, the two young ladies built themselves a bower in a very retired and romantic spot called the Burnbraes, about three-quarters of a mile westward from Lynedoch House, where they resided for some time, supplied with food, it is said, by a young gentleman of Perth, who was in love with them both. The disease was unfortunately communicated to them by their lover, and proved fatal, when, according to custom in cases of the plague, they were not buried in the ordinary parochial place of sepulture, but in a sequestered spot called Dronach Haugh, at the foot of a brae of the same name, upon the banks of the river Almond. Some tasteful person, in modern times, has fastened a sort of bower over their double graves, and there " violets blue and daisies pied " will for ever blow over the remains of unfortunate beauty.

The following pathetic little ballad, which Allan Ramsay supplanted by his lively song, has fortunately been recovered by Mr Kirkpatrick Sharpe :—

> " O Bessie Bell and Mary Gray,
>   They war twa bonnie lasses,
> They biggit a bower on yon burn side,
>   And theekit it ower wi' rashes.
> They theekit it ower wi' rashes green,
>   They theekit it ower wi' heather;
> But the pest cam frae the burrows-town,
>   And slew them baith thegither.
>
> They thocht to lie in Methven kirkyard,
>   Amang their noble kin ;
> But they maun lie in Lednock braes,
>   To beek forenent the sun.

LEAVING Dunkeld, the road passes for some miles along
the eastern bank of the Tay, and at the distance of five
miles reaches Dowally Kirk. On the opposite side of the
river are seen Dalguise, (Stewart, Esq.) and Kinnaird
House, (Duke of Atholl.) A little farther on is Moulin-
earn Inn. A mile farther is Donavourd, (Macfarlane,
Esq.,) on the right, and Dunfallandy, (General Ferguson,)
on the western bank of the Tummel. A mile beyond is
the village of Pitlochrie, and a little farther, on a low
tongue of land formed by the junction of the Tummel
and the Garry, is Fascally House, (Butter, Esq.,) surrounded by wooded hills, forming a most romantic and
attractive scene.* Proceeding onward, at the distance
of a mile, the traveller enters the celebrated pass of
KILLIECRANKIE, which stretches for the space of a mile
or more along the termination of the river Garry. The
hills which, on both sides, approach very near, are covered
with natural wood, and descend in rugged precipices to
the deep channel of the river. At the bridge over the
Garry, near the entrance of the pass, a road leads on the
left to the districts of the Tummel and Rannoch. The
north end of this pass is the well-known scene of the battle fought, in 1689, between the Highland clans under
Viscount Dundee, and the troops of King William, com-

> And Bessie Bell and Mary Gray,
>   They war twa bonnie lasses ;
> They biggit a bower on yon burn side,
>   And theekit it ower wi' rashes.
>   PENNANT's *Tour.* CHAMBERS' *Ballads*, p. 146.

* On the estate of Fascally, upon the high ground about a mile from Pitlochrie,
on the road from Dunkeld, is a pretty little waterfall called the Black Spout.

manded by General Mackay. A stone is pointed out at
Urrard House, on the right, which marks the spot where
Dundee received his death-wound.* Several villas adorn

* "Dundee," says Sir John Dalrymple, "flew to the Convention, and demanded justice. The Duke of Hamilton, who wished to get rid of a troublesome adversary, treated his complaint with neglect ; and, in order to sting him
in the tenderest part, reflected upon that courage which could be alarmed by
imaginary dangers. Dundee left the house in a rage, mounted his horse, and
with a troop of fifty horsemen, who had deserted to him from his regiment in
England, galloped through the city. Being asked by one of his friends who
stopped him, where he was going ? he waved his hat, and is reported to have
answered, 'Wherever the spirit of Montrose shall direct me.' "—*Memoirs*, 4to
edit. vol. i. p. 287. Dundee immediately proceeded to collect the army with
which he fought the battle of Killiecrankie. This incident has been commemorated by Sir W. Scott in the following spirited Song :—

" To the Lords of Convention, 'twas Clavers who spoke,
  Ere the King's crown go down, there are crowns to be broke,
  So each cavalier, who loves honour and me,
  Let him follow the bonnet of bonnie Dundee.

    Come, fill up my cup, come, fill up my can,
    Come, saddle my horses, and call up my men ;
    Come, open the West Port, and let me gae free,
    And it 's room for the bonnets of bonnie Dundee.

Dundee he is mounted, he rides up the street ;
The bells are rung backward, the drums they are beat ;
But the Provost, douce man, said, Just e'en let him be ;
The town is weel quit of that deil of Dundee,
    Come, fill up, &c.

As he rode down the sanctified bends of the Bow,
Each carline was flyting and shaking her pow ;
But some young plants of grace, they looked couthie and slee,
Thinking—Luck to thy bonnet, thou bonnie Dundee !
    Come, fill up, &c.

With sour-featured saints the Grassmarket was panged,
As if half of the west had set tryst to be hang'd ;
There was spite in each face, there was fear in each ee,
As they watch'd for the bonnet of bonnie Dundee.
    Come, fill up, &c.

The cowls of Kilmarnock had spits and had spears,
And lang-hafted gullies to kill cavaliers ;
But they shrunk to close-heads, and the causeway left free,
At a toss of the bonnet of bonnie Dundee.
    Come, fill up, &c.

the terraced sides of the valley approaching the pass, viz. Urrard House, (Alston, Esq.,) Killiecrankie Cottage, (Hay, Esq.,) Strathgarey, (Stewart, Esq.,) &c. Passing Lude, (M'Inroy, Esq.,) the road descends into the valley, and crosses the river at the Bridge of Tilt, where there is a neat village, and an excellent inn. The beauties of Glen Tilt, and the Falls of Fender, formed by a burn falling into the water of Tilt, will amply repay a visit. A little further on, the road reaches the village and inn of Blair, and, in the neighbourhood, the noble old castle of Blair, now called Atholl House, the ancient residence

He spurr'd to the foot of the high castle rock,
And to the gay Gordon he gallantly spoke ;
Let Mons Meg and her marrows three volleys let flee,
For love of the bonnets of bonnie Dundee.
    Come, fill up, &c.

The Gordon has ask'd of him whither he goes—
Wheresoever shall guide me the soul of Montrose ;
Your Grace in short space shall have tidings of me,
Or that low lies the bonnet of bonnie Dundee.
    Come, fill up, &c.

There are hills beyond Pentland, and streams beyond Forth ;
If there 's lords in the Southland, there 's chiefs in the North ;
There are wild dunniewassals three thousand times three,
Will cry *Hoich !* for the bonnet of bonnie Dundee,
    Come, fill up, &c.

Away to the hills, to the woods, to the rocks,
Ere I own a usurper, I 'll couch with the fox :
And tremble, false Whigs, though triumphant ye be,
You have not seen the last of my bonnet and me.
    Come, fill up, &c.

He waved his proud arm, and the trumpets were blown,
The kettle-drums clash'd, and the horsemen rode on,
Till on Ravelston crags, and on Clermiston lee,
Died away the wild war-note of bonnie Dundee.

Come, fill up my cup, come, fill up my can,
Come, saddle my horses, and call up my men ;
Fling all your gates open, and let me gae free,
For 'tis up with the bonnets of bonnie Dundee.

of the Dukes of that name. It is a long narrow building of three storeys. It was formerly much higher, and
a place of considerable strength, but was reduced in
height in consequence of the attacks of the Highlanders
in 1716. Blair is celebrated for its noble old woods.

FALL OF BRUAR.

In the immediate neighbourhood there is a number of
interesting waterfalls. Three miles to the westward are
those of Bruar. The streamlet makes several distinct
falls, and rushes through a rough perpendicular channel
above which the sloping banks are covered with a fir
plantation formed by the late Duke of Atholl, in compliance with the request of Burns in the well-known
" Petition." And now, according to the poet's wish,—

" lofty firs and ashes cool,
The lowly banks o'erspread,
And view deep-bending in the pool,
Their shadows' watery bed !

z

> Here fragrant birks in woodbines drest,
>   The craggy cliffs adorn,
> And for the little songster's nest,
>   The close embow'ring thorn."

A walk has been cut through the plantation, and a number of fantastic little grottoes erected, and a carriage-
road leads as far as the second set of falls. From Blair-
Atholl a road leads through Glen Tilt, and over a wild
mountainous district, to the Braes of Mar. Leaving
Blair-Atholl, the tourist passes through a wild Alpine
territory, and, proceeding along the banks of the Garry,
at the distance of ten miles and a half, reaches the inn
of Dalnacardoch. The country between Dalnacardoch
and Dalwhinnie, (thirteen miles,) presents a most desolate and cheerless aspect. Half way there are two
mountains, named the Badenoch *Boar* and the Athol
Sow, at which the mountain streams part in opposite
directions, some running eastward to join the Truim and
the Spey, while others fall into the Tay. This spot is
the proper separation between the counties of Inverness
and Perth: The savage pass between Dalnacardoch and
Dalwhinnie is called Drumouchter. The inn of Dalwhinnie is surrounded by a young plantation, the only
green and pleasing object on which the eye can rest for
many miles around. It is situated at the distance of
about a mile from the head of Loch Ericht, on the north
side of which is the mountain Benalder. A cave exists
in this mountain in which Prince Charles Stuart found
refuge for a short time after the battle of Culloden. At
Dalwhinnie, a road parts off by Laggan and Garviemore,
and over the difficult hill of Corryiarick to Fort-Augustus. Leaving Dalwhinnie, at the distance of six miles,
the road crosses the Truim, and four miles farther crosses

the Spey. At Invernahavon, near the junction of these
rivers, a celebrated clan battle was fought in the reign
of James I. between the Mackintoshes and Camerons.
Glen Truim is the property of Captain Ewen M'Pherson. The mountains which skirt the road on both sides
are bleak and bare, and dull and uninteresting in their
forms. Passing the village of Newton of Benchar,*
commenced not long since by the late Mr. M'Pherson of
Belleville, the tourist reaches Pitmain Inn, where he
will enjoy an extensive view of the valley of the Spey
and of the high black rock of Craig Dhu, the rendezvous
of the M'Phersons. Badenoch was anciently the possession of the great family of the Cumings, who ruled here
during the reigns of the early Scottish sovereigns. The
remains of many of their numerous fortresses are still
visible. The vast possessions of this family were forfeited on account of the part which they took in the
wars between Bruce and Baliol. Badenoch now belongs
to his Grace the Duke of Richmond. A mile beyond
Pitmain is the village of Kingussie, opposite to which,
on the other side of the Spey, are the ruins of Ruthven
Barracks, destroyed by the Highlanders in 1746. On
the same mount once stood one of the castles of the
Cumings. It was at this place that the Highlanders re-
assembled to the number of 8000 two days after their
defeat at Culloden, and here they received from Prince
Charles the order to disperse. About two miles distant,
on the north side of the Spey, is Belleville, the seat of
Macpherson, the translator of Ossian, now occupied by
his daughter, Miss Macpherson. It stands on the site of

---

* From Newton of Benchar the road to Fort-William by Loch Laggan strikes
off. Here are relics of a Roman encampment, of which the lines are still discernible.

the ancient castle of Raits, the principal stronghold of the Cumings. A little farther on, a view is obtained of Invereshie, the seat of Sir George Macpherson Grant of Ballindalloch, on the south bank of the Spey of Loch Insh, through which the river passes, and of some of the highest of the Grampians. A short way beyond is Kinrar, the favourite seat of the late Duchess of Gordon. The high rocky crag on the north banks of the Spey is Tor Alvie. On its eastern brow is a rustic hermitage, and at the other extremity of the ridge, an enormous cairn of stones, on one side of which is a tablet with an inscription to the memory of the heroes of Waterloo. On the left of the landscape is the beautiful Loch Alvie, with its neat manse and church. The magnificent scenery around Kinrara has been very correctly described by Dr. Macculloch.—"A succession of continuous birch forest, covering Kinrara's rocky hill and its lower grounds, intermixed with open glades, irregular clumps, and scattered trees, produces a scene at once Alpine and dressed, combining the discordant characters of wild mountain landscape, and of ornamental park scenery, while the variety is, at the same time, such as is only found in the most extended domains." Beyond Kinrara, on the right, are the great fir woods of Rothiemurchus,* (Sir J. P. Grant,) supposed to cover from fourteen to sixteen square miles.

---

* The reader may, perhaps, recollect Sir Alexander Boswell's lively verses :—

"Come the Grants of Tullochgorum,
Wi' their pipers gann before 'em,
Proud their mothers are that bore 'em.—
Feedle-fa-fum.!

Next the Grants of Rothiemurchus,
Every man his sword and dirk has,
Every man as proud 's a Turk is.—
Feedle-deedle-dum!"

The Spey here takes several majestic sweeps, and supplies a noble foreground to these forests. The road now enters Morayshire, and, thirteen miles from Pitmain, reaches Aviemore Inn, opposite to which is Cairngorm Hill, famous for a peculiar kind of rock crystals. The mountains on the left are extremely bare and rugged, but towards the west they terminate in the beautiful and bold projecting rock of Craig Ellachie (the *Rock of Alarm,*) the hill of rendezvous of the Grants. " Stand fast Craig Ellachie," is the slogan or war-cry of that clan, the occupants of this strath.—" From its swelling base and rifted precipices the birch trees wave in graceful cluster, their bright and lively green forming a strong contrast in the foreground to the sombre melancholy hue of the pine forests, which in the distance stretch up the sides of the Cairngorms." * At Aviemore a road leads along the banks of the Spey to Grantown and Castle Grant, the residence of the Earl of Seafield. The road now leaves the Spey, and, at the Bridge of Carr, eight miles from Aviemore, crosses the Dulnain; near this place another road strikes off on the right to Grantown. The country around is barren and uninteresting, but some burnt stumps sticking above the moor, and a few hoary and stunted pine trees are still to be seen, the solitary remains of those immense forests which once covered the surface of the country. The road now passes through the deep and dangerous pass called Slochmuicht, (the boar's den or hollow,) which was the favourite haunt of banditti even so late as near the close of last century. Four miles from the Bridge of Carr it re-enters Inverness-shire; and two miles farther on crosses the rapid river Findhorn. The banks of the Findhorn

* Anderson's Guide to the Highlands, p. 81.

are in general highly romantic, but at this spot they are by no means interesting.

In the month of August 1829, the province of Moray, and adjoining districts, were visited by a tremendous flood. Its ravages were most destructive along the course of these rivers, which have their source in the Cairngorm Mountains. The waters of the Findhorn and the Spey, and their tributaries, rose to an unexampled height. In some parts of their course these streams rose *fifty feet* above their natural level. Many houses were laid desolate, much agricultural produce was destroyed, and several lives were lost. The annexed Plate represents the situation of a boatman called Sandy Smith, and his family, in the plains of Forres. " They were huddled together," says the eloquent historian of the Floods, " on a spot of ground a few feet square, some forty or fifty yards below their innundated dwelling. Sandy was sometimes standing and sometimes sitting on a small cask, and, as the beholders fancied, watching with intense anxiety the progress of the flood, and trembling for every large tree that it brought sweeping past them. His wife, covered with a blanket, sat shivering on a bit of a log, one child in her lap, and a girl of about seventeen, and a boy of about twelve years of age, leaning against her side. A bottle and a glass on the ground, near the man, gave the spectators, as it had doubtless given him, some degree of comfort. Above a score of sheep were standing around, or wading or swimming in the shallows. Three cows and a small horse, picking at a broken rick of straw that seemed to be half afloat, were also grouped with the family."* The account of

* An Account of the Great Floods in the Province of Moray and adjoining Districts. By Sir Thomas Dick Lauder, Bart. of Fountainhall, F.R.S.E. Edin. 1830.

SCENE IN THE MORAYSHIRE FLOODS.

the rescue of the sufferers is given with a powerful dramatic effect, but we cannot afford space for the quotation. The courageous adventurers who manned the boat for this dangerous enterprise, after being carried over a cataract, which overwhelmed their boat, caught hold of a floating hay-cock, to which they clung till it stuck among some young alder trees. Each of them then grasping a bough, they supported themselves for two hours among the weak and brittle branches. They afterwards recovered the boat under circumstances almost miraculous, and finally succeeded in rescuing Sandy and his family from their perilous situation.

After crossing the Findhorn, the road passes Corybrough House (Smith, Esq.) and a short way beyond reaches the inn of

FREEBURN,

about nine miles from Bridge of Carr. Near it are the house and plantations of Tomatin (Duncan Macbean, Esq.) The small estate of Free is the property of John Mackintosh, Esq. of Holm. All the rest of the adjoining lands, on the north side of the Findhorn, belong to the Mackintosh estate. Three miles and a half beyond this, on the right, is the castle of Moy, the ancient residence of Mackintosh, the chief of the clan Chattan, a confederation of the clans of Mackintosh, Macpherson, and others of less consequence. It stands on an island in the midst of a small gloomy lake, called Loch Moy, surrounded by a black wood of Scotch fir, which extends round the lake, and terminates in wild heaths, which are unbroken by any other object as far as the eye can reach. Near the southern end of the lake is a small artificial islet of loose stones, which the former chiefs of Moy used as a place of confinement for their prisoners. On

the largest island, a handsome granite obelisk, seventy
feet high, has been erected to the memory of the late Sir
Æneas Mackintosh, Bart. chief of the clan. On the west
side of Loch Moy are the church and manse of Moy, and
at the head of the lake, Moy Hall, the family residence
of Mackintosh of Mackintosh. Here is preserved the
sword of Viscount Dundee, and a sword sent by Pope
Leo X. to James V., who bestowed it on the chief of
clan Chattan, with the privilege of holding the king's
sword at coronations. Leaving Loch Moy, the road enters Strathnairn, and passes for three miles through a
bleak and heathery plain till it crosses the river Nairn,
called in Gaelic *Kis-Nerane*, or the Water of Alders.
The road now passes, on the right, Daviot House, the
residence of Æneas Mackintosh, Esq. Here stood the
ancient castle of Daviot, founded, it is said, by David Earl
of Crawford, who, by his marriage with Catherine, daughter of Robert II., acquired possession of the barony of
Strathnairn. Passing Leys Castle, the seat of Miss Baillie of Leys, and various other mansions, the tourist, at
the distance of six miles, enters the royal burgh of

INVERNESS,

situated on both sides of the river Ness, at the spot where
the basins of the Moray and Beauly Friths and the Great
Glen of Scotland meet one another. Inverness is a thriving town, though from its rich natural advantages, capable of much greater improvement as a seat of trade
and commerce. It is generally considered the capital of
the Highlands, and contains a number of well built streets
and elegant houses. The public buildings are spacious,
and some of them elegant. A fine stone bridge of seven
arches was erected over the Ness in 1685, between the
second and third arches of which there is a vault, for-

merly used as a jail, and latterly as a madhouse, which was only shut up about twenty years ago. At the door of the Town-Hall is a strange blue lozenge-shaped stone, called Clach-na-Cudden, or " stone of the tubs," from having served as a resting-place on which the women, in passing from the river, used to set down the deep tubs in which they carried water. It is reckoned the palladium of the town. In the wall above are the royal arms, with those of the town, beautifully carved. Inverness contains a flourishing Academy, incorporated by Royal Charter; a public Seminary, endowed from a bequest of £10,000 made by the late Rev. Dr. Andrew Bell; a public News-room; six Banking-houses; several printing establishments; and three weekly newspapers. It carries on a respectable trade with London, Leith, and other places; and a regular communication by steam is kept up between Inverness, Leith, and Glasgow. The tonnage of all the shipping belonging to the port is about 4300 tons, and the number of vessels sixty. In 1831, the population of the parish amounted to 14,324, that of the town alone being 9663. It unites with Forres, Nairn, and Fortrose, in electing a member of Parliament.

Inverness is a town of great antiquity, but the exact date of its origin is unknown. On an eminence to the south-east of the town stood an ancient castle, in which it is supposed that Duncan was murdered by Macbeth. It is highly probable that Macbeth had possession of this castle, and it is certain that it was destroyed by the son of the murdered king, Malcolm Canmore, who erected a new one on an eminence overhanging the town on the south. This latter edifice continued for several centuries to be a royal fortress. It was repaired by James I., in whose reign a Parliament was held within its walls, to which all the northern chiefs and barons were summoned, three of whom were executed here for treason. In 1562, Queen Mary paid a visit to Inverness, for the purpose of quelling an insurrection of the Earl of Huntly. Being refused admission into the castle by the governor, who held it for the Earl, she took up her residence in a house, part of which is still in existence. The castle was shortly after taken by her attendants, and the governor hanged. During the civil wars this castle was repeatedly taken by Montrose and his opponents. In 1715, it was converted into barracks for the Hanoverian soldiers, and in 1746, it was blown up by the troops of Prince Charles Stuart, and not a vestige of it now remains. On the site of this ancient edifice, a handsome .castellated building has been erected, from a design by Mr. Burn, architect, consisting of the Court-House, County Buildings, &c. On the north side of the town, near the mouth of the river, Cromwell erected a fort at an expense of £80,000. The stones employed in its construction were procured from the monasteries of Kinloss and Beauly, and the Greyfriars' Church. This fortress was demolished at the Restoration, but a considerable part of the rampart still remains. Within the area of the citadel, a hemp manufactory is carried on. The environs of Inverness are remarkably fine, and the scenery on the banks of the river Ness presents a striking mixture of beauty and grandeur. At a little distance to the west of the town is a singular hill, called Craig Phadric, crowned by a splendid vitrified fort. The view from the summit is varied and extensive. The sides of the hill are covered by fine woods, in the midst of which stands the handsome house of Muirton, the seat of Mr. Huntly Duff, the great grandson of Catherine Duff, Lady Drummuir, in whose house both Prince

Charles and the Duke of Cumberland lodged during their residence in Inverness. *

A mile to the south-west of Inverness is a strange wooded hill, called Tom-na-heurich (the hill of fairies), shaped like a ship with its keel uppermost. The walks all around it and on the banks of the Ness, are extremely beautiful.

One of the most interesting objects in the neighbour-hood of Inverness is Culloden Moor, the scene of the final defeat of the Highland army under Prince Charles Stuart. This memorable spot lies about five miles to the south-east of the town. It is a vast and desolate tract of table land, traversed longitudinally by a carriage road, on the side of which are a number of green trenches marking the spot where the heat of the battle took place. On the north it is flanked by the Firth and the table land of the Black Isle. On the south-east by the ridges of Strathnairn, and its extremities are bounded on the west-ward by the splintered and serrated heights of Stratherrick. In the opposite distance, the moor is lost in a flat bare plain stretching towards Nairn,—one old square tower, the castle of Dalcross, a hold of the clan Chattan, rising upon the open waste with a unique and striking effect. The level nature of the ground rendered it peculiarly unfit for the movements of the Highland army, against cavalry and artillery. According to the general accounts, about 1200 men fell in this engagement. The number killed on both sides was nearly equal.

The victory at Culloden finally extinguished the hopes

* The bustle and confusion occasioned in the house by its distinguished ten-ants, made the proprietrix very testy; she used to say: "I have had twa kings' bairns for my guests, and trowth I never wish to hae another." This house was, at the period in question, the only one in Inverness which contained a parlour without a bed.

of the house of Stuart, and secured the liberties of Britain, but the cruelties exercised by the Duke of Cumberland on his helpless foes have stamped his memory with indelible infamy; and there are few who will not join in the sentiments expressed in the concluding stanza of Burns' pathetic song on the Battle of Culloden.

> " Drumossie muir, Drumossie muir,
>   A waefu' day it was to me,
> For there I lost my father dear,
>   My father dear and brethren three.

> " Their winding sheet the bluidy clay,
>   Their graves are growing green to see,
> And by them lies the dearest lad
>   That ever blest a woman's e'e.

> " Now wae to thee, thou cruel Duke,
>   A bluidy man I trow thou be,
> For monie a heart thou hast made sair,
>   That ne'er did wrang to thine or thee."*

* On the road leading from the battle-field to Inverness, there is an old farm-steading with trees about it, like a small laird's dwelling. On the day succeeding the battle, the body of a youth of the better class was carried here shrouded in a plaid: " My darling! my darling!" said the pitiful matron, to whom the stranger's corpse was brought, "some mother's heart is lying with thee." It was her own son, whom she fancied safe away with her relations in Glen Urquhart. The following beautiful and pathetic song, of which Culloden is the scene, has never before (as far as we are aware) been in print. It was written, we believe, by a young man of the name of Blair, belonging to Dunfermline.

> " Again the laverock seeks the skies,
>   And warbles dimly seen,
> And summer views wi' sunny joys
>   Her gowden robe o' green.
> But, ah! the summer's blythe return,
>   In flowery pride array'd,
> Nae mair can cheer this heart forlorn,
>   Nor charm the Highland maid.

> " My father's shielin' on the hill
>   Is cheerless now and sad,
> The breezes round me whisper still,
>   I 've lost my Highland lad.

A mile to the north of Culloden Moor is Culloden
House (Forbes, Esq.), which, at the time of the rebellion, belonged to the celebrated Duncan Forbes, Lord
President of the Court of Session. Here Prince Charles
lodged the night before the battle. Since 1745, it has
been renewed in a very elegant style.

Fort-George, distant about twelve miles from Inverness, is another interesting object in this neighbourhood.
It is situated on the extremity of a low sandy point which
projects far out into the Moray Firth opposite Fortrose.
At this spot the breadth of the firth is only about a mile.
Fort-George was erected immediately after the suppression of the Rebellion, for the purpose of keeping the
Highlanders in check. The fortifications, which are constructed on the plan of the great fortresses of the Continent, cover about fifteen English acres, and afford accommodation for about 3000 men. The establishment is
kept in excellent order. At the bottom of the peninsula
is Campbelton, a modern fishing village named from the
Campbells of Cawdor. The Earl of Cawdor has an ancient residence near this place, Cawdor Castle, which has
still its moat and drawbridge, tower and " donjon keep,"
as in the days of antiquity. It is the most perfect specimen now remaining of the old feudal fortress. Some

His bonnet blue has fallen now,
　　And bloody is the plaid,
Where oft upon the mountain's brow
　　He row'd his Highland maid.

" The lee-lang night for rest I seek,
　　The lee-lang day I mourn,
The smile upon my wither'd cheek
　　Can never mair return.
Upon Culloden's fatal heath
　　He spak o' me, they said ;
And falter'd, wi' his dying breath—
　　Adieu ! my Highland maid."

ancient timber trees (which attracted the admiration of
Dr. Johnson himself), surround the castle, and the scenery of the neighbourhood is wild and romantic.

A delightful excursion may be made to the little town
of Beauly, situated at the head of the frith which bears
its name, twelve miles west from Inverness. It has been
justly said that there are not many rides of a more various
and animating kind than that from Inverness westward
to Beauly. Leaving Inverness, the tourist crosses the
Caledonian Canal. The beautiful wooded hill in front is
Craig Phadric, and the turreted mansion close by the
road, embowered among trees, is Muirtown, the seat of
Mr. Huntly G. Duff. The road now passes on the right
the basin and village of Clachnaharry,* and enters on the
Aird, the richest and most beautiful district in Inverness-
shire, and the land of the clan Fraser, studded with man-

* Clachnaharry derives its name (Clach-na-herrie, or the Watchman's Stone)
from the rough impending rocks to the westward, where, in the days of blackmail and reivers, a watchman used to be stationed to give notice of the approach
of the Highland clans from Ross or the west coast. On the highest pinnacle of
the rock a column was erected by the late Major Duff of Muirtown, to commemorate a sanguinary engagement fought here between the Munroes of Foulis
and the clan Chattan. It is thus described by Mr. Anderson in his *Historical
Account of the Family of Fraser*, p. 54. "The Munroes, a distinguished tribe
of Ross, returning from an inroad they had made in the south of Scotland,
passed by Moyhall, the seat of Mackintosh, leader of the clan Chattan ; a share
of the booty, or road-collop, payable to a chief for traversing his dominions, was
acceded to ; but Mackintosh's avaricious spirit coveting the whole, his proposal met with contempt, and Mackintosh summoned his vassals to extort
compliance. The Munroes pursuing their journey, forded the river Ness,
a little above the island, and dispatched the cattle they had plundered
across the hill of Kinmylies to Lovat's province. Their enemy came up to
them at the point of Clachnahayre, and immediately joined battle ; the conflict
was such as might have been expected from men excited to revenge by a long
and inveterate enmity. Quarter was neither sought nor granted ; after an obstinate struggle, Mackintosh was killed. The survivors of this band retraced
their steps to their own country. John Munro, tutor of Foulis, was left for
dead upon the field ; his kinsmen were not long of retaliating. Having collected
a sufficient force, they marched in the dead of the night for the Isle of Moy,
where the chief of the Mackintoshes resided. By the aid of some planks which
they had carried with them, and now put together, they crossed to the isle, and
glutted their thirst for revenge by the murder or captivity of all the inmates."

sions, comfortable farm-houses, and snug cottages. The
opposite shore of the firth is singularly rich and picturesque, and the background is occupied by the lofty
mountains of Ross-shire. To the north is the huge form
of Ben Wyvis and the heights of Strathglass and Strath-
connan close the horizon to the west. The northern
shore of the Firth, called the Black Isle, is adorned with
the mansion of Redcastle, the seat of Colonel Hugh Baillie, M. P. for Honiton, anciently the property of a family
sprung from the second son of the Laird of Kintail, chief
of the clan Mackenzie. Three miles from Inverness is
the wooded promontory of Bunchrew, once the property
and the favourite retreat of President Forbes of Culloden.
It is now little more than a picturesque ruin in a dell or
cleugh, covered by a perfect bewilderment of grotesque
ancient trees, mossy springs, and tangled plants. The
tourist now enters on the possessions of Lord Lovat ;
and on the next promontory will perceive the house of
Phopachy, which has long been the property of an old
branch of the clan Fraser, ancestors of the Frasers of
Torbreck. At Bogroy, seven miles from Inverness, a
fine view is obtained of a ridge which rises from the bank
of the river Beauly, crowned with luxuriant woods, and
adorned with elegant mansion-houses, among which are
those of Mr. Fraser of Newton, and Mr. J. Baillie Fraser of Reelig, the distinguished Persian traveller and
author. From Bogroy there are two roads which lead
to Beauly,—the post-road, which keeps along the low
ground, and passing the houses of Easter and Wester
Moniack, surrounded by fine scenery, crosses the river
Beauly by the handsome Lovat Bridge, built in 1810,
and reaches Beauly village. The old road passes several
of the seats before alluded to, and the church and manse

of Kirkhill, and leads over the summit of the hill where
the old church of Wardlaw stood. The chapel which
occupies the site of that building has been for many generations the burying place of the family of Lovat, and
the walls are hung round with escutcheons and tablets,
memorials of the chiefs of former days. From this spot
a magnificent view is obtained of the valley of Beauly,
traversed by the broad winding river, the village and the
old priory, Beaufort Castle, and other mansions, embosomed in woods, and in the distance the rugged heights
of Strathglass and Glenstrathfarrar.

Crossing the ferry, the tourist reaches the inn and village of Beauly, worthy of its name,—Beau-lieu, *fine
place*. Close by the village, on the brink of the river,
are the ruins of the priory founded by John Bisset of
Lovat, in 1230, and peopled at first by monks from
France, belonging to the order of Valliscaulium, a reform
of the Cistercians. Only the walls and nave and transepts of the chapel now remain. The internal area is
used as a burying-place by the clan Fraser, the Chisholms, and other families in Strathglass. The north aisle
belongs exclusively to the Mackenzies of Gairloch. The
priory is overshadowed by some fine old trees, which
have a pleasing effect.

The tourist, while in this district, may visit Dingwall, nine miles
north from Beauly, and the scenery around Strathpeffer. On quitting Inverness-shire, the road at Beauly enters Ross-shire by a flat
dull tract called the *Muir of Ord*, once the scene of the clan battles of the Frasers, Macleods, and Mackenzies, now distinguished
for its large cattle-markets. About three miles farther on, the
tourist reaches the banks of the Conon, a stream flowing through a
beautiful valley, richly studded with mansion-houses, woods, ham-

lets, and farms. On the left is Highfield (Gillanders, Esq.) beyond it Fairburn, (Miss Macpherson of Belleville,) and in the centre of the plain, Castle Brahan, the seat of the Right Hon. J. Stewart Mackenzie of Seaforth, now Governor of the Ionian Islands, an imposing structure, with charming grounds.* Some delightful views are obtained of the grand scenery of Wester Ross-shire. The road now passes Conon House, the mansion of Sir Francis Mackenzie of Gairloch, and descends to the Bridge of Scuddel, where it joins the road from Inverness by Kessock Ferry, which is eight miles shorter than the road by Beauly. Here also a road strikes off to the west by Brahan to Contin Inn (five miles distant) where it joins the road from Dingwall to Loch Carron. Three miles beyond, the road reaches the royal burgh of Dingwall, the capital of Ross-shire. Dingwall is a neat town, containing about 1000 inhabitants. It lies in a low situation near the opening of the valley of Strathpeffer. The scenery around is remarkably beautiful. In the neighbourhood of the town formerly stood the castle of the powerful Earls of Ross; but of that once princely structure scarcely a vestige now remains. From Dingwall the great road to the west coast of Ross-shire leads through a succession of valleys. Strathpeffer, the first of these, is a fair flat fertile valley, broad and open, stretching from Dingwall about four or five miles. At an obtuse angle it joins Strathconon, from which it is separated by Knockfarrel. On the other side of the open strath rises Ben Wyvis, the

---

* Brahan Castle was built by Kenneth, the founder of the clan of the Mackenzies. The father of Kenneth, an Irishman, of the house of Geraldine, married the only daughter and heiress of *Coinneach Grumach, i. e.* "Kenneth the morose," chief of the clan Mathieson. Kenneth was named after his grandfather, and given up as heir-apparent to his management. According to clan traditions, Coinneach Grumach was assassinated through a perfidious plot of the chief of Glengarry with whom he was at feud about the lands of Lochalsh. At the same time, nearly the whole of his clan were murdered by the Macdonalds in cold blood in their beds. Young Kenneth alone escaped through the affection and fidelity of his nurse. At a royal hunting match held in Kintail by Alexander III., the king having been accidentally separated from his attendants, was put in peril of his life by a stag, when young Kenneth sprang to the rescue of the monarch, exclaiming, "*Cudich an Righ! Cudich an Righ!*" and getting between Alexander and the deer, the youth, with his naked sword in his hand, severed its head from its body at one stroke. The *caber fae* (the deers' head) ever after formed his crest, and his motto *Cudich an righ!* Such was the respect of the clan for the roof-tree of Kenneth I. that it is said the heads of the different Mackenzie families at one time forcibly interfered to prevent the Earl of Seaforth from pulling down Brahan Castle.

king of the mountains on this side of the island, divided from it
by an advanced hill, on which hangs Tulloch Castle, (D. Davidson, Esq.) surrounded by fine plantations. At the head of Strathpeffer is an excellent and fashionable mineral well, and a number
of villas and neatly built houses have lately sprung up around it.
In the immediate vicinity of the Spa is the venerable baronial
mansion, the seat of the ancient Earls of Cromarty, and now the
property of the Hon. Mrs. Hay Mackenzie of Cromarty, to whom
the greater part of Strathpeffer belongs. The surrounding scenery
affords ample scope for excursions.*

Leaving Strathpeffer, the road leads us to the banks of the
Conon, passing by the church and manse of Contin, standing on
an island of the river embowered among trees and shrubs, and
Coul House, the mansion of Sir George S. Mackenzie, Bart. the
principal proprietor of this fine woodland district. A little to the
east of Contin village, the fine streams of the Conon and the Garve
or Blackwater unite. At the church of Contin, the Parliamentary
Road from Dingwall is joined by the other branch from Scuddel
Bridge before noticed.† Exactly opposite the Inn of Contin rises
the shapely and graceful hill of Tor Achilty, lightly sprinkled with
birches and pines, and young oak copses. From this spot a road

---

* Strathpeffer was about the year 1478 the scene of a bloody conflict between
the Macdonalds of the west coast and the Mackenzies. It is thus described by
Messrs. Anderson in their Guide to the Highlands, p. 559.—"Strathpeffer, now
the resort of the fair and the gay, as well as the sick and decrepit, was, in days
of yore, about the year 1478, the scene of a bloody conflict between the Macdonalds of the west coast and the Mackenzies, who were aided by parties of
their neighbours, the Dingwalls, Baynes, Maccullochs, and Frasers, in which
the latter were victorious. Gillespie Macdonald, the nephew, or, as some say,
the brother of the Lord of the Isles, headed one party, and the chief of the
Mackenzies, whose residence stood on an island in the small adjoining lake of
Kinellan, commanded his troops in person.

"This chief had, for a slight offence, repudiated his wife, a sister of the Macdonald, and married another lady, a daughter of Lord Lovat. The clan, in revenge for the injured honour of their chieftain, Macdonald, laid waste the lands
of the Mackenzies. It is said they were challenged by the latter to meet them
on the spot, and the combat which ensued was most desperate. A thousand
of the islesmen are said either to have been killed or drowned in the river
Conon while attempting to escape. This conflict is generally known as the
battle of Blar-na-Parc."

† Contin is only sixteen or eighteen miles distant from two points where the
Edinburgh and London steamers touch,—Invergordon, on the Cromarty Firth,
and Kessock Ferry, opposite Inverness. From Kessock a coach (the *Caberfae*)
proceeds in summer to Dingwall every afternoon through the Black Isle.

strikes off to the west, which leads past Loch Achiltie and Comrie
to Strath Conon, and the Falls of the Conon. Passing Craigdar-
roch, a lovely villa lately purchased by Sir George S. Mackenzie,
and now occupied by Horatio Ross, Esq. of Rossie, the tourist
reaches Loch Achiltie, " the most enchanting small lake in Great
Britain," one of those exquisitely beautiful spots where, if

> " Art ere come, 'tis with unsandall'd feet."

" It is literally embosomed among hanging glades, and shrubby
crags, and birchen knolls, rising in every light, graceful, and fanciful form, which, however, come not so near as to trouble or dim its
bright loveliness there where it reposes

> " A mirror in the depths of sylvan shelves,—
> So fair a spot of earth, you might, I ween,
> Have deem'd some congregation of the elves,
> To sport by summer-moons, had shaped it for themselves."

Loch Achilty is about three miles in circumference, its margin
is broken into caves, islets, and promontories, luxuriantly clothed
with trees, shrubs, and herbage, while in the extreme distance
tower the " aërial or hazily empurpled summits ". of Scuirvullin in
Strath Conon. The road skirts the northern shore, and, leading
past a series of little lochs, at the distance of two miles, enters the
soft meadow holms of Comrie, and the sweet valley of Scatwell,
watered by the combined streams of the Conon and Meig. The
former river descends from Loch Luichart, the latter flows through
Strath Conon, and rushes along at the bottom of a narrow savage
gorge, presenting the appearance of a continuous cataract nearly a
mile in length. There is a regular ferry-boat, which will conduct
the tourist across the river, opposite Milltown of Scatwell. The
road leads along the south side of the valley over a bare rocky
ridge, and, at the distance of about a mile, enters Strath Conon, a
narrow valley, the sides of which are fringed with alder trees and
birch copse. This glen formed part of an estate, which was forfeited on account of the participation of its proprietor in the rebellion of 1745. The numerous patches of bright verdure which are
seen here and there amidst the heathery or russet pasturages of the
extensive sheep farms, show how populous this strath has once
been. But it is now lone and desolate, and the interesting race
who once peopled it have found a new Strath Conon beyond the
western waters.

" A noble race, but they are gone,
    With their old forests wide and deep,
And we have *fed our flocks* upon
    Hills where their generations sleep.

Their fountains slake our thirst at noon ;
    Upon *their* fields our harvest waves ;
Our shepherds woo beneath their moon,—
    Ah ! let us spare at least their graves."

The tourist may either return to Contin by the way he left it, or he may proceed directly across the northern shoulder of Scuirvullin, and join the parliamentary road from Dingwall to Lochcarron, half way between Auchnanault and Auchnasheen.

Leaving the inn of Contin he proceeds up Strathgarve, winding through birch and pine woods. The picturesque Falls of Rogie, which have been likened to those of Tivoli in Italy, lie down the wooded steeps under the road. Loch Garve is a fine sheet of water about two miles in length. Near the head of the loch is the inn of Garve, which was sometimes the sojourn of Sir Humphrey Davy. The scenery beyond this point is uninteresting.

The most prominent object all through this tract of country is the mountain Ben Wyvis, not so much on account of its height as from its enormous lateral bulk. Sir Hugh Munro of Foulis, the principal proprietor of Ben Wyvis, holds his estate in Ross-shire by a tenure binding him to bring three wainloads of snow from the top of that mountain whenever his Majesty shall desire. It has never been entirely free from snow within the memory of man, except in September 1826.

About two miles west from Beauly are the lower falls of Kilmorack. They lie immediately under the garden of the manse, and are best viewed from it. The falls themselves are of no great consequence, " but the whole scene,—the full river toiling through the deep tortuous chasm, and escaping in smooth lapses,—the rough rocky steeps, and hanging woods and green margins,—is beautiful and striking." It used to be a favourite sport to catch the salmon at this place, as they struggle to ascend the river over the rocky ledges ; and it is said that the Lords Lovat of the olden time, by a particular contrivance, made the salmon leap into a boiling kettle which was kept suspended over the bank. On the opposite side of the river, close by the saw-mills, are the ruins of the old church and the deserted manse of Kiltarlity.

A little below the falls, on the right bank of the river, is Beaufort Castle, the seat of Lord Lovat, the chief of the clan Fraser. It was erected on the site of the old fortress of Beaufort, which belonged to the powerful family of Bizzet or Bisset. The possessions of this family extended over the Aird, and a great part of Stratherrick and Abertarff on Loch Ness, but, being implicated in the rebellion of Donald, Lord of the Isles, their estates were bestowed on the Frasers, who emigrated to the north from Peebles and Tweeddale about the year 1296. Beaufort was besieged by Edward I. in 1303, and also by Oliver Cromwell, who blew up the citadel. It was completely destroyed by the royal forces in 1746, after the battle of Culloden.

About three miles above the church and falls of Kilmorack, there is another succession of falls, at a place called " the Drhuim," where the valley has narrowed to a gorge, and completely shut out the view of frith and champaign. " The hilly banks, luxuriantly wooded, are lofty and steep, and high pyramids of rock, in every fantastic shape, shoot up like glaciers from the choked though wide-spread bed of the river, which here boils and chafes in fury, and there, when its rage is spent, sleeps in dreamy dark pools among the banks of the loveliest moss and freshest verdure, as if mustering its force for another fierce encounter.

" The broad rocky bed of this powerful river, in which
are united the Glass and the Farrar, and many smaller
tributaries, is studded by innumerable shrubby islets,
which throw a wild profusion of intermingled boughs
and plants into the translucent water, with exquisite
effect in reflection and colouring." On one of these, (the
island of Aigas,) which is, in fact, a river-girt and wooded
hill, the notorious Simon Lord Lovat, in 1697, concealed
the dowager Lady Lovat, whom he had forced to become
his wife.   On this romantic little island is·built a handsome house, occupied by Charles Edward Stuart, Esq.,
and his brother John Sobieski Stuart, gentlemen who
claim to be descendants of the royal family of Stuart,
and who always wear the Highland dress.   Half way up
the strath is an enchanting Highland residence, called
Teanassie, often occupied in summer as a shooting lodge.
Proceeding a few miles up the valley, the tourist reaches
Erchless Castle, the seat of Chisholm, the chief of a
small clan who came from the Borders.   The family
estates lie on the north side of the Beauly, and in Strathglass.   The late chief (A. W. Chisholm, Esq.) died suddenly at the early age of twenty-eight, whilst M.P. for
Inverness-shire, and was interred on a small wooded
mount, a solitary spot, near the family residence.   His
premature death was much regretted.   In front of Erchless Castle, the Farrar and the Glass unite, and form the
river Beauly.   Near the junction a handsome stone bridge
of five arches was erected a few years ago, and adjoining
it stands Struy House, till lately the seat of the ancient
branch of the Frasers, next heirs of entail to the estate of
Lovat after the present Lord and his heirs-male.   Struy
Bridge is about ten miles from Beauly.   Here the valley
or strath of the Beauly river divides itself into two glens,

Glenstrathfarrar and Strathglass. The former extends along the base of the mountain Benevachart for a distance of about nine miles. It is lone and wild, rocky and lavishly wooded, but of exquisite beauty, and, alternately narrowing and expanding, presents a great variety of landscape. At its further extremity is Loch Miulie, in which is a small island that afforded shelter to Lord Lovat after the battle of Culloden.

Strathglass stretches nearly southwest, and is traversed by the stream whose name it bears. In ancient times large pine forests stretched along the valley up to the summits of the hills. These have long ago been destroyed, but the sides of the glen are still fringed with beautiful birch trees. A fine road has lately been made through what is termed Chisholm's Pass, which passes along some splendid mountain scenery. About fifteen miles from Struy Bridge, the tourist reaches the elegant mansion-house of Guisachan, the seat of William Fraser, Esq. of Culbockie. The grounds are in a high state of cultivation, and their luxuriant vegetation is very unlike what we might have expected in such a remote district. The scenery around is uncommonly magnificent. The distance from Guisachan through Glen Affrick to Dornie in Kintail, is only a forenoon's journey. The route lies along a series of lochs through a hoary primeval pine forest. The scenery is of a kindred nature to that of the Trosachs, but greatly surpasses it in wildness, grandeur, and extent.

Until the parliamentary road was opened through Glen Moriston and by Cluny into Glen Sheil, this was the principal route from Inverness and Ross-shires into Kintail and the surrounding parts of the west coasts.*

* It may be easily believed that no one was permitted in those days to enter

There are various roads which lead across the hills from Strathglass into Urquhart and Glen Moriston.

Kintail whose visits were not perfectly acceptable to the natives. "When the estates of the Earl of Seaforth were forfeited after the rebellion of 1715, and the foolish attempt at invasion which succeeded it in 1719, it was found quite impracticable for the government to collect any rents in Kintail. A Mr. Ross, the first gentleman sent to make the attempt, was attended by a select party of soldiers, whom the Kintail men—to save them the needless trouble of coming through Glen Affrick, on a bootless errand—met at Lochan Cloigh, in the heights of Strathglass, where an admonitory bullet, sent from an overhanging thicket, grazed the neck of the collector of his Majesty's exchequer. He, however, was a Highlander, though a Whig; and he gallantly advanced three or four more miles, when his son was fired at from another ambuscade, and mortally wounded. The *soldiers* became alarmed, and their leader capitulated, and retreated as wise as he came. Another attempt to enter Kintail next rent-time, made by a more northerly route, was met in the same manner: the military leader was wounded and forced to return. Yet all this while the rents were duly collected among the devoted tenantry of Seaforth—the Macraws of Kintail; and, by some means or other, duly transmitted to France to the forfeited Earl, by a Donald Murchieson, the memory of whose military and business talents, and attachment to the chief, are still embalmed in the hearts of the elders among the Kintail tribes. The natives felt not a little pride, that, though worsted in the open fight of Glenshiel, they for years contrived, by means of their fastnesses, and the mountain passes into their country, to baffle the agents and troops of the government.

"We were informed that it is not yet easy to execute even a civil process on this west coast, if against a popular character. The minions of the law coming from Inverness or Dingwall, are as well known in the hills, and not much more beloved, than the *gaugers*. As soon as they are discovered descending the heights, their errand is guessed; and, though open deforcement is rarely ventured upon, the fiery cross is secretly speeded on to the individual in peril of the law, while the emissaries are detained at fords, ferries, and clachans, rivers, and arms of the sea. No boat tackle is ready—ponies are on the hill and cannot be caught, until the safety of the party is secured! when the beagles, after beating about for some days, may return from whence they came, and draw out their bill of costs for travelling to Loch Broom or Loch Carron."—*Tait's Magazine*.

FOURTEENTH TOUR.

*** A Chart of this Tour will be found on page 302.

THE tourist may leave Inverness by a very delightful route, which leads along the banks of the Caledonian Canal. There are two roads along the opposite sides of Lochs Ness and Oich, but the north-west road is by far the more picturesque. Leaving Inverness by the old bridge, and leaving the peculiarly-shaped hill called Tomnaheurich, the tourist, at the distance of about a mile from the town, crosses the canal, and ascends the undulating face of Torvain. On this hill, in 1197, there was fought a desperate battle between Donald Bane of the Isles and a body of troops from the castle of Inverness. Passing the house of Dunain (W. Baillie, Esq.,) the tourist comes in sight of the beautiful little lake— Dochfour. On its banks is Dochfour House, the seat of Evan Baillie, Esq., surrounded by fine parks and magnificent trees. A monumental pillar has lately been erected, near the house, to the memory of the late proprietor, Evan Baillie, Esq., who was at one time M.P. for Bristol, and died in his native glen at the advanced age of ninety-five. Nearly opposite, in a sequestered bay which forms the narrow eastern extremity of Loch Ness, is

Aldourie, the seat of W. F. Tytler, Esq., where Sir James
Mackintosh was born, and in the immediate neighbourhood
of which he spent several years of his childhood.   For
the first few miles along the shores of Loch Ness, the
hills are bare and very steep.   They are called Craig
Derg, or the Red Rocks, from their reddish tint.   The
inhabitants of these *braes* were formerly noted for smuggling whiskey.   About fifteen miles from Inverness,
Glen Urquhart opens up from the lake.   This glen,
which has been pronounced the fairest, the richest, and
the most splendid in its beauty among Scotland's glens,
is about ten miles in length, and is luxuriantly wooded.
At the mouth of the glen there is an excellent inn called
Drumindrochet.   In the centre of the vale there is a
small but very pretty lake, having the mansions of Lake-
field, Lochletter, and Sheuglie, scattered around its borders.   About two miles from the inn, a small burn falls
over a lofty ledge of rock forming the falls of Divach.   A
small bay runs up from the loch for about two miles into
the valley, receiving the united waters of the Coiltie and
Enneric.   On the western promontory of this bay are the
ruins of the castle of Urquhart, rising finely over the dark
waters of the loch, which, at this point, is 125 fathoms
in depth.   It appears to have been once a strong and
extensive building.   It was besieged and taken by the
troops of Edward I. in 1303.   In 1509, it fell, along
with the barony of Urquhart, into the hands of the chief
of the clan Grant, and it still continues in the possession
of that family, who have a residence in it called Balma-
caan.   The road from Drumindrochet to Invermoriston
—thirteen miles—is one of remarkable beauty.   It is
cut in the mountain side, plunging into hollows and climbing sharp acclivities, sometimes bordering the loch, but

more frequently proceeding at a considerable elevation above its level, and winding through the most luxuriant woods of oak, birch, alder, and pine. It skirts the base of the high and naked mountain, Mealfourvonie, which separates the two glens of Urquhart and Moriston. Mealfourvonie rises almost perpendicularly from the lake to the height of 3060 feet. The opening of Glen Moriston is a very picturesque scene.* In the foreground is the mansion of James Murray Grant, Esq., proprietor of the glen. The situation is very fine. On the opposite side of the river, and twenty-six miles from Inverness, is the inn of Invermoriston, a small but comfortable house. Immediately below it, the river Moriston falls over a considerable precipice, forming a very beautiful and picturesque waterfall. Glen Moriston is a serene and beautiful valley, watered by the Moriston, a wild, foaming, impetuous stream, which has its origin in Loch Cluny and the distant mountains of Glenshiel. From Invermoriston a road leads through the glen to Glenelg and the Isle of Skye. Proceeding along the side of Loch Ness, the tourist crosses the river Oich and reaches Fort Augustus, distant thirty-two miles from Inverness. This fort, which was built shortly after the rebellion of 1715, is situated at the west end of Loch Ness, on a high peninsula between the rivers Tarff and Oich, and commands a noble sweep of the lake and mountains. It forms a square, with four bastions at the corners, and the barracks are constructed for one field-officer, four captains, twelve subalterns, and 280 rank and file. A few soldiers are stationed in the fort, but the guns have been removed to Fort-George, and the magazine is empty. Fort-Augustus is

* It was in Glen Moriston that a young man was killed by the royal troops in 1746, under the mistake that he was Prince Charles.

useless as a place of defence, being completely commanded
by the surrounding hills and eminences. There is a pleasant little village in the neighbourhood. From Loch Ness
to Loch Oich, the next and smallest of the chain, is a distance of five miles. The old road leads along the south
side of Loch Oich, but the tourist should follow the new
one on the opposite side. The scenery on the banks of this
loch is finer than at any other part of the Great Glen.
Glen Garry, which opens upon Loch Oich, is a charming valley, abounding in the most fascinating scenery.
" Less splendid than Glen Urquhart, less diversified than
Glen Moriston, it has, in its beautiful Loch Garry, and
its endless succession of birch-clad knolls and eminences,
and, above all, in the magnificence of the mountain vista
to the west, a character quite peculiar." In the birch-
woods which adorn this romantic glen the trees have
attained a size and luxuriance equal to the finest of the
pines of Rothiemurchus, or the beeches of Athole. Near
the mouth of the Garry, and close to the loch, are the
ruins of the ancient castle of Invergarry, situated on a
rock. It was burnt by the Duke of Cumberland after
the rebellion of 1745. In the immediate neighbourhood of the castle is Invergarry House, lately the residence of the chief of the Macdonells, who, in 1839,
sold his estate of Glenquoich to Edward Ellice, Esq., and
emigrated, along with a considerable part of his clan, to
Australia. Invergarry inn, one of the best in the Highlands,
which stands a little way up the glen, is about seven and
a half miles from Fort Augustus, and about the same distance from Letterfinlay inn on the banks of Loch Lochy.
A little way from Invergarry Castle is a small monument
erected by the late Colonel Macdonell of Glengarry over
the " well of seven heads," commemorating the summary

vengeance inflicted by a former chief of Glengarry " in
the swift course of feudal justice," on the perpetrators of
the foul murder of the Keppoch family. This eccentric
chief was the original of the character of Fergus M'Ivor,
who occupies such a prominent place in the novel of Waverley. The distance between Lochs Oich and Lochy is
about two miles. In 1544 Kinloch Lochy was the scene
of a bloody encounter between the Frasers and a much superior force of the Macdonalds of Clanranald. On account
of the heat of the weather, the combatants threw off their
coats and fought in their shirts, whence the battle received the name of " Blar-na-leine," or " the Field of
Shirts." Lord Lovat and his eldest son, together with
most of the principal gentlemen of the clan, were slain
in this engagement. Fourteen miles from Fort-Augustus, on the south side of Loch Lochy, is the inn of Letterfinlay. On the opposite side of the Loch is the bay of
Arkaig, at a short distance from which, in Glen Arkaig,
is Achnacarry, the mansion of Lochiel, chief of the clan
Cameron. It is delightfully situated, and completely
embosomed in wood.* The hills which environ Loch

* The district of Lochaber has for ages been the residence of this clan. Their
name was originally MacMartin, but they are said to have adopted the name
Cameron on the marriage of a daughter of their chief with a gentleman named
Camarriens or Chambers. MacMartin of Letter Finlay, however, still retains
the original patronymic.

Close beside the present building are the walls of the old mansion, burned
by the Duke of Cumberland in 1746.

In the bottom of the valley lies Loch Arkaig, a beautiful sheet of water, about
two miles distant from Loch Lochy. It is fourteen or fifteen miles long, and
from one to one and a half broad. It is surrounded with dark and lofty mountains, and its banks were, till lately, covered with a magnificent oak and pine
forest, now cut down: but the shoots and saplings rising from the old stock are
already covering the sides of the hills. The banks of the lake are frequented
by herds of Lochiel's celebrated red-deer. A small wooded island at the lower
end of the lake has been for ages the burying-place of the family of Lochiel.
On the shores of Loch Arkaig, Prince Charles more than once found shelter
after his defeat at Culloden. It was here, too, that after the suppression of
the rebellion, Major Munro of Culcairn was shot by one of the clan Cameron in

Lochy are wild and stupendous, and but scantily wooded.
It is ten miles in length, and the depth is, in some places,
from seventy to eighty fathoms. Seven miles from Letterfinlay the tourist crosses the deep and rocky channel of
the Spean by a picturesque-looking bridge, called High
Bridge, which was built by General Wade. At this spot
hostilities first commenced in the Rebellion of 1745.
Here a road strikes off on the left to Glen Roy, celebrated for its parallel roads. Proceeding onward, the
road opens upon the river Lochy, and keeping along its
banks, the tourist reaches the ruins of Inverlochy Castle,
about two miles distant from Fort-William. It consists
of four large towers, the western and southern of which
are nearly entire. Inverlochy is supposed to have been
built by the powerful family of Cuming. It was the
scene of a bloody engagement, during the reign of James
I., between Donald of the Isles and the Earls of Mar
and Caithness, in which the latter were defeated, and the
Earl of Caithness slain. Here also, in 1645, the Marquis
of Argyle was defeated with great slaughter by the Marquis
of Montrose. This engagement is described at great length
in the "Legend of Montrose."

A mile and a half from Inverlochy Castle, the tourist
reaches

FORT WILLIAM,

situated at a bend of Loch Eil, twenty-nine miles from
Fort Augustus and sixty-one from Inverness. The fort

revenge for the death of his son, who had been basely murdered by an officer of
the name of Grant. Major Munro had unfortunately borrowed the white horse
on which Grant rode, and thus met the fate which was intended for another.
Glen Arkaig is divided at the opening, by a ridge of hills, into two valleys of
unequal breadth. The southern contains the mansion of Lochiel. The other,
which is called Mill-dubh, or the Dark-mill, is a narrow pass, completely overshadowed by the branches of the trees by which the perpendicular barriers of
rock on each side are clothed to the summit.

was erected in the reign of William III., from whom it derived its name. It contains a bomb-proof magazine, and the barracks are intended to accommodate ninety-six private soldiers, with the proper number of officers. In 1715, and again in 1745, the Highlanders besieged it, but without success. The adjacent village of Maryburgh, named in honour of Queen Mary, contains a population of about 1500 persons, who are for the most part engaged in the herring fishery. There is an excellent inn at Neptune's Staircase, at which most of the tourists prefer stopping rather than at Fort William. The celebrated mountain, Ben Nevis, which rises from the plain to the east of Fort William, having been already minutely described in the Ninth Tour, demands no additional notice in this place.

The road from Fort William to Oban, along the shores of Lochs Eil and Linnhe, is a continued succession of romantic scenery.

A parliamentary road leads from Fort William to Arisaig, distant forty miles, where there is a ferry to Skye. This road passes through the lovely vale of Glenfinnan, in which there is an inn, remarkable as the place where Prince Charles Stuart first raised his standard, August 19, 1745. At Borrodale, on the shore of Loch na Nuagh, he first disembarked on the mainland of Scotland, and from the same spot he finally embarked for France, after the failure of his unfortunate enterprise. A monument has been erected by the late M'Donald of Glenaladale, on the spot where the standard was unfurled, to the memory of those " who fought and bled " in this rebellion.

Leaving Fort William, the road proceeds along the south side of Loch Linnhe, and, at the distance of nine miles, reaches Coran Ferry ; thence it leads a short way along the north shore of Loch Leven, a branch of Loch Linnhe, extending in a straight line between the counties of Inverness and Argyle. "From its mouth to its farther extremity," says Dr. Macculloch, " Loch Leven is one continued succession of landscapes." On both sides it is bounded by lofty mountains. Fourteen miles from Fort William, the tourist crosses Loch Leven at Ballachulish Ferry. About two miles from the Ferry are the celebrated slate quarries of Ballachulish, which give employment to about 200 people. The road now proceeds for about four miles along the southern shore of Loch Leven, and enters the vale of

GLENCOE,

celebrated both for the grandeur of its scenery and its historical recollections. The lower part of the glen, next Loch Leven, is covered with rich verdure, while the character of the upper portion is unmingled wildness and grandeur. In the middle of the valley is the small lake Treachtan, from which issues the wild stream of Cona, celebrated by Ossian, who is said to have been born on its banks. On both sides of this river the hills shoot up perpendicularly to a tremendous height, casting a deep gloom on this wild vale, calculated to strike the traveller with the deepest awe. From one end of the vale to the other only one solitary farm-house is to be seen.* The well-known massacre of Glencoe, which casts so deep a

---

* "As a piece of perfectly wild mountain scenery, Glencoe has no superior that I know of. In the Alps there are many ravines and valleys immensely larger, but I am not aware of any which has better claims to attention in all that relates to the fantastical disposition of barren rocks of great magnitude, tossed indiscriminately about by the hand of Nature."—*Captain Basil Hall's Patchwork*, vol. ii. p. 268.

stain on the character of King William and his ministers, happened at the north-west end of the vale. At the farthest extremity of Glencoe is the rugged mountain of Buchael Etive, the road over which, from its steepness, has been denominated *The Devil's Staircase.* Proceeding onward through a barren district, the tourist arrives at King's House, distant twenty-eight miles and a half from Fort-William. The road then crosses a tedious hill called the Black Mount ; and, nine and a half miles from the King's House, reaches Inverouran, on the banks of Loch Tulla. Two miles beyond this, the road crosses the river Orchy, which waters the pretty valley of Glenorchy, and, seven miles farther, reaches

TYNDRUM,

situated at the head of Strathfillan, in Perthshire. A short distance from Tyndrum, at a place called Dalrigh, or the King's Field, King Robert Bruce was encountered and repulsed, after a very severe engagement, by the Lord of Lorn. " Bruce's personal strength and courage," says Sir Walter Scott, " were never displayed to greater advantage than in this conflict. There is a tradition in the family of the MacDougals of Lorn, that their chieftain engaged in personal battle with Bruce himself, while the latter was employed in protecting the retreat of his men ; that MacDougal was struck down by the king, whose strength of body was equal to his vigour of mind, and would have been slain on the spot, had not two of Lorn's vassals, a father and son, whom tradition terms M'Keoch, rescued him, by seizing the mantle of the monarch, and dragging him from above his adversary. Bruce rid himself of these foes by two blows of his redoubted battle-axe, but was so closely pressed by the other followers of

2 B

Lorn, that he was forced to abandon the mantle, and broach which fastened it, clasped in the dying grasp of the MacKeochs. A studded broach, said to have been that which King Robert lost upon this occasion, was long preserved in the family of MacDougal, and was lost in a fire which consumed their temporary residence."* Ac-

---

* This exploit is celebrated by Sir Walter Scott in the following song, entitled "THE BROACH OF LORN," supposed to be sung by the bard of Lorn at his chieftain's request :—

> "Whence the broach of burning gold,
> That clasps the chieftain's mantle-fold,
> Wrought and chased with rare device,
> Studded fair with gems of price,
> On the varied tartans beaming,
> As, through night's pale rainbow gleaming,
> Fainter now, now seen afar,
> Fitful shines the northern star?

> "Gem! ne'er wrought on Highland mountain,
> Did the fairy of the fountain,
> Or the mermaid of the wave,
> Frame thee in some coral cave?
> Did in Iceland's darksome mine
> Dwarf's swart hands thy metal twine?
> Or, mortal-moulded, comest thou here,
> From England's love, or France's fear?

> "No! thy splendours nothing tell
> Foreign art or faery spell.
> Moulded thou for monarch's use,
> By the overweening Bruce,
> When the royal robe he tied
> O'er a heart of wrath and pride;
> Thence in triumph wert thou torn,
> By the victor hand of Lorn!

> "When the gem was won and lost,
> Widely was the war-cry toss'd!
> Rung aloud Bendourish fell,
> Answer'd Douchart's sounding dell,
> Fled the deer from wild Teyndrum,
> When the homicide, o'ercome,
> Hardly 'scaped with scathe and scorn,
> Left the pledge with conquering Lorn!

> "Vain was then the Douglas brand,
> Vain the Campbell's vaunted hand,

cording to the account given in Barbour, three of the
strongest among Lorn's followers resolved to rid their
chief of this formidable foe. " They watched their opportunity until Bruce's party had entered a pass between
a lake (Loch Dochart probably) and a precipice, where
the King, who was the last of the party, had scarce room
to manage his steed. Here his three foes sprung upon
him at once. One seized his bridle, but received a wound
which hewed off his arm ; a second grasped Bruce by
the stirrup and leg, and endeavoured to dismount him,
but the King, putting spurs to his horse, threw him down,
still holding by the stirrup. The third taking advantage
of an acclivity, sprung up behind him upon his horse.
Bruce, however, whose personal strength is uniformly
mentioned as exceeding that of most men, extricated himself from his grasp, threw him to the ground, and cleft
his skull with his sword. By similar exertion he drew
the stirrup from his grasp, whom he had overthrown,
and killed him also with his sword as he lay among the
horse's feet."

Two miles from Tyndrum is St. Fillan's Church. Here
there is a linn in the river Etterick, called St. Fillan's

> Vain Kirkpatrick's bloody kirk,
> Making sure of murder's work ;
> Barendown fled fast away,
> Fled the fiery De la Haye,
> When this broach, triumphant borne,
> Beam'd upon the breast of Lorn.

> " Farthest fled its former Lord,
> Left his men to brand and cord,
> Bloody brand of Highland steel,
> English gibbet, axe, and wheel.
> Let him fly from coast to coast,
> Dogg'd by Comyn's vengeful ghost,
> While his spoils, in triumph worn,
> Long shall grace victorious Lorn ! "
> _Lord of the Isles_, canto ii. stanza 11, and Notes.

Pool, in which a considerable number of lunatics are annually immersed, and then bound hand and foot, and laid all night in the churchyard of St. Fillans in the expectation of effecting a cure. Two miles farther is Crianlarich inn, from which the tourist may either proceed through Glenfalloch to the head of Loch Lomond, or by Glen Dochart and Glen Ogle to Lochearnhead, and join the route described p. 370.

FIFTEENTH TOUR.

STEAM-BOAT TOUR FROM NEWHAVEN TO ABERDEEN, INVERNESS, WICK,
ORKNEY AND SHETLAND ISLANDS.

AFTER leaving Newhaven, the first object of interest is
the island of Inchkeith, which received its name from the
ancient family of Keith, to whom it formerly belonged.
It was fortified by the English in the reign of Edward
VI., but the fortifications were afterwards demolished by
order of the Scottish Parliament. During the regency of
Mary of Guise, it was occupied by the French, who de-
signted it L'Isle des Chevaux, because the grass which
it produced formed a nutritious food for horses. Inchkeith possesses several fine springs of water, and maintains a few sheep and rabbits. The lighthouse on this
island is a work of great neatness, and the machinery
by which the lights revolve, is very interesting. A fine
view is obtained from the middle of the Firth, of the
city of Edinburgh, with the harbours of Leith and Newhaven, and the coast of Fife, thickly studded with towns.
In allusion to this striking characteristic of Fife, King
James VI. is said to have likened it to " a gray cloth
mantle with a golden fringe." A little to the west is
Burntistand, nearly opposite is the inn of Pettycur,* and

* Pettycur is supposed to have derived its name (petit corps) from the land
ing of a small body of French troops during the regency of Mary of Guise.

a little farther east is the royal burgh of Kinghorn,[*]
which gives the title of Earl to the Earls of Strathmore.
About half a mile west of the town is a precipice called
King's Woodend, where Alexander III. was thrown
from his horse and killed, 16th March 1285. Below
Kinghorn is a square tower, the remains of Seafield
Castle. A short way farther on is the " lang town of
Kirkaldy," a royal burgh of great enterprise and trade.
Its streets are extremely irregular, narrow, crooked, ill-
paved, and dirty. Dr. Adam Smith, author of the
" Wealth of Nations," was a native of this town. Bal-
wearie, in this neighbourhood, was the birth-place of Sir
Michael Scott, the famous wizard immortalised in the
Lay of the Last Minstrel. The ruins of the old tower of
Balwearie are still to be seen. On a rising ground
behind Kirkaldy is Raith House, the handsome seat of
Colonel Ferguson, M. P. for the Kirkaldy burghs. The
situation is commanding, and the pleasure grounds are
extensive, and very beautiful. At a short distance is
Dunnikier House, the seat of Lady Oswald. To the
east of Kirkaldy is Ravenscraig Castle, the property of
the Earl of Rossyln, situated upon a rock overhanging
the sea. It has been in the possession of the St. Clair
family since the reign of James III., and was entire and
habitable till the time of Cromwell. About half a mile
farther on is Dysart House, a seat of the Earl of Rosslyn,
and close to it is the town of Dysart,[†] a royal burgh of

[*] The parish church of Kinghorn is without a spire. This, and some other
circumstances, supposed to be characteristic of the town, have given rise to the
following couplet:—
        " Here stands a kirk without a steeple,
        A drucken priest, and a graceless people."

    [†] " The canty carles o' Dysart,
            The merry lads o' Buckhaven,
            The saucy limmers o' Largo,
            The bonny lasses o' Leven."—*Old Song.*

great antiquity, and two or three centuries ago a place of considerable trade. It now exports coals and salt.* Two miles farther on is West Wemyss, a burgh of barony, containing about 600 inhabitants, a dingy, dirty, ruinous looking place. The steamer now passes Wemyss Castle, the seat of Captain Erskine Wemyss, M.P., Lord Lieutenant of Fife, situated on a steep rock overhanging the sea. In this castle Darnley was first introduced to Queen Mary. Farther on is Easter Wemyss, a burgh of barony principally occupied by weavers. Wemyss derives its name from the number of caves on this part of the coast,— *Weem* or *Wemyss* being the Gaelic word for a cave. One of these, called the King's Cave, received its designation from an adventure related of James IV. Travelling through Fife on foot, and incognito, that monarch happened to be benighted, and was obliged to enter a cave for shelter. He found it already occupied by a band of robbers, but having gone too far to retreat, he was under the necessity of joining the company. After some time, supper having been served up, two of the gang approached him with a plate on which lay two daggers,— a signal that he was to be put to death. He instantly snatched a weapon in each hand, laid the two robbers prostrate at his feet, and rushed through the rest toward the mouth of the cave. Having fortunately succeeded in making his escape, he returned next day with a sufficient force, and captured the whole band. A short way

---

* " Then from her coal-pits Dysart vomits forth
Her subterranean men of colour dun,
Poor human mould-warps, doom'd to scrape in earth
Cimmerian people, strangers to the sun;
Gloomy as soot, with faces grim and swarth,
They march most sourly leering every one,
Yet very keen at Anster loan to share
The merriments and sports to be accomplish'd there."

TENNANT'S *Anster Fair.*

farther east are the ruins of Macduff's castle, said to have
been built by Macduff, created Thane of Fife about the
year 1057. A mile farther down is Buckhaven, a curious
antique fishing village, inhabited by a most extraordinary
race, supposed to be the descendants of the crew of a
vessel from the Netherlands, which was wrecked near
this place in the reign of Philip II. They were severely
ridiculed more than a century ago in a celebrated satirical
pamphlet called the " History of the College of Buckhaven, or the Sayings of Wise Willie and Witty Eppie,"
well known to the book-stall collectors of pamphlets and
broadsides. Buckhaven is, however, a place of considerable wealth. A mile farther on is the small village of
Methill, and, at the distance of another mile, the thriving
village of Leven, situated at the mouth of the river of the
same name, which issues from Loch Leven. Though it
has a course of only twelve miles, it receives an immense
number of tributary streams. The principal of these are
enumerated in the following rhyme :—

> Lochtie, Lochrie, Leven, and Orr,
> Rin a' through Cameron Brig bore.

Leven contains about 1200 inhabitants, who are principally engaged in weaving linen. A short way in the interior is Durie House, the seat of C. M. Christie, Esq. of
Durie. The steamer is now in Largo Bay, familiar to
every Scotsman, from the allusion made to it in the fine
old song, " Weel may the boatie row." In the centre of
the bay is the village of Lower Largo, the birth-place of
Alexander Selkirk, whose singular adventures form the
groundwork of Defoe's charming novel of " Robinson
Crusoe." The chest and cup which he used on the
uninhabited island are still in possession of his family,
and the gun with which he killed his game, now belongs

to Major Lumsden of Lathallan. Upper Largo was the birth-place of Sir Andrew Wood, the celebrated Scottish Admiral, who received the barony of Largo from James IV. as a reward for his services at sea against the English. Largo also gave birth to Sir John Leslie, the celebrated philosopher. Near Upper Largo, in the midst of a beautiful park, and surrounded by trees, stands Largo House, the seat of Thomas Durham, Esq. To the north of the village, the fine hill called Largo Law rises to the height of 1000 feet above the level of the sea. A short way to the west of Largo, in the midst of a park, are three straight sharp stones, several yards high, called " the Standing Stanes o' Lundie." They have attracted considerable notice, and are supposed to be of Roman origin. Four miles east from Largo is a neat little town called the Elie. Elie House, the seat of Sir W. C. Anstruther, stands close to the town. Two miles farther on is St. Monance, noted for its curious little old Gothic church. The ruins of Newark Castle, the seat of the famous General Leslie, stand on a bold part of the shore, about a mile to the west of the village. A mile to the east is the ancient royal burgh of Pittenweem. Here are the ruins of some curious antique religious buildings. Pittenweem contains the house in which Wilson and Robertson committed the robbery upon the Collector of Excise, which led to the famous Porteous Mob. A mile from Pittenweem there are two or three towns placed together in a cluster. The first is Wester Anstruther, or Anster, a royal burgh, with a population of about 420,* then Easter Anstruther, also a royal burgh, with a population of 1000.

* It is said that a clergyman of Easter Anster, during the last century, used to say of the Magistrates of Wester Anster, that instead of their " being a terror to evil doers," evil doers were a terror to them.

Anstruther was the residence of the renowned " Maggie Lauder," commemorated in the popular song of that name, and " Anster Fair," has been made the subject of an amusing poem by Mr. Tennant, Professor of Oriental Languages in the University of St. Andrews.   Opposite to this part of the coast is the Isle of May.   It is about three miles in circumference, and was formerly the seat of a considerable religious establishment. It is now inhabited only by the persons who attend upon the lighthouse, which was first built in the reign of Charles I. A fine view is obtained here of North Berwick Law, the Bass, and the coast of East Lothian.   About a mile farther down the coast stands Kilrenny, another royal burgh, with a population of about 1500. The next town to the east is Crail, a venerable and decayed burgh, formerly a place of considerable importance, but now greatly diminished. It contains about 2000 inhabitants. It was in the church of Crail that John Knox, on the 29th of May 1559, preached a sermon against popery, which so inflamed the populace, that they immediately rose, and, in a very short time, demolished all the churches in Crail, Anstruther, and the adjacent towns along the coast.   Crail was famous for its *capons*, a kind of dried haddocks prepared by a peculiar mode of cookery.*   The notorious Archbishop Sharpe was at one time minister of

---

* " Next from the well-air'd ancient town of Crail,
    Go out her craftsmen with tumultuous din ;
  Her wind-bleach'd fishers sturdy-limb'd and hale ;
    Her in-knee'd tailors garrulous and thin ;
  And some are flush'd with horns of pithy ale ;
    And some are fierce with drams of smuggled gin ;
  While, to augment his drouth, each to his jaws
  A good Crail capon holds at which he rugs and gnaws."
                                        Anster Fair.

There is a strange old song called " Crail Town," of which the following ar
the introductory stanzas :—

this parish. About a mile to the east of Crail is the East Neuk of Fife, which gives name to a popular Scottish air. Beyond this promontory the coast stretches away towards the north-west, forming the extensive bay called St. Andrew's Bay. At the bottom of this bay, on a ridge of rock projecting into the sea, stands the ancient city of

ST ANDREWS,

with its venerable towers and numerous spires. St. Andrews was formerly a place of great importance, and was the seat of the primate of Scotland. It is about a mile in circuit, and consists of three principal streets, intersected by a few considerable lanes. Of late years a number of elegant houses have been erected, and the streets have been repaired and lighted with gas. The principal street, it has been justly said, for length, straightness, and uniformity, may be reckoned as, even at this day, one of the best in Scotland. It is entered at the west end by a massive antique portal, which the magistrates have with great taste preserved unimpaired,—its other extremity terminates in the ruins of the cathedral, church, and monastery. The city abounds in curious antique houses, which were once occupied by persons of rank, both in church and state, and it has an air of seclusion and quiet that, together with its colleges and memorials of antiquity, gives it an appearance not unlike some of the cathedral towns of England. The origin of St. Andrews is invol-

> " And was you ere in Crail toun ?
>   Igo and ago ;
> And saw ye there Clerk Dishington,
>   Sing irom igon ago.
> His wig was like a doukit hen,
>   Igo and ago ;
> The tail o't like a goose pen,
>   Sing irom igon ago," &c.

It appears to have served as a model for Burn's lines on Captain Grose.

ved in obscurity, but it is justly believed to have been at a very early period the seat of a religious establishment. It was originally denominated Muckross. According to the common tradition, about the end of the fourth century it became the residence of St. Regulus, who was shipwrecked here. The ruins of the chapel, and an entire tower, known by the name of St. Regulus or St. Rule, are still to be seen near the cathedral. On the union of the Scottish and Pictish kingdoms, the name of the city was changed to St. Andrews. The famous priory of St. Andrews was erected by Bishop Robert, in the reign of Alexander I., about the year 1120. It was made a royal burgh by David I. in the year 1140. The charter of Malcolm II., written upon a small bit of parchment, is preserved in the tolbooth. In 1471, it was erected into an archbishopric by Sextus IV. at the request of James IV. It is not known with certainty at what time its church became metropolitan, but it must have been at a very early period. St. Andrews contains many interesting memorials of antiquity. The chapel of St. Regulus is, without doubt, the oldest relic of ecclesiastical architecture in the kingdom. The oldest Scottish writers agree in admitting, that it is at least as ancient as the end of the fourth or beginning of the fifth century. The tower is a square prism 108 feet in height, the side of the base being 24 feet. A winding stair leads to the summit, from which a most delightful view is obtained. The stone of which this building is composed, is of so excellent a texture, that although it has been exposed to the weather for so many centuries, it still remains quite entire and unimpaired. The chapel to the east of the tower, which was the principal one, still remains; but of a small chapel to the west, which formerly existed, there is now no trace. The cathedral was founded in the year

1159 by Bishop Arnold, but it was not finished till the time of Bishop Lamberton, who completed it in 1318. This magnificent fabric, the work of several ages, was demolished in a single day by an infuriated mob, excited by a sermon of John Knox against idolatry, preached in the parish church of St. Andrews.* It was an edifice of great extent, the length being 350 feet, the breadth 65, and the transept 180 feet. The eastern gable, half of the western, part of the south side wall, and of the

* This event is graphically described by Professor Tennant in his poem entitled "Papistry Stormed; or the Dinging Doun o' the Cathedral." We may give a short extract as a specimen of the poem :—

> "I sing the steir, strabash, and strife,
> Whan bickerin' frae the towns o' Fife
> Great bangs o' bodies, thick and rife,
>   Gaed to Sanct Andro's town.

> "And wi' John Calvin in their heads,
> And hammers in their hands, and spades,
> Enraged at idols, mass, and beads,
>   Dang the Cathedral down.

> "I wot the bruilzie then was dour,
> Wi' sticks, and stanes, and bluidy clour,
> Ere Papists unto Calvin's power
>   Gaif up their strongest places.

> "And fearfu' the stramash and stour
> Whan pinnacle cam down, and tow'r,
> And Virgin Marys in a shower
>   Fell flat, and smash'd their faces.

> "The copper roofs that dazzlit heaven,
> Were frae their rafters rent and riven,
> The marble altars dasht and driven,
>   The cods wi' velvet laces;

> "The siller ewers and candlesticks;
> The purple stole and gowden pyx;
> And tunakyls and dalmatycks
>   Cam tumbling frae their cases.

> "The devil stood bumbased to see
> The bonnie cosie byke where he
> Had cuddlit monie a century,
>   Rip't up wi' sic disgraces."

transept, are all that now remain of this once splendid
pile.

The other religious houses in St. Andrews were the
convent of the Dominicans, founded in 1274 by Bishop
Wishart ; the convent of Observantines, founded by
Bishop Kennedy, and finished by his successor, Patrick
Graham, in 1478—a collegiate church, which stood immediately above the harbour, and a priory. Slight vestiges of the latter, which was the most important of these
foundations, may be traced to the south of the cathedral.
It was of great extent, and richly endowed. Its boundary wall is still nearly entire, and seems to have enclosed all the east quarter of the town. The prior of
St. Andrews had precedence of all abbots and priors,
and on festival days had a right to wear a mitre and all
Episcopal ornaments.

" On the north-east side of the city are the remains
of the castle, on a rock overlooking the sea. This fortress was founded about the year 1200, by Roger, one
of the bishops of St. Andrews, and was repaired towards
the end of the 14th century by Bishop Trail, who died
in it in 1401. He was buried near the high altar of the
cathedral, with this singular epitaph :

> Hic fuit ecclesiæ directa columna, fenestra
> Lucida, thuribulum redolens, campana sonora.

" James III. was born in the Castle. It was the residence of Cardinal Beaton, who, after the cruel execution
of the celebrated reformer George Wishart in front of it,
was afraid of the fury of the people ; and his knowledge
of this, joined to his apprehension of an invasion from
England, induced him to strengthen the fortifications,
with a view of rendering the castle impregnable. In this

fortress he was surprised and assassinated by Norman Lesley, aided by fifteen others. Early in the morning of May 29, 1546, they seized on the gate of the castle, which had been left open for the workmen who were finishing the fortifications; and having placed sentinels at the door of the Cardinal's apartment, they awakened his numerous domestics one by one, and, turning them out of the castle, without violence, tumult, or injury to any other person, inflicted on Beaton the death he justly merited. The conspirators were immediately besieged in this castle by the regent, Earl of Arran; and although their strength consisted of only 150 men, they resisted his efforts for five months, owing more to the unskilfulness of the attack than the strength of the place, for in 1547, the castle was reduced and demolished, and its picturesque ruins serve as a land-mark to mariners."*

The University of St. Andrews, which is the oldest establishment of that nature in Scotland, was founded in 1411 by Bishop Wardlaw. It consisted formerly of three colleges:—1. St. Salvator's, which was founded in 1458 by Bishop Kennedy. The buildings of this college formed an extensive court or quadrangle about 230 feet long, and 180 wide, and a gateway surmounted by a spire 156 feet high. On one side is the church, on another what was the library of St. Salvator's, the third contains apartments for students, the fourth is unfinished. The buildings connected with this college have fallen into a state of decay, and a grant was made by Parliament for erecting a new structure. One half of the proposed buildings for the United College have been erected, but the rest of the funds appointed to complete the works having unfortunately been diverted to another purpose,

* Encyclopædia Britannica, seventh edition, vol. iii. p. 121.

the structure remains incomplete. 2. St. Leonard's College, which was founded by Prior Hepburn in 1532. This is now united with St. Salvator's, and the buildings sold and converted into private houses. 3. New, or St. Mary's College, which was established by Archbishop Hamilton in 1552, but the house was completed by Archbishop Beaton. The buildings of this college have lately been repaired with great taste.

In the United College the languages, philosophy, and the sciences are taught. St. Mary's, which stands in a different part of the town, is reserved exclusively for theology. The classes and discipline of the two colleges are quite distinct, each having its respective Principal and Professors. They have a common library, containing upwards of 35,000 volumes, which, till lately, was entitled to a copy of all new books entered in Stationers' Hall, but by an Act of Parliament, passed in 1837, that right was abolished, and in lieu of it, the library receives from the Treasury the sum of £600 annually for the purchase of books.

Seventy-one bursaries or endowments are connected with the university, and are conferred upon the students. Of these, sixteen are foundation bursaries belonging to the college, and fifty-five were established at different times by various benefactors, and are in the gift of different patrons. In St. Mary's College there are nine foundation bursaries, which extend their benefit to about twenty individuals.

The system of instruction carried on in the United College is excellent. From the sequestered character of the town, the absence of all manufacturing establishments, and of those temptations incident to large cities, there are few seminaries where youth are better pro-

tected from idle and vicious habits, or where greater
facilities are afforded for acquiring a sound and compre-
hensive education. The moderate number attending the
College enables the Professors to become personally acquainted with each of the students ; and, while advancing
their literary and scientific proficiency, their instructors at
the same time exercise a wholesome control over their
moral habits. Previous to 1824, the attendance at the
United College averaged about 70. In session 1824-5
there were 220 students. Since that period the numbers
have gradually declined, though they are still far above
what they were in former times. The average number
of students attending St. Mary's College is about 30.

The Madras College was established in the year 1833
by the late Dr. Andrew Bell, a native of St. Andrews,
and inventor of the monitorial system of education which
bears his name, who bestowed the munificent sum of
£120,000 in three per cent. stock for its establishment.
The buildings, which are very splendid, stand on the site
of the Blackfriars' monastery, and in front of it is the fine
old ruin of the chapel connected with that monastery.
The course of education comprises the Classics, the
English and other modern languages, Mathematics, Natural Philosophy, Chemistry, Music, and Drawing. The
fees being low, and in many cases not exacted, the institution has been very successful, the number of scholars
averaging about eight hundred.

St. Andrews contains six places of worship—the parish
church, the college church, an episcopal, secession, and independent chapel, and a new chapel in connection with the
established church which was opened in August 1840. The
parish church is a spacious structure, 162 feet in length,
by 63 in breadth, and is large enough to accommodate

2500 persons. It contains a lofty monument of white marble, erected in honour of Archbishop Sharpe, who, in revenge for his oppressive conduct, was murdered by some of the exasperated covenanters. On this monument is a bas relief representing the tragical scene of the murder. To the north is situated the college church, which belongs to the united college of St. Salvator and St. Leonard. It was founded in 1458 by Bishop Kennedy, and contains a beautiful tomb of its founder, who died in 1466. It is a piece of exquisite Gothic workmanship, though much injured by time and accidents. About the year 1683, on opening this tomb, six highly ornamented silver maces were discovered, which had been concealed there in times of trouble. Three of these maces are still preserved in the university, and one was presented to each of the other three Scottish universities. The top has been ornamented by a representation of our Saviour, with angels around, and the instruments of his passion; with these are shewn some silver arrows with large silver plates affixed to them, on which are inscribed the arms and names of those who were victors in the annual competitions of archery, which, after having been discontinued for half a century, were again revived in 1833. Golf is now the prevailing game in St. Andrews. It is played on a piece of ground called the Links, which stretches along the sea-shore to the extent of nearly two miles. A considerable number of golf-balls are manufactured in St. Andrews. Besides the consumption of the town, about 9000 are annually exported to various other places.

The trade of St. Andrews was once very considerable. The shipping of the port now consists of a few vessels employed in the coasting trade. The harbour is guarded by piers, and is safe and commodious ; but it is difficult of access, having a narrow entrance, and being exposed to the east wind, which raises a heavy sea on the coast. The shore of the bay is low on the west side, but to the south it is precipitous, bold, and rocky ; and, in severe storms, vessels are frequently driven on it and lost. St. Andrews unites with Cupar, Anstruther, Pittenweem, Crail, and Kilrenny in returning a member to Parliament. The population of the town is 4300.

About two miles from St. Andrews is the estuary of the river Eden ; and a short distance inland the village of Leuchars. A little to the east of Leuchars is Tents-moor Point, the south-eastern point of the frith of the Tay, and on the opposite shore, in Forfarshire, is Button Ness, the north-eastern point of the same estuary. There are two light-houses on this promontory, and two others on the south shore, nearly opposite to Broughty Ferry, a thriving village, much frequented by strangers in summer for bathing quarters. About six miles up the Firth of Tay, on the north shore, is

DUNDEE,

the fifth town in Scotland in wealth and population. It is also a place of great antiquity, deriving its origin from Malcolm Canmore, and erected into a royal burgh by William the Lion. The population of the town and parish, according to the census of 1841, amounts to 62,000. The trade of Dundee has long been extensive, and has rapidly increased in late years. Its manufactures are chiefly brown and bleached linen, canvass and cotton bagging, for the home and foreign market, great quantities of which are exported directly to France, and to North and South America. This town, indeed, may be considered the principal seat of the linen trade of

Britain, and the great emporium for flax and hemp.   In
1839, its imports of these articles amounted to 32,462
tons, value £1,017,242, and the value of its exports of
manufactured goods and yarns in the same year was
£1,810,466.   In the town and neighbourhood are about
50 spinning-mills, all of which are worked by steam.
There are also several extensive iron founderies and
establishments for the manufacture of steam-engines and
machinery.

The grandest and most important feature of Dundee
is its harbour, with its magnificent wet docks, and a
number of spacious quays, patent slip, graving dock, &c.
spreading along the margin of the Tay, and terminated
on the west by the Craig Pier, which is exclusively appropriated to the use of the ferry.   These splendid works
have cost no less than £486,991 to April 1841.   An
elegant building is contracted for, and will be begun
immediately, for a Custom House, Excise Office; also
premises in the same for the accommodation of the harbour trustees, and officers connected with the establishment.   The number of vessels belonging to the port in
1839 was 325, their tonnage being 44,882.*   Of these
two are employed in the whale fishery, and many of
them in the Baltic and American trade.   In the London
trade, besides a number of sailing smacks, there are
three splendid steam-vessels, of 300 horse power, each
of which was built at an expense of £20,000.

The streets are for the most part narrow and irregular,
except in the modern portions of the town.   " The market-place, or High Street, is a spacious square, 360 feet

* Shipping registered at the port in August 1840 was, 324 vessels, 51,135 tons.
Since then (April 1841,) upwards of 18 vessels have been added to these, making at least 3000 tons additional.   Several have, however, been lost during the
same period.

long by 100 broad, from which diverge the Nethergate, Seagate, Overgate, and Murraygate, the principal streets, which run from east to west, nearly parallel to the river. Castle-street leads from the south-east end of the High-street to the new docks on the south, and contains, among other neat buildings, an Episcopal chapel and a theatre. At the south-east corner is an elegant building in the Grecian style, erected for an exchange and reading-room. On the south side of the market-place or square stands the Town-hall, surmounted by a steeple, and having piazzas below; it was built in 1743. Opposite to this building is a spacious new street, named Reform Street; at the north end of which, and fronting the Town-hall, is an elegant edifice, in the Grecian style of architecture, for an academy and public schools. At the east end of the High Street, and rather obstructing the entrance to the Murraygate, stands the Trades' Hall, a plain edifice, with pilasters of the Ionic order, the principal apartments of which are now used as an office by the Eastern Bank of Scotland. A little to the west of the High Street, in the Nethergate, are the remains of an old cathedral, which contained four places of worship, one of which was built in the finest Gothic style, the groining of the arches being much admired. Three of these churches were completely destroyed by fire on Sunday morning, the 3d January last ; negotiations are in progress for repairing or rebuilding two of them. This structure is said to have been originally built by David, Earl of Huntingdon, in 1185. On the west end of these churches stands a magnificent Gothic tower 156 feet high. There are several other churches and chapels connected with the Establishment, beside one Episcopal chapel, one elegant Roman Catholic chapel, lately erected in the Nethergate, and many other places of worship for Dissenters, who form a very considerable part of the population. Among the public institutions may be mentioned a Lunatic Asylum, an Infirmary, which has a a Dispensary for out-patients, and an Orphan Institution ; a Chamber of Commerce, the Society of Writers, incorporated by royal charter, and a Mechanics' Institution. Dundee has three joint-stock banking establishments, viz., the Dundee Bank, the Union Bank, and the Eastern Bank of Scotland. Besides these, there are agencies for the British Linen Company, the National Bank of Scotland, the Bank of Scotland, and the Royal Bank. There is a native establishment for fire insurance, and three for sea insurance ; also several agencies for fire, life, and sea offices. There are four weekly newspapers published in this place." * A railway was opened some years ago between Dundee and Newtyle, a village in Strathmore, ten and a half miles distant, with branches to Cupar Angus and Glammis, which lays open the traffic of that extensive agricultural district ; and another double line to Arbroath, seventeen miles in length, was opened in 1840.

Dundee was anciently fortified with walls ; but of its walls or gates no traces now remain, except the Cowgate Port, from which Wishart the martyr is said to have preached to the people during the plague of 1544. At the period of the Reformation, it was the first town in Scotland which publicly renounced the Roman Catholic faith : and so zealous was the spirit of its Protestantism, that it acquired the name of " *the second Geneva.*" In 1651, the town was sacked, with circumstances of revolting cruelty, by General Monk ; and so great was the

* Encyclopædia Britannica.

amount of plunder, that each of his soldiers is said to
have received £60 sterling as his share. According to
tradition, the indiscriminate carnage which took place on
this memorable occasion was continued till the third day,
when a child was found sucking its murdered mother.

About twelve miles east from this part of the coast is
the famous BELL ROCK,* or Inch Cape Rock, which, from
a very remote period, has been the cause of numerous
shipwrecks. The top of the rock only being visible at
low water, one of the abbots of Aberbrothock attached
to it a frame-work and a bell, which, being rung by the
waves, warned mariners to avoid the fatal reef. A tradition respecting this bell has been embodied by Dr.
Southey in his ballad called "Ralph the Rover." A
famous pirate of this name is said to have cut the bell
from the frame-work "to plague the Abbot of Aberbrothock," and some time after to have received the just
punishment of his malice by being shipwrecked on the
spot. An elegant light-house, 115 feet high, has now
been erected by Government at an expense of £60,000.
It is one of the most prominent and serviceable beacons
on the Scottish shores, and has been the means of preventing innumerable shipwrecks.† About nine miles
from Button Ness is the royal burgh of Aberbrothock or

---

* The Bell Rock is 24 miles east of Dundee Harbour, 12 from the Buoy of
Tay, 12 from Arbroath, and 12 from Fifeness.

† The following beautiful lines were written by Sir Walter Scott in the
Album kept by this light-house:—

PHAROS LOQUITUR.

Far on the bosom of the deep,
O'er these wild shelves my watch I keep ;
A ruddy gem of changeful light,
Bound on the dusky brow of night;
The seaman bids my lustre hail,
And scorns to strike his tim'rous sail.

ARBROATH,

a neat and thriving sea-port town, situated at the distance
of 58 miles N.N.E. from Edinburgh. The harbour is
an artificial one, and though neither safe nor spacious,
possesses considerable trade. Here are the ruins of a
magnificent abbey, founded by William the Lion in
1178, and dedicated to the celebrated primate Thomas-
à-Becket. The founder was interred within its precincts, but there are no remains of his tomb. The last
abbot was the famous Cardinal Beaton, who was at the
same time Archbishop of St. Andrews. King John of
England granted this monastery extraordinary privileges,
for, by a charter under the Great Seal, he exempted it
from taxes in trading to every part of England, except
London. The ruins of the Abbey are greatly dilapidated.
The Scottish nobility met here in 1320, and drew up a
spirited remonstrance to the Pope against the claims
made by Edward II. upon the sovereignty of the kingdom. Arbroath is a royal burgh, and unites with Forfar, Inverbervie, Montrose, and Brechin, in sending a
Member to the British Parliament. The population of
the parish in 1831 was 11,211.*

---

* Fifteen miles north-west of Arbroath lies Forfar, the county town. It is a
burgh of great antiquity, and was a royal residence in the time of Malcolm Canmore. It is a neat and clean-looking town, and the inhabitants are principally
engaged in weaving and the manufacture of *brogues.* About a century ago,
Forfar was the scene of the murder of the Earl of Strathmore. That nobleman
was returning with a party of gentlemen from attendance upon a *dredgie,* or
funeral entertainment, when one of them, Mr. Carnegie of Finhaven, being
tossed by another into the gutter, rose, bespattered and blinded with mire, and
mistaking the Earl for the offender, ran him through the body. He was tried
for the crime, and narrowly escaped the gallows. On a mount to the north of
the town was the castle in which King Malcolm resided, and his queen lived in
a nunnery which stood on a small artificial island near the north side of the
loch. In the steeple of Forfar is preserved a curious instrument, called "the
Witches' Bridle," which was placed on the head of the miserable creatures
burnt in Forfar for the imaginary crime of witchcraft, and acted as a gag to
prevent their cries during the dreadful process of incremation. There are a

Leaving Arbroath, at the distance of two miles and a half, is Carlinheugh Bay, and a short way farther on,

number of pleasant anecdotes connected with Forfar, but it is somewhat curious, as has been noticed by Chambers, that they all refer to drinking or to public houses. The legal gentlemen of this town, indeed, are characterized as the "drucken writers of Forfar." Their tippling habits are finely illustrated by an anecdote of the late Earl of Strathmore. The town is a good deal annoyed with a lake in its neighbourhood, which the inhabitants have long had it in contemplation to drain, and which would have been drained long ago but for the expensiveness of such an undertaking. At a public meeting, held some years ago for the discussion of this measure, the Earl said, that he believed the cheapest method of draining the lake would be, to throw a few hogsheads of good mountain dew into the water, and set the *drucken writers* of Forfar to drink it up.*

The chief magistrate of Forfar, in the time of King James VI., kept an alehouse. His Majesty, in the course of his first journey to London, having been entertained with great splendour by the mayor of an English town, who, in honour of the occasion, kept open house for several days, some of the courtiers hinted that such examples of munificence must be very rare among the civic dignitaries of Scotland. "Fient a bit o' that are they," cried the King; "the provost o' my burgh of Forfar, whilk is by nae means the largest town in Scotland, keeps open house a' the year round, and aye the mae that comes the welcomer."

It was in Forfar that the famous case occurred which led to the decision of the Court of Session, that no charge could be made for a stirrup-dram. A brewster-wife in Forfar, previous to the Restoration, having one day "brewed a peck o' maut," and set it out to the door to cool, a neighbour's cow passing by drank the whole browst. The injured alewife had recourse to the law for satisfaction, and in process of time the case came before "The Fyfeteen," when that learned body decided, that as, by the immemorial custom of the land, nothing is ever charged for a standing drink, otherwise called a *deoch-an-dorras*, or stirrup-dram, the defendant ought to be absolved from the charge in dependence, seeing that she swallowed the browst standing, and at the door.

Forfar is situated in the beautiful valley of Strathmore, which gives title to the noble family of Lyon. The seat of this family, the celebrated castle of Glammis, stands near the village of the same name, about five miles and a half south-west of Forfar. It is situated in the midst of a park, one hundred and sixty acres in extent, and containing a considerable number of fine old trees.

GLAMMIS CASTLE.

* Chambers' Rhymes of Scotland, p. 117. Picture of Scotland, vol. ii. p. 290.

Ethie House, the seat of the Earl of Northesk. About a mile beyond is the promontory of Redhead, 250 feet high. The coast now bends inward, forming the fine bay of Lunan. Six miles from Redhead is the mouth of the South Esk river, and near it the new parish church of Craig, on an elevated situation, and Rossie Castle, (Horatio Ross, Esq.) On the north side of the mouth of the South Esk stands the royal burgh of

MONTROSE,

twelve miles north from Arbroath. Behind the town the river expands into a spacious basin, which forms a sort of road-stead to the port. At high water, it has a peculiarly striking and beautiful effect. The South Esk is crossed by a very magnificent suspension bridge, the distance between the points of suspension being 432 feet.

The castle is an edifice of great antiquity, and has a princely and antique appearance. The walls in some places are fifteen feet thick, and the height is such that the stair which leads to the top contains 143 steps. Glammis was anciently used as a royal residence, and was the scene of the death of Malcolm II., who was mortally wounded by assassins on the Hunter's Hill in this neighbourhood. Macbeth, as the readers of Shakspeare know, was thane of Glammis, and after his death it reverted to the Crown. It was given by Robert II. to John Lyon, who married the king's second daughter by Elizabeth Mure, and became the founder of the present family of Strathmore. On the barbarous execution of the young and beautiful Lady Glammis for witchcraft, in 1537, Glammis was once more forfeited to the Crown, and was for some time a residence of James V. (*the Gudeman of Ballangeich*,) but was afterwards restored to the family. It contains a valuable and extensive museum of ancient curiosities, old armour, and a collection of portraits, amounting to about a hundred in number, principally of the most distinguished characters in the reign of Charles II. The view from the top of the castle is remarkably splendid and extensive. Near the castle stand the figures of four lions rampant, each supporting in their forepaws a dial facing the four cardinal points. The figures are extremely curious, and well deserve the attention of the tourist.

Finhaven Castle, the once magnificent residence of the powerful family of Lindsay, is frequently visited by tourists. It is situated about six miles from Forfar, on the new road to Brechin. The ruins, which now consist of little more than a square tower, stand on a steep bank of the small river Lemno, near the place where it joins the South Esk. To this castle, Alexander, Earl of Crawford, popularly known by the appellation of Earl Beardie, retired in disgrace after the battle of Brechin, in 1452, and here he feasted James II. in the most magnificent style, after his reconcilement to that monarch.

Montrose is a remarkably neat town, and carries on a considerable trade. It has been connected with a number of interesting and important events in Scottish history. From this place Sir James Douglas embarked in 1330 on a pilgrimage to the Holy Land, carrying along with him the heart of Robert Bruce. It was the birthplace of the celebrated Marquis of Montrose. It was the first port made by the French fleet in December 1715, with the Chevalier St. George on board; and that personage embarked at the same place 14th February 1716, having spent the previous night in the house in which Montrose was born. The principal public buildings are the town hall, the parish church, the episcopal chapel, the public schools, the academy, the lunatic asylum, and the office of the British Linen Company. In 1831 the population of Montrose was 12,055.*

About four miles and a half from Montrose, the North Esk joins the ocean, and immediately behind it commences Kincardineshire or the Mearns. The scenery along the coast is peculiarly desolate. Passing the fishing village of Milltown, and the manufacturing village of Johnshaven, the royal burgh of Inverbervie is seen, situated on the river Bervie. It received its charter from David II. in 1362, on account of the kindness which the poor fishermen of Bervie displayed to him when forced

* Eight miles west from Montrose is 'the ancient royal burgh of Brechin, romantically situated on the banks of the South Esk. In ancient times there was an abbey of Culdees in his place, and a bishopric was established here by David I. in 1150. On the edge of a precipitous bank descending towards the river, stood the Cathedral, a stately Gothic fabric, but its architectural symmetry has of late been almost entirely destroyed by the wretched taste displayed in repairing it as a modern place of worship. Brechin contains one of those round towers, which, like that of Abernethy, have proved such stumbling blocks to antiquaries. Brechin Castle, the ancient seat of Lord Panmure, stands on a precipitous rock in the immediate neighbourhood of the town. It underwent a siege of twenty days, in 1303, from the English army under Edward I., and only surrendered on Sir Thomas Maule, its brave governor, being killed.

to land here by stress of weather. About two miles and a half farther on are the remains of Whistleburg Castle, and, in the immediate vicinity, the church of Kinneff, beneath the pulpit of which the regalia of Scotland were concealed, when they had been secretly conveyed from Dunnotar Castle.

All along this district the coast is bold and precipitous. Upon the top of a stupendous insulated rock, 160 feet above the level of the sea, stand the ruins of the celebrated CASTLE of DUNNOTAR, the seat of the ancient family of the Keiths, Earls Marischal. The area of the castle measures about three acres, and the rock bears a considerable resemblance to that on which Edinburgh Castle is built. It is divided from the land by a deep chasm, and the only approach is by a steep path winding round the body of the rock. Dunnotar was built by Sir William Keith, then Great Marischal of Scotland, during the wars between England and Scotland in the reign of Edward I. In 1296 it was taken from the English by Sir William Wallace.* Edward III. re-fortified it in his progress through the kingdom in 1336, but as soon as he quitted the kingdom, it was again captured by Sir Andrew Murray, Regent of Scotland. During the time of the Commonwealth, it was selected as the strongest place in the kingdom for the preservation of the Regalia. The garrison, under the command of Ogilvy of Barras, made a vigorous resistance to the English army, but were at

---

* Though the place is almost inaccessible, Wallace and his followers found their way into the castle, while the garrison, in great terror, fled into the church or chapel, which was built on the very verge of the precipice. This did not save them, for Wallace caused the church to be set on fire. The terrified garrison, involved in the flames, ran, some of them upon the points of the Scottish swords, while others threw themselves from the precipice into the sea, and swam along to the cliffs, where they hung like sea-fowl, screaming in vain for mercy and assistance."—*Tales of a Grandfather.*

length compelled to surrender by famine. Previously to this, however, the regalia had been secretly conveyed away, and buried beneath the pulpit of the church of Kinneff, by Mrs. Grainger, the wife of the minister of that parish. At the Restoration, all the persons connected with this affair were amply rewarded. Ogilvy was made a baronet; the brother of the Earl Marischal was created Earl of Kintore; and Mrs. Grainger was rewarded with a sum of money. During the reign of Charles II. Dunnotar was used as a State prison for confining the Covenanters. It was dismantled soon after the Rebellion of 1715, on the attainder of its proprietor, James Earl Marischal, " The battlements with their narrow embrasures, the strong towers and airy turrets, full of loop-holes for the archer and musketeer; the hall for the banquet, and the cell for the captive, are all alike entire and distinct. Even the iron rings and bolts that held the culprits for security or torture, still remain to attest the different order of things which once prevailed in this country. Many a sigh has been sent from the profound bosom of this vast rock,—many a despairing glance has wandered hence over the boundless wave,— and many a weary heart has there sunk rejoicing into eternal sleep."*

About a mile and a half from Dunnotar is the seaport of Stonehaven, situated in the bottom of a bay at the mouth of a stream called the Carron. It has a safe and commodious harbour, and contains a population of upwards of 2000. The tract of country which extends between Stonehaven and Aberdeen is remarkably bleak and sterile, presenting, for the most part, barren eminences, and cold swampy moorlands. The only object

* A Summer Ramble in the North Highlands.

worthy of notice is the fishing village of Finnan, remarkable for the dried fish called Finnan Haddocks.* At the
northern extremity of this barren tract is Aberdeenshire,
and passing Girdleness, the eastern termination of the
great chain of the Grampians, on which an elegant light-
house has recently been erected, the tourist reaches the
city of

ABERDEEN,

which ranks next to Edinburgh and Glasgow, in point of
general importance, and is considered the capital of the
North of Scotland. It is situated on a cluster of eminences, which rise along the northern bank of the river
Dee, in the immediate vicinity of its confluence with the
German Ocean. On approaching the city, along the
principal line of communication from the southward, the

---

* In a very amusing and well-written work, entitled " The Book of Bon Ac-
cord : or a Guide to the City of Aberdeen," we find the following glowing apo-
strophe to these far-famed fish :—"FINNAN, *magnum et venerabile nomen!*
' To abstract the mind from all local emotion,' says the moralist, ' would be
impossible if it were endeavoured, and would be foolish if it were possible. Far
from me and from my friends be such frigid philosophy. That man is little to
be envied, whose patriotism would not gain force upon the plain of *Marathon,*'
or whose appetite would not grow keener among the huts of *Finnan.* Its un-
lettered sages will impart wisdom which will be vainly sought in elaborate dis-
sertations on culinary science. ' Finnan Haddocks,' says a lady who cooks
upon principles of economy, ' are served at breakfast in Scotland to eat with
bread and butter, either *cold* or *just warmed* through, and moistened with one
or two *drops of sweet oil*!' This nauseous and abominable libel may be for-
given in an author born on the wrong side of the Tweed ; but it is not easy so
leniently to overlook the blunders of Mrs. Margaret Dods of St. Ronan's, whose
recommendation is, that ' Finnans be taken from the gridiron when just done,
and *dipped in hot water, if dry or hard,* and wrapped in a cloth to *swell and soften
them*!' With becoming diffidence, it is surmised that mine Hostess of the
Cleikum knows as much about Finnans, as a bare-legged Nereid of Port Lethen
knows of Parisian *entremets,* or of the Chinese luxury of edible bird's nests.
Before your Finnan becometh ' dry or hard,' or needeth to be recovered by
blankets and hot baths, you will nose him as you go up stairs, and may rely
that a certain convocation of politic worms are e'en at him. Worthy Mrs. Margaret must have mistaken him for a *Pin-the-Widdie,* or other member of the
same dessicated family. A similar mistake has led Sir Walter Scott to protest,
in the name of his country, against Dr. Johnson's taste ; but the philosopher's
' disgust' was virtuous,—for it was expressed against *Buckie* haddocks."

tourist is forcibly struck with the scene which bursts upon his view, after a long and rather dreary transit across the Grampians, at a point where their mountainous character is lost, but from which some of their sublimer features are distinctly visible in the far west. The traveller is here suddenly admonished of his approach to an important city; its more prominent buildings, scattered here and there, indicating its imposing magnitude; the numerous vessels in the harbour bearing testimony to the extent of its commerce and trade; while the high cultivation of the surrounding district is evidently tributary to the requirements of a large municipal population. The county of Aberdeen is bounded, on the south, by the Dee, which the tourist crosses by a fine old bridge of seven arches, erected about three centuries ago, by Bishop Dunbar. In the days of the Covenant, it was the scene of more than one tough contest between hostile parties. It is rather deficient in width; but the removal of this inconvenience is already in progress. A drive of a mile through the western suburbs of the city, which boast many elegant private buildings, brings the traveller to one extremity of Union Street, terminating, at the other, in Castle Street, and presenting a vista which is generally and justly admired, whether regard be had to the spacious dimensions of the street itself, the beauty and regularity of the buildings which line it on each side, the splendour of many of its shops, or the bustle which constantly enlivens it. The three chief inns of the city are situated in it, in either of which, not to mention the attractions of the minor hostelries, the stranger may well seek, and " take his ease." Curiosity will probably first direct his steps towards Castle Street, the *Plàce* of the city. Here he will find the Town House, a

plain but commodious building, of date 1730. It contains the Town-Hall, Council Chamber, &c., to which
ready access may be obtained. The hall is a spacious
apartment, and contains one or two good paintings, three
superb lustres, and some other matters worthy of inspection. The Council Chamber contains a fine head, by
Jameson. On the east end of the Town-House is a
square tower, of ancient date, which has been recently
faced up with granite in a very tasteful style. It is surmounted by a spire, 120 feet high, of singularly elegant
proportions. Contiguous to the tower, on the east, are
the new offices of the North of Scotland Banking Company, a fine building in the Grecian style, of beautifully
dressed granite. The principal entrance is under a cur-
ved portico, supported by granite columns of the Corinthian order, the capitals being executed with a delicacy
and precision hitherto deemed unattainable in that stubborn material. On the opposite side of the street stands
the Aberdeen Bank, a very chaste building, erected some
forty years ago, from a design by Mr. Burn of Haddington.
At the west end of Castle Street is the Athenæum, or Public News Room, to which a stranger may be introduced by
any of the subscribers, with free access to it for a fortnight.
It is a fine room, and well supplied with newspapers, and
the best periodicals. In the centre of Castle Street are
situated the Plainstones, and the Cross. The latter is well
worthy of notice. It was built, in 1686, by John Montgomery, a country mason of the district. It is one of the
most beautiful structures of the kind. It is adorned
with large medallions of the Scottish monarchs, from
James I. to James VII., and from the centre springs a
splendid column of the composite order, surmounted by
the royal unicorn, rampant, and bearing a shield. From

the centre of Castle Street, there are fine views of Union Street and King Street, which were both laid out, nearly forty years ago, at an expense of about £170,000. In the latter are situated some public buildings, worthy of inspection, viz. the Medical Hall, the North Church, and St. Andrew's Chapel. From Union Street, already referred to, diverges, on the south side, a new street, forming a more convenient access to the quay and harbour than any previously existing. In this street there are in progress of erection a new Post-office, and Public Markets, the latter projected by a joint-stock company, to supply what has long been a local desideratum. On the north side of Union Street are situated the East and West Churches, surrounded by a cemetery, which is separated from the street by a very beautiful façade of the Ionic order. The West Church is a building in the Italian style, from a design by the celebrated Gibbs, who was a native of Aberdeen. It contains a very fine monument, in white marble, to the memory of a lady, executed by Bacon, at an expense of £1200 ; a curious monumental plate of brass, commemorative of the death of Dr. Duncan Liddel, founder of the professorship of Mathematics in Marischal College ; and a stone effigy of Sir Robert Davidson, Provost of Aberdeen, who fell at Harlaw in 1411. The East Church is a modern building, in the Gothic style, from a design by Mr. Archibald Simpson. It is deservedly much admired. The churches are separated by Drum's Aisle, so called from its being the burial-place of the ancient family of that name. It formed the transept of the original church of St. Nicholas, a fabric of the twelfth century. The only part of the old structure is the central tower, in which hang the bells. The original date of the great bell, Laurence, which

weighs 40,000 lbs., is 1352.   In the churchyard reposes
the hallowed dust of the poet of " The Minstrel," of Principal Campbell, the learned Blackwell, and Dr. Hamilton,
the well-known author of the celebrated work on the
National Debt.   Part of Union Street is carried over a
deep ravine, by means of a magnificent bridge, consisting
of one arch of 130 feet span, 44 feet in breadth, and 50
feet above the surface of the ground below.   It is built
of dressed granite, and surmounted with a cornice, parapet, and ballustrades.   It cost £13,342.   Westward of
the bridge, at some distance, are situated the Public Rooms.
In beauty of architecture, and splendour of internal deco-
ration, they are inferior to none in the kingdom.   The
banqueting-room contains a portrait of the late Duke of
Gordon, by Lawrence, and another of Provost James
Hadden, by Pickersgill.   To these will soon be added
another, by the latter artist, of the Hon. Captain Gordon,
who has, for many years, represented the county in Parliament.   The other public buildings which particularly
merit the attention of the stranger, are the New Infirmary, the Lunatic Asylum, Gordon's Hospital, the New
Female Orphan Asylum, the New Hall of the Society of
Advocates, the Trades' Hall, and Marischal College.
Gordon's Hospital is an institution similar to that founded
in Edinburgh by George Heriot.   Upwards of 120 of
the sons or grandsons of burgesses are educated in it.
It owes its foundation to Robert Gordon, a descendant
of the Straloch family, who starved himself, that he might
accomplish his charitable design.   The Orphan Asylum
is a similar institution for females, recently built and endowed by Mrs. Elmslie, a native of Aberdeen, who is
understood to have appropriated £30,000 for that purpose.   Marischal College has been in progress of erection

for some years, and is now nearly completed. It is a building of imposing dimensions, and magnificent architectural effect. It is in the Gothic style, simplified, and adapted to the capabilities of the material (granite) of which it is built. It forms three sides of a quadrangle, and rises to the height of two lofty storeys, presenting unbroken ranges of mullioned windows, which have a fine effect. From the centre of the building springs a splendid tower, to the height of 100 feet from the ground. It contains the principal entry, and the staircase leading to the Hall, Library and Museum. Each of these rooms is 74 feet long, by 34 feet wide, and upwards of 30 feet in height. There are, besides, a Common Hall and 16 class rooms, to each of which is attached a private room for the professor. The total expense of the building is estimated at about £30,000. It is from a plan by Mr. Archibald Simpson. The old buildings, which were mostly of the seventeenth century, were neither elegant nor commodious, and had latterly become ruinous. The College was founded in the sixteenth century by one of the Earls Marischal. It ranks among its alumni many who have distinguished themselves in every department of science and literature. The traveller will, of course, not omit to visit the Harbour, with its noble quays and extensive pier, stretching into the sea upwards of 1200 feet. Vast sums of money have been expended on the improvement of the harbour, and still farther improvements, on an extensive scale, are in contemplation. The annual revenue, from dues, &c., is about £17,000. The tonnage of vessels registered as belonging to the port is about 39,000 tons. There are in the city many extensive

manufactories of flax, cotton, wool, and iron, which employ an aggregate number of hands, amounting to about
14,000. We would particularly recommend to the
stranger a visit to Bauner Mill, which is perhaps the
most extensive and best arranged cotton manufactory in
the kingdom. There are various other branches of commerce and trade successfully prosecuted in the city, the
extent of which may be inferred from the fact, that the
tonnage of all the vessels actually arriving in the port,
is about 210,000 tons. Large steamers ply regularly
between it and London, Leith, and Hull. The adoption
of steam navigation has been of the greatest advantage
to the city and county, and particularly to the agricultur-
ist. Cattle are thus shipped in large numbers, and at all
seasons, for the London market. The accommodation
for passengers is excellent. In the course of three or four
days may the care-worn denizen of the metropolis escape
from its din and dust, to " the land of the mountain and
the flood," there to inhale its invigorating breezes, enjoy
the splendid sports offered by its heaths and streams, and
admire the magnificent scenery of " dark Lochnagar."
The population of the city is supposed to be about 80,000.
It is a city of high antiquity, its earliest charter extant
being one granted by William the Lion in 1179. Previously to that early period, however, it was a place of
comparative importance, and enjoyed, for so remote an
age, a rather extensive commerce. At a subsequent
period, it stood high in the favour of " The Bruce," who
bestowed on it many important privileges, and a large
extent of lands in its vicinity, in consequence of the devotion shown by its inhabitants to his cause. The history of Aberdeen exhibits it participating largely in the

successive vicissitudes of the times; but, under all circumstances, its inhabitants have generally been distinguished for their loyalty, prudence, and enterprise.

Old Aberdeen, which is situated about a mile to the
north of the city, contains the Cathedral and King's College, both of which will amply reward a visit. The nave
of the former is used as the parish church, and is in
excellent repair. The style is rather plain, but it boasts
a glorious western window, and a carved roof, in the
most exquisite style of ancient art. It is a building of
the fourteenth century. King's College was founded in
1494 by Bishop Elphinstone. Its buildings are well
worthy of notice. It contains a fine Library, Hall,
Chapel, and Museum. The Chapel has recently undergone renovation. In it are to be seen the tombs of the
founder, and of Hector Boethius, the first Principal. The
crown, which surmounts the tower on the west end of
the Library, is a perfectly unique specimen of architecture. The top is 100 feet above the ground. For rich-
ness of ornament, beauty of design, and general effect, it
has, perhaps, no parallel. The tourist must not omit a
visit to the far-famed " Brig o' Balgownie," which Byron
refers to in a well-known stanza. It was originally built
in the twelfth century by Bishop Cheyne. The surrounding scenery is such as was well calculated deeply
to impress the mind of the youthful poet; presenting, as
it does, a venerable structure, which the lapse of many
generations has assimilated with the everlasting rock on
which it is founded—a deep and dark stream stealing
silently to the blue ocean, descried in the distance, amid
the attendant pomp of beetling crag and thick-embowered
wood—and the repose of profound seclusion which is
breathed over, and hallows the whole!

The Dee, which falls into the sea on the south side of New Aberdeen, is a river of great note in Aberdeenshire. It has its source in Lord Fife's forest, in the parish of Crathy, at the point where the south-western extremity of Aberdeenshire unites with Inverness-shire. The total length of the Dee, from its source to its mouth, following its various windings, is about eighty miles. It is distinguished by its rapidity, its broad and capacious channel, and the limpid clearness of its waters. It is skirted with fine natural forests, and extensive plantations. There is but little alluvial land on its banks, but its salmon-fisheries are very valuable. Hence the old rhyme,—

> " A rood o' Don's worth twa o' Dee,
>   Unless it be for fish and tree."

The Don rises on the skirts of Ben Avon, on the confines of Aberdeenshire and Banffshire. Its total course is about sixty-one miles. It is a much less rapid river than the Dee, and flows, for a considerable part of its course, through rich valleys. About a mile from Old Aberdeen the Don is crossed by the " BRIG OF BALGOWNIE," celebrated by Lord Byron in the tenth canto of Don Juan.

> " As ' auld lang syne' brings Scotland, one and all,
>   Scotch plaids, Scotch snoods, the blue hills and clear streams,
>   The Dee, the Don, Balgownie's Brig's black wall,
>   All my boy-feelings, all my gentler dreams,
>   Of what I then dream't, cloth'd in their own pall,
>   Like Banquo's offspring ;—floating past me, seems
>   My childhood, in this childishness of mind :
>   I care not—'tis a glimpse of ' Auld lang syne.'"

" The Brig of Don," adds the poet in a note, " near the Auld Town of Aberdeen, with its one arch, and its black deep salmon stream below, is in my memory as

ABERDEEN, BALLATER, BRAEMAR, GLEN TILT, BLAIR ATHOLL.

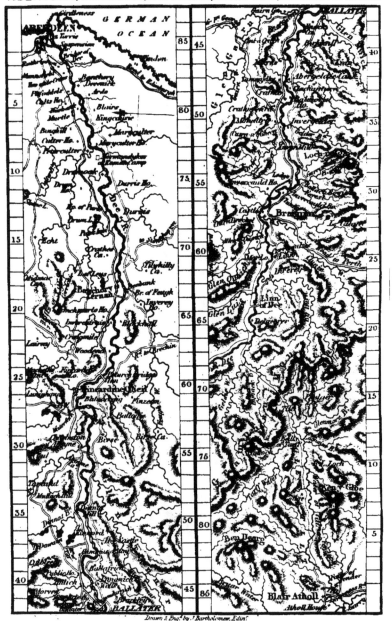

Drawn & Eng.ᵈ by J. Bartholomew, Edinᵗ

Edinburgh, Published July 1, 1841 by Adam & Charles Black, 27 North Bridge

yesterday. I still remember, though perhaps I may mis-quote, the awful proverb which made me pause to cross it, and yet lean over it with a childish delight, being an only son, at least by the mother's side. The saying, as recollected by me, was this, but I have never heard nor seen it since I was nine years of age :

> " Brig of Balgownie, black's your wa',
>   Wi' a wife's ae son, and a mare's ae foal,
>   Doon ye shall fa' ! "

The bridge was built by Bishop Cheyne, in the time of Robert Bruce, and consists of one spacious Gothic arch, which rests on a rock on each side.*

* From Aberdeen a very interesting tour may be made up the Dee to Ballater and Castleton of Braemar. The district of country which this route gives the tourist an opportunity of visiting is peculiarly wild, exhibiting scenes of savage grandeur unequalled in any other part of Scotland.

Although Aberdeen is made the starting point in this excursion, we shall advert, in our progress, to other routes by which the various interesting spots mentioned in it may be reached, without passing through Aberdeen.

TOUR TO THE HIGHLANDS OF DEESIDE AND THE CAIRNGORM MOUNTAINS.

On leaving Aberdeen there are two routes as far as Upper Banchory—one on the north, the other on the south side of the Dee. The latter is sometimes adopted by pedestrians and horsemen, but the former is the usual turnpike road, and is not only the shorter, but the more interesting of the two in its command of prospect. Opposite the third mile there is the kirk and village of Banchory Devenick on the south bank of the river ; and a little farther on is a bridge across the river, built at the private expense of Dr. Morison, the clergyman of the parish, for the use of his parishioners. For several miles after leaving the town there is a succession of small patches of landed property, with handsome houses, generally having lawns and pleasure grounds sloping towards the river. Near the sixth mile-stone, on the south bank, is the Roman Catholic College of Blairs, endowed by the munificent Mr. Menzies of Pitfodels. In its close vicinity the churches of Mary Culter and Peter Culter front each other—the former on the south, the latter on the north side of the river. A little farther on,

After leaving Aberdeen, and passing a number of fishing villages and Cruden Boy, the old castle of Slaines is

the road descending into a ravine, crosses the burn of Culter by a
massive stone bridge. The banks are steep and wooded, and refreshing to the tourist's eye, as the first specimen of picturesquely broken
ground which he passes on this jaunt. On a bare flat heathy hill, of
slight elevation, between this spot and the Dee, the antiquarian will
find an object of considerable interest in an undoubted Roman camp
in good preservation. It is called Norman Dikes, (supposed to be a
corruption of Roman Dikes.) A minute account of it will be found
in Chalmers' Caledonia. It has been maintained to be the site of the
Roman town and station of Devana, but the ramparts, which are
distinctly traceable, are neither in their size nor strength such as to
justify the supposition that the Romans had a permanent station within them. In a wooded elevation to the north-east of Norman Dykes
there is an oblong space, enclosed by a rampart, which, however, from
its irregular construction, appears to be of British origin. It is called
Kemp (viz. Camp) Hill. Apropos to this subject, it may be mentioned
that the antiquary will find, a few miles to the north-west, in the vicinity of Skene, one of the most remarkable fortified remains in existence.
It consists of five concentric ramparts of stone, enclosing the summit
of a steep conical hill, which, in reference to these works, is called
the Barmekyne (viz. Barbican) of Echt. The outside ring is nearly
a mile in circumference, and the inmost encloses about an acre of
level land ; after toiling up the steep ascent which leads to it,
one is astonished by the traces of the mechanical skill, energy,
and patience, which must have been combined in the construction
of works so gigantic on such a spot. The whole of this neighbourhood bears traces of ancient and long forgotten conflict. There
are many minor fortifications and camps, and the peasantry frequently turn up flint spear and arrow heads of exquisite proportion
and finish, remnants of an ancient and partial civilization, that must
have passed away long before the commencement of Scottish history.
At the tenth mile is the house or castle of Drum, (Alex. Irvine,
Esq.) boldly looking out from a noble hill slope among scattered forest
trees. The most remarkable part of the building is the old keep or
donjon, a massive square tower, with rounded corners, which looks as
if it had been built to give battle to earthquakes. The walls are
twelve feet thick, and thus, though the outside circumference is considerable, the interior merely consists of a small gloomy vaulted
chamber in each floor. The family of Drum is of considerable antiquity, and great fame in local history. It is the subject of a multi-

seen standing on a steep precipice overlooking the sea. This fortress was destroyed in 1594, when James VI.

tude of traditions, the more striking of which concern a long deadly feud with the Keith family, and the great battle of Harlaw. A little beyond the tenth mile are Mains of Drum Inn and Drumoak Church and Manse. Opposite the eleventh mile-stone there is, on the south bank of the river, the House of Durris, (Anthony Mactier, Esq.) and a little farther on the Kirk of Durris, or, as it is pronounced in the vicinity, Dores. On the north side of the river, and between it and the road, is Park House, (A. Kinloch, Esq.) a somewhat more dapper and villa looking edifice than the majority of the Deeside buildings. About the 15th mile, Crathes Castle, (Sir Robert Burnett, of Leys, Bart.) looks majestically forth from a sloping mass of thick woodland. It is one of those old Flemish buildings which, rising as it were from a solid root and stem, becomes, as it ascends, broken into a varied picturesque cluster, of turrets chimneys and peaked gables. There are, unfortunately, some modern additions sadly out of keeping with the picturesque character of the older part. Here, as at Drum, there is abundant traditionary lore, both in prose and song.*

At eighteen miles from Aberdeen is the village of Banchory Ternan or

UPPER BANCHORY,

the first of the genuine pleasure-trip places on Deeside. It enjoys a considerable share of the beauties of water, wood, and mountain.

---

* Of the latter, there is a somewhat humorous ballad, called " The Baron o' Leys," in which a hopeful heir of the family, having got inveigled in some foreign liaison, is represented as mystifying the object of his affections on the subject of his identity, by successively representing himself as the proprietor of very grotesque and unreasonable names. The dialogue proceeds thus :—

" Some ca's me this, some ca's me that,
  Whatever may best befa' me ;
But when I'm in Scotland's King's high court,
  Clatter-the-speens they ca' me.

" O waes me now, O Clatter the speens,
  And alas! that ever I saw thee ;
For I'm in love, sick sick in love,
  And I kenna well fat to ca' thee.

" Some ca's me this, some ca's me that,
  I carena what they ca' me ;
But when wi' the Earl o' Murray I ride,
  Its Scour-the-Braes they ca' me.

" O waes me now, O Scour the Braes, &c.

marched north after the battle of Glenlivat, to reduce
Huntly and Errol to obedience.   The Errol family then

The older part of the village consists of venerable sturdy gloomy
houses, that have been built for genuine residenters, and to suit the
humours of no capricious city lodger.   The newer part contains
several stylish "boxes," with gardens, and neat lodging houses.   A
new Gothic church, in good taste, terminating the steep bank of the
river, along which the straggling village runs, gives a finished landscape air to the whole.   The Dee is here joined by the Feugh, an
angry moss-stained stream, which comes thundering down from the
Braes of Angus, lashing its black waters into foam, as it quarrels with
the surly rocks.   Near its junction it crosses a stony barrier, where,
after a succession of broken foaming torrents and inky pools, it casts
itself over the brow of a rock, and makes a stormy cascade—its last
act of independent turbulence, before its troublesome spirit is sub-
dued by intermixture with the more dignified and placid waters of
the Dee.   Looking up in the direction whence this stream runs, the
traveller will see the broken outline of the hills from which its
waters are supplied, and towering above the others is the characteristic summit of Cloch-na-ben, with a great stone like a gigantic wart
projecting from its brow.   Four miles north from the village is the
Hill of Fare, wide and flat, and not very elevated, presenting little
attraction to the searcher after the romantic.   A hollow on the north
side, however, is not unfrequently visited, from its being the battle-
field of Corrichie, where Murray and Huntly fought in 1562, under
the eye of Queen Mary.   A small fountain near the spot is called
Queen Mary's Well.   In a densely wooded recess on the northern
declivity of this hill rises an oriental looking cluster of turrets, forming the mansion or castle of Midmar.

A little more than a mile beyond Banchory, on the south bank, is
the modern castellated mansion of Blackhall, (Colonel Campbell,) a
parkish looking place, with a long wide avenue, bordered by magnificent trees.   On the north bank is Inchmarlo, (D. Davidson, Esq.)
About a mile farther on is Woodend Cottage, peeping from a
plantation sloping finely to the Dee.   At the 24th mile is the Brig of
Potarch, where the old south and north road, still used by drovers,
crosses to the Cairn O'Mont, Fetter Cairn, and Brechin.*   The Dee,

* If any one wishes to experiment on a really old fashioned Scottish country
inn, equally unknown to tourists and commercial travellers, we would recommend him to the hostel of Cutties-Hilloc on this road, should it still remain
the respectable relic of former hospitality which we remember it to have been
but a few years ago.

removed to their present habitation, a collection of low
houses forming a quadrangle, one side of which is built

where it is spanned by this bridge, is hurried between two rocks,
which leave but a space of twenty feet for its ample waters. According to Mr. James Brown's Guide Book—of which anon—a caird, or
gipsey, called John Young, pursued for murder, escaped, by leaping
this wild chasm.* Twenty-six miles from Aberdeen is the village of
Kincardine O'Neil, where we could not have wished the traveller
better fortune than to find the worthy Mrs. Gordon still presiding
over her well-conditioned inn, venerable in the administration of hospitalities, from which the profuseness and cheapness seemed to remove
all mercenary character. Mrs. G. has, we understand, retired from
her important duties; and we doubt not her successor will feel a stimulus in the ambition to rival so distinguished a predecessor. This
remote locality is connected with one of the most remarkable incidents in Scottish history. The pursuit and death of Macbeth, transferred by Bœce, and the other fabulous annalists whom Shakespeare
read, to Perthshire, took place, according to the earlier and more
credible chroniclers, in the vicinity of Kincardine. Wyntoun says,

> " And owre the mownth thai chast hym than
> Til the wode of Lunfanan.
> *   *   *   *
> This Macbeth slewe thai there
> Into the wode of Lunfanan,
> And his hewyd thai strak off thare,
> And that wyth thame fra thair thai bare
> Til Kynkardyn, quhare the King
> Till thare gayne come made byding.

It is a singular coincidence between tradition and history, that in the
sterile alley of Lumphanan, some miles to the north, where Shakespeare, Bœce, and Wynton, are alike unknown, and where neither
tourist nor antiquary has taught the simple inhabitants to drive a
trade in associating their neighbourhood with great events, a small
mound of stones still bears the name of Cairn-beth. This neighbourhood, like that mentioned a little above, is rife with the reliques
of ancient warfare. There are several remains of fortification on the

---

* Young was a man of many feats in Aberdeenshire story, and is the same
to whom was attributed the bold practical joke of releasing all the prisoners in
the jail of Aberdeen, (himself included,) and placarding the door with the ad-
vertisement " ROOMS TO LET."

on the very verge of the precipice overhanging the ocean.
The coast here is very rocky, but the rocks being soft,

hills, and weapons of rude workmanship have frequently been turned
up by the plough. *

A little below the twenty-seventh mile-stone the road crosses a
stream, on which, some 200 yards or so up, will be found a small
cataract, called the Slog of Dess. The Parliamentary Road to Bridge
of Alford and Huntly here strikes off to the right. Thirty-one miles
from Aberdeen is Charleston of Aboyne, a village surrounded by wide
stretches of forest land and picturesquely broken ground. There is
here a good inn, and a handsome suspension bridge across the Dee,
the successor of a less solid structure, swept away by the great flood of
1829. Aboyne Castle, one of the seats of the Marquis of Huntly, rears
its many heads from the woods on the right. It is an irregular structure, built apparently at different periods, and though imposing in size,
scarcely to be characterised as either picturesque or elegant. After
leaving the shady woods of Aboyne, the traveller enters a wild and
desolate heath, called the Muir of Dinnet, a sort of debateable land,
separating the Highlands from the Lowlands, where, to beguile the
time, he may speculate on the character of the population he has
been passing through. He will have remarked, that on Deeside
there are few large farms, and that where the land can be termed
fertile, the crofters' and small farmers' houses are numerous. If he be
a pedestrian, he will have had many opportunities of personal intercourse with the swains who cultivate these patches, and after he has
mastered their energetic northern dialect, will have found them to be
a shrewd, civil, and independently courteous people. Interviews are
spoken of as a thing that must, in the ordinary course of circumstances, take place, for no man can walk Deeside without either
committing a woful breach of etiquette or exchanging courtesies
with those he meets. Nor, however humble may be the peasant who
says " a fine day," and perhaps offers his " sneeshen mull," will much
servility be found in his deportment. There is, in fact, an independence of demeanour in these worthy fellows, which, backed by their
energetic accent, has a somewhat repulsive appearance to strangers ;
yet, from the genuine kindness met at every turn, wherever there is an

* In the parish of Leochel, immediately adjacent, is the Castle of Craigievar,
(Sir John Forbes, Bart.) a grim old Flemish building, suited to the character
of the place, and worth mentioning were it only for the expressive motto in
large and very legible characters over the heavy door-way of the keep,

DO NOT WAKEN SLEEPIN DOUGS.

are wasted and corroded by the constant action of the
waves, and the fragments which remain where the soft

opportunity to call it forth, such a feeling must soon disappear. The
hospitalities of the Deeside peasantry are, however, by no means of
the kind which would generally be called refined, in high life. As an
illustration of their courtesies, it is said that a weary pedestrian from
Aberdeen, who had lost his way, and was kindly provided with a
night's lodging, was not a little astonished in stepping out of bed to
find himself up to the knees in water—the night had been rainy. On
appearing before his entertainers in a pitiable plight, and representing
to them that such an inroad of the element in such a quarter was an
uncommon event, which required some peculiar explanation, he met
the excuse justificative in these terms, " Oh, man, you surely forgot
to look for the stappin stons."

To the north of the Muir of Dinnet lies the district of Cromar and
the village of Tarland. The highest summit in this direction is the
Hill of Morven, round, and somewhat flat in its outline ; and a glimpse
is just caught from the road of a pretty sedgey sheet of water, called
the Loch of Kinnord. The monotony of the progress through the dreary
muir is gradually relieved by the opening prospect of the hills, which
rise, terrace above terrace, like mounds thrown up for an audience of
Titans. Highest of all, a long gracefully waving outline, bending on
either side from a sharp peak, characterises the mountain monarch
of the district, Lochnagar. If the atmosphere be clear, the line of
precipice which constitutes its eastern wall may be seen from summit to base, clear and smooth ; but most generally it suits not the
monarch to unveil his fearful beauties, and a mass of black cloud
hovers round his summit, within whose mysterious folds proceeds the
manufacture of elemental wrath. As the traveller approaches closer
to the base of the series of mountain terraces, he perceives a little
fertile plain reposing beneath their huge shadows, and edged by the
clear waters of the Dee. When the eye is sufficiently accustomed to
the large masses by which it is surrounded to detect minuter objects,
a small spire may be seen rising very distinct from the plain, round
it curls a light smoke, indicative of the dwelling of human beings,
and finally, rows of small houses, like so many pebbles that might
have rolled from the hills, come into distinct view. This is the
village of

BALLATER,

Forty-two miles from Aberdeen. Ballater is a very important place,
—the Tunbridge Wells and the Keswick of Aberdeenshire, where
people resort both to drink the waters and to rove among hills. It has

parts have been washed away, have assumed the appearance of old Gothic towers. In this neighbourhood is

an excellent inn, where there is, or used to be, an ordinary—a shop
or two of all wares, a baker, butcher, tailor, and shoemaker, a parish
school, manse, lodge, and post office, besides a commodious church.*

* To the useful little work called the "Guide to Deeside," by James Brown,
formerly car-man on Deeside, and now, we believe, gardener in the Botanical
Garden of Edinburgh, we have, on several occasions, trusted in the above sketch
for the spelling of names, or for distances, when our own memory or notes
happened to be at fault. We cannot avoid here quoting his description of
Ballater, which is in his best and most emphatic manner.

"As Aberdeen is the chief town of the shire, so Ballater is the capital or metropolis of Deeside, an honour which in every respect it is well worthy to enjoy.
Though Ballater and Aberdeen are both chief towns, it is altogether out of the
question to compare them together in respect of size, number of inhabitants,
or stateliness of buildings—for Aberdeen is the capital of a whole shire, with
hills, valleys, muirs, and plains, altogether unspeakable, while Ballater is but
the metropolis of one single valley, with its parts and pertinents. Surely, therefore, it is a vain thing to think that Ballater should be a town any thing like so
large as Aberdeen, or yet so well built; but this I will say, that Ballater, for the
extent of ground to which it is the renowned metropolis, is in proportion little
behind Aberdeen. As for grandeur and beauty of situation there is no comparison whatsoever—the stance on which Aberdeen stands being just as much
inferior to the stance on which Ballater stands as the Broad-hill of the Links is
inferior to Lochnagar or Ben-Muick-dhui. And farther I will take it upon me
to say, that in point of renown Ballater is very little if any thing inferior to
Aberdeen—its fame as a fashionable watering place being spread far and wide
to the uttermost corners of the earth, as may be known by the number of
strangers coming to see it from all parts of the world, and among others from
the Isle of Sky and the Cape of Good Hope. As for pleasantness and agree-
ableness, every one must admit that Ballater has the advantage, else why do
such numbers of Aberdeen people leave their homes there and come out here
every summer to take up their abode—while few or none of the Ballater people
ever visit Aberdeen, except upon urgent business?—a thing which can be accounted for in no way whatever but by allowing Ballater is out of all sight a
much more agreeable and pleasant town to dwell in than Aberdeen. What
with many Aberdonians is a matter of great reproach to Ballater is that its
steeple is only a timber steeple; but the Ballaterians have no reason to be
ashamed of their steeple, and the Aberdonians in objecting to it only show that
they can see their neighbour's faults but not their own—for it is perfectly notorious that some of the steeples of Aberdeen are timber as well as the Ballater
steeple—from which they differ in no respect except that they are covered with
lead, and have clocks, which it must be confessed Ballater steeple has not.
Nevertheless, for all that, it is as excellent a steeple as any body need wish to
look at, and if not covered with lead, is so curiously painted that it looks just as
well as if it were real stone. Indeed, many of those who now scoff at it, at first mis-
took it for stone. As for other things with which Aberdeen people taunt the
Ballaterians—saying that they have no fine streets, or noble buildings, or stately
bridges, such as Aberdeen has, we can show hills and mountains, and woods

that wonder of nature, the BULLER OF BUCHAN. It is a huge rocky caldron, into which the sea rushes through a

The Dee, in its immediate vicinity, was formerly crossed by a fine stone bridge, which being destroyed by the floods of 1829, has been replaced by a structure partly of wood. The ostensible object of the Ballater visitors—the medicinal Wells, are at a spot called Pananich, about two miles to the east, on the south side of the river. Their virtues are long famed in Highland tradition, and bring multitudes from the far off hills to partake of their healing influence ; and if the water, unadulterated by any artificial admixture, produced all the joviality that may be witnessed among the groups that sometimes congregate round the brinks of the wells in a sunny evening, it would probably acquire a still more extensive reputation.

From Ballater there are many pleasing detours. The first task of the visitor is invariably to climb Craigendarroch, (the rock of oaks,) a steep round knob, about the height of Arthur Seat, i. e. 800 feet, and rising right up from the village. Its celebrity consists in a rather uncommon qualification to be applied to a hill—its smallness. It is, in fact, the lowest hill in the vicinity that one can get satisfactorily to the top of ; and it is many a one's sole premises for the satisfactory conclusion of being " able to say" he has climbed a Highland hill. It is in this respect a valuable appendage to Ballater, but it is not without its own merits,—the view is magnificent, and few so wide and varied can be purchased with so small an expenditure of climbing. Immediately at its foot is Ballater Cottage, belonging to Mr. Farquharson. To the north Craigendarroch is separated from a loftier ridge of rock by a precipitous chasm, called " The Pass of Ballater." Another rocky hill, about four miles from the village, is frequently scaled, not so much for its own intrinsic merit, perhaps, as because Byron said of it,

" When I see some dark hill point its crest to the sky,
   I think of the rocks that o'ershadow Culbleen."

From like associations, the farm house of Ballatrich on the south side of the river, where Byron lived, " rude as the rocks where his infancy grew," is often visited. But a spot worthy of admiration on its own account, for the ages before the bard existed, and which will

and valleys, and rocks and lochs, with which Aberdeen has nothing to compare, and which every one will allow are much better worth looking at than any streets, bridges, or buildings any where in the whole world, not to speak of Aberdeen. So much for the comparison which has been made between Ballater and Aberdeen."

natural arch or rock. There is a path around the top which in one place is only two feet wide, with a mon-

continue so when he is forgotten,—if the land be inhabited when that comes to pass, is another object of his Highland muse—Lochnagar. From Ballater to the summit is considered about ten miles; but miles, where there is no turnpike, are terribly long in the Highlands. Those who are not accustomed to hard walking should take Highland ponies with them, and all should make it a day's work, chusing a clear one for the purpose. In itself, the ascent is a stony, boggy, toilsome business; but to all who can admire a run of precipice, varying from 1200 to 900 feet high, with a cold inky lake at its base, and the gorgeous prospect of half Scotland spread below, the toil will not seem mis-spent. The summit is 3800 feet above the level of the sea. It has been only on a few very warm summers that the snow has ever en-tirely deserted Lochnagar, and considerable fields of it are generally to be seen in midsummer; it is much prized by knowing tourists as an ingredient in iced grog. Another detour from Ballater is to the Linn and Loch of Muick. This stream joins the Dee at Ballater, and the traveller has but to keep by its rocky banks, along which there is a tolerable road. At the Linn, the Muick, in a considerable body, hurls itself over a precipice into a black hopeless-looking pool. The Loch is a considerable sheet of water, but somewhat sombre in its scenery, except in certain spots, where, over its rounded banks, the precipices of Lochnagar may be seen frowning grim and close. The adventurous traveller should not be content with Loch Muick, but ought to ascend a stream at its upper extremity, by which, after passing some miles of wildly broken ground, where cataracts start as it were every now and then at his feet, he will be led to the Dhu Loch, a smaller lake than that of Muick, but incomparably grander in its scenery,—its banks, except where the stream issues, being a circum-vallation of huge black precipices, on the same scale with those of Lochnagar. A journey from Ballater of considerable labour, but much interest, is across Mont Keen, (3180 feet above the sea,) to Lochlee, in the Braes of Angus, classical as the residence of Alexan-der Ross, the author of the Fortunate Shepherdess. The southern descent of Mont Keen is by a seried mass of stones, like a ruined stair-case, not unaptly called "the Ladder," and its descent brings the traveller to a succession of wild narrow broken glens, noisy with a succession of waterfalls, which at last open on the pastoral valley of the North Esk and the pretty lake of Lochlee. It is right to men-tion that this is a path by which Ballater and the Highlands of Dee-side may be reached from the south by way of Brechin. One more

strous precipice on either side. In the side of the caldron there opens a huge black cavern. In high gales,

object of interest to be mentioned before we leave Ballater is the
Burn of the Vat, so termed from its perforating diagonally a huge
natural well of perpendicular rock. The visitor creeps through the
channel of the burn by a narrow stony orifice, and looks up astonished
through this Barclay-and-Perkins looking freak of nature to the clear
heavens, with nothing to interrupt the circular smoothness of the
rocks but some birch trees in invisible fissures, that hang from the
height like little tendrils.

There are two roads from Ballater up the Dee, one on the north, the
other on the south bank—the former is generally preferred. It will be
remarked, that the mile-stones on it, (where any happen to remain,)
calculated direct from Aberdeen by the old road through the pass,
make no allowance for a divergence of a mile and a half at Ballater.
Sweeping round Craigendarroch, the water of Gairn is crossed at a
point about equidistant from Aberdeen with Ballater. About a mile
farther on, on the north side, is Craig Youzie, (the rock of firs,) a
round knob, something like Craigendarroch. About the forty-fifth
mile is a pristine Highland Clachan, not yet brushed up by tourists,
called the Micras. Rather more than a mile farther on is Abergeldie
Castle, (M. F. Gordon, Esq.) with an old turreted square tower and
some modern additions of various dates,—a formidable place in the
rieving days, when it was held that

> " He should take who had the power,
>   And he should keep who can.

Hitherto the traveller will have observed the birch trees thickening
as he proceeds, and here he will find them at their climax of dense
luxuriance and beauty, covering almost every spot, save where the
broad river sweeps along the bottom of the glen, or the hills carry
their broken rocky heads to the clouds. Abergeldie owes no good
turn to Burns, who, finding it worthily possessed of the old air of
" The Birks of Abergeldie," with the despotism of genius, transferred
its leafy honours, without a moment's warning, to his nearer neighbour Aberfeldy. About a mile farther en are two localities respec
tive y bearing the expressive denominations of " The Thief's Pot " and
" The Gallow's Hill." These classic spots are held sacred to the
memory of that great effort of political subordination and marital affection which prompted the high-souled Highland spouse to say to her
rebellious husband, " Get up, John, and be hanged, and dinna anger
the laird ; " but, as in the case of other heroic acts, Deeside is not
without competitors for this honour.

2 E

the waves rush in with incredible violence, and fly over
the natural wall of the Buller, which is at least two

Between the forty-eighth and forty-ninth mile are the kirk, manse
and school of Crathie, on the north side, and the old mansion of Bal-
moral, belonging to the Earl of Fife, lately fitted up as a shooting
lodge by Sir Robert Gordon, on the south side. A little below the
manse the river is crossed by a suspension bridge. About a mile
farther on to the right, a road strikes off to Corgarff, on the Don, (a
tower used as a small military station,) and thence to Fort-George.
To the westward are the remains of the House of Monaltrie, which
having been burned down in 1745, is now fitted up as a farm house.
A small village in the neighbourhood is called the Street of Monaltrie. A little farther on is the mound called Cairn-a-quheen, (the
cairn of remembrance,) which was used in the foraying days as
the great gathering cry of Deeside when the crossteric passed. A
small inn on the way side, called Inver, may here not be without its
attractions to the pedestrian. At the fifty-fourth mile-stone, the traveller on the north side of the river will have to cross by the Bridge
of Invercauld, thrown over a rapid and rocky strait of the river. It
will have been noticed that the soft birch foliage has been gradually
giving place to the sturdier and statelier pine, of which there are here
many fine trees, masses of which spread up the glens to the south,
where they form the great forest of Ballach-bowie. Soon after crossing the bridge, the road winds round the foot of Craig Cluny, an
abrupt ascent clothed with pine much farther up than the eye can
individualise single trees, but raising a sharp bare granite peak, that
nearly abuts across the road, to a much greater height. The foundation of an old tower, called the Laird of Cluny's Charter-Chest, about
a third of the distance to the top, may be reached by an enterprising
scrambler. It is worth visiting, as a specimen of old Highland engi-
neering. How it could have been possible to reach it if any one
wished to keep intruders down, none but cats or tigers can tell ;
from an assault above, it is protected by the superincumbent rock
bulging over. At the foot of Craig Cluny, and on the opposite side
of the road, lies a stone about the size of a three-storey house, which
has dropped some day or other from the edge of the rock. It would
have astonished the outsiders of a stage-coach, if any such had been
passing. Beyond Craig Cluny the strath opens, showing at the bend
of the northern sweep Invercauld House, an irregular pile of considerable size, but dwarfed by the majestic scale of the scenery.
About the centre of the strath, and on the south side of the river, is
Braemar Castle, a high bare walled tower, with a venerable Flemish

hundred feet high. Rounding the promontory of Buchanness,—the most easterly point of land in Scotland,—the

expression about it, though not dating back so far as " the '15."
Immediately beyond, and fifty-seven miles from Aberdeen, is the village of

CASTLETOWN OF BRAEMAR,

a straggling collection of primitive looking houses, on a piece of broken rocky ground, where the turbulent stream of the Cluny clatters
down in a great hurry to trouble the Dee with the care of its fidgetty
existence. The Castletown is in its pristine state as an old Highland
village, the capital of the Strath. It has few if any new lodging-
houses for health-seeking citizens ; but it has two excellent inns for
the tourist, where he may be positively on occasion saturated with
venison and grouse. In the close vicinity are the remains, little beyond the foundation, of the old Castle, where the Earl of Mar
raised the standard of rebellion in 1715. However adventurously
disposed, the traveller should take up his central position in Braemar, as, without crossing the great mountain barriers to the basins
of the Tay or the Spey, he will find no other home near the wild
scenery of the higher Grampians. It may be mentioned that it
is by no means necessary that the journey to Braemar from the south
should be made *via* Aberdeen and along Deeside. From Dunkeld or
Blairgowrie it may be easily reached through Spital of Glenshee,
where there is a good inn. The distance from Blairgowrie to Braemar by this route is about thirty-five miles ; viz. Brig O'Cally, (where
there is an inn,) six miles ; thence to Spital, fourteen m. ; thence
to Braemar, fifteen m. By another and wilder road, Braemar may
be reached through Blair-Athol, by following the Tilt to its source,
and descending the streams that run to the Dee. The distance is
estimated at twenty-eight miles from Blair-Athol.

To begin with the smaller objects of interest near Braemar : About
four miles east, on the declivity of the dusky pine forest of Ballach-
bowie, is seen a white streak, which forms the cataract of the Garrawalt.
It is easily approached by drives constructed along the natural terraces
of the forest banks. There is here a considerable supply of water
rolling over a bank of great height, which, though not perpendicular,
gives a thundering and foamy torrent ; but, as a cataract, it is rather
deficient in interest, from its not disgorging itself into one of those
black cauldrons, which give a mysterious, frightful, and characteristic
feature to most of the Highland falls. It has a rustic bridge, and a
fog-house to make it " tural lural," as the cockney said when he tried

tourist comes in sight of Peterhead, the fifth sea-port in Scotland, and, as a whale-fishing port, inferior only to

to utter 'truly rural' with his mouth full of strawberries. Between three and four miles west of Braemar, there are two other waterfalls, one on the south, the other on the north side of the river. The former is termed Corramulzie,—exactly the sort of spot where old painters send fawns to sleep in hot days. It is a deep gash in the rock, narrow and precipitous, but having all its asperities softened off by the profusion of birches and creeping plants with which it is matted. The fall (which one often forgets, for it has so little of the terrible in it, though of considerable height, and very steep,) slides down pearly white through a winding slit in the rock, where its gentle surface is in close companionship with the tender wild flowers that are kept in eternal green by its spray. The Linn of Quoich, on the other side of the river, (a couple of miles below the Earl of Fife's hunting seat, Mar Lodge,) is of a different character. It is on one of those powerful streams that tumble from the Cairngorm Mountains, and the cataract is formed by a succession of precipitous ledges. The schist rock is perforated in many places by the whirling waters into deep circular holes, from the appearance of which some man of gigantic dram-drinking visions is presumed to have christened the fall by its name of the Quoich. The next waterfall to be visited is the Linn of Dee itself, about eight miles from Braemar. It is not the height of fall, but the contraction of the stream, that is the object of interest ; indeed, when the water is swollen, the ledges over which it falls almost disappear, the corners being rounded off as it were by the thickness of the watery drapery. One may descend to the river's edge, and the furious mass of waters, crushed and huddled together by the impregnable granite walls, raves with a wild and deafening fury, that dizzies the brain, and excites a sort of apprehension that the exasperated element may leap from its prison, and overwhelm the spectator as he is coolly gazing on its agony. It is easy to step from the north bank to the south ; but the adventurer should adopt the old counsel of looking before leaping. The southern ledge is very narrow, and the rock rises perpendicularly over it. It may happen that, as the leap back is upwards, the adventurer may feel it beyond his power, and there is then nothing for it but to climb up the face of the rock, with the hungry Linn below. Instances have been known of lovers of the *juste milieu*—people given to half measures—constituting animal bridges for some length of time across this piece of pleasant scenery.

To conclude with Deeside,—we must now give the traveller the briefest possible sketch of the features of that huge mountain desert lying

Hull. It possesses a highly accessible, safe, and commodious harbour, and its inhabitants are remarkable for their

between the Straths of the Dee and Spey, which, presenting a district totally uninhabited, and containing no traces of the foot of man, has more association with the solitudes of distant unpeopled wastes than any one who does not know the place would anticipate in the land of spinning-jennies and steam. The mountains, which here rise almost from one root, form the loftiest cluster in the united kingdom. Among them are, Ben-muich-dhui, 4390; Brae-riach, 4280; Cairn-toul, 4230; Cairngorm, 4050; Ben-a-bourd, 3940; and Bena'an 3920. Their sides present perpendicular precipices of great height, and the valleys between them form gloomy ravines, narrow and dark, from the nearness of the hills to each other. Although no part of this district is within the line of perpetual congelation, the snow lingers in the hollows during the summer in such vast quantities, as to give a perfectly wintry aspect to the higher shaded glens. Down the sides of these mountains there are several cataracts of great height and no small bulk. But the scenery is not without its softer features. Many of the most rugged are relieved by the gentle weeping birch. Glen Zui, one of the entrance-avenues from Deeside to this lonely district, presents a wide plain of green turf as bright and almost as smooth as a shaven lawn, while a pellucid stream ripples through it over yellow sand, or among sedges and waterflowers, as gentle and modest as if it could not have come roaring down just ten minutes before from the black precipices of Ben-muich-dhui. The old weatherbeaten pines are a curious feature of some of these glens. By Deeside, the trees, lofty and grand as many of them are, have more an air of good keeping about them; they are more park-like. In Glen Quoich and Glen Derry, they are scarred by centuries of contest with the mountain storms. Some are bowed to the earth, others twisted round and round like the horn of a sea-unicorn, and others stripped bare still stand erect, like mammoth skeletons set on end. On the lower declivities of the hills, and on the skirts of the forest land, may be occasionally seen those noble troops of red deer, which, since the days of sheep farming and black cattle, are scarcely to be found elsewhere in the Highlands, in their ancient glory. By Deeside you may see a shy stag or so looking down on you from a bank; but even there the air is tainted to their nice senses; it is in Glen Lui or Glen Derry that they congregate in droves; and though they seldom approach very close to the wanderer, he will frequently see their graceful forms and stately antlers on the edges of the heights between him and the setting or rising sun.

activity and public spirit.   The Chevalier St. George'
landed at Peterhead in the disguise of a sailor, on his
fruitless expedition to Scotland in 1715.   Eighteen miles

To see all the characteristic portions of this wild district, the adventurer should make two or three detours from Braemar, unless he
can manage to sleep on the heather, and so take the stages successively. One special object of attention should be Loch A'an. The
best means of reaching it is by proceeding up the Glen Lui already
mentioned, and at the point where the glen diverges into two others,
following that to the right, Glen Derry.   When the head of this glen
is reached, the mound must be ascended, and then descended on the
other side by the stream, the Alt-dhu-lochan, which runs towards
the Spey, the mound forming the water-shed between the Straths of
Dee and Spey. After descending a considerable way, and winding to
the left among precipitous banks, Loch A'an is reached, a sheet of
water about two miles long, bedded in the precipices of Ben-muich-
dhui and Bena'an, which rise in varied and grotesque forms to the
height of from 1000 to 1500 feet. Loch A'an may be reached by following the Quoich instead of the Lui, and crossing the water shed.
as above. It may also be reached by descending Ben-muich-dhui,
Near the top, and on the eastern declivity, there is a field of snow,
out of which comes a pellucid stream, which, gathering other friendly
rills into a considerable joint-stock torrent, tumbles down into the
lake. The descent may be followed by a skilful cragsman ; but it is
to any one a perilous and tedious business. When the lake is reached,
the series of torrents above look like one waterfall from the top to the
base of the mountain, and when swollen with melted snow, it must
form one of the most stupendous cataracts in Europe. Before this
descent is attempted, Ben-muich-dhui must of course have been
climbed. With all his ruggedness, this is not a difficult matter, if the
old "black hog" (this it seems is the English of his name) be taken in
the right way, like others of his species. One method is by Glen
Lui, the left-hand path being taken, up Glen Lui-beg, where the
glens diverge, instead of the right hand by Glen Derry. Another
method is by ascending right up from the most northern well of the
Dee, and there is another by climbing over the banks of the Dee a
little above the Linn. Ben-muich-dhui being the centre of the group,
and its highest member, cannot easily be mistaken, if the weather be
clear,—if it is foul the ascent should not be attempted. The source
of the Dee, with Bræ-riach and Cairn-toul deserve a special visit.
Where the streams of the Dee beyond the Linn separate,—by keeping
all along by the right-hand stream, a circular well is reached, where

forth from Peterhead is Fraserburgh, a considerable
town, and burgh of regality, of which Lord Saltoun is
superior, and chief proprietor. It has risen into considerable importance in consequence of the construction
here, during last war, of a large harbour for the reception of ships of war. The old castle of Fraserburgh,
which is now converted into a light-house, stands on
Kinnaird-head, about a mile north of the town, and is a
picturesque object seen from the sea. Twenty-one miles
from Fraserburgh is the royal burgh of BANFF, the capital
of the county which bears its name. It is an old-
fashioned, but clean and neat town, containing about
3000 inhabitants. At the distance of a mile, on the opposite bank of the Deveron, is the modern village and
seaport of Macduff. In the immediate neighbourhood is
Duff House, the magnificent mansion of the Earl of Fife,
surrounded by extensive plantations. The park is fourteen miles in circumference. About a century ago Banff
was the scene of the execution of a noted robber, named

the water bubbles up clear and full from the interior of the mountains. The stream here passes between what are well called

> " The grisly rocks that guard
> The infant rills of Highland Dee—

viz. on the east, Ben-muich-dhui, and on the west, Brœ-riach, which
rises in one black smooth perpendicular precipice, extending for two
miles, and calculated by Dr. Skene Keith and others at 2000 feet
high. By mounting the Garachary, which disputes with the stream
just described the title to be the principal source of the Dee, the top
of Brœ-riach may be reached. On the way up, the stream is joined by
the Guisachan from a small lake on Cairn-toul, called Loch-na-Youan
whence it tumbles by a fall of about 1000 feet, as measured by Dr.
Keith. The other branch of the stream then falls over a succession
of ledges, making in all 13,000 feet, according to the same authority.
The wells at the top were found to be 4068 feet above the sea level.
Dr. Keith, who made the ascent in the middle of July, found the
stream at its commencement passing under an arch of snow.

Macpherson, whose "farewell" has been made the subject of a spirited song by Burns.

About seven miles from Banff is Portsoy, a small irre-
gularly-built town, with a thriving port. A few miles
farther is the royal burgh of Cullen, where the queen of
Robert Bruce died, and was buried in the eastern aisle
in the old church. Behind the town is Cullen House,
the splendid mansion of the Earl of Seafield. It contains
a valuable collection of paintings. The other towns
round the coast are Garmouth, a neat modern town on
the left bank of the Spey; Burghead, a thriving seaport
with a considerable trade in ship-building, and herring-
fishing; Nairn, a royal burgh, and capital of the county.
After leaving Aberdeen, the Orkney steamer does not
touch at any intervening place till it reaches Wick, a
royal burgh, and the county town of Caithness. It is a
thriving town, and is the principal seat of the herring-
fishery in the north of Scotland.

After leaving Wick, the steamer proceeds to Kirkwall,
the principal town in the ORKNEY ISLANDS. The Orkney
and Shetland Islands lie in two groups to the north of
Scotland, and form between them a county which returns
a member to Parliament. The former, which are the most
southerly, are separated from the county of Caithness by
the Pentland Firth, which is about six miles broad. Their
number is estimated at sixty-seven, of which twenty-seven
are inhabited. They comprise an area of about 281,600
acres, and their population, in 1831, amounted to 28,847.
The more important islands are about twelve in number,
of which Pomona, or the Mainland, is decidedly the
largest. Kirkwall, the chief town, contains upwards of
3000 inhabitants. The most important public building
is St. Magnus's Cathedral, a stately pile, which was

founded about the year 1138, and is still quite entire. There are also some interesting remains of the Bishop's Palace, and of the Earl's Palace, built by the infamous Patrick Stuart, who obtained the earldom in 1600. The general aspect of the country is bare and dreary, and there is a total absence of trees. In some places, however, the land is fertile, and produces good crops. The herring fishery has greatly increased of late, and straw-plaiting for bonnets is carried on to a considerable extent. The total amount received in Orkney, in 1833, for the exports of farm produce, manufactures, fisheries, &c. was £60,114.

The SHETLAND or ZETLAND ISLES, supposed to be the *Ultima Thule* of the ancients, are separated from the Orkneys by a channel 48 miles across. They exceed 100 in number, but of these only between 30 and 40 are inhabited. " The climate," says Dr. Edmonstone, a native of the county, " is very variable and damp, although by no means generally unwholesome to the inhabitants. Spring can scarcely be said to commence until April, and there is but little general warmth before the middle of June. The summer terminates for the most part with August, though sometimes it continues through September. Autumn is a very uncertain period, and winter commences with the middle of October, and occupies the remaining months of the year." Lerwick, which is the capital, contains about 2700 inhabitants. In the Lowlands it would be only entitled to the name of a thriving village, very irregularly built. " The opposite island of Bressay forms Bressay Sound, one of the finest harbours in the world, and the rendezvous of all the vessels destined for the north, and the whale fishery. Off Bressay is the most remarkable of the rock phenomena

of Shetland ; the Noss, a small high island, with a flat
summit, girt on all sides by perpendicular walls of rock."[*]
It is only 500 feet in length, and 170 broad, and rises
abruptly from the sea to the height of 160 feet. The
communication with the coast of Bressay is maintained
by strong ropes stretched across, along which a cradle or
wooden chair is run, in which the passenger is seated.
It is of a size sufficient for conveying across a man and
a sheep at a time. The purpose of this strange contrivance is to give the tenant the benefit of putting a few
sheep upon the Holm, the top of which is level, and
affords good pasture. The animals are transported in
the cradle, one at a time, a shepherd holding them upon
his knees in crossing.

NOSS HOLM, SHETLAND.

" The temptation of getting access to the numberless
eggs and young of the sea-fowl which whiten the surface
of the Holm, joined to the promised reward of a cow,
induced a hardy and adventurous fowler, about two centuries ago, to scale the cliff of the Holm, and establish a
connection by ropes with the neighbouring main island.
Having driven two stakes into the rock, and fastened his

* Murray's Encyclopædia of Geography. Lond. 1834.

ropes, the desperate man was entreated to avail himself
of the communication thus established in returning across
the gulf. But this he refused to do, and, in attempting
to descend the way he had climbed, he fell, and perished
by his fool-hardiness." *

There are scarcely any roads in Shetland, and travelling is usually performed on those hardy, spirited little
horses known by the name of *shelties,* which are bred
in Shetland, and are exported in considerable numbers.

SHETLAND PONEY.

The trade and exports of Shetland are much the same
as those of Orkney. These islands formerly belonged to
the kingdom of Denmark, but, in 1468, on the marriage
of James III. with the Princess Margaret of Denmark,
they were given in pledge for the payment of her dowry,
and have never since been disjoined from Scotland. They
were at various times bestowed by the Crown on different persons, some of whom subjected the inhabitants to
great oppressions. At length, in 1707, James Earl of

* Anderson's Guide to the Highlands.

Morton obtained them from the Crown in mortgage, which was rendered irredeemable in 1742, and in 1766 he sold the estate for £60,000 to Sir Lawrence Dundas, the ancestor of the Earl of Zetland, their present proprietor.

ITINERARY.

I. EDINBURGH.—GALASHIELS.—MELROSE.—JEDBURGH.—51 MILES.

ON RIGHT FROM EDIN.	From Jed.	EDINBURGH.	From Edin.	ON LEFT FROM EDIN.
		Leave Edinburgh by New-ington.		
Grange House, Sir Thos. ck Lauder, Bart.	49	Powburn.	2	
	48	Libberton vill. & Kirk.	3	
	47	Gilmerton.	4	Eldin, —— Clerk, Esq.
In the neighbourhood is slin Castle and Chapel.	45	Lasswade.	6	Melville Castle, Lord Melville.
Hawthornden, once the at of Drummond the	43	cr. South Esk.	8	Newbattle Abbey, Marquis of Lothian.
et; under the house are veral curious caves.	42	Dalhousie. Kirkhill vill. & Kirk.	9	Powder Mills, the oldest in Scotland.
Dalhousie Castle, Earl of lhousie, an ancient seat odernised.	39¾	Fushie Bridge.	11¼	Ruins of Borthwick Castle, with Borthwick Kirk. The Castle is very entire, and was inhabited for a short time in 1567 by Queen Mary and Bothwell.
	38	Middleton.	13	
Arniston, —— Dundas, q.	31	Crookston.		
Heriot House.		cr. Heriot Water.		
Heriot Kirk and Manse. Bowland, —— Walker, q.	27	cr. Crookston Wat.		
		Gala bank Inn.	24	
		Torsonce Inn.	25	Crookston House, —— Borthwick, Esq.
Torwoodlee and Fernie-, —— Pringle, Esq.	25½	Stow vill.	25½	Pirn, —— Tait, Esq.
Galashiels is separated om this line of road by e Gala, which joins the weed about a mile below.	20½	Buckholm Farm. Laudhopeburn House.	30½	
Gala House, —— Scott, q.		Langhaugh.		Langlee House, —— Bruce, Esq.
Across the river may be en Abbotsford, the seat Sir Walter Scott.		cr. Allan Water.		Pavillion, L. Somerville. The vale of the Allan is supposed to be the "Glendearg" of the Monastery.
Melrose Abbey, the fin-t specimen of Gothic chitecture in Scotland.	15	cr. Tweed. Darnick vill.		
In St. Boswell's Village great annual fair is held the 18th of July for rses, cattle, sheep, &c.	13	MELROSE. Eildon vill.	36	Near Melrose are the Eildon Hills, on which are the remains of Roman Camps.
Ancrum House, Sir Wm. ott, Bart.	10	Newton, Dryburgh. St. Boswell's.	38 / 41	Dryburgh Abbey is beautifully situated on the left bank of the Tweed. Sir Walter Scott was interred here. Farther down the Tweed is Mertoun, the seat of Lord Polwarth.
Near Ancrum the Battle Lilliards Edge was ught in 1545, where a dy of English troops, nder Lord Evers and Sir rian Latoun, were completely defeated by the arl of Angus.	3 / 2	Ancrum, where the Ale joins the Teviot. Teviot Bridge. cr. Teviot. Bonjedward. cr. Jed Water. JEDBURGH.	48 / 49 / 51	Near Ancrum the Roman road from York to the Firth of Forth passes.

edburgh is situated on the west bank of the Jed, in the midst of a country beautifully ooded. It is a royal burgh of very ancient erection, and was one of the chief Border towns, d a place of considerable importance before the Union. After that period its trade was, a great measure, destroyed; it has now, however, greatly revived. The remains of the obey form the principal object of curiosity in Jedburgh. It was founded either in 1118 or 47, and, after various damages in the course of the Border wars, was burnt by the Earl of ertford in 1545. It is a magnificent ruin, and is considered the most perfect and beau-ul specimen of the Saxon and early Gothic in Scotland. Part of the west end is fitted up a parish church. The Castle of Jedburgh, situated on an eminence at the town head, was fortress of very great strength. The ground is now occupied by a Jail. The environs of dburgh abound in rich woodland scenes. Some remains of the famous ancient forest are be seen in the neighbourhood of the half ruined castle of Ferniehirst, belonging to the arquis of Lothian, and the original seat of his ancestors, the Kers. Jedburgh contains ove 4000 inhabitants, and joins with Haddington, North Berwick, Dunbar, and Lauder, in ecting a member of Parliament.

II. EDINBURGH.—DALKEITH.—LAUDER.—KELSO.—42 Miles.

On right from Edin.	From Kelso.	EDINBURGH. Leave Edinburgh by Hope Park Chapel.	From Edin.	On left from Edin.
	41¾	Gibbet Toll.	¼	
Inch, Little Gilmour, Esq.	41	Salisbury Green.	1	
	40¾	cr. Pow Burn.	1¼	Ruins of Craigmillar Castle, a residence of Queen Mary.
Said to have acquired its name from the French attendants of Queen Mary.	39½	Little France.	2½	
Drum, Miss Innes, formerly a seat of the Somerville family.	36	cr. N. Esk River and enter Dalkeith.	6	Population 5596; votes with the county for M.P.
Melville Castle, Lord Melville.		cr. South Esk.	6¼	Dalkeith Palace and grounds, Duke of Buccleuch.
Newbattle Abbey, Marquis of Lothian.	32	Cranstoun Kirk.	9	Oxenford Castle, Sir J. Dalrymple.
Near Crichton Castle, once the residence of Chancellor Crichton.	30	Pathhead.	10½	
		cr. Fala Water. Fala vill.		
	27	Blackshiels Inn.	15	Soutra Hill, 1209 feet above the level of the sea, where there was once an hospital built in 1164 by Malcolm IV.
		cr. Soutra.		
		Enter Berwickshire.		
		cr. Red Brae.		
		cr. Channelkirk Burn.		
	20¾	Carfrae Mill Inn.	21	
	20½	cr. Leader Wat.		
Lauder is a royal burgh. Population 2063. Joins with Haddington, North Berwick, Dunbar, and Jedburgh in electing M.P.	16¾	LAUDER.	25¼	Cochrane, Earl of Mar, and other favourites of James V. were hanged by the factious nobles over Lauder bridge.
		cr. Leader Wat.		
	14¼	Thirlestane.	27¾	Close beside Lauder stands Thirlestane Castle, an ancient and spacious edifice, the seat of the Earl of Lauderdale.
—— Spottiswoode, Esq. lineal descendant of Archbishop Spottiswoode the historian.	12¾	Spottiswood.	29	
	12½	Whitburn Inn.	29¼	
	10¾	Legerwood Kirk.	31¼	Hume Castle seen on a height to the left. Also Mellerstain House, Geo. Baillie, Esq. of Jerviswood.
The original residence of the Gordon family, and from which their title of Duke was derived.	7¾	Gordon Kirk, and vill. of West Gordon.	34¼	
		cr. Eden.		
The scene of the boyhood of Sir Walter Scott.	6¾	Smailholm vill. and Tower.	35¼	
	4	Nenthorn vill. & Kirk.	38	Nenthorn House, Ro. Esq.; formerly possessed by a branch of the powerful family of the Kers.
Fleurs, Duke of Roxburghe.		cr. Eden.		
		KELSO.	42	

Kelso is a handsome town, containing a spacious square or market-place, in which stand the town-house, and many elegant houses and shops. The Tweed is here crossed by a handsome bridge of Rennie's construction, from which the view, looking westward, and taking in Fleurs the seat of the Duke of Roxburghe, is extremely beautiful. Kelso Abbey is well deserving of attention for its venerable antiquity, and the purity of its Saxon architecture. It was founded in 1128 by David I. who dedicated it to the Virgin Mary and St. John, and endowed it with immense possessions and privileges. In this Abbey James III. was crowned in 1460. The ruins of Roxburgh Castle, so celebrated in Scottish history, are situated about a mile from Kelso, near the junction of the Tweed and Teviot. Kelso contains above 4000 inhabitants: it votes with the county for M.P.

III. EDINBURGH.—SELKIRK.—HAWICK.—LONGTOWN.—85¾ Miles.

On right from Edin.	From Longtown		From Edin.	On left from Edin.
		For the space between Edinburgh and Galashiels, 30½ miles, see No. 1. A new road from Galashiels to Selkirk was formed in 1829, now crossing the Tweed and Ettrick by two handsome bridges. It leaves the old road at Crosslee toll-bar, three miles from Galashiels.		
A little above Yair is Ashiestiel, formerly the residence of Sir W. Scott.	53	Whitebank.	29	
		cr. Gala Water.		
Near Selkirk is Bowhill, a seat of the Duke of Buccleuch.	50	cr. Tweed at Yair Bridge.	32	
	49	Sunderland.	33	Sunderland Hall, Plomer.
Philiphaugh, a plain to the north of the junction of the Ettrick and Yarrow, was the scene of the famous battle between the army of the Marquis of Montrose, and a body of horse commanded by General Leslie, in which the former was completely defeated.	46	cr. Ettrick Wat. and enter SELKIRK. Immediately beyond Selkirk, pass the Haining, —— Pringle, Esq.	39¼	Selkirk is a royal burgh, containing a population of 1800. A band of Selkirk burgesses behaved with great gallantry at Flodden. A standard was taken by them, which is still preserved by the corporation. A great business in shoemaking was formerly carried on. The electors of Selkirk vote with those of the county.
	41	cr. Ale Water.	44¼	
Wool, Scott, Esq.	40½	Ashkirk.	44¾	Sinton, Scott, Esq.
Thirlestane, Lord Napier.				
Wilton House, across the Teviot.	34½	Wilton Kirk.	50¼	
Near Hawick, on the banks of the Teviot, stands Branxholm Castle, belonging to the Duke of Buccleuch, and the chief scene of the Lay of the Last Minstrel.	34	cr. the Teviot, and enter HAWICK.	50¾	Population, 4970; a remarkably active manufacturing town, chiefly producing hosiery. Votes with the county.
		Junction of Borthwick and Teviot.		
	32	cr. the Teviot.	52¾	Goldiland's Tower, celebrated in Border ballads.
Here Johnny Armstrong and his men were hanged by the summary justice of James V.	26	Carlinrig Ch. in ruins.	58¾	
	22	Mosspaul Inn.	63¾	On the heights where the counties of Roxburgh and Dumfries meet.
Mickledale, Beatty, Esq.	16	Ewes Kirk.	69¾	
Langholm Lodge, a minor seat of the Duke of Buccleuch.		cr. Ewes Bridge.		
	11¼	Langholm vill.	73¾	Broomholm, —— Maxwell, Esq.
	9½	cr. Esk River.	75½	The banks of the Esk are here romantically beautiful.
Near Hollows is Gilnockie Tower, the ruined stronghold of Johnny Armstrong.	8	Hollows vill.	77	
		cr. Canobie Wat.	78	
	6	Canobie vill.	79	
	3½	Scots Dyke toll-bar, Where English ground commences.	81½	Across the Esk is Netherby, the beautiful seat of Sir James Graham.
	2½	Kirk Andrews.	82½	
		cr. the Esk, and enter LONGTOWN.	85¾	

IV. EDINBURGH.—MUSSELBURGH.—HADDINGTON.—DUNBAR.—BERWICK.
57½ Miles.

ON RIGHT FROM EDIN.	From Berwick	EDINBURGH.	From Edin.	ON LEFT FROM EDIN.
		Leave Edinburgh by Regent Bridge.		
Fine view of Arthur's Seat and St. Anthony's Chapel.		**Jock's Lodge.** Portobello. Duddingstone Salt Pans.	3	Restalrig. Lochend House. Piershill Barracks, with accommodation for 10 Cavalry.
New Hailes, Miss Dalrymple. Pinkie House, Sir John Hope, near the spot where the battle of Pinkie was fought in 1547.	52	cr. Esk Bridge. **Fisherrow and** MUSSELBURGH.	5½ 6	Portobello, much sorted to by the inhabitants of Edinburgh for sea-bathing. Musselburgh Race course, upon which the Edinburgh Races are run annually.
Coalston, Earl of Dalhousie.	48	Tranent.	10	On the coast, Prestonpans village.
Lennox Love, L. Blantyre. In Haddington the chief object of interest is the old Franciscan Church. Here, according to some writers, John Knox was born.	45 41	Gladsmuir. HADDINGTON. A royal burgh; population 5583.	13 17	Gosford House, Earl of Wemyss. The battle of Preston, in which the Royal troops under Sir John Cope, were defeated by the Highlanders under Prince Charles Stuart, was fought in this neighbourhood. The house of Colonel Gardiner, and the spot where he fell, as well as the tree under which Prince Charles stood during the battle, are still pointed out.
Amisfield, E. of Wemyss. Ruins of Hailes Castle, the seat of the Earl of Bothwell, husband of Queen Mary.	37½ 35½	Hailes. Linton. cr. River Tyne.	20½ 22½	
A mile to the south is Traprain Law.	33¾	Gateside Inn.	24	
Biel, Mrs. Ferguson Nisbet.	31½	West Barns. cr. Belton Water.	26	
Belton Place, —— Hay, Esq.		Belhaven vill.		A short distance from Dunbar is Broxmouth, a large mansion of the Duke of Roxburghe, surrounded with wood.
Lochend House, Sir G. Warrender, Bart.	29¾	DUNBAR.	28	
Two celebrated battles have been fought in the neighbourhood of Dunbar, the first in 1296, when the Scotch were defeated by the English under Earl Warren, and the second in 1650, when they were defeated by Cromwell.	27 26¼ 24¾ 22½	East Barns vill. cr. Dryburn Wat. Thornton Bridge. cr. Innerwick Wat. cr. Dunglas Burn, and enter Berwickshire.	30¾ 31½ 33 35½	The ruins of Dunbar Castle, about 300 yards west of the town. Here Edward II. found refuge after his defeat at Bannockburn. To the north of the town is Dunbar House, a seat of the Earl of Lauderdale.
Dunglas House, Sir John Hall, Bart. situated amidst beautiful plantations. It stands on the site of an old castle which was originally a strong fortress of the Earls of Home.	18½ 16½ 12½	cr. Penmanshiel Bridge. cr. Peas Burn. Grant's Inn. Houndwood.	39½ 41½ 45½	A little below, on the old road, is the celebrated Peas Bridge, consisting of two arches 300 feet long and 240 feet in height, supported in the centre by one of the loftiest piers in the world.
Houndwood House, Mrs. Coulson, said to have been a hunting seat of the Scottish monarchs.	7½ 6¾	Ayton vill. cr. Ay Water. Fleemington.	50 51	
Remains of Lamerton Kirk, where James IV. of Scotland was married by proxy to Margaret, eldest daughter of Henry VII. of England.	3	Liberties of Berwick. BERWICK.	55 58	

The town of Berwick is more remarkable for its historical recollections than for its present importance. It is 23 miles distant from Kelso, and 58 from Edinburgh, and is a respectable looking town, containing about 8000 or 10,000 inhabitants. It is still surrounded by its ancient walls, which only of late years ceased to be regularly fortified. Its principal trade is the export of salmon.

V. EDINBURGH.—LINLITHGOW.—FALKIRK.—STIRLING.—35¼ MILES.

ON RIGHT FROM EDIN.	From Stirling.	EDINBURGH.	From Edin.	ON LEFT FROM EDIN.
		Leave Edinr. by west end of Prince's Street.		
Corstorphine Hill, richly wooded and studded with gentlemen's seats and villas.	33¾	cr. Coltbridge.	1	
	33¼	cr. Water of Leith.	2	
	31¼	Corstorphine vill.	4	On the right bank of the Almond, before crossing the bridge, is a rude monument, called the Catstane, commemorative of a battle fought in 995.
	27¾	cr. Almond Water, and enter Linlithgowshire.	7½	
	26¼	Kirkliston vill.	9	
At Winchburgh, Edward II. first halted after his defeat at Bannockburn.	23¾	Winchburgh vill.	11½	Ruins of Niddry Castle, where Queen Mary first slept after her escape from Lochleven.
		cr. Union Canal.		
	22¼	Three-Mile-Town.	13	Linlithgow Bridge was the scene of a battle fought between the Earls of Arran and Lennox in the minority of James V.
Champfleurie, Johnston of Straiton.		cr. Haugh-burn.		
Linlithgow, a town of great antiquity. In its streets the Regent Moray was shot. The palace is the chief object of interest. In it Queen Mary was born. The church is a fine specimen of Gothic architecture.	18½	LINLITHGOW.	16¾	
	17¼	cr. Avon by Linlithgow Bridge and enter Stirlingshire.	18	Callander Ho., Forbes, Esq., formerly the seat of the Earl of Kilmarnock.
	14	Polmont vill.	21¼	Falkirk, an ancient town, celebrated for a defeat sustained in its neighbourhood by Wallace, in a battle with Edward I. Also the scene of an engagement between the rebel and the royal armies in 1746, when the latter was defeated. The town has now acquired a more peaceful celebrity, by its trysts or cattle markets. At a short distance from the village of Bannockburn, is the field of Bannockburn, where Robert Bruce, with 30,000 men, defeated Edward II. with 100,000. At Milton, in the same neighbourhood, is the scene of James Third's assassination after his defeat at Sauchie.
		cr. Castle Water.		
	13½	Lauriston.	21¾	
		cr. Burn Water.		
	10¾	FALKIRK.	24	
	10¼	cr. under Canal.	25	
A mile from Camelon the Carron Iron Works are easily distinguishable by the smoke and flames.	9¼	Camelon vill.	26	
		cr. Carron Water.		
	8¼	Larbert.	27	
At Torwood stood the tree in which Wallace used to conceal himself when hard pressed by his enemies. Here Mr. Cargill, in 1680, excommunicated King Charles II. the Duke of York, and the Ministry.	6¼	Torwood.	29	
	1¾	Bannockburn vill.	33½	
		cr. Bannockburn.		
	1	St. Ninian's vill.	34¼	
		STIRLING.	35¼	

The central and original part of Stirling bears an appearance rather antique than elegant, but there are several good streets, and a great number of neat villas in the outskirts. The church is a handsome old Gothic fabric, and includes two places of worship called the East and West Churches. The former was erected by Cardinal Beaton, the latter by James IV, in 1494. The celebrated Ebenezer Erskine, founder of the Secession Church, was for some time minister of the West Church.

The most conspicuous object in Stirling is the Castle. It was a favourite residence of the Scottish monarchs, and a stronghold of great importance. Many events of historical interest are associated with this fortress. Here James II. murdered William Earl of Douglas for refusing to withdraw himself from a rebellious association with other Scottish nobles; in revenge for which the friends of Douglas burnt the town. Here also James IV. was born, and James V. crowned. The prospect of the surrounding country from the castle is magnificent, combining every element of beauty and of grandeur. A visit to Demyat, one of the Ochils, will amply repay the labour of the tourist, as this hill commands one of the noblest views any where to be met with.

*** Tourists proceeding from Stirling to Callander and the Trosachs, are referred to page 204 for a description of the route.

VI. EDINBURGH.—PEEBLES.—MOFFAT.—DUMFRIES.—74 Miles.

ON RIGHT FROM EDIN.	From Dumfries	EDINBURGH. The road leaves Edinburgh by Nicolson Street.	From Edin.	ON LEFT FROM EDIN
Morton Hall, —— Trotter, Esq.	72	Powburn.	2	At a little distance, the ruins of Craigmillar Castle, Gracemount, Mrs. Hay, St. Catherine's, Sir Wm Rae.
Burdiehouse House, a corruption of Bourdeaux House, some French Protestants having emigrated hither from Bourdeaux after the revocation of the edict of Nantes in 1685.	71 70½ 69 68	Libberton Kirk. Burdiehouse. Straiton vill. Pass Bilston Toll-bar, where road to Roslin parts off to left.	3 3½ 5 6	Near Straiton was fought the second of three conflicts which took place in one day in 1303, styled the battle of Roslin.
At a little distance, Woodhouselee, F. Tytler, Esq. Glencorse House and Church.	67 64	Greenlaw. Auchindinny. Penicuik.	7 10	Dryden House, G. Meikar, Esq. Built as a depot for French prisoners during the late war.
Penicuik, Ho., Sir George Clerk, Bart.	63 62	cr. North Esk. Wellington Inn.	11 12	
Where the direct road to Dumfries parts off on the right. Early Vale.	61 60	Leadburn Inn. Kingside Edge. cr. Eddleston Wat.	13 14	Pass through a considerable tract of moorish country. Close to the village of Darnhall, a seat of Lord Elibank.
	56	Eddleston vill.	18	
An ancient royal burgh beautifully situated on the Tweed. Population of the parish 2750. Votes with the county for a Member of Parliament. From this is six miles along the north bank of the Tweed to Innerleithen, a village much resorted to for its mineral springs, and for rural recreations.	52 51 49 46½ 46 44½ 42½	PEEBLES. cr. Lyne Wat. Stobo Kirk. Stobo Castle, Montgomery, Bart. New Posso, Nasmyth, Bart.	22 23 25 27½ 28 29½	A little beyond is the Cottage, Mackenzie Portmore, Esq. On the left Nidpath Castle, nearly in ruins, a most romantic situation. Barns, Burnet, Esq. Across the Tweed, the Vale of Manor, in which lived David Ritchie, the original of the Black Dwarf.
Drummelzier Castle was formerly the property of the powerful family of Tweedie, from whom it went to the family of the Hays. It is now the property of White, Esq.	37 28 21	Drummelzier Kirk. Crook Inn. Tweed Shaws. cr. Annan.	31½ 37 46 48	Oliver Castle Ruins Tweedie, Esq. Polmood House, Captain Forbes. On the left, the remarkable hollow called the Devil's Beeftsand.
		MOFFAT.	53	Moffat is a pleasant town, noted for its medicinal waters. Populated about 1400.
There is another road from Edinburgh to Moffat and Dumfries, which leads by the Pentland Hills, Glencross, Linton, and Broughton villages, and joins the other road about 31 miles from Edinburgh. The distance between Edinburgh and Dumfries by this road is 71 miles.	19½ 17½ 6½ 5 3	Beatock Inn. Kirkpatrick Juxta. cr. Water of Æ. Amisfield House, with the old ruined tower of Amisfield. Tinwald Kirk. DUMFRIES.	54½ 56½ 67½ 69 71 74	Amisfield is the seat of the ancient family of Charteris. Tinwald was the birthplace of Paterson, the projector of the banks of England and Scotland, and likewise of the Scottish expedition to Darien.

Dumfries was made a royal burgh in the thirteenth century. It contains few monuments of antiquity, except an excellent bridge of three arches, which has stood for nearly 900 years. The most interesting circumstance connected with Dumfries is its having been the residence and burial place of Burns. St. Michael's church yard contains an extraordinary number of monuments of fine proportions and decorations. Dumfries unites with Annan, Kirkcudbright, Lochmaben, and Sanquhar, in returning a Member of Parliament. Population 11,606.

VII. EDINBURGH.—MID CALDER.—STRATHAVEN.—GALSTON.— KILMARNOCK.—AYR.—72 MILES.

ON RIGHT FROM EDIN.	From Ayr.	EDINBURGH. Leave the city by Princes St.	From Edin.	ON LEFT FROM EDIN.
Near Merchiston Ho., Walker, Esq.	69½	Gorgie Mills. cr. Wat. of Leith. Loanend.	½	Dalry House, Walker, Esq.
Saughton Hall, Baird, Bart.	66	Long Hermandston vill.	6	Riccarton, Sir James Gibson-Craig, Bart.
Saughton, Watson, Esq.	64	Addiston. } Earl of		
	63½	Dalmahoy. } Morton.	7½	
		cr. Gogar Burn.		
Hatton, Captain Davidson; formerly a residence of the Lauderdale family.	63	Burn Wynd Inn.	9	
	61½	Wester Cocksiedean.	10¼	
The Church of Mid Calder is a fine specimen of an old parochial place of worship in the Gothic style. The father of Archbishop Spottiswoode officiated here, being Minister of Calder.	60	East Calder. MID CALDER. From Mid Calder proceeds also the southern line of road to Glasgow. See No. XIII. cr. Almond Wat.	12	Close to Mid Calder is Calder House, the seat of Lord Torphichen, where John Knox preached, and where the only authentic portrait of him exists. The scenery around Mid Calder is of a very romantic description.
	55½	West Calder vill. Here commences an extensive moor, unenlivened by any object of interest. At length, after passing near the extensive iron work of Shotts, the road begins to descend by the minor vale of Calder into the valley of the Clyde.	16½	
A new road leads from this to Strathaven, crossing the Clyde by the Garion Bridge; another road, somewhat less direct, leads by Hamilton. The former is used by the stage coaches to Ayr.	44	Allanton, Lady Seton Stuart.	28	
	43	Bonkill.	29	
	42	Newmains Inn. On left of Garion Bridge the vill. of Dalserf.	30	The road now passes over a long tract of moorish land, enlivened only by the towering form of Loudon Hill, where Ayrshire is entered.
		Stonehouse vill.		
Wallace's Cairn, marking the scene of a conflict between that hero and a party of English.	32	STRATHAVEN.	40	
	22	Priestland.	50	
	21	Darvel vill.	51	The more direct road to Ayr from this point, leads by Fail and St. Quivox, saving two miles.
A mile and a half to the right is Drumclog, the scene of the battle of that name, in May 1679, in which Claverhouse was defeated by the Covenanters.	17	Newmills vill.	55	Kilmarnock is eminent as a seat of various branches of woollen manufacture. It now rivals Kidderminster in the manufacture of carpets. The cotton manufacture has also been introduced with marked success, and the town now produces shawls, gauzes, and muslins of the finest quality. The external appearance of Kilmarnock is very pleasing.
	12	GALSTON.		
	11	KILMARNOCK. cr. Irvine Water, and pass through	60	
London Castle, the magnificent seat of the Marquis of Hastings.			61	
		Riccarton vill.		
	7	Symington Kirk.	65	
For the Description of Ayr, see No. XVIII.	4	Monkton vill.	68	
	2¾	Priestwick vill.	69¼	
		AYR.	72	

VIII. EDINBURGH.—CARNWATH.—DOUGLAS MILL.—CUMNOCK.—AYR.—76¾ M.

ON RIGHT FROM EDIN.	From Ayr.	EDINBURGH. Leave the city by the Lothian Road and Port-Hopetoun.	From Edin.	ON LEFT FROM EDIN.
Merchiston Castle, Lord Napier.				Craig Ho., Gordon.
		Pass under the Union Canal.		
Baberton, Christie. Charles X. and his family occupied this house for some time as shooting quarters.	73¾	Slateford vill.	3	Overhung by a splendid aqueduct bridge of the Union Canal, which here crosses the Water of Leith.
	70¾	Currie vill.	6	
	69	Ravelrig.	7¾	At a little distance on the left, Colinton village.
At a little distance, Riccarton, Gibson-Craig, Bart. Lumphoy Castle, ruins. Malleny, General Scott. Dalmahoy Crags, 866 feet above the sea. Meadowbank, Maconochie, Lord Meadowbank.	65¾	Little Vantage Inn.	11	Lennox Castle in ruins on a fine situation, commanding an extensive view. It has been a place of great strength.
	64¾	Morton Castle Ruins.	12	
	62¾	Causewayend Inn.	14	
	61¾	cr. Linhouse Wat.	15	
	59¼	Crosswood Hill.	17½	Easter Colzium, Linning, Esq.
		cr. Dryburn Burn.		For many miles before and after this point, the road passes over a dreary moor.
	54¾	cr. Medwen Wat.	22	
	51¾	Carnwath vill.	25	
	48¼	Carstairs vill.	28½	Kersewell, Capt. Bertram.
Carnwath Ho., Macdonald Lockhart, Bart.	47¼	Ravenstruther Toll.	29½	Carstairs Ho., Monteith, Esq.
		cr. Clyde.		At the distance of 3 miles is Lanark, an ancient royal burgh; population of the parish 7672. The falls
	44¾	Hyndford Bridge Inn.	32	
	41¼	Hecklebirny.	35½	of the Clyde at Bonnington and Cora are about 2 miles
Here was the original seat of the family of Douglas. In the vicinity of the town stands Douglas Castle, a seat of Lord Douglas. A part of the old church is still kept in repair, on account of the monuments in it and the burying vault.	38¼	Douglas Mill Inn.	38½	from Lanark, approached by a road leading through New Lanark village, where the celebrated cotton mills formerly conducted by Mr. Robert Owen, are to be seen.
	36¼	Douglas.	40½	
		cr. Douglas Wat.		
	25¾	Muirkirk.	51	Between Cumnock and Muirkirk lies the extensive morass denominated Air Moss, where, on July
		Muirmill Bridge.		
Cumnock is celebrated for the manufacture of those curious little cabinets known by the name of Cumnock snuff-boxes.	20¾	cr. Ayr Wat.	56	1680, a skirmish took place between a body of dragoons commanded by Bruce of Earlshall, and sixty-four Covenanters, under the conduct of Hackstoun of Rathillet and Mr. Richard Cameron.
	15¼	CUMNOCK.	61½	
	9¾	Ochiltree.	67	
		cr. Burnock Wat.	.	
	5¾	Drongan House.	71	
For the Description of Ayr, see No. XVIII.	4¾	cr. Kyle Wat.	72¾	
	1	Shawwood.	75¾	
		AYR.	76¾	

IX.—EDINBURGH.—QUEENSFERRY.—INVERKEITHING.—KINROSS.—
PERTH.—44 MILES.

ON RIGHT FROM EDIN.	From Perth.	EDINBURGH.	From Edinb.	ON LEFT FROM EDIN.
		Leave Edinburgh by Queensferry road.		
St Bernard's Well. Dean House, Sir J. Nisbet. Craigleith Park, Bonar, Esq. Craigleith Quarry.		cr. Water of Leith by Dean Bridge, a superb edifice of four arches, each 90 feet in span.		The old road passes between John Watson's Hospital, and the Orphan Hospital; both buildings of great elegance. Ravelston, Lady Murray Keith.
Barnton, W. R. Ramsay, Esq.	40	Barnton.	4	Craigcrook, Lord Jeffrey. Craigiehall, Hope Vere, Esq.
Village of Cramond on the shore to the right.	39	cr. Almond by Cramond Bridge.	5	Dalmeny Kirk.
Dalmeny Park, Earl Rosebery.		Hawes Inn.		
A little to the south are the ruins of Dundas Castle, a building of great antiquity, which has been in the Dundas family upwards of 700 years.	35	QUEENSFERRY. Cross Ferry.	9	Queensferry was erected into a royal burgh by Malcolm Canmore, and derived its name from Margaret his Queen, sister of Edgar Atheling. Here are the ruins of a monastery of Carmelite Friars, erected in 1330.
	33¾	North Queensferry Inn.	10¼	
Donnibrissel House, Earl of Moray. Donnibrissel House was the scene, in 1592, of the murder of the Earl of Moray by the Marquis of Huntly. This melancholy event is commemorated in the ballad of "The bonnie Erle of Moray."	31¼	INVERKEITHING. Crossgates.	12½	A very ancient royal burgh, erected, it is said, by William the Lion. The bay is large and safe. Great quantities of coal and salt are annually exported here. Population, 3189.
	27		17	
Fordel, Sir J. Henderson. Lochgelly, Earl of Minto. Lochore, Sir Walter Scott.	25	Cowden Beath Inn.	19	
		cr. Orr.		Kirk of Beath.
		cr. Kelty Water.		Maryburgh, the birth-place of the two brothers Adam, the distinguished architects.
		Benarty Hill.		Blair - Adam, Sir C. Adam, M.P.
	10	Gairney Bridge hamlet.	25	
	17	KINROSS. Population, 2017.	27	
Burleigh Castle.	15	Milnathort.	29	
Kinross is situated on the beautiful banks of Lochleven. Lochleven Castle, remarkable for its great antiquity, and as being the place where Queen Mary was imprisoned. The trout produced in Lochleven are of acknowledged excellence.	11½	Damhead Inn.	32¾	The road now enters Glenfarg, a beautiful little valley, enclosed by the Ochils. To the right Abernethy, the capital of the Pictish kingdom.
	4	Bridge of Earn.	40	In the neighbourhood of Bridge of Earn is Pitcaithly Well, celebrated for its medicinal waters.
		Moncrief Hill, On whose shoulder the traveller first comes in sight of Perth.		
		PERTH.	44	

Perth is one of the handsomest and most ancient towns in Scotland. It is beautifully situated on the west bank of the Tay, having the spacious plains of the North and South Inches extending on each side. On account of its importance, and its vicinity to the royal Palace of Scone, it was long considered the capital of Scotland, before Edinburgh acquired that distinction. Here, too, the Parliaments and national assemblies were held, and many of the nobility took up their residence. A splendid bridge of ten arches, and 900 feet in length, leads across the Tay to the north. Perth contains several beautiful streets and terraces, and a number of splendid public buildings. It is peculiarly rich in objects of historic and picturesque interest. Of Gowrie House, the scene of a well known mysterious incident in Scottish history, most unfortunately not a vestige remains. In Blackfriars Monastery, which once stood at the north side of the town, James I. was assassinated by a band of conspirators. The principal and oldest public building is St John's Church, in which the demolitions of the Reformation commenced, in consequence of a sermon preached by John Knox.

X. PERTH.—CUPAR-ANGUS—FORFAR.—BRECHIN.—STONEHAVEN.—
67 Miles.

ON RIGHT FROM PERTH.	From Stonehaven.	PERTH. Leave Perth by Bridgend.	From Perth.	ON LEFT FROM PERTH.
	65¼	Pass through Scone vill.	2	Scone Palace, Earl of Mansfield. It is a heavy modern building, occupying the site of the ancient palace, where the kings of Scotland at an early period used to be crowned. In the modern house much of the old furniture has been preserved. At the north side of the house is a small eminence said to have been composed of earth from the estates of the different barons who here attended the early kings. About 50 yards from the house there is an old aisle, the last remaining portion of the Abbey of Scone.
Dunsinnane Hill, on the top of which the circumvallations of what is said to have been Macbeth's Castle may still be traced. It commands an extensive view.	61¾	St. Martin's vill.	5¼	
	60½	Dunsinnane.—Nairn.	6½	
		The road now passes through the valley of Strathmore, having on the right the Sidlaw Hills, on the left the Grampians.		
Belonging to Lord Willoughby D'Eresby.	57	Burrelton vill.	9½	
Cupar-Angus is a neat town of about 6000 inhabitants, situated on the border of Forfarshire, and partly within Perthshire.	54	CUPAR-ANGUS.	13	
Belmont Castle, Lord Wharncliffe.	50½	Junction of the Isla and Ericht.	16½	Kinloch—Kinloch, Esq. Here is obtained a fine view of Strathmore.
Meigle is remarkable on account of some very antique monuments in the church-yard, which the common people assert to denote the grave of Queen Vanore, the wife of King Arthur. The stones bear a variety of hieroglyphical figures with representations of animals and men.	48	Meigle vill.	19	
	43½	Essie Kirk.	23½	
	41¼	Glammis vil.	25¾	The celebrated Castle of Glammis, the seat of the Earl of Strathmore, is situated within a park of 160 acres. It is an edifice of princely and antique appearance. Glammis was the scene of the murder of Malcolm II. in 1034. The armoury contains a vast assortment of ancient armour. The rooms contain about 100 portraits of great value. The view to be obtained from the *leads* of the Castle is splendid and extensive.
Forfar, the county town of Forfarshire has a pleasant appearance. It is a burgh of great antiquity, and was a royal residence in the time of Malcolm Canmore. About a mile to the east of Forfar stand the ruins of the ancient Priory of Restennet, one of the three churches founded in Scotland by Boniface at the beginning of the 7th century.	36	FORFAR. Popularly denominated "Brosie Forfar."	31	
	30	Finhaven Castle ruins.	37	
		☞ cr. South Esk.		
	25¾	Cariston.	41¼	Finhaven Castle, the once magnificent residence of the powerful family of Lindsay, is an object much visited by the tourist.
The ancient royal burgh of Brechin is romantically situated on some high ground overhanging the north bank of the South Esk. The Cathedral was a stately Gothic fabric 166 feet in length and 61 broad. Brechin was one of the seats of the Culdees. (Brechin Castle, the seat of Lord Panmure, is in the immediate neighbourhood of the town.) Population 6508.	23½	BRECHIN.	43½	
	22	Keithock Hall-Know.	45	
	20	Strickathrow vill.	47	In the church-yard of Strickathrow King John Baliol was divested, by command of Edward I. of all the ensigns of royalty.
	18¼	☞ North Esk Bridge.	48¾	
	13	Laurencekirk vill.	54	Laurencekirk was the birth place of Dr. Beattie. The illustrious Ruddiman was once schoolmaster there. The town is remarkable for a manufacture of snuff-boxes.
		STONEHAVEN. Thence to Aberdeen, as No. XV.	67	

XI. PERTH.—DUNKELD.—BLAIR ATHOLL.—INVERNESS.—119 Miles.

ON RIGHT FROM PERTH.	From Inverness	PERTH. Leave Perth by the North Inch.	From Perth	ON LEFT FROM PERTH.
Balhousie.	109½	Palace of Scone.	2½	Tulloch Printfield.
Luncarty Bleachfield, near which is the scene of the battle of Luncarty, between the Scots and the	109	cr. Almond Wat.	3	Earl of Mansfield. Feu House,—Nicol, Esq. Near Birnam Hill and
	106	cr. Shochie Wat.		Birnam Road.
	103	New Inn.	6	The walks through the
Danes. Near Stanley Mills, celebrated for their enormous wheels, and the Linn of Campsie.	100	Auchtergaven vill. Murthly Castle. (—— Stewart, Bart.)	9 / 12	policies of Dunkeld are upwards of 50 miles.
Another road parts off directly east to Blairgowrie. The present route passes for some miles along the east bank of the Tay.		Little Dunkeld. cr. the river Tay.		From this point a road proceeds by the west side of the river to Logierait, and thence by Aberfeldy to Kenmore.
Dunkeld is a place of great antiquity, and was at one time the capital of ancient Caledonia. One of the principal objects of curiosity here, is the ruined Cathedral. It must have been a fine pile of building. The architecture is partly Gothic, partly Saxon.	98 / 93 / 92 / 90½	DUNKELD. Dunkeld Ho., Duke of Atholl. Dowally Kirk. Near Dalguise Ho., Stewart, Esq. Kinnaird House. Logierait, where Prince Charles kept the prisoners whom he had taken at Prestonpans. Moulinearn Inn.	14 / 19 / 20 / 22½	Eight miles above Dunkeld the united waters of the Tummel and Garry fall into the Tay. The site of Faskally is of a peculiarly romantic character. It stands at the junction of three deep and confined valleys, and is encircled on all sides by diverging mountains.
The road now enters the pass of Killiecrankie, a narrow glen, at the bottom of which runs the Tummel water.	84 / 81½ / 77	Faskally, Butter, Esq. Lude, M'Inroy, Esq. cr. the Tilt Wat. BLAIR ATHOLL.	28 / 30½ / 33 / 35	In front, on the ascent to Urrard House, is the scene of the battle of Killiecrankie, fought July 26, 1689, between the High-
The vale of the Tilt is celebrated for its fine scenery, and for geological wonders. At the Bridge of Tilt is an excellent inn.		The road now passes through a wild Alpine territory, almost to Inverness.		landers under Dundee, and the forces of King William under Mackay, the former
The noble old Castle of Blair, (Duke of Atholl,) is in the neighbourhood.	69½	Dalnacardoch Inn. Dalnaspidal.	42½	being killed, and the latter defeated.
About two miles from Blair Atholl, the road crosses the Bruar, where that river makes a series of cascades, which enjoy extensive celebrity.	67½ / 56½	cr. Edendon Wat. Enter Inverness-shire. Drumochter Forest. Dalwhinnie Inn.	44½ / 55½	From Dalwhinnie the mountain of Benalder may be seen, situated on the north side of Loch Ericht. Here a road parts off by
Near Etrish there is a beautiful waterfall.	50	In front is Ben Chruben. Etrish.	62	Laggan and Garvamore, and over the difficult hill of Corriarrack to Fort
Across the Spey, ruins of Ruthven Castle and Barracks, destroyed by the Highlanders in 1746.	46	cr. Truim Wat. Bridge of Spey. Newton of Benchar.	66 / 66½	Augustus. From Pitmain may be seen the rocky barrier of Craig Dhu towards the
Across Spey, Invereshie, Sir Geo. M'Pherson Grant of Ballindalloch.	43½ / 42	Pitmain Inn. Kingussie Kirk & vill.	68½ / 70	west, the gathering-place of the M'Phersons. Belville, the seat of
Rothiemurchus, Grant, Esq.	37	Kincraig, Built on the site of an ancient monastery.	75	M'Pherson, the translator of Ossian, now possessed by Miss M'Pherson.
Opposite Aviemore is Cairngorm Hill.	20½	Aviemore Inn. cr. the Dolnain.	91½ / 99	Inverness is a royal burgh of the first reformed class, joining with Forres, Fortrose, and
Near Moy Hall, M'Intosh of M'Intosh. Here Prince Charles Stuart was nearly taken by surprise in February 1746.	18 / 6	Freeburn Inn. Daviot Kirk. INVERNESS.	106 / 112	Nairn in electing a Member of Parliament. Population 14,394. Inverness is considered the capital of the Highlands, being the only town of importance beyond Aberdeen. For further description see page 408.

XII.—EDINBURGH TO GLASGOW BY RAILWAY.—46 Miles.

ON RIGHT FROM EDINB.	From Glasgow.	EDINBURGH.	From Edinb.	ON LEFT FROM EDINB.
Coltbridge.	45		1	
Beechwood, Dundas, Bart.		cr. Water of Leith.	1½	
Corstorphine Hill, beautifully wooded.	43½		2½	Saughton House, Ramsay.
Corstorphine village.	43		3	
	41½		4½	Gogar Bank House, and Harmiston vill.
Kirkliston village, formerly called Temple-Liston, because its church and a great part of the parish belonged to the Knights Templars.	39		7	Ratho vill.
	38	cr. Almond Water, viaduct of 36 arches, each of 50 feet span, and from 60 to 80 feet high.	8	Canal Aqueduct.
		cr. Viaduct of 7 arches over Glasgow road.	8½	
Newliston House, Hog.	37		9	Broxburn vill.
Ruins of Niddry Castle, where Q. Mary first slept after her escape from Lochleven.	36	Tunnel.	10	Binny Crag, at which is a fine freestone quarry.
			10½	
Winchburgh vill. at which Edward II. first drew bridle after his defeat at Bannockburn.	35		11	Uphall vill.
Linlithgow is a town of great antiquity. In its Palace Q. Mary was born, and in its principal street the Regent Moray was shot. Its chief manufacture is the tanning and preparing of leather, and its principal trade is in shoes, made for Edinburgh and other markets. It has also two distilleries and a brewery, but upon the whole its trade is inconsiderable. Population of the parish in 1831 was 4874.	31	LINLITHGOW.	15	Champfleurie, Johnston, Esq.
	29		16½	The road by Torphichen to Bathgate here branches off.
			17	
	28	cr. Avon Water by viaduct of 25 arches, each 50 feet span, and from 70 to 80 feet high.	18	
Polmont House, Davidson.	25	Redding vill.	21	
	24		22	
Overton, R. Warden.	23½		22½	
Knowhead, Sir T. Livingston.	22½	Tunnel, 800 yards.	23½	Canal Tunnel.
	22		24	
Half a mile to the right is the town of Falkirk, celebrated for its trysts, or cattle markets. Here Edward I. gained a decisive victory over the Scots in 1298, and here also Prince Charles Stuart defeated General Hawley in 1746.		Here the Railway to Falkirk branches off.	24½	
	20½	cr. Viaduct over Union Canal, 102 yards.	25½	
Bonnymuir, Henry Salmon.	19		27	
Castle Cary Bridge and vill.	15½	cr. Red Burn Viaduct, 50 feet span, 100 feet high.	30½	Road to Cumbernauld. On the farm of Carrickstone, west of the parish church, is a stone called the Standing Stane, having a hole in it, in which Robert Bruce is said to have planted his standard before marching to Bannockburn.
Netherwood, J. S. More.	14½		31½	
Drumgrew, Capt. Murray.	10	Drumshanty Moss.	36	Dumbreck, C. Stewart.
	8½	cr. Luggie Water.	37½	
Woodley Quarry.	7	cr. Monkland and Kirkintulloch Railway.	39	
	3	Bishop Briggs vill.	43	
Here the road to Kirkintulloch branches off.	1½	Cowlair's Station.	44½	
	1	Tunnel, 1100 yards.	45	
		GLASGOW.	46	

XIII. EDINBURGH.—MID CALDER.—KIRK OF SHOTTS.—HOLYTOWN.—GLASGOW.—44 MILES.

ON RIGHT FROM EDIN.	From Glasgow.	EDINBURGH. For a description of the road from Edinburgh to Mid Calder, see No. VII.	From Edin.	ON LEFT FROM EDIN.
	32	Howden.	12	
	29	Kirk Livingston.	15	
		Cowsland.		
	26¾	Seafield.	17¼	
	25¼	Blackburn.	18¾	
	25	Lathbrae.	19	
	24	Swan Inn.	20	
Polkemmet House, Baillie, Bart.; remarkable for the quantities of game in the neighbourhood.	23	Whitburn vill.	21	
	22	Half-way-house.	22	
	19	Badweather.	25	
	17	Kirk of Shotts Inn.	27	Here the traveller is on the highest ground between the Forth and Clyde in this direction.
	13¾	Newhouse Inn.	30¼	
Lachup House, Robertson, Esq. Woodhall, Campbell of Shawfield.	11	HOLYTOWN, Where a road turns off to Hamilton.	33	
		cr. Shirle Water.		
Tollcross Ho., Dunlop, Esq.	9	Bellshill vill.	35	
	2¾	cr. Calder Wat.	41¼	One mile to the left, are the Clyde Iron Works, where 12,500 bars of iron were produced in 1835, a greater amount than the aggregate production of any other work in Scotland.
Jeanfield, Finlayson, Esq.		Tollcross vill.		
Newlands and Borrowfield Houses, Hozier, Esq.	1½	Parkhead.	42½	
		Camlachie.		
		GLASGOW.	44	

XIV. EDINBURGH.—LINLITHGOW.—FALKIRK.—CUMBERNAULD.—GLASGOW.—46¾ MILES.

ON RIGHT FROM EDIN.	From Glasgow.	EDINBURGH. For a description of the road between Edinburgh and Falkirk, see No. V.	From Edin.	ON LEFT FROM EDIN.
Larbert Ho., Stirling, Bart. Dunipace, Spottiswoode, Esq.				
Underwood House.		Camelon.	26	
Knowhead Ho., Patrick, Esq.		Cumbernauld Inn.		Merchiston Hall.
Castle Cary House.		cr. Bonny Wat.		Woodside Ho., Russell, Esq.
Cumbernauld House, Admiral Fleming.	14¼	CUMBERNAULD.	32½	Bankhead Ho., Cuthill, Esq.
		cr. Logie Water.		
Dunbeath Tower in ruins, once the property of the Kilmarnock family.	9¾	Bedlay Inn.	37	Mayothill Ho., Graham, Esq.
	8¼	Christon vill.	38½	Frankfield Loch.
Frankfield Ho., Millar, Esq.	4¼	Frankfield House.	42½	Kennyhill Ho., Stewart, Esq.
Rosemount Ho., Millar, Esq.	2¾	Provan Mill.	44	Whitehill Ho., Graham, Esq.
Garnkirk, Sprott, Esq.		cr. Monkland Canal.		Dunchattan and Cudbear Manufactories.
Riddry Park, Miss Provan.		GLASGOW.	46¾	Broom Park.

XV. EDINBURGH.—UPHALL.—BATHGATE.—AIRDRIE.—GLASGOW.—42¾ Miles.

ON RIGHT FROM EDIN.	From Glasgow.	EDINBURGH. Leave the city by Princes St.	From Edin.	ON LEFT FROM EDIN.
Murrayfield, W. Murray, Esq.		For 4½ miles the road is the same as in No. V.		Rosebery House, Balfour, Esq.
Beechwood, Dundas, Bart. Corstorphine House, Keith, Bart.	37¾	North Guile.	5	Saughton House, Baird, Bart. Milburn Tower.
Clermiston, Paterson, Esq.	36¾	Nether Gogar.	6	Gogar Camp, Osborne, Esq.
		cr. Gogar Burn.		
Gogar House, Ramsay, Esq.	36¼	Mount Gogar.	6½	Wardlaw, Esq.
Ingliston, Gibson, Esq.		Golf Hall.		Norton House, Norton, Esq.
Newliston, James Hog, Esq., once the seat of the great Earl of Stair.	35¼	Middle Norton.	7½	
		cr. Almond Wat.		Clifton Hall, Sir A. Gibson Maitland, Bart.
Kirkhill, the ancient family seat of the Earl of Buchan.	32¾	cr. Broxburn.	10	
	31¾	Broxburn.	11	Kinpunt House, which once gave the title to an Earl. It is now the property of Earl Hopetoun.
In Uphall Kirk lie interred the Hon. Henry Erskine, and Lord Erskine, his brother.	30¾	UPHALL.	12	
		West Mains.		Middleton, Thriepland, Esq. Houston, Shairp, Esq.
A thriving burgh of barony; population 5593, supported mostly by weaving, and partly by the adjacent coal and lime works.	24¾	BATHGATE.	18	Robert Bruce gave the barony of Bathgate as a portion with his daughter Marjory, who married Walter, the High Steward, in 1315. Walter died at his castle here, the remains of which are still pointed out.
	20¾	Armadale Inn.	22	
Bedlormie, Livingstone, Bart.		cr. Craigs Water.		
Auchingray, Haldane, Esq.		West Craigs Inn.		
The road is here skirted by a fine sheet of water, from which the Canal is supplied.	18¾	Auchingray.	24	The country is here generally a moorish upland, variegated by few objects.
		Blackrig.		
Woodhall, Campbell of Shawfield.	13¾	Pass Calder Water.	29	Moffat Hills in the south.
Airdrie is a thriving modern town, which has been called into existence chiefly by the neighbouring iron works and collieries. It is situated between two rivulets on a rising ground, and is a handsomely built town. The parish of New Monkland, in which Airdrie is situated, contains 9867 inhabitants.		Clerkston vill.		Airdrie Place, Miss Mitchelson.
	10¾	AIRDRIE.	32	
	9¼	Cairnhall.	33½	
	7¾	Longloan.	35	Drumpellier Ho., Buchannan, Esq.
	6¾	Drumpellier.	36	Barracknie, Hamilton, Esq.
	3	Shettlestone.	39¾	Glenduff Hill, Tod, Esq.
Summerlee House, M'Braire, Esq.		Joins the Mid Calder road.		Larch Grove, Scott, Esq.
Bailliestoun Ho., Maxwell, Esq.		Camlachie.		Wellhouse, Millar, Esq. Greenfield, M'Nairn, Esq.
Mount Vernon, Buchannan, Esq.		GLASGOW.	42	Carntyne House, Gray, Esq.

XVL EDINBURGH.—KIRKALDY.—CUPAR.—DUNDEE.—ARBROATH.—STONE-
HAVEN.—ABERDEEN.—109¼ MILES.

ON RIGHT FROM EDIN.	From Aberdeen	EDINBURGH. Newhaven to Pettycur by steam-boat.	From Edin.	ON LEFT FROM EDIN.
	100¼	Kinghorn.	9	
At the east end of the town Ravenscraig Castle in ruins, formerly the seat of the family of St. Clair.	98¼	KIRKALDY.	11	An ancient royal burgh. Population of the parish 2579.
	97¼	Pathhead vill.	12	
	95¼	Galatown.	14	
	89¾	Plasterer's Inn.	19½	Raith, Robert Ferguson, Esq.
		✦ cr. Leven Wat.		Leslie House, Earl of Rothes.
Near Markinch Kirk, where General Leslie, the leader of the Cove-	87½	New Inn	22	Balbirnie, Gen. Balfour.
nanting army, lies interred. Cults Kirk. Cults Manse, the birth place of Sir David Wilkie, R.A.	85½	Kettle vill.	24	On left, two miles dis- tant, bye-road to Perth, Falkland, and Falkland
	84½	Pitlessie.	25	Palace.
		✦ cr. Eden Wat.		Rankeillour, Maitland M'Gill Crichton, Esq.
The Mount, the patri- monial estate of Sir David	79½	CUPAR.	30	Crawford Priory, Earl of Glasgow.
Lindsay, is about four miles	76	Dairsie Kirk.	83½	
to the west of Cupar, but	75¼	Osnaburgh vill.	33¾	Cupar is a handsome town,
no old building exists at the place.	72¼	St. Michael's Inn.	37	of modern and thriving ap- pearance. The Town Hall
		Newport,		and County Hall are ele- gant buildings. An emin-
	69¼	Where embark in a steam- boat, and cross the Tay to	40	ence at the east end of the town was the site of a for-
Dundee is the chief seat	67¼	DUNDEE.	42	tress of considerable impor-
of the linen manufacture	65¼	✦ cr. Dighty Wat.	44	tance, of which no trace
in Britain, and one of the	54¼	Muirdrum vill.	55	now exists.
most prosperous towns in the empire. The principal		Panbride Kirk.		Near Cupar, in ruins, Airdit Ho., Stewart, Esq.
objects are the Town Hall, Exchange Reading Rooms,		✦ cr. Elliot Wat.		Fintry, Graham, Esq.
(open to strangers,) Aca-	50¼	ARBROATH.	59	The most interesting
demy, the Howf or Bury- ing Ground, the Tower of	44¼	Chance Inn.	65	object in Arbroath is the venerable ruins of the
the old Church, and the		✦ cr. Lunan at		Abbey. It was founded
Law, from which a most extensive view is to be seen.		Lunan Kirk.		by William the Lion, who is interred here.
		✦ cr. South Esk to		The rock on which the Bell Rock Lighthouse is
	37½	MONTROSE.	71½	founded, is about 12 miles
Ethie, Earl of Northesk.		✦ cr. North Esk.		from the shore at Arbroath
The road, for some miles,	32½	St. Cyrus Kirk.	77	Montrose is a remarkably
passes near the sea coast.	28¼	Johnshaven.	81	neat, and even handsome town. The river is crossed
Kaim of Mathers, Adam.				by a fine suspension bridge
Ruins of Dunnotar Castle.	24¼	INVERBERVIE.	85	Population 12,055.
Dunnotar was built by an		✦ cr. Bervie Wat.		Aberdeen is a large and ele-
ancestor of the Marischal family about the time of		STONEHAVEN.		gant city of great antiquity, possessing many handsome
the contest between Bruce	15	✦ cr. Carron and	94¼	streets and splendid public
and Baliol. Before the use		Cowie Waters.		buildings. The large propor- tion of eminent Scotsmen who
of fire arms, it was con- sidered as almost impreg-		Muchals House.		have been produced in this city, is very remarkable, and can
nable, and was used as the	11	✦ cr. Dee, and enter	98¼	only be attributed to the pre-
deposit of the Regalia of Scotland, to preserve them		ABERDEEN.	109¼	sence of its Universities. In Old Aberdeen are to be seen the
from the English army un- der Cromwell, in 1651.				remains of the Cathedral. The scenery in the neighbourhood is remarkably interesting.

ON RIGHT FROM INVERN.	From Thurso	INVERNESS. Leave Inverness by the Bridge over the Ness, and cross the Caledonian Canal.	From Invern.	ON LEFT FROM INVERN.
Chachnaharry Basin, the end of the Canal.				Muirtown, Duff.
Popachie, Fraser. Across Beauly Firth, Redcastle, the seat of the late Sir William Fettis, Bart.	170	Bunchrew, Forbes.	2	Bunchrew, or Bunchrive, was long the residence of President Forbes.
Near the road, at the point where it enters Rossshire, are two upright stones, standing in a due line east and west, which mark the scene of a conflict between the Frasers and M'Kenzies.	165½ 162	Kirkhill Kirk. cr. Beauly river, and enter BEAULY.	7½ 10	Near Auchnagairn, Relig, Warrenfield, and Fingask. Beauly, a pleasant village, with the ruins of Beauly Priory, and at no great distance Kilmorack waterfalls. Farther up the Beauly, Beaufort Castle, the seat of Lord Lovat.
Tannadale, Baillie. Road to Fortrose. Highfield, M'Kenzie.		Enter Ross-shire.		
One of the most remarkable things in the eye of a stranger, all through this tract, is the enormous mountain Ben Wyvis. Sir Hector Munro of Foulis, the proprietor of this mountain, holds his estate in Ross-shire, by a tenure from one of the early Scottish kings, binding him to bring three wain-loads of snow from the top of the hill, whenever his majesty shall so desire. *	160 158 154 153	Gilchrist Kirk. Urray Kirk. Bridgend vill. Pitglassie vill.	12 14 18 19	Ord House, M'Kenzie. Brahan Castle, Lady Hood M'Kenzie. Conon, M'Kenzie.
Dingwall Castle was formerly the residence of the Earls of Ross.	150½	Dingwall.	21½	Dingwall was erected into a royal burgh by Alexander II. in 1226. Near the town are the ruins of the ancient residence of the Earls of Ross. Near the church is an obelisk, fifty-six feet high, though only six feet at the base, intended to distinguish the burial-place of the Cromarty family.
Inchculter, Fraser; and Culcairn and Novar, Munro.	148½ 147	Ardulie, and Foulis, Munro, Bart.	23½ 25	Near Tulloch, Davidson. At the head of Strathpeffer, about four miles from Dingwall, there is an excellent and well-frequented mineral well, round which are congregated a considerable number of buildings.
Near Castle Leod, the ancient seat of the Cromarty family, and Cowl House, M'Kenzie, Bart.	142½ 138	Alness Kirk. Rosskein Kirk.	29½ 34	
Invergordon Castle, M'-Leod, Esq.	136½ 135	Invergordon vil. & seaport. Kilmuir Kirk.	35¼ 37	There are some fine views of the opposite coast through the Sutors of Cromarty.
Tarbet House was once the seat of the Cromarty family, and whence the first Earl took his first title of Viscount Tarbet.	134 128½	Tarbet House. Knockbreck House.	38 43½	

The top of Ben Wyvis was never known to be uncovered by snow, till the memorably warm summer of it was quite bare.

INVERNESS TO THURSO—*Continued.*

ON RIGHT FROM INVERN.	From Thurso.		From Invern.	ON LEFT FROM INVERN.
The road from Tain to Dornoch is a very singular one. The distance between the two towns, straight across the firth, is only four miles, but, instead of going directly across the water, the coach winds round the bed of the firth, a distance of thirty-one.	125 123	**TAIN.** On right Meikle Ferry of Dornoch, which, if adopted, cuts off 19 miles of road. The mail proceeds by the route now described.	47 49	Tain is an irregularly built town, with several new and handsome houses. It is situated on the margin of the Dornoch Firth. The ancient church of Tain was collegiate, and dedicated to St. Duthus. James IV. performed pilgrimage to the shrine of
The Castle of Lochlin is a remarkable building; it has stood 500 years. Sir George M'Kenzie, (popularly denominated *The Bloody M'Kenzie*,) King's Advocate in the reign of Charles II., was born there. Bonar Bridge is a strong and magnificent structure, composed of iron. It cost £14,000. Near Crach Church is an obelisk, eight feet by four, erected in memory of a Danish chieftain. Here, on the summit of a hill, which juts out into the firth, is a noted vitrified fort, called Dun Creech.	122 115 114½ 112¼ 100¾	Edderton Kirk. West Fearn. Kincardine Inn. cr. Firth of Dornoch, by Bonar Bridge. Bonar Inn. Clashmore Inn.	50 57 58½ 59¾ 71½	this Saint, to whose honour several churches were at different times built in this place. Near Fearn, there are the ruins of an abbey of great antiquity, founded by the first Earl of Ross. Patrick Hamilton, an abbot of this place, was the first who suffered in this country for the Reformed religion. Near the abbey is a high square column, covered with Saxon characters. Near Skibo, Dempster, Esq.
	97¾ 95	**Dornoch.** cr. Loch Fleet, By a stupendous mound, built to dam out the sea—Cost £9000.	74½ 77	Dornoch is, without exception, the most miserable of all our royal burghs. It is nevertheless, the county town of Sutherland, and formerly was the seat of the bishopric of Caithness. Part of the cathedral still serves as the parish church.
From Golspie, all the way to Brora, the road is skirted with neat cottages, surrounded by shrubberies and covered with honeysuckle. Brora is one of the new villages built by the Duke of Sutherland. It is situated at the mouth of the river Brora, which descends from a vale of the most romantic and savage character.	86¾ 83 82 80½ 77 71¼	Golspie vill. Brora. Kirk of Clyne. Kinkradwell. Loth Kirk. Helmsdale.	85¼ 89 90 91 95 100¾	Dunrobin Castle, the seat of the Duke of Sutherland, occupies an eminent site upon the shore, a little beyond Golspie, and is surrounded by some fine old wood, besides extensive modern plantations. It is said to have been founded in the 13th century by one of the earliest Earls of Sutherland. About a mile farther on, between the road and the beech, stands one of those unaccountable relics of antiquity, called Picts Houses. Adjoining Helmsdale, are the ruins of a romantic old castle, once the seat of an extensive proprietor of the name of Gordon.

ON RIGHT FROM INVERN.	From Thurso.		From Invern.	ON LEFT FROM INVER.
In the immediate neighbourhood of Berridale, on a high crag, stand the remains of a castle, once the residence of the Sutherlands of Langwell, the ancient Lords of Berridale, and, according to tradition, a very gigantic race. One of them, William More Sutherland, is reported to have been upwards of nine feet high. Swiney, Gordon.	61½	Berridale Inn.	110½	
		🏇 cr. Dunbeath water.		
	60¾	Dunbeath Inn.	116¼	
	52	Kirk of Latheron.	120	Latheron House, Sinclair.
	49	Swiney Inn.	123	Nottingham House, Sutherland.
	48		124	Near Stempater and Rangog Lochs. Near the former is a Druidical temple and the Arch-Druid's house.
	46	Clyth, Henderson.	126	
	37	Hempriggs, Dunbar, Bart.	135	
	36	Newton.	136	
		🏇 cr. the Wick river, by a 🏇 to		
From Wick, the mailroad to Thurso proceeds from a point south of the river, keeping by the south side of the Loch of Watten, and twenty-one miles in extent, Watten Inn being situated about midway. The road by Duncansbay Head and John O'Groat's House, proceeds by the coast. On right, upon the coast, the ruins of Girnigo and Sinclair Castles. Also, Akergill Tower, Dunbar, Bart.	34½	WICK.	137½	Wick is the principal seat of the herring fishery in the north of Scotland. It is a thriving and fast increasing town. Piers and other erections have lately been built at the harbour, costing upwards of £13,000.
		Werter House and Loch.		
	32		142	
	25	Miltown.	147	Kliss House, Macleay, and Kliss Castle ruins, formerly the seat of the Earl of Caithness.
	23	Freswick, Sinclair.	149	
Near Duncansbay Head and John O'Groat's House. Ratter, Earl of Caithness.	18	Houna Inn.	154	Bucholis Castle ruins.
	16½	Cannisbay Kirk.	155½	Moy Castle, Stirling, Bart.
	8	Dunnet Kirk.	164	
Thurso is a burgh of barony, holding of Sir George Sinclair of Ulbster. Thurso Castle, his residence, is in the neighbourhood, along with a highly ornamental structure, which the late Sir John built to the memory of Harold Earl of Caithness, who was slain and buried on the spot upwards of six centuries ago. The coast to the west increases in terrific wildness and grandeur till it terminates at Cape Wrath.	1	Thurso Castle.	171	
		THURSO.	172	

XVIII. GLASGOW.—PAISLEY.—GREENOCK.—LARGS.—KILWINNING.—AYR.— 72 Miles.

ON RIGHT FROM GLASGOW.	From Ayr.	GLASGOW.	From Glasgow.	ON LEFT FROM GLASGOW.
	70	Leave Glasgow by the New Bridge, and pass through Tradestown.	2	Parkhouse, Walkinshaw, Esq.
	69		3	
Paisley, a celebrated seat of manufacturing industry. Placing the factories out of view, the most interesting object of curiosity in Paisley is the Abbey church, which is still a magnificent and impressive object. Attached to its south side there is a small chapel, where it is said Marjory, daughter of King Robert Bruce, was interred. This chapel possesses a remarkably fine echo.	64¼	PAISLEY.	7¾	Cardonald, Lord Blantyre.
	61	Johnston vill. where cr. Black Cart River.	11	Crookston Castle in ruins. A place deriving interest from its connexion with Queen Mary.
	58½	Kilbarchan vill.	13½	
	58	Bridge of Weir; where cr. Gryfe Water.	14	A thriving village, engaged in the cotton manufacture. The course of the Gryfe, to its junction with the Cart, is a tract of beautiful scenery.
	53¼	Kilmalcolm vill.	18¾	
Greenock is a large and populous town, the first seaport in Scotland. The situation of Greenock is remarkably beautiful. The principal branches of its commerce have reference to the East and West Indies, the United States, and British America. The Custom House is a beautiful building. There is also an elegant Exchange.	49¼	Port Glasgow.	22¾	A populous sea-port erected by the merchants of Glasgow, as an appropriate place for the shipping of goods. On the shore, at a little distance to the east, is situated the deserted Castle of Newark, formerly a place of great strength. Near Innerkip, Ardgowan, Shaw Stewart, Bart. and Kelly, Wallace, Esq.
	46½	GREENOCK.	25½	
	43½	Gourock.	28½	
	40½	Innerkip vill.	31½	
	38½	cr. Kelly Water.	33½	
	32¾	cr. Nodle Water.	39¼	
Largs stands on a beautiful plain, surrounded by mountains on the land side. Near this place, in 1263, in the reign of Alexander III., was fought the battle of Largs between the Scots and Danes.	32	LARGS.	40	Brisbane Ho., Brisbane, Bart. Kelburn Ho., Earl of Glasgow.
	29¾	Fairley.	42¼	Fairley Castle in ruins.
		cr. Rye Water.		
	26¼	West Kilbride.	46¾	Near ruins of Ardrossan Castle. The Harbour of Ardrossan possesses advantages superior to all the other harbours in the Frith of Clyde.
A few miles to the north of Ardrossan, stands the ruined Castle of Portincross, rendered memorable by the frequency of the visits of the first Stuart sovereign to it. Its situation on a bare rock projecting into the sea, is singularly wild and picturesque.	20	Ardrossan.	52	
	18½	Saltcoats.	53½	
	14	KILWINNING.	58	Eglinton Castle, Earl of Eglinton; a splendid structure.
		cr. Garnoch Wat.		
	11	Irvine.	61	Irvine was the birth-place of John Galt, and James Montgomery, the poet. Burns was, for a short time, engaged in business in Irvine as a flax-dresser,
		cr. Irvine Water.		
Kilwinning is remarkable as the first settlement of Free Masons in Scotland.	3	Monkton.	69	
		AYR.	72	

Ayr is a handsome old-fashioned town, skirted with modern streets of considerable elegance. It dates as a royal burgh from 1202, and was the scene of several remarkable exploits of Sir William Wallace. Many of the localities of Ayr and its vicinity are rendered interesting by their association with the life and poems of Burns. The poet was born in a clay-built cottage, about two miles and a half from the town. At a little distance are the ruins of Alloway Kirk, the Auld Brig of Doon, Burns' Monument, &c.

488

XIX. GLASGOW.—AYR.—MAYBOLE.—GIRVAN.—PORTPATRICK.—94 MILES.

ON RIGHT FROM GLASGOW.	From Portpat.	GLASGOW. Glasgow to Ayr, see No. XVII.	From Glasgow.	ON LEFT FROM GLASGOW.
The native cottage of Burns, his monument, the old bridge of Doon, and other objects deriving interest from the life and writings of the poet.	60½ 59	Alloway Kirk. cr. Doon by new Bridge, and skirt along Brown Carrick Hill.	33½ 35	Blairston, Cathcart. Maybole is a burgh of barony, and obtained its privileges in 1516. It carries on a woollen manufacture to a considerable extent. The Mansion House of the Cassilis family is the finest surviving specimen of the twenty-eight winter seats of noble and baronial families formerly existing in Maybole. It is said to have been the residence of the repudiated Countess of Cassilis, whose story was the subject of the well known ballad of Johnny Faa. Burns received part of his education in Kirkoswald. Girvan, a place of considerable antiquity, situated at the mouth of Girvan Water, the banks of which abound in fine scenery, and in fine seats. Carleton Castle, ruins, Cathcart, Bart. Stinchar Castle ruins, an ancient seat of the Kennedys of Bargany. Such is the irregularity of the rivulet which runs through Glenapp, that the road crosses it at least half a dozen times within the extent of half a dozen miles. Near Stranraer, Castle Kennedy and Culhorn, Earl of Stair. Stranraer is a thriving and handsome seaport town, uniting with Wigton, New Galloway, and Whithorn, in returning a Member to Parliament. In the centre of it stands a tall strong edifice, originally a castle. There are several seats in the neighbourhood adorned with all the charms of nature and of art. Dunskey Castle ruins, finely situated on a very high rock overhanging the sea.
	56	Grange House. Torrence, M'Micken, Esq.	38	
Crossraguel Abbey, founded in 1244; part of the cloisters remain, and the Abbot's house is entire. The last Abbot was famed for his disputation with John Knox. The ruin is preserved with great care. Some miles to the right of Kirkoswald, is Colzean Castle, the splendid mansion of the Marquis of Ailsa. It is built on the brink of a perpendicular precipice; under it are the celebrated caves of Culzean, penetrating 200 feet into the rock. On the coast, the ruins of Turnberry Castle, a seat of Robert Bruce when Earl of Carrick.	51½ 49 47 41 39 36½ 34	MAYBOLE. Population 6287. Ruins of Crossraguel Abbey. Kirkoswald. Chasel House. cr. Girvan Wat. Girvan vill. The road now keeps close by the coast for many miles. Ardmillan. Crawford, Esq. Carleton Bay.	42½ 45 47 53 55 57½ 60	
The village of Ballantrae is situated close to the mouth of the Stinchar water, and picturesquely overhung by the ruins of an old castle. It was formerly a great haunt of smugglers. It has a good sea and salmon fishery.	26½ 24	Ballantrae vill. cr. Stinchar Wat. Glenapp, A romantic glen.	67½ 70	
View of the beautiful Bay of Lochryan, celebrated in the fine old pathetic ballad, entitled "The Lass of Lochryan."	16½ 15	Enter Wigtonshire. Cairn.	77½ 79	
Portpatrick is a thriving town of considerable size. The channel between Great Britain and Ireland is here only 21 miles across. Portpatrick possesses an excellent harbour and reflecting lighthouse.	9 6	Stranraer. Population 3390. Lochan's Bridge. PORTPATRICK.	85 88 94	

XX. GLASGOW.—RUTHERGLEN.—HAMILTON.—LANARK.—PEEBLES,— SELKIRK—HAWICK.—83½ MILES.

ON RIGHT FROM GLASGOW.	From Hawick.	GLASGOW. Leave Glasgow by the Calton. At Barrowfield take to the left.	From Glasgow.	ON LEFT FROM GLASGOW.
Near the ancient royal burgh of Rutherglen, of date 1196, now chiefly occupied by weavers. Population of the parish in 1831, 5503.	80	cr. Clyde at Dalmarnock Bridge. Cambuslang vill.	3½	On the left, at a distance, Clyde Iron Works. Remarkable for a great revival of religion, which occurred there in consequence of the preaching of Whitefield.
Dechmont Hill is here a conspicuous object, it commands a very extensive view.	75½	Blantyre vill. and Priory on the left.	8	The remains of Blantyre Priory are delightfully situated on the banks of the Clyde, opposite to Bothwell Castle. In the neighbourhood there is a large cotton mill, which gives employment to 900 persons. Near Mauldslie Castle, Nisbet, Esq. once the seat of the Earls of Hyndford.
Numerous neat villas on both sides of the road.	74¼	HAMILTON.	9¼	
Hamilton unites with Falkirk, Airdrie, Lanark, and Linlithgow in sending a representative to Parliament. Population of the parish in 1831, 9513. Close to the town is Hamilton Palace, the superb seat of the Duke of Hamilton. The interior of the palace is fitted up in the most gorgeous style; and the collection of paintings has long been considered the best in Scotland. Within the grounds, on the banks of the river Avon, the ruin of the ancient Castle of Cadzow is perched on the top of a rock 200 feet above the water.	67 60¾ 59¼ 58½	Dalserf vill. Nethanfoot. Soon after pass Stonebyres Fall. cr. Clyde Water by Lanark Bridge. LANARK.	16½ 22¾ 24½ 25	Stonebyres Fall, so named from the adjacent estate of Stonebyres, a cataract of eighty-eight feet in height. Lanark is a very ancient royal burgh containing about 4000 inhabitants.
Twenty-two miles from Glasgow stands Craignethan Castle, on a lofty eminence near the conflux of the Nethan and the Clyde. This fortress, now in ruins, was once the seat of the celebrated personage called the Bastard of Arran.	48 41	cr. Clyde by Hyndford Bridge. Biggar. cr. Biggar Water. Broughton.	35½ 42½	About a mile from Lanark, there is a profound ravine through which the Mouse water descends to join the Clyde. The precipitous sides of the ravine are the celebrated Cartland Crags, in which Wallace found refuge on several occasions.
Vale of Manor, in which lived David Ritchie, the original of the Black Dwarf.	39½ 39	Stobo Castle. Stobo Kirk. cr. Lyne Water.	44 44½	Montgomery, Bart.
	33	PEEBLES.	50½	Nidpath Castle, nearly in ruins, a most romantic situation.
Innerleithen, a favourite resort of the citizens of Edinburgh, is a handsome village full of neat houses; its situation is very beautiful.	27 18	Innerleithen vill. and Mineral Wells. Fernalie or Yair Bridge.	56½ 65½	Horsburgh Castle in ruins. Cardrona, Williamson, Esq.
Traquair House, Earl of Traquair.	12	SELKIRK. For the route between Selkirk and Hawick, see No. III.	71½ 83½	

XXI. GLASGOW.—DUMBARTON.—TARBET.—TYNDRUM.—FORT WILLIAM.—103 MILES.

ON RIGHT FROM GLASGOW.	From Fort Wil.	GLASGOW.	From Glasgow.	ON LEFT FROM GLASGOW.
		Leave Glasgow by Anderston.		
Cranston Hill, Houldsworth, and numerous other villas, belonging to the wealthy citizens.	99½	cr. Kelvin Water.		
		White Inch.	3½	
Jordanhill, Smith, Esq.	93½	Kilpatrick vill.	9½	Dalnottar.
Dumbarton is one of the four fortresses stipulated by the articles of Union to be kept up, and accordingly is still in repair, and occupied by a garrison.	92	Dunglas Castle ruins.	11	Near the termination of the Forth and Clyde Canal.
	88½	DUMBARTON.	14½	
		cr. Leven Water.	―	Levensido, Ewing.
Cardale Ho., Stirling, Esq. Bonhill, Smollet, Esq. Balloch Castle Stott. Loch Lomond is on the right for many miles.	86½	Renton vill.	16½	Near Smollet's monument, and Dalquhurn House, where he was born.
	85	Alexandria.	18	Broomley, Miss Alston. Tillichewen Castle.
Cameron Ho., Smollet, Esq.	84	Lower end of L. Lomond.	19	Woodbank, Miss Scott. Bellretiro, Miss Rowet.
Rosdew, Colquhoun, Bart.	82	Arden, Buchannan.	21	Glen Fruin was the scene of a bloody conflict between the M'Gregors and Colquhoun in 1602.
Luss is beautifully situated; the waters of the Luss run through it, and fall into Loch Lomond.	78	cr. Fruin Water.	25	
	76½	Luss vill. and Inn.	26½	For crossing Loch Lomond to Rowardennan, where the ascent to Ben Lomond is usually commenced.
	79½	Inveruglas Ferry.	30½	
Nearly opposite Inveruglas Island, in a hollow above a small cascade, are the ruins of Invernaid Fort, an old military station, chiefly designed to keep the Clan Gregor in check.	68½	Tarbet Inn.	34½	Three miles above Tarbet is a small wooded island called Inveruglas, and about two miles farther, another called Eilan; on each of which are the ruins of a stronghold of the family of Macfarlane.
		Keep along the side of Loch Lomond.		
	65	Across the loch is Invernaid Mill.	38	
	60	Head of Loch Lomond.	43	
	58	Auldtarnan Inn.	45	
About half way between Crianlaroch and Tyndrum, there is a linn in the river called the Pool of St. Fillan's, which is to this day not unfrequently the scene of the observance of a degrading superstitious rite. Here St. Fillan, so noted in the Highlands for works of piety and sacred gifts, is said to have lived.	57	Glenfalloch, Campbell.	46	On the right a road proceeds to Killin.
		Proceed up Glenfalloch to Crianlaroch Inn.		
	52		51	Strathfillan was the scene of a battle of Robert Bruce.
		Take to the left up Strathfillan.		
	47	Tyndrum Inn.	56	Tyndrum Ho., Marquis of Breadalbane.
	38	Inverouran Inn.	65	Between Inverouran and King's House, the road crosses a lofty hill called the Black Mount. From the top an extensive view is obtained of the Moor of Rannoch, the largest tract of the kind in Scotland.
In the neighbourhood of Ballachulish, is a cavern of such difficult access, that nobody of late has ventured to explore it.	28½	Mountainous scenery to King's House Inn.	74½	
	26	Foot of the steep road to Fort William, called the Devil's Staircase.	77	Glencoe is famous for its singularly wild Alpine scenery, and the historical event connected with it. The massacre of Glencoe in King William's reign, took place at the northwest end of the vale.
		Enter Glencoe.		
So called from the tradition of Patrick, a Danish Prince, having been drowned there.	14½	Ballachulish Inn.	88½	Maryburgh contains about 1500 inhabitants, and two respectable inns.
	13	The Ferry of Calas-ic Phatric.	90	
Fort William is situated on the shore of Loch Eil, at the distance of about two miles from the termination of the canal of Corpach. It was erected in the reign of William III. for the purpose of keeping down the Jacobite clans of the west.	11	ONICH.	92	It contains a bomb-proof magazine, and the barrack is calculated to accommodate 96 men. The fort was besieged in 1745-6 by the Camerons, but without success. It is now almost in a state of disuse.
	7½	Coran Ferry across Loch Eil.	95½	
	½	Maryburgh.	102½	
		FORT WILLIAM.	103	

XXII. ABERDEEN.—KINTORE.—INVERURY.—HUNTLY.—KEITH.— FOCHABERS.—57 MILES.

ON RIGHT FROM ABERD.	From Focha.	ABERDEEN.*	From Aberd.	ON LEFT FROM ABERD.
Mugiemoss, L. Ja. Hay.		Cross the hill of Tyrebagger, *i. e.* Tirebeggar.	4½	Craibstone, Mrs. Dr. Scott.
Caskieben, Dr. Henderson.				Glasgow Forest, Mrs. Brebner.
Glasgowego, Wilson, Esq.	45	KINTORE,	12	Benachie rises to the
Greenburn Inn.		A borough of considerable antiquity.		height of 1420 feet. On the east end is a remarkable
Balbethan, Gen. Gordon.		Cross Don by a handsome ▭ of 3 arches,		rock, rising perpendicularly on three sides 180 feet,
Keith Hall, Earl of Kintore.	41¾	built in 1798.	15¼	it is only accessible on one side; it has been fortified,
The Bass, a conical mount of considerable elevation, said to be artificial. The river Ury runs close to it. Tradition says the pestilence was buried in it. Thomas the Rhymer has predicted:	41¼	INVERURY. Pitcaple Inn. At some distance, on the opposite side of the Ury, the battle of Harlaw was fought.	15½	tradition says, by the Picts. A borough of considerable antiquity. Here Robert Bruce gained a victory over the English. Here, in 1745, the rebels defeated a party of the King's troops.
" Dee and Don shall run in one, And Tweed shall run in Tay, And the bonnie water of Ury Shall bear the Bass away."		" July 24, St. James's even, Harlaw was fought fourteen hundred and eleven."		Maner, Gordon, Esq. Balquhain, Leslie, Esq. Pittodrie, Erskine.
The first part of the prediction was fulfilled by the Inverury Canal.				
Pitcaple, Lumsden, Esq.				
Logie, Elphinstone, Bart.	36	The Church of Oyne to the west 1 mile.	21	Old castle of Harthill.
	35	▭ cr. the Gadie.	22	
		" Oh an I were where Gadie rins, At the back of Benachie."		
Pitmachie Inn.	33		24	
Newton, Gordon, Esq.	31	Vill. of Old Rain.	26	At a distance may be seen the hill of Dunideer,
Williamston, Fraser, Esq.	30½	▭ cr. Kelloch.	26½	*i. e.* Dun d'Ore; on the top
Freefield, Gen. Leith.				of which are the ruins of an old castle, said to have
Enter the Glens of Foundland, through which the road passes for some miles. In stormy weather it is frequently shut up.	25	▭ cr. the Ury, Here called the Glen Wat. On the left is the hill of Foudland, celebrated for its slate quarry, some of which are of the finest quality.	32	been the palace of King Gregory the Great about 300. It has been surrounded by a double rampart. The walls, after encountering 1000 winters, are so hard that the smallest
Huntly Castle, a ruin partly built by George first Marquis of Huntly, whose name, and that of his wife, Hen. Stewart, daughter of Esme Duke of Lennox, are in the hall. The extensive estates of the Gordon family have now devolved upon the Duke of Richmond.	19	▭ cr. Bogie. " I'll o'er Bogie wi' my love." HUNTLY, pop. 3000. Once celebrated for its linen manufacture, and still for its bleaching.	38	stone will break rather than be separated from the mass; large masses of vitrified stone are scattered over the level top of the hill, and marks of many buildings.
A handsome Church.	18	Huntly Lodge.		Many years the residence of the last Duke of Gordon when Mar. of Huntly.
About a mile distant, the vill. of New Mills.	9	▭ cr. Deveron.	39	A short way below the
Shortly after leaving Keith, the road enters upon the property of the Duke of Richmond, and continues to Fochabers; close to which stands Gordon Castle, 560 feet in length. The park is 18 miles in circumference.	8	Keith vill. ▭ cr. Isla. Fife Keith vill. Barren moor to FOCHABERS.	48 / 49 / 57	Deveron is joined by the Bogie, and afterwards by the Isla, and after a course of 90 miles it falls into the Moray Firth at Banff.

* The Great North Road from Aberdeen to Inverness, at the distance of 8½ miles from the former, divided into two, one branch by Turriff, Banff, and Cullen, being 72 miles; the other by Kintore, Invery, Huntly, and Keith, being 57 miles to Fochabers, where the roads again unite. The latter being the shortest line, is the mail coach road, and is now chiefly used by travellers.

XXIII. ABERDEEN.—BANFF.—CULLEN.—ELGIN.—FORRES.—NAIRN.— INVERNESS.—126 MILES.

ON RIGHT FROM ABERD.	From Inver.		From Aberd.	ON LEFT FROM ABERD.
		Leave Aberdeen, and pass for several miles along the bank of the Inverury Canal.		Hilton, Johnston, Bart.
Persley, Haddin, Esq. Woodside, Kilgour, Esq. Waterton, Pirie, Esq. Parkhill, Skene, Esq.		Dyce vill.	6	Kirkhill, Bannerman, Esq. Fintry House, Forbes, Bart. Kinmundy, E. of Aberdeen. Elrick House, Burnett, Esq.
		cr. the Don.		Straloch, Ramsay, Esq.
		New Macher Kirk.	9	Barra, Ramsay, Esq.
Tillygreig, Harvey, Esq. Pittrichie, Milne, Esq. Udney Castle, Col. Udney. Kilblain, Manson, Esq.	111	Leithfield.	14½	Fingask, Elmslie, Esq. Tulloch, Kilgour, Esq.
	108	Old Meldrum vill.	18	
Haddo House, Earl of Aberdeen.		Meldrum Ho., Urquhart, Esq.		
	101½	Fyvie Kirk.	24½	
	99½	Fyvie Castle, Gordon of Fyvie, on the right.	26½	Fyvie Castle is a princely looking building, beautifully situated on a small eminence in the centre of a large amphitheatre of fine grounds, skirted with woods on the heights around, and the river winding through the centre.
	95½	Towie, The native place of the father of Barclay de Tolly, i.e. Towie, the Russian general.	30½	Gask, Earl of Fife.
Hatton Castle, Duff, Esq.		cr. Turriff Water.		
" When ye're at the Brig o' Turay, Ye're half-way between Aberdeen and Elgin o' Murray."		Muiresk, Spottiswood, Esq. Laithers, Stuart, Esq.		
Delgatty Castle, Earl of Fife, a mile from Turriff; not seen from the road.	93	Turriff. Pronounced Turay. Forglen House, Abercromby, Bart., about a mile from Turriff.	33	
	91½	On the left Monthlairy, Morison, Esq. and Eden, Duff, Esq.	35½	Banff, the county town, is agreeably situated on the side of a hill at the mouth of the river Deveron. It was founded by Malcolm Canmore in 1162.
Craigston Castle, Urquhart, Esq. Forglen Church on the north side of the river Deveron.	88	cr. King Edward.	38	There have been large additional piers built to the harbour here, but, owing to the sandy bottom, the bar is often much filled up.
	79	cr. Deveron River, and enter BANFF.	47	On the left on entering the town is Duff House, the elegant mansion of the Earl of Fife.
Between Boyndie and Portsoy are the ruins of Boyne Castle, Lord Seafield, once the finest seat in the North of Scotland, but destroyed in the civil war.	75½	New Kirk of Boyndie.	50½	Durn Park, Gordon, Esq.
Along this line of road the Earls of Fife and Seafield, and the Duke of Richmond, are the chief proprietors.		cr. Boyne Streamlet by of Broadlie.		Durn, Earl of Seafield.
From Banff to Fochabers (26 miles) the road passes at no great distance from the sea-coast.	70	Portsoy, A small irregularly built town, with a thriving port; population 2000.	56	Glasshaugh, Abercromby, Esq.
				Birkenbog, Abercromby, Bart.
	65	CULLEN, A royal burgh in the Elgin district, population 1686.	61	Cullen House, Earl of Seafield, a large and venerable building. The grounds are fine.
Near village of Buckie.	61	Letterfourie, Gordon, Bart.	65	Cairnfield, Gordon, Esq.
Near village of Port Gordon.	52	Fochabers vill.	74	On the right from Aberdeen, and at the back of Fochabers, is Gordon Castle, Duke of Richmond; a magnificent mansion, erected by Alexander Duke of Gordon, who died in 1827. The ancient seat of the family was Huntly Castle, now in ruins; near it Huntly Lodge, Duchess of Gordon.
Speymouth Kirk. The royal burgh of Elgin is an old fashioned and impressive place. The remains of the Cathedral form the chief object of attraction in Elgin. It was founded in 1224 by the Bishop of Moray. The great tower fell in 1711. The Cathedral, when entire, was exactly a model of Lichfield. Elgin has been much improved of late years by the erection of various public buildings.		cr. Spey River, enter Morayshire.		
	48	Urquhart vill.	78	
	46	Kirk of St. Andrews.	80	
	43	ELGIN Joins with Banff, Cullen, Inverary, Kintore, and Peterhead, in electing an M.P.; population 4500.	83	

ON RIGHT FROM ABERD.	From Inver.		From Aberd.	ON LEFT FROM ABERD.
		cr. the Lossie.		A little to the south of Forres, and near the road, stands the remarkable obelisk, usually called Sweno's Stone; it is above 20 feet high; it has a number of figures cut on it, which are still remarkably distinct. There are various traditions respecting it; one is, that it was erected to commemorate the murder of King Duffus in the castle of Forres, and the execution of the murderers; another, that it commemorates a victory over the Danes under Sweno, in the time of Malcolm II., about the year 1010. The character of the figure seems to favour the former tradition, the name of the obelisk the latter.
	40	Newton House, Fortaath; a little farther, Thunderton, Dunbar, Bart.	86	
	38	Kirk of Alves.	88	
On the right, ruins of Abbey of Kinloss.		Burgie Castle, Brodie. At distance, see Findhorn vill.	91	
The genius of Shakspeare has immortalised the town of Forres. It was on a waste, two or three miles on the road to Inverness, that Macbeth and Banquo were said to have met the weird sisters.	31	FORRES, A royal burgh, in the Inverness district. Population 3395.	95	
On a small conical hill, about a mile south of Forres, is erected a tower to commemorate the victory of Trafalgar.	30	Moy, Grant, on the right.	96	
	29½	cr. Findhorn River.	96½	
Darnaway Castle, Earl of Moray, not seen from the road. It is four miles from Forres. The great hall was built by the celebrated Regent Randolph, the nephew of Bruce. It contains the dais of feudal times. The original roof, which is of dark oak, still remains. The Findhorn flows by it through a well wooded park. Immense plantations of oak, pine, larch, &c. cover the whole country side, and conceal the castle from view.	27½	Kirk and vill. of Dyke, enter Nairnshire.	98½	Brodie House, Brodie, Esq.
	23½	Auldearn vill.	104	Auldearn was the scene of a victory gained, May 4, 1645, by the Marquis of Montrose over an army of the Covenanters, under Sir John Hurry.
		cr. Nairn Water.		In the neighbourhood of Nairn is Cawdor Castle, the seat of the Earl of Cawdor. It is one of the most ancient and entire baronial residences in Scotland. It stands upon a low rock overhanging the bed of a torrent, and is surrounded by the largest sized forest trees. It is enclosed within a moat, and is approachable only by a drawbridge. Macbeth was " Thane of Cawdor."
	20	NAIRN, A royal burgh of very old fashioned appearance. Population 3665.	105	
	18	Firhall.	106	
	14	Ardersier Kirk.	112	
	12	Campbellton vill.	114	
On right 5¾ miles from Inverness, Castle Stewart, Earl of Moray, a ruin.	11	Connage.	115	At no great distance is Fort George, remarkable as the only regular fortification in the island, and as a complete architype in miniature of the great fortresses of the continent. Fort George is a mile N.W. of Campbellton, 3 miles from Inverness.
Inverness contains a number of goodly streets, and has the usual public buildings of a large county town. The whole environs are beautiful in a high degree, and there is no town in Scotland which enjoys so many fine walks. The famous Castle of Inverness, which was the property and residence of Macbeth, stood on an eminence to the east of the town, termed the Crown. This castle was destroyed by Malcolm Canmore, who soon after built another to serve as a royal residence and fortress. This edifice was destroyed, in 1746, by the troops of Prince Charles Stuart, and only the wall of an interior rampart now remains.		Culloden House. INVERNESS. The remains of the Fort which Oliver Cromwell built at Inverness are to be seen at the place where the Ness joins the sea. The most remarkable natural curiosity in the neighbourhood of Inverness is a strange oblong mound called Tom-na-heurich (hill of the fairies.) Inverness joins with Forres, Nairn, and Fortrose in electing a M. P. The population of the town in 1831 was 9663.	126	The scene of the Battle of Culloden is a mile to the left of Culloden House, about 4 miles from Inverness. The most distinguished seats in the neighbourhood of Inverness are, Culloden House, Raigmore (Mackintosh, Esq.), Derroch Villa (Dowager Lady Saltoun), Leys (Miss Baillie), and Muirton (Mr. Huntly Duff).

INDEX.

CPSIA information can be obtained
at www.ICGtesting.com
Printed in the USA
BVHW090123111122
651563BV00003B/53